# THE
# HEART
# DOCTRINE

## Mystical Views of the
## Origin and Nature
## of Human Consciousness

*Christopher P. Holmes*

# Within-Without from Zero Points

**Book I**
## THE HEART DOCTRINE
Mystical Views of the Origin and Nature
of Human Consciousness

**Book II**
## MICROCOSM-MACROCOSM
Scientific and Mystical Views on the
Origin of the Universe, the Nature
of Matter & Human Consciousness

**Book III**
## TRIUNE MONADS IN
## SEVEN DIMENSIONAL HYPERSPACE
Scientific and Mystical Views of the Multidimensional
Nature of Human Existence

**Book IV**
## A FOOL AT THE ZERO POINT
An *Autobiographic* Tale
of the Strange Case of Professor Z,
the Mysteries of Love, the Ecstasies of the
Heart & the Horror of It All

ZERO POINT

Institute for Mystical and Spiritual Science
Box 700, 108 Clothier Street East,
Kemptville, Ontario, Canada K0G 1J0
zeropoint@bell.net
(613) 258-6258
Visit: www.zeropoint.ca

*Within-Without from Zero Points*

Book I:
# THE HEART DOCTRINE
Mystical Views of the Origin and Nature
of Human Consciousness

## ©2010 by Zero Point Publications

Cover Illustration: *Veiling of the Soul*, Rassouli, www.Rassouli.com
Book Design & Layout: Groundhog Computing Services, groundhogcs@cogeco.ca
Set in Arno Pro with titles in Berkeley Retrospective SSi.

1st Printing – 2002
2nd Printing – 2010

## National Library of Canada Cataloguing in Publication

Holmes, Christopher P.
The heart doctrine: mystical views of the origin and nature
of human consciousness / Christopher P. Holmes.
(Within-without from zero points; 1)
Includes bibliographic references.
ISBN 978-0-9689435-0-2
1. Mysticism. 2. Consciousness. I. Title. II Series: Holmes
Christopher P. . Within-without from zero points ; 1.
BF311.H64 2002    149'.3    C2002-901750-5

" ..."material points without extension" are Leibnitz's monads, and at the same time the materials out of which the 'Gods' and other invisible powers clothe themselves in bodies ... ."
H. P. Blavatsky, *The Secret Doctrine*, Vol. I. <u>Cosmogenesis</u>, 1888 (p. 489)

"... such a point of transition must certainly possess special and not readily discoverable properties." (*S. D. I.*, p. 628)

"BEHOLD HE THEN RESTRICTED HIMSELF, IN THE MIDDLE POINT WHICH IS IN HIM, PRECISELY IN THE MIDDLE, HE RESTRICTED THE LIGHT. AND THE LIGHT WAS WITHDRAWN TO THE SIDES AROUND THE MIDDLE POINT. AND THERE HAVE REMAINED AN EMPTY SPACE, ATMOSPHERE, AND A VACUUM SURROUNDING THE EXACT MIDDLE POINT."
Kabbalist Isaac Luria

"The secret of secrets is the divine spark within each of us. Remembrance is remembering that which we already know. It is to get in touch with that divine spark that God has placed within each human being. ... And that divine spark is the secret of secrets. ... And it's within every one of us. Who we are is far more than who we think we are."
Robert Frager/Sheikh Ragip, psychologist and Sufi (Cott, 2005)

"... the divine spark [is] buried deep in every soul. ... we must leave the physical world of matter far behind and rise to the luminous world above to attain the divine principle of our superior soul. ... I ... engraved the symbol of the knowledge of the Initiates: a circle with a point in the center. ... Understand me once and for all: I am speaking from experience, for me it is not mere theory, all my life has been based on this symbol of the circle with its central point. This center which is in us, we must find ...."
Michael Aivanhov, 1976

"When God created the world, He had to limit Himself. From being Infinity ... He decided to limit Himself, to become concentrated, and He gathered Himself into a single Point from which He now projects Himself into the whole universe."
M. Aivanhov, 1977

"The zero-dimension or the point is a *limit*. This means that we see something as a point, but we do not know what is concealed behind this point. It may actually be a point, that is, a body having no dimensions and it may also be a whole world, but a world so far removed from us or so small that it appears to us a point... seven cosmoses related to one another in the ratio of zero to infinity."
P. D. Ouspensky & G. I. Gurdjieff, 1949

# Preface by
## A Fool at the Zero Point

*We speak the wisdom of God in a mystery....*
*If any man among you seemth to be wise in this world,*
*let him become a fool, that he may be wise.*
—Corinthians I, 7/18

*Within-Without from Zero Points* explores the mysteries. These are the mysteries of the mind and of the heart, of life and death, of being and non-being, of science and religion, of human consciousness and cosmic creation, and ultimately–the mystery of God. Let us dare to assume the role of fools—by dismissing no possibilities in this search for truth. By admitting to ourselves how little we ultimately know about life and creation, we might become wise. It is essential to approach the *Within-Without from Zero Points* series with an open heart and mind.

Over thirty five years ago, when I began to study mystical and esoteric teachings, I could not have imagined where that path would eventually lead. Mystical realizations involve transformations of consciousness, experiences of awakening and enlightenment, and the realization of the subtle faculties of the heart and mind. Awakened states attest to the unity of life and to the existence of deeper metaphysical and spiritual forces, principles and dimensions within life and Self. Such profound experiences can occur in glimpses and flashes or as sustained experiences of the inner light and the multidimensional nature of being. Mystical experiences reveal the limits and illusions of so-called normal consciousness and common thought, while pointing to the need for a more inclusive and illuminating paradigm of scientific and individual understanding.

By penetrating different veils of nature, the mystic attains a more objective knowledge about the nature of Self and the world, and directly experiences spiritual and metaphysical realities. In fact, we already experience such realities but we are simply not conscious of what we are in our being. People do not ordinarily understand anything of how the world is produced, informed and sustained by higher dimensional dynamics. It is precisely because humans are so deeply asleep and under spells of illusion that they are so unaware of the mystical inner realities which inform and sustain Self within the world.

The *Within-Without from Zero Points* series is the product of a search for truth concerning the mysteries of life, consciousness, science and God. I hope that this work encourages others to investigate these areas and contribute to the development of a mystical perspective and paradigm within psychology, philosophy, science and education. On an individual level, I hope that the profound nature of the material will inspire you to deepen your understanding of consciousness within yourself. *Within-Without from Zero Points* provides practical insights into your being and your possibilities for awakening and self-realization. To understand mystical teachings, we must experience directly the transformation of consciousness, heart and mind that they prescribe and through which the hidden truths are revealed.

The sacred teachings of the wisdom traditions provide a striking alternative to science's materialist views and reductionist methods. A mystical perspective reveals many limitations, enigmas and fundamental errors within modern scientific and psychological theories, and allows for an intriguing re-interpretation of scientific issues and discoveries. In fact, the ancient wisdom teachings allow one to approach any domain of human life, science and knowledge from an extraordinary and provocative perspective.

Those scientists and philosophers, who consider mystical ideas to be irrational, unintelligible or pseudo-scientific, are simply uninformed about that which they so easily dismiss. This reflexive denial of mysticism is a distinctly modern prejudice and like all prejudices, it cannot withstand a careful and impartial examination. Contrary to what critics of mysticism believe, there is nothing especially comforting about esoteric teachings, nor are they easily and readily apprehended. On the contrary, people are unable to grasp the profound meaning of mystical insights and truths because of the sleepwalking condition which characterizes so-called *'normal human consciousness.'* If we live and interpret life and our place in the cosmos in terms of our acquired psychological makeup, we will attain nothing more than sleepwalkers' guesses at to what is and is not 'real.' To understand the mysteries of consciousness and the heart demands that these be awakened and realized within oneself.

The primary hypothesis of the *Within-Without from Zero Points* series is that consciousness and life within a human being emerge within-without from a point source rooted into higher space dimensions. Strangely enough, this dynamic parallels that which modern science posits in describing how the universe emerged from a point source singularity out of the quantum vacuum. Each such 'Son' in turn becomes a world. Although consciousness is distributed throughout the body, mind and soul during our life, its ultimate origin is from a zero point source within the heart, wherein it is rooted into higher space dimensions and the mystical void/plenum. This point source of light is a substantive consciousness principle "enthroned" within the sacred space of the Heart. As it happens, understanding this profound teaching is a very subtle and difficult undertaking. There is a vast inner cosmos of consciousness which is not simply the product of the material brain but rather originates within-without through the higher dimensional physics and metaphysics of the human heart!

*Within-Without from Zero Points* is an extremely provocative and unusual series. By juxtaposing the most advanced concepts in modern science with the wisdom of mystical and spiritual teachings, it raises intriguing questions as to the ultimate nature of human consciousness and reality. This series is for those brave souls who in seeking after truth recognize that the depths of the unknown are much greater than anything ordinarily imagined. Somehow, people feel in their hearts that there is something profoundly mysterious lying behind the seemingly familiar and mundane reality which meets the senses, engages the desires and preoccupies the mind. In this spirit of wonder, *Within-Without from Zero Points* provides a sweeping scope of inquiry into the ultimate mysteries of existence. I wish you well in your efforts to penetrate the wisdom, understanding and knowledge embodied within this series.

The 'heart doctrine' is a unifying esoteric teaching found within the world's primary religions. The phrase 'the heart doctrine' is drawn from *The Voice of the Silence* (1889) of H. P. Blavatsky, while the term 'zero point' is derived from Blavatsky's *The Secret Doctrine* (1888). However, this series draws from Judaism and Christianity, Hinduism and Tibetan Buddhism, Islam and Sufism, Native spirituality, and additional sources to illustrate the hidden teachings of the heart. Whereas religions may differ in their external forms, dogmas and names, the essential inner esoteric teaching of the heart is a common element. Thus, spiritual psychologies pose a viewpoint which significantly challenges the so-called 'scientific' approach to the study of human consciousness that focuses exclusively on the brain as the site and source of mind and regards humans as nothing more than biological organisms.

The *Within-Without from Zero Points* series puts forth an original perspective on consciousness studies and a theoretical model of 'intelligent design'—allowing for a novel view of the relationships between science, religion and mysticism. I would argue that much of what is touted as 'science' is in fact pseudo-science or 'quack science' and that much of what is claimed simply to be religious dogma is actually quite scientific. H. P. Blavatsky stated in 1888 that: *"… the occult side of Nature has never been approached by the Science of modern civilization."* (p. viii)

Nearly, one hundred and twenty-five years later, Blavatsky's assertion continues to describe modern science's profound ignorance and indefensible prejudices regarding the occult, the esoteric and mystical—especially as pertains to the issues of the origin and nature of consciousness and the mysteries of the human heart.

The *Within-Without from Zero Point* series is dedicated to H. P. Blavatsky for her monumental work, *The Secret Doctrine* (1888). In addition, I have valued extensive studies of G. I. Gurdjieff, rascal sage and author of *Beelzebub's Tales to His Grandson* (1950), his student P. D. Ouspensky, Kabbalist and Judaic scholars, Swami Prabhupada and the Vedic-yogic teachings, contemporary native elder Sequoyah Trueblood, Heart Master Adi Da, Michael Aivanhov, Sufi saints—and other musical poets of the heart and soul. A wide range of individuals and esoteric teachings have influenced and inspired my individual efforts to penetrate the awesome mysteries that we face as human beings in the grand scheme of creation.

On an individual level, I would like to thank Anita J. Mitra for her love, support and struggle through twenty years together—as well as for her illustrations. I would like particularly to thank James A. Moffatt for his help over many years in editing this book and always demanding that the quality of the writing match the profound nature of the subject matter. Jim and I met in high school, befriended at University and have since shared through our lives in the thrills of mystical and esoteric studies. Jim, more than any other, because of his breadth of knowledge and reading, has appreciated the significance of this work and helped to motivate me in its refinement. Thirdly, I would like to thank Karen T. Hale, who has embodied the teachings of this work and helped me understand what they mean in life amidst the madness about us within the world. I would like further to acknowledge my five children—Alison, Matthew, Timothy, Peter and Daniel—who all lost their father too much to his work and life concerns; but who all know that I love and care for them; and lastly, my loving parents who provided a positive early Christian upbringing and support through lean years.

As fools and seekers after truth, we must realize that by attempting to understand the origin and nature of human consciousness, we become participants in a profoundly subtle and intricate mystery play. The mind longs to know the wisdom of the heart and the deep nature of the Spaces within which we live, move and have our being.

Christopher P. Holmes, Ph. D. (Psych)
Kemptville, Ontario, Canada, 2010

"Learn above all to separate Head-learning from Soul-Wisdom, the "Eye" from the "Heart" doctrine. But even ignorance is better than Head-learning with no Soul-wisdom to illuminate and guide it. ... The "Doctrine of the Eye" is for the crowd, the "Doctrine of the Heart," for the elect. ... "Great Sifter" is the name of the "Heart Doctrine ... ."

Blavatsky, *The Voice of the* Silence, 1889

"... you ... of interior knowledge ... Say, then, from the heart that you are the perfect day and in you dwells the light that does not fail. ... They are the ones who appear in truth since they exist in true and eternal life and speak of the light which is perfect and filled with the seed of the Father,and which is in his heart and in the pleroma,while his Spirit rejoices in it and glorifies the one in whom it existed ... ."

Christ, Gospel of Truth (Nag Hammadi Library, Robinson, 1981)

"I am the Self, O conqueror of sleep, seated in the hearts of all creatures. I am the beginning, the middle and the end of all beings." (10, 20)
"I am that Lord represented as the Supersoul, dwelling in the heart of every embodied being."

Bhagavad-Gita (8, 4)

"Within the lotus of the heart he dwells, where, like the spokes of a wheel in its hub, the nerves meet. ... This Self, who understands all, who knows all, and whose glory is manifest in the universe, lives within the lotus of the heart."

*Mundaka Upanishad*

"Many seem wide awake to the life without, but asleep to the life within; and though the chamber of their heart is continually visited by the hosts of heaven, they do not know their own heart; they are not there. ... if the heart of man were expanded, it would accommodate the whole universe, just like a drop in the ocean. The heart can be so large that it can hold the whole universe, all."

Hazrat Inayat Khan (1982, 1960)

"The heart is the treasury in which God's mysteries are stored; Seek the purpose of both the worlds through the heart, for that is the point of it."

Sufi poet, Lahiji

"The heart must make of itself a hollow space wherein Godliness can be revealed in stages. Thus the heart (binah) corresponds to the hollow of Creation ... the Vacated Space. Binah, then, is conceptually the Vacated Space wherein the formation of all the Universe takes place."

Kabbalist & Judaic scholar, C. Kramer, 1998

# THE HEART DOCTRINE

## Mystical Views of the Origin and Nature of Human Consciousness

### 0
### Preface by ... A Fool at the Zero Point

### I
### THE ORIGINS OF HUMAN CONSCIOUSNESS

### I I
### THE PROBLEM OF GOD'S CONTRACTING UNIVERSE

# III
# THE HEAD DOCTRINE
## Modern Views on the Origin and Nature of Human Consciousness

# IV
# THE HEART DOCTRINE
## Mystical Views on the Origin and Nature of Human Consciousness

# V

# MYSTICAL DIMENSIONS
## of Consciousness, the Heart and the Cosmos

# V I

# FOOL AT THE ZERO POINT
## Within-Without and the Mysteries of Creation

# I
# The Origin of Human Consciousness

*"… when I die, the 'I' will be lost forever, too."*
—Isaac Asimov, material scientist

*"What he sees in the inmost recesses of his heart is his real "I," his God."*
—Sri Chinmoy, mystic

*"… the Monad … is not of this world or plane,
and may be compared only to
an indestructible star of divine light and fire,
thrown down on to our Earth."*
—Blavatsky, 1888

# 1. The Mysteries of Consciousness

What is the nature of human consciousness? Psychologists, scientists and philosophers use this term in a hundred and one ways—with a thousand and one meanings and interpretations. Within the scientific and popular literature as well as in common discussion, there is widespread confusion and misunderstanding regarding the issues of consciousness. Further, people do not generally even question the nature of consciousness within themselves or have a language in which to talk about such things.

The contemporary scientific literature demonstrates how much scientists are in the dark about the mysteries of consciousness. This is exemplified by a *Scientific American* article—*"The quest to find Consciousness"*—published in a special issue of MIND (2004). The most certain comments offered by author G. Roth regarding consciousness are that *"a true understanding of the phenomenon remains elusive,"* and further that, *"For now, no definitive explanations exist...."* Science journalist John Horgan in *The Undiscovered Mind* (1999) came to a similar conclusion: *"Mind-scientists and philosophers cannot even agree on what consciousness is, let alone how it should be explained."* (p. 228) The Dalai Lama simply states: *"I do not think current neuroscience has any real explanation of consciousness itself."* (2005, p. 130)

In his investigations of consciousness, John Horgan quotes Harvard psychologist, Howard Gardner, who suggests that someone may find *"deep and fruitful commonalities between Western views of the mind and those incorporated into the philosophy and religion of the Far East."* Gardner states that a fundamentally new insight is necessary in order to understand consciousness; although unfortunately, *"we can't anticipate the extraordinary mind because it comes from a funny place that puts things together in a funny kind of way."* (p. 260) These comments are ironic, as indeed there is a fundamental difference between Western scientific views of consciousness and the mind as centred in the brain and both Eastern and Western spiritual traditions with their emphasis upon the heart. Understanding this difference between *the head doctrine* and *the heart doctrine* will certainly provide a novel perspective on the issues of consciousness and put things together in a *"funny kind of way."*

What are the nature and origin of human consciousness? These are big league issues of profound importance not only to science, but also to us individually—in terms of understanding the meaning and significance of our human life. Unfortunately, the whole basis of the modern scientific approach to consciousness has been fundamentally flawed and misguided. The mysteries of consciousness are far deeper than imagined by author Roth—who ends up associating the "seat of consciousness" with the association areas of the cerebral hemispheres in interaction with other mid-brain structures. Roth embodies 'the head doctrine.' Further, scientists have no idea of the profound alternative mystical and spiritual viewpoints on these issues of consciousness.

James Moffatt (2003) offers an amusing perspective on the intriguing enigmas of consciousness:

> "Consciousness"—what do I mean when I use that term? What is consciousness? Well, that is the big question. As far as questions go, it is pretty much in a class of its own. It is the World Series, the Stanley Cup, the Superbowl, the Greater Intergalactic Open, and the heavyweight championship of the world of Big Questions all rolled into one. People win Nobel Prizes, receive huge research grants, become knights of the realm, gain international acclaim and celebrity as scholars and thinkers, and much, much more—just for beating around consciousness' bushes or hanging out under its porch light looking for its keys. Mathematicians forge its signature; physicists trace its shadow. Chemists scour its soup pot; biologists listen to its heartbeat, draw its bloodlines, and chart its pulse. In the most remote ranges of the Himalayas, there are said to be monks who draw closer to consciousness' door simply by chanting its postal code. ... Ah, consciousness ... the cosmic key that unlocks the doors to eternal mysteries ... the straw that stirs the universal fluids ... the meaning of meaning ... the mirror with which God does His tricks ... but what, pray tell, is it? You can know it—more or less. You can lose it—without missing it—for the longest time. You can focus it, reflect on it, summon it ... elevate, expand, and divide it ... .You can refine it, define it ... you can wine & rhyme & divine it ... you can even make space and time for it ... but the one thing you can never do is to know consciousness when you do not have it. Pretty tricky business—trying to think of what consciousness may or may not be. Questions about the nature of consciousness have stymied some major league thinkers, driven others to the intersection of Angst & Despair, and simply worn out the rest. (p. v)

The issues of the origin and nature of consciousness indeed pose big league questions. Moreover, these subjects have to be approached from various perspectives in order to wine, dine and then divine them. The issues of nature of human consciousness are also central to the contemporary debate between science and religion, and to the issue of the existence of God. The debate between science and religion hinges on the issue of the origin and nature of consciousness—because this is linked to that of the existence or non-existence of the human spirit, soul or divine nature. Is consciousness a product of material processes as science claims or does it originate from within a spiritual, metaphysical or divine realm?

To begin, the term consciousness can be taken generally to refer to the inner awareness of being, which each of us has or is within our lives. Although we might see another persons' physical body, we can never directly view their inner world of consciousness or their inner experience of being. Yet, in a very real sense, it is within this inner world that each of us has our existence. Hence, in order to understand consciousness, we must make an effort to understand it within ourselves—through direct inner awareness and experience. This approach is necessary to supplement other scientific approaches which rely upon external observers and intellectual theories. It is also the essential method of the mystics, yogis and masters of the esoteric traditions who study consciousness within themselves. Such self study explorations of consciousness have been hardly considered within the mainstream of modern thought, which also propagates varied misleading ideas on the subject. As the Dalai Lama explains, *"it is clear that the third-person method—which has served science so well in many areas—is inadequate to the explanation of consciousness."* (2005, p. 133)

The issues of consciousness are profoundly important from both a scientific and an individual perspective. What is "I" in me—this inner self awareness? Could there be some type of mystical I, that is not simply a collection of molecules or a pack of neurons? Where could such come from and what types of experience are possible for human beings—during life and after death? *The Heart Doctrine* is an inquiry into the ultimate origin and nature of human consciousness, as well as into the issues of the existence or non-existence of the human spirit and soul. The approach is to contrast 'the head doctrine'—the major twentieth century scientific theory of consciousness—with 'the heart doctrine' derived from ancient and modern mystical and spiritual teachings. This comparative study provides a profoundly valuable alternative approach to the deep mysteries and enigmas of consciousness and it highlights many of the assumptions underlying the modern scientific views. We must at least sound the postal codes of consciousness or beat around its bushes.

# 2. The Head Doctrine

For decades, psychologists dismissed the study of consciousness as it was too difficult to study empirically and borders on such unscientific pursuits as religion and metaphysics. Behaviourist John Watson remarked that no one had seen a soul in a test tube and that the study of consciousness was just as elusive as that of the soul. Nevertheless, in the second half of 20th century, consciousness re-emerged within psychology and neuroscience as a legitimate area of study. However, scientists embraced an extremely limited conceptualization of consciousness and most often equated it with thinking and other cognitive processes of the mind or the electromagnetic activities of the brain. It was assumed that consciousness is produced by the brain's material neurological processes and/or by their information processes. *The head doctrine* became the most commonly accepted western scientific and psychological model of consciousness. However, the nature of consciousness has remained the most mysterious of all psychological phenomena.

The *MIND* article by Roth, *The Quest to find Consciousness,* is illustrated by an artist who depicts *"the mysterious brain activity involved in consciousness."* (2004). The image is of the top portions of a human skull with the interior brain illuminated yellow, red and orange, and with lightening bolts extending from the brain into surrounding space. Although Roth comments that *"a true understanding of the phenomenon remains elusive,"* and further that, *"For now, no definitive explanations exist ...,"* it is simply assumed that the consciousness is generated somehow within the brain from material processes. Many modern books on human consciousness and the mind are illustrated simply with pictures of the head and/or the brain on the front cover.

If we read Roth's article for scientific insights into consciousness, we come up quite empty handed. A small table in Roth's article is entitled *"FAST FACTS: The Rise of Awareness"* and includes these three points:

1. How does consciousness, with its private and subjective qualities, emerge from the physical information processing conducted by the brain? ...

2. Recently neuroscientists have focused on the neural correlates— the activities in the brain that are most closely associated with consciousness.

3. To date, no "centre" for the phenomenon has revealed itself, but advances in imaging have helped in the study of the brain areas that are involved during consciousness. (p. 34)

Of course, there is not a single 'fact' in the table but only questions or assumptions. There is no "proof" that consciousness emerges *"from the physical information processing"* in the brain or from *"the neural correlates."* Although these views are presented as *'fast facts,'* they are really nothing more than simple assumptions.

The basic assumption that the brain produces consciousness seems most reasonable and few scientists question it—despite the fact that they are completely unable to establish how or where the brain produces consciousness or what exactly this consciousness is. Nevertheless, putting aside these uncertainties, theorists share the view of prominent neurologist Roger Sperry, who remarked: *"I don't see any way for consciousness to emerge or be generated apart from a functioning brain."* (1984)

While most people would consider that understanding human consciousness is somewhat irrelevant to their life apart from posing issues in science, this is simply not the case. In fact, if the strictly material conceptualization of consciousness is true, then this has profound implications for the nature and significance of human existence. Isaac Asimov identifies the most important of these implications:

> "The molecules of my body, after my conception, added other molecules and arranged the whole into more and more complex forms, and in a unique fashion, not quite like the arrangement in any other living thing that ever lived. In the process, I developed, little by little, into a conscious something I call "I" that exists only as the arrangement. When the arrangement is lost forever, as it will be when I die, the 'I' will be lost forever, too." (Asimov, 1981, p. 158)

This is the gist of the head doctrine. Human beings are material beings who live and die with their functioning brains. When the molecules or neurons are destroyed, consciousness is no more and so life ends at death and the "I" is lost forever.

In the same vein, Carl Sagan elaborated a strictly materialist position:

> the mind is merely what the brain does. There's nothing else, there's no soul or psyche that's not made out of matter, that isn't a function of 10 to the 14th synapses in the brain. (*Psychology Today*, 1995, p. 65)

In this view, human consciousness and the mind are nothing more than electrical processes within the brain, which generate the experience of consciousness and "I" for a limited period of time until they are extinguished at death. There is no individual singular 'I' in a living being and we are instead nothing but a 'pack of neurons' or an arrangement of material molecules.

When it comes to 'states of consciousness,' Roth offers a pretty limited scheme of consideration from a so-called scientific perspective:

> Any effort to understand consciousness must begin by noting that it comprises various states. ... At one end of the spectrum is the so-called alertness (or vigilance) state. States of lower consciousness include drowsiness, dozing, deep sleep and on down to coma. (p. 34)

A normal state of 'alertness' is put at one end of the continuum, as if this is the highest possible state of consciousness a human being can experience and the other levels are below it—down into coma and the extinction of consciousness in death. It is assumed that there are no states of consciousness beyond basic vigilance—hence no 'Self consciousness,' cosmic consciousness, spiritual or God consciousness.

Current scientific thinking also tends to regard consciousness as *non-substantive*—that is, as nothing in itself. According to this conception, there is no way for consciousness to exist separately from or beyond the mind and the body, because consciousness has literally no substance in itself—it is no thing. It is an epiphenomena produced by material and electrical processes. Psychologists and scientists reject animistic or vital principles in the life of human beings and deny the existence of soul. There is no modern psychology as a science of the soul. Similarly, scientists have banished spirit from their considerations of nature and the universe. Life is regarded as having been created according to natural laws and principles rather than being created by any form of supernatural or metaphysical means. Given the extraordinary achievements in many areas of the physical sciences over the course of the past century, there seems to be little reason to question the basic assumptions and methods of science. However, when it comes to the central enigma of modern psychology and science concerning the origin and nature of consciousness, scientists have made no progress at all and in fact have many different wrong ideas and misguided theories.

Whereas humans used to invoke God or gods to make sense of the unknown and to interpret the meaning of life in terms of supernatural forces, scientists suppose that their discoveries of natural forces and laws have done away with the need for such religious and mythic explanations. Carl Sagan, the esteemed popular science writer, gave voice to this spirit when he declared: *"As we learn more and more about the universe, there seems less and less for God to do."* (1979)

According to the mainstream of contemporary science, human beings are material biological beings, the result of the blind evolutionary processes of random mutation and natural selection. In fact, all the phenomena in nature are believed to have occurred in a God-less Universe, governed by chance and the mechanical functioning of natural laws. In this view, human life and the life of the universe are the fortunate by-products of material processes—ranging from those of subatomic physics to those of evolution and neurology. Consciousness and mind are most frequently equated with the sum of neurological and psychological processes located within the material brain centred in the head. This is the basic 'head doctrine' of modern science and there is considered to be no real 'I' within a human being.

# 3. The Diagnosis of Modern Psychology

In a *Psychology Today* interview (1976), Guru Bawa, an Eastern wise man, made these rather startling comments about western psychology and the common misunderstanding of Self. According to the guru, psychologists are quite deluded about the origin of the mind (or consciousness):

> "I studied psychology once, and I became crazy," Bawa responded in a playful tone. "I lost all my powers. ... Psychologists don't know where the mind is. Some think it is in the brain. Others think it is in the genitals. Others think it is in the ass. But the mind is in the heart, and that is what psychologists do not know. Unless the heart opens, you will be driven crazy by the monkeys of the mind." (April 1976)

This is a telling diagnosis of modern psychology and science. Certainly scientists are in a sad predicament if they do not know where the mind is or where consciousness originates! Yet, from a mystical and spiritual perspective, this is precisely the case. There are fundamental errors in modern scientific approaches to understanding consciousness and the mind.

Guru Bawa describes some psychologists as thinking that the mind is in the brain—as in the modern head doctrine. Others relate it to the genitals—in reference to Freudian psychology with its focus on human sexuality; or 'in the ass' —in reference to the Kundalini, a primordial instinctual energy locked within the root chakra, as described in yoga psychology. However, Bawa insists: *"The mind is in the heart."* The deepest, most essential Mind and Self are established within the heart and are more primary than what the yogis refer to as the *"monkeys of the mind."* In this viewpoint, mainstream psychology, philosophy and science alike are fundamentally mistaken about the nature of consciousness, mind and self. They are not *'Knowers of Self'* as described throughout the mystical literature.

Sri Chinmoy, another contemporary spiritual teacher, stresses the heart doctrine and also diagnoses human beings' *common ignorance* as to the true nature of self:

> He does not know himself precisely because he identifies himself with the ego and not with his real 'I.' What compels him to identify himself with this pseudo 'I'? It is Ignorance. And what tells him that the real 'I' is not and can never be the ego? It is his self-search. What he sees in the inmost recesses of his heart is his real 'I,' his God. (1970, p. 16)

Human beings lack true self-knowledge and are asleep to their deeper nature as spiritual beings. According to the mystics, we live in *ignorance*— identifying Self with the thoughts, feelings, desires and sensations which make up the contents of the mind and the personal daily life dramas. All the while, we do not know Self or "real I"—as related to the subtle mystical dimensions of the heart.

Ramana Maharshi, an Indian sage and mystic, similarly described the Self as related to the Heart Centre—deeper than the personal or ego level of the mind centred in the head:

> the final goal (of yoga, or life) may be described as the resolution of the mind in its source which is God, the Self; in that of technical yoga, it may be described as the dissolution of the mind in the Heart lotus. ... The mind and the breath spring from the same source. They arise in the heart, which is the centre of the self-luminous Self. ... Where the 'I' thought has vanished, there the true Self shines as 'I.' 'I' in the heart. ... The 'I,' the Self, alone is real. As there is no other consciousness to know it, it is consciousness. (1977, pp. 90-1)

Ramana Maharshi makes a number of important points concerning consciousness and self. Firstly, "I" or "Self" is identified most intimately with the spiritual and soul dimensions of the heart, and is connected therein to God. Secondly, the goal of yoga is the dissolution of the mind into its source—within the heart lotus or centre. Thirdly, the Self is "self-luminous" and "shining"— having an inherent light nature. Fourthly, the self-luminous Self is "consciousness itself." Consciousness is the light of Self.

If scientists and psychologists are unable to locate consciousness, the soul and spirit in the material brain processes, perhaps they are looking for it in the wrong place: firstly, in the head, rather than within the heart and secondly, in the materiality of the physical world rather than in the subtle matters and metaphysical dimensions which underlie and sustain the physical dimensions. The Heart, not the mind, is the centre of a human being considered as a whole electromagnetic quantum system, as a living breathing being or as a spiritual being ensouled through the heart. Modern psychology and philosophy has failed to explore the psychology of the heart and soul and therefore is faced with such enigmas as to how and where the brain is producing consciousness.

# 4. The Heart Doctrine

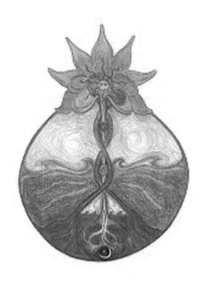

"Speak to us of Self-Knowledge."
And he (the prophet) answered,
saying: "Your hearts know in
silence the secrets of the days and
the nights. But your ears thirst
for the sound of your heart's
knowledge."
Kahil Gibran, *The Prophet*
(1968, pp. 54-55)

Mystical and esoteric teachings and practices can enable an individual to overcome the illusions, conditioning and limitations of *pseudo-I*—the sense of ego or I associated with the personality and mind centred within the head brain—and to realize the deeper dimensions of "I" within the heart. The realization of Self within the Heart is the basis for the mystical declaration *"I AM."*

The heart doctrine is found throughout eastern and western religious teachings—including Hinduism, Tibetan Buddhism, Islam and Sufism, Judaism and Christianity, as well as in numerous other esoteric mystical and spiritual teachings—from *The Secret Doctrine* of Blavatsky, to A. Crowley and Kabbalah. The heart doctrine is illustrated most simply in this Aboriginal tale about creation and the gods:

> One day...the gods decided to create the universe. They created the stars, the sun and the moon. They created the seas, the mountains, the flowers, and the clouds. Then they created human beings. At the end, they created Truth.

> At this point, however, a problem arose: where should they hide Truth so that human beings would not find it right away? They wanted to prolong the adventure of the search.

> "Let's put Truth on top of the highest mountain," said one of the gods. "Certainly it will be hard to find it there."

> "Let's put it on the farthest star," said another.

> "Let's hide it in the darkest and deepest of abysses."

> "Let's conceal it on the secret side of the moon."

At the end, the wisest and most ancient god said, "No, we will hide Truth inside the very heart of human beings. In this way they will look for it all over the Universe, without being aware of having it inside of themselves all the time." (Mills, 1999)

Truth, wisdom and understanding are all associated with the awakening of the Heart. The Self within the heart has inner connections to the universe, to spiritual realities and even to God.

In the *Upanishads* of ancient India, the heart doctrine is elaborated most eloquently:

Within the lotus of the heart he dwells, where, like the spokes of a wheel in its hub, the nerves meet. ... This Self, who understands all, who knows all, and whose glory is manifest in the universe, lives within the lotus of the heart, the bright throne of Brahman. ... Self-luminous is that Being, and formless. He dwells within all and without all. ... The Self exists in man, within the lotus of the heart, and is the master of his life and of his body. ... The knot of the heart, which is ignorance, is loosed, all doubts are dissolved ... . *Mundaka Upanishad* (Prabhavananda & Manchester, 1957, pp. 45-6)

As large as the universe outside, even so large is the universe within the lotus of the heart. Within it are heaven and earth, the sun, the moon, the lightning, and all the stars. What is in the macrocosm is in this microcosm ... All things that exist ... are in the city of Brahman. (*Chandogya*, ibid, 1957, pp. 74)

Sacred religious texts from the world's religions associate states of illumined, spiritual and cosmic consciousness with the sacred space of the Heart. Such teachings suggest that there is a deep holographic physics and metaphysics to the human heart and Self.

These teachings have practical application within self study, as is evident if we consider these profound comments provided by a yogi and medical doctor Dr. R. Mishra:

The physical heart and physical consciousness are related. In the same way, the spiritual heart and spiritual consciousness are related. ... Life and consciousness are byproducts of the heart. ... Biological heart and consciousness are physical in nature and they depend on the metaphysical heart and consciousness. In reality, consciousness is not created but manifested and this manifestation depends on the evolution of the nervous system ... and blood ... Your principle aim is to reach the spiritual heart and spiritual consciousness by means of the physical heart and physical consciousness. (1969, pp. 139-40)

Mystical teachings elaborate an alternative model of the higher dimensional origins of human consciousness and self. Whereas modern science presupposes that material processes within the brain produce consciousness and the experience of self, mystical perspectives suggest that consciousness 'comes from above' or from *'within-without'* through some incredibly profound physics and metaphysics of the human heart. These claims will be elaborated throughout this *WWZP* series and illustrated with references to the sacred literature of the world's religions and mystical teachings, as well as through explorations of modern physics and science.

Mystical teachings suggest profound possibilities for states of awakened consciousness, enlightenment, illumination and liberation—associated with the awakening of the heart and the illumination of higher centres. These provide an alternative viewpoint to those perspectives offered by so-called "exact science" —with its denial of spirit, soul and any transcendental or religious principle. If we speak off the tops of our heads, we can simply assume that the head-brain produces consciousness and mind, but if we penetrate to the heart of being, to the Heart of ourselves, might we indeed become *"Knowers of Self?"* H. P. Blavatsky, a prominent occult scholar, notes, *"Learn above all to separate Head-learning from Soul-Wisdom."* (1877) and quotes the ancient *Stanzas of Dyzan*: *"The Sons expand and contract through their own Selves and Hearts ... each a part of the web,"* as woven between spirit and matter.

From a mystical and spiritual perspective, modern psychology and philosophy are filled with head knowledge but lack the secret wisdom of Self within the Heart. Consciousness and Self are substantive and should not simply be used as generic terms to identify the flow of thoughts, feelings and sensations that occur within subjective experience generated by the brain. There is something far deeper happening within a human being as concerns the origin and nature of consciousness.

Ramana Maharshi elaborates upon the mysteries of the heart. He explains how the Self emerges as a point source of light and consciousness associated with the true Heart centre and that its influences circulate as light throughout the interior dimensions of a human being:

> The effulgent light of active-consciousness starts at a point and gives light to the entire body even as the sun does to the world. When that light spreads out in the body one gets the experiences in the body. The sages call the original point *'Hridayam'* (the Heart). ... The Individual permeates the entire body, with that light, becomes egocentric and thinks that he is the body and that the world is different from himself. ... The association of the Self with the body is called the *Granthi* (knot). ... When Atma (the Self) alone shines, within and without, and everywhere ... one is said to have severed the knot .... (Bhikshu, 1966, pp. 39-42)

The Self is inherently self-illuminating and this light emerges from a point source within the heart and then permeates the body and mind. This light is associated with consciousness itself. A human being is thus 'ensouled' through the electromagnetic activities of the heart, the breath and the blood flow.

Yogic and mystical teachings articulate also that the light energies of Self are dispersed through three major channels to seven major wheels or chakras within the subtle anatomy of human beings. The Heart Chakra is the central and original chakra with three above and three below.

The Self exists in relationship to a hierarchy of interpenetrating world orders—spiritual, divine and metaphysical dimensions of being, which underlie and sustain the realm of gross matter. These dynamics allow for afterlife existence and for complex relationships of the individual to the Sun, to the larger Universe, and most importantly to spiritual and divine realities.

These seemingly preposterous claims about humans' miraculous possibilities simply cannot be weighed properly without a detailed examination of what exactly mystical and spiritual teachings say about these invisible worlds and hidden realities. These teachings present a complex physics and metaphysics of consciousness, the heart and the universe. We will need to take such teachings and examine them in light of modern ideas in physics, science and cosmology in order to more deeply understand their meanings. Unfortunately, modern science lacks the wisdom of the heart and soul, and fails to consider the inner light and spiritual life. Further, we do not realize the Creator manifesting in all things and assume blindly that the world is simply what it appears to be to us in our conditioned states of vigilance or awareness—dominated by ten thousand and one worries, anxieties, life interests and habits.

The origin and nature of human consciousness are very deep mysteries, which can only be understood through the awakening of consciousness and the psycho-spiritual and alchemical transformation of the heart. The awakening of the Heart is the basis for the experience of Self-realization.

# 5. Zero Point Origins

"material points without extension" are Leibnitz's monads, and at the same time the materials out of which the 'Gods' and other invisible powers clothe themselves in bodies. ... the entire universe concentrating itself, as it were, in a single point."
H. P. Blavatsky, *The Secret Doctrine,*
Vol. I. <u>*Cosmogenesis,*</u> 1888 (p. 489)

"... such a point of transition must certainly possess special and not readily discoverable properties." (I, p. 628)

The term *"zero point"* was used by the mystic scholar Helena P. Blavatsky, founder of the Theosophical Society (1875) and author of *The Secret Doctrine* (1888). Blavatsky does not elaborate extensively upon zero point dynamics within *The Secret Doctrine* or elsewhere, but her few discussions are immensely valuable. The zero point teaching has been largely overlooked within modern theosophical studies. In the *Within-Without from Zero Points* series, the obscure zero point teaching extrapolated from *The Secret Doctrine* is illustrated by explorations of modern science and physics, and through consciousness studies.

Volume I of *The Secret Doctrine* is entitled *Cosmogenesis* and deals with the origin of the universe and creation metaphysics. Blavatsky used the symbol of a point within a circle to represent the zero point origin of the cosmos—a point source of unfolding wherein the finite Kosmos emerged from the Infinite at the beginning of time. The Kosmos expands within-without when the *Breath of the Father* is upon it and then eventually contracts without-within when the *Breath of the Mother* touches it. The Kosmos returns to a neutral zero point centre at the end of time. Relative space-time worlds, or 'Sons,' emerge out of an underlying *Eternal Parent Space* and eventually return again to it. Cycles of the Seven Days and Nights of Brahma occur with Days of creation or *Manvantara*, alternating with Nights of Brahma—a period of Pralaya, or rest. Blavatsky depicted innumerable worlds over eons of time being created in cycles from such zero point sources or 'laya centres.'

Blavatsky uses various terms to depict these invisible points—labeling them also as *"layu centers"* and *"laya centers."* The influences of divine or spiritual realms upon the physical realm emerge through these laya centres, which exist at or beyond the level of material differentiation.

the Laya condition, the point from which, or at which, the primordial substance begins to differentiate and thus gives birth to the universe and all in it. (*Transactions of the Blavatsky Lodge*, 1889, p. 5)

Laya does not mean any particular something or some plane or other, but denotes a state or condition. It is a Sanskrit term, conveying the idea of something in an undifferentiated and changeless state, a zero point wherein all differentiation ceases. (p. 7)

from the "Zero-state" (or *layam*) it becomes active and passive, ... and, in consequence of this differentiation (the resultant of which is evolution and the subsequent Universe),—the "Son" is produced, the Son being that same Universe, or manifested Kosmos, till a new Mahapralaya. (p. 38)

Not only did Blavatsky depict the point source origin of the universe, but also she described zero point laya centres as existent in all living beings— including ourselves. It is through zero point laya centres and dynamics that ""*the "Gods" and other invisible powers clothe themselves in bodies.*"

Zero points are beyond the level of material differentiation:

The chemist goes to the *laya* or zero-point of the plane of matter with which he deals, and then stops short. ... But the full Initiate *knows* that the ring "Pass-Not" is neither locality, nor can it be measured by distance, but that it exists in the absoluteness of infinity. In this "Infinity" ... there is neither height, breadth nor thickness, but all is fathomless profundity, reaching down from the physical to the "para-para-metaphysical." (*S.D., I*, p. 131)

What Blavatsky describes as the *zero point* or the *Ring Pass Not* is at the level of the Planckian units in physics, beyond which physical measurement becomes impossible. In fact, one might find zero point transitional states and dynamics at varied levels within the Aethers of Space.

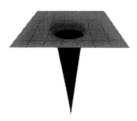

The true Atoms for Blavatsky exist at zero point levels in the unmanifest condition—in the *laya state*. Beings differentiate from a Laya condition or centre at the beginning of each new Manvantara or age, to manifest as a Kosmos, Son or quanta. At the end of time, elements resolve back into the laya state with the dissolution or ingathering of the cosmos. For Blavatsky, atoms are eternal in the laya or zero point condition, prior to physical differentiation. All material matter is impermanent and will ultimately return to the laya state. This is a remarkable alternative concept of the nature of cosmoses, quanta and atoms, and the teaching can also be applied to human beings.

The informing life principle withdraws into the neutral laya centre at the dissolution of the Cosmos *"at the hour of the Pralaya."* Blavatsky describes the "path onward" from matter into Spirit, and further, *"... the necessary gradual and final reabsorption into the laya state, that which Science calls in her own way "the point neutral as to electricity" etc., or the zero point. Such are the Occult facts and statement."* (S.D., I, p. 551)

Blavatsky gives this overview of the evolution and dissolution of the Cosmos:

> evolution ... may be thus formulated as an invariable law; a descent of Spirit into Matter, equivalent to an ascent in physical evolution; a re-ascent from the depths of materiality towards its *status quo ante*, with a corresponding dissipation of concrete form and substance up to the LAYA state, or what Science calls "the zero point," and beyond. (S.D., I, p. 620)

*The Secret Doctrine* postulates the dissolution of the universe, or Son, into a Laya Centre or neutral zero point centre at the end of time.

When examined from a physical perspective, zero points are infinitely small and disappear from view. Zero points mark the transition between varied world orders within the hierarchies of creation. They are points at which something passes over from this world to THAT; where the physical dissolves back into the metaphysical or the material resolves back into the spiritual and divine. Somehow, it is as if as Blavatsky suggests: *"... the entire universe concentrates itself, as it were, in a single point."* Zero points are rooted into higher dimensional Space. The actuality of human beings being based upon such a multidimensional physics of zero point dimensions allows for a much expanded view of human nature.

A century after the publication of *The Secret Doctrine*, theories in modern physics and cosmology now illustrate Blavatsky's seemingly bizarre concepts of the zero point origins of the Kosmos. In modern cosmology, the universe is described as emerging from *a singularity point*, $10^{-33}$ cm in diameter at the beginning of time, $10^{-45th}$ of a second. It emerged out of the quantum vacuum—a seeming void and plenum, a realm of hidden dimensions of being and non-being. Scientists have traced material nature back to its origins and passed from physical to metaphysical dimensions at the singularity. Modern scientists consider that the universe emerged from such a singular point and it could ultimately return to such a dreaded singularity at the end of time, in what is referred to as the 'big crunch' to contrast with the 'big bang' creation event. *The Secret Doctrine* similarly described creation emerging from such a point source and eventually returning to such a state. However, in *The Secret Doctrine*, the zero point or laya centre is not just there at the beginning and end of time, as the alpha and omega points, but instead it exists throughout. It is the means by which the higher dimensional intelligences fashion and bring life into the material coverings or bodies. It is the means by which the entire universe concentrates itself in a single point!

Within the metaphysical teaching of Blavatsky's *The Secret Doctrine*, a Kosmos is labeled as a *"Son,"* as a *"wink of the Eye of Self-Existence"* and as a *"spark of eternity."* It is suggested that there are such zero point laya centres, elements and dynamics within all living beings.

A Monad is such a zero point source of light and life within self. Blavatsky wrote: *"... the Monad ... is not of this world or plane, and may be compared only to an indestructible star of divine light and fire, thrown down on to our Earth."* (1888) Just as the Macrocosm might have a first point of supernal *lux*, so also does the Microcosm of a living breathing human being. This is in accord with the mystical axiom *"As above, so below."* Thus, there might theoretically at least be a "God spark" or divine element, or jivatma, within a living human being. This would constitute an 'I' unlike any of the materialist scientists which are only the impermanent and illusory composites of molecules, cell or neurons in the brain. A zero point laya centre within the heart would be an "I" for which there could be a whole inner physics and metaphysics.

It is suggested that such elements at zero point levels are the true *'atoms'* within living beings.

"MATTER IS ETERNAL, becoming atomic (its aspect) only periodically." (*I*, p. 552)

"Matter is eternal," says the Esoteric Doctrine. But the matter the Occultists conceive of in its *laya*, or *zero state*, is not the matter of modern science; ... when the adept or alchemist adds that, though matter is eternal, for it is PRADHANA ('original base'), yet atoms *are born at every new manvantara,* or reconstruction of the universe. (*S.D.,* I, p. 545)

*The Secret Doctrine* maintains that the universe is founded upon an original zero point and the laws of nature are based upon a further differentiation into *seven zero point centres.* Whether a Universe, a quantum or an individual divine spark, the laws of nature manifest in the material worlds are due to Divine and spiritual forces and intelligences emerging within/without through seven dimensional zero point dynamics. Blavatsky describes seven minute *'holes dug in space'* as the means by which higher dimensional forces sculpt the void through the processes of creation. Blavatsky offers this explanation of the *"Forces of Nature"*:

> all the so-called Forces of Nature ... are *in esse,* i.e., in their ultimate con-stitution, the differentiated aspects of that Universal Motion. ...Fohat is said to produce "Seven Laya Centres" ... the GREAT LAW ... modi-fies its perpetual motion on seven invisible points within the area of the manifested Universe. *"The great Breath digs through Space seven holes into Laya to cause them to circumgyrate during Manvantara."* (Occult Catechism). We have said that Laya is what Science may call the Zero-point or line; the realm of absolute negativeness, or the one real absolute Force ... the neutral axis, not one of the many aspects, but its centre. ... "Seven Neutral Centres," then are produced by Fohat .... (*S.D.,* I, pp. 147-8)

Blavatsky describes the great Breath or Law as *"digging holes in Space"* to channel intelligence and influences into the material realm. Thus, seven invisible zero point *holes dug in space* are established as a foundation for physical manifestation and the laws of nature. Any Cosmos, any Universe, any Monad (a

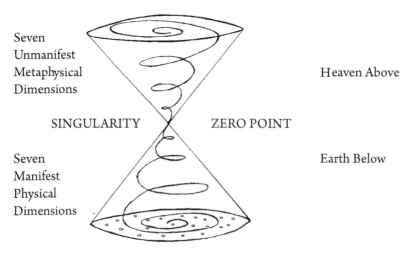

Seven Unmanifest Metaphysical Dimensions — Heaven Above

SINGULARITY — ZERO POINT

Seven Manifest Physical Dimensions — Earth Below

divine or spiritual spark), any atom or quantum, is thus *"worked and guided from within outwards"* through the dynamics of such zero point centres.

A zero point is not exactly a 'thing' in itself—as much as it is a condition or a place at which certain processes occur. Divine and Spiritual Intelligences above ensoul the material body through such zero point dynamics. A zero point can be considered as a 'point particle'—like a monad in hyperspace, or as a portal or transitional point between dimensions. In fact, there could be multiple zero point transitions between dimensions and lives. The human being is ensouled through zero point dynamics and a higher dimensional holographic physics of the heart.

Another *Stanza of Dzyan*, from Blavatsky's *The Secret Doctrine* (1888) reads: *"The Sons expand and contract through their own selves and hearts; they embrace infinitude. ...Each is a part of the web. Reflecting the "Self-existing Lord" like a mirror, each becomes in turn a world."* (p.489) The expansion and contraction of the Sons is through the zero point laya centre associated with the heart and each individual in turn becomes a world. At the heart of the universe, a galaxy, the sun, a quantum and a human being are such zero point laya centres, whereby the gods and other invisible powers clothe themselves in bodies. Thus, life within a living being originates within/without out of higher space dimensions through the dynamics of a multidimensional heart.

According to the heart doctrine, a *divine spark* is the essential point source of individual light consciousness and of the life force within a living being. There is a "quantum Self" or real "I," a Monad or jivatma, established within the higher seven dimensional Space embodied within the Heart. This 'God spark' or divine source emanation is brought down into a spiritual world, then a psychical (soul) world and embodied as the electromagnetic centre within the physical heart. The presence of Self initiates the heartbeat and diffuses the light of consciousness and life energies through the blood and subtle matters to various levels of the body and psyche. The presence of the Self as a 'self-illuminating element,' the Sun of the body, serves to illuminate the psychological and psychic processes within the inner world.

The idea of a living human being growing within/without from a point source is actually illustrated by the dynamics of the conception and growth of the physical body. A fertilised ovum is barely visible to the naked eye—essentially a zero point source. In turn, the ovum is a whole world into itself on a different scale of being from our usual perception. By some unexplained magic, a human being's physical body grows from an original zero point condition, as did the universe. It is not constructed from without, by external shaping or building, but it unfolds from within/without.

P. D. Ouspensky (1949) wrote: *"The zero-dimension or the point is a limit. This means that we see something as a point, but we do not know what is concealed behind this point. It may actually be a point, that is, a body having no dimensions and it may also be a whole world, but a world so far removed from us or so small that it appears to us a point."* This description of a point source as being a whole world in itself certainly applies to a fertilised ovum and to the emergence of the universe.

Although the scientist must concede that the body of a physical human being and the body of the Universe grow from such zero poivnt sources, they do not imagine that human consciousness might similarly be understood in terms of such zero point dynamics. In this view, the origins of human consciousness are traced to the higher dimensional physics and metaphysics of the human heart and the heart chakra; while the seven fold zero points form the centres of the seven chakras.

Consciousness does not arise from material, neurological activity within the material brain. The mind merely reflects the light which originates from within the spiritual heart and space itself. Mystics compare the mind to the moon, which has no light of its own but simply reflects the light of the sun. Similarly, the egoic mind reflects the light of the self within the heart. The zero point centres are inherently "living" and "self-illuminating" and the heart is the Sun of the body.

The mystical conjunction of zero point divine sparks within the nothingness and hyperspace dimensions associated with the heart ultimately gives rise to human consciousness. The zero point divine spark is a quantum self—a point source of divine light and life and of spiritual consciousness. It is the source of the "I" that "I AM," the hidden Self pointed to by mystics and sages throughout the ages. There is an inner physics and metaphysics to such zero point dynamics, light and the higher dimensions of the human heart.

# 6. The Mysteries of Space & the Aether

Space *is, ever was, and ever will be,* and you cannot make away with it.
(Blavatsky, 1888, p. 12)

In order to understand zero points dynamics, we have to consider the nature of space, as the zero point centres exist within the 'medium' of space. This includes the three dimensional space with which we are familiar (or the four-dimensional space-time continuum) and the subtle, higher dimensional Space which underlies and sustains it. The mysteries of consciousness are intimately interrelated to the mysteries of space and the hidden dimensions of being.

Each divine spark "reflects" the life of the "Self-Existing Lord," as a point source of supernal (or supernatural) light arising out of a sea of infinite light. These sparks are the sources of consciousness or divine light *"emanating"* out of hidden dimensions of higher dimensional Space. The individual experience of consciousness arises from the conjunction of such divine sparks within the Divine Mother, the Aether of Space itself. The zero point reflects the qualities of the Divine Father, the Self Existing Lord, a point source of supernal light. The sacred Aether of Space embodies the mysteries of the Divine Mother—the akasha, the Aether or ether—the medium of space itself, within which we live, move and have our being. Understanding the conjunction of the zero points within the heart space is a key to unlocking the mystical origins of consciousness and self, as well as that of life and the universe. Mystical teachings depict a world of profoundly subtle dimensions, interpenetrating and sustaining life through the mysteries of the heart.

The zero point is *a portal* by which influences of higher dimensions are channelled into physical manifestation. Without, the zero point dynamics gives rise to the four dimensional space-time complex, while within, the zero point is established within a seven dimensional Aether of Space. According to Blavatsky, the sevenfold nature of creation and of Space is a basic teaching of the divine wisdom. Blavatsky offered these profound comments on the nature of Space:

> Space is ... a 'limitless void' (and) a conditioned fullness ... the Plenum, the absolute Container of all that is, whether manifested or un-manifest. ... Space is called in the esoteric symbolism "the Seven-Skinned Eternal Mother-Father." It is composed in its undifferentiated to differentiated surface of seven layers. (*The Secret Doctrine*, p. 8)

> The whole range of physical phenomena proceeds from the *Primary* of Ether—Akasa .... Modern science may divide its hypothetically conceived ether in as many ways as it likes; the real Aether of Space will remain as it is throughout. It has seven principles, as all the rest of Nature

has, and where there was no Ether *there would be no sound,* as it is the vibrating soundboard in nature in all of its seven differentiations. This is the first mystery the Initiates of old have learned. (*The Secret Doctrine,* p. 536)

In the *Cosmogenesis* of *The Secret Doctrine,* a key to the mysteries of creation lies within this arcane teaching of the *seven-skinned Eternal Parent Space.* In this view, the entire phenomenal world is regarded as an outgrowth or unfolding of patterns of creation inherent within this root principle of the divine essence. The *Eternal Parent Space* is the ultimate Aether or hyperspace dimension, which sustains physical reality. Blavatsky maintains that the sevenfoldness of things is latent in the Eternal Parent Space and then manifest within all realms of nature and creation.

Blavatsky was highly critical of the scientific views of her era, particularly when it came to conceptualizing "space." She wrote: *"...Space is, in the sight of the materialists, one boundless void in nature—blind, unintelligent, useless."* (p. 587) Blavatsky explains that instead of regarding Space as an *"abyss of nothingness,"* the occultist regards it as a substantial living Entity, the *"real world"* in contrast to the illusory world of visible causes and effects. Space is the Plenum, the Unity in which there is an interconnectedness of all matters and forces. It is the container and body of the universe with its seven principles. In the language of modern physics, Blavatsky's *Eternal Parent Space* refers to the void/plenum of the quantum vacuum as a hyperspace with an inherent seven dimensional nature.[1] Without this Aether of Space, there would be no forces of nature, elements or creation.

According to Madame Blavatsky, cosmic manifestation—within both spiritual and material dimensions of creation—entails the unfolding or expansion of this inherent sevenfold nature. *"Everything in the metaphysical as in the physical Universe is septenary."* (Blavatsky, *S.D.* p. 158) In the process of cosmic creation, the *"first born"* are Seven Luminous Sons, or the Seven Lords, or Seven Logi, or Seven Rays. These Seven Divine Intelligences are *"the builders of form from no-form."* The seven Luminous Sons sculpt the void through inner processes of quantized geometric differentiation. Seven Sons are born from the Web of Light, which manifests out of the Darkness of Non-Being and the Eternal Parent Space. Blavatsky explains that the Divine Essence then becomes *"Seven Inside, Seven outside."* Sevenfoldness is inherent in the Eternal Parent Space, which gives birth firstly to the Seven Luminous Sons, which in turn create seven Laya Centres and materialize within the seven dimensional patterns of manifest existence.

The multidimensional holographic universe consists then of a realm of primary creation, in light and spirit, and a realm of secondary creation, in darkness

---

1    This is the case in the eleven dimensional K. K. theory and M-theory proposed to unify the known laws of physics. This model of higher space dimensions outlines four large dimensions sustained by seven hidden compacted dimensions existing at every point within external space.

and matter. Thus, God creates the Heavens and the Earth. The Sevenfoldness is evident throughout and even in the Eternal Parent Space before the emergence of the Universe. The Seven inside inform the Seven outside. Blavatsky describes the seven inside as *"digging holes in Space"* to channel their intelligence/influences into the material realm. Thus, Seven Laya Centres, seven invisible zero points, are established as the foundation for physical manifestation; seven invisible centres beyond the level of physical differentiation. The causative forces within the four dimensional spacetime thus emerge from within/without from zero point dynamics and an individual is 'clothed' in different bodies.

Blavatsky's archaic doctrines are beautifully illustrated by modern physical and cosmological theories. Scientists have penetrated into the void/plenum and hyperspace in their attempts to unify the physical laws and to understand the creation of the universe. In doing so, they have arrived at singularities, the quantum vacuum, seven dimensional hyperspace and a hierarchy of broken symmetries, which generate form from formlessness, matter from nothingness to sculpt the void. Blavatsky explained similar concepts over a hundred years ago. Of course, Blavatsky expected the rejection of such concepts in her time but predicted that *"in the twentieth century of our era scholars will begin to realize that The Secret Doctrine has neither been invented or exaggerated, but, on the contrary, simply outlined."*

Scientists and consciousness researchers should take up Blavatsky's challenge to science and explore the depths of occult wisdom. The materialistic conception of blind matter moving about in empty four-dimensional space-time is no longer valid even within the domain of established science. The concepts of zero-point centres, the seven-skinned Eternal Parent Space and the void/plenum are the stuff of science and mysticism. Generally, of course, the physicist remains ignorant of the relationships of contemporary theories to the ancient wisdom and the issues of consciousness are left to the neurologists and psychologists to think about.

Mystics suggest awesome possibilities for human consciousness and experience in a profoundly deep universe. Humans live in forgetfulness and are ignorant of the true nature of self and the higher dimensional Space within which we live, move and have our being. The mysteries of consciousness as light and the zero point centres are intimately tied into the mysteries of the Aether of space.

In the *Transactions of Theosophical Society*, Blavatsky provides some commentaries on the nature of the real 'atoms' and of matter:

> the hypothetical atom, a mere mathematical point, is not material or applicable to matter, or even to substance. The real atom does not exist on the material plane. The definition of a point as having position, must not, in Occultism, be taken in the ordinary sense of location: as the *real* atom is beyond space and time. ... the atom is in its eternal state, invisible even to the eye of an Archangel; and becomes visible to the latter only periodically, during its life cycle. ... An atom may be compared to ... the

seventh principle of a body or rather a molecule. (1889, pp. 107-109)

In the symbol of the Theosophical Society, the Self is depicted by the ankh as the seventh principle within the six sided seal of Solomon or the Star of David. The ankh represents the eternal life principle in Egyptian magic. The Snake swallowing its own tail represents the processes of creation and dissolution or involution and evolution of the whole; while the swastika represents the four elements of nature and the four worlds. This is a profound symbolic representation of the monadic essence established within the seven fold higher dimensional physics of the human heart. This image depicts what might be such a 'wink of self-existence' as referred to by HPB. In reference to the Sun, Blavatsky notes: *"The Sun has but one distinct function; it gives the impulse of life to all that breathes and lives under its light. The sun is the throbbing heart of the system; each throb being an impulse. But this heart is invisible; no astronomer will ever see it. ... This impulse is not mechanical but a purely spiritual, nervous impulse."* (p. 117)

Zero point laya centres are established within the Eternal Parent Space as the true Atoms, or I's. Blavatsky describes the Eternal Parent Space as the "upper space."

the "upper space" is the space "within," however paradoxical it may seem, for there is no *above* as no *below* in the infinitude; but the planes follow each other and solidify *from within without*. It is in fact, the universe as it first appears from its laya or "zero" state, a shoreless expanse of spirit, or "sea of fire." (p. 119)

Living beings have such zero point laya centres, the means by which the universe somehow concentrates itself as it were into a single point. The metaphysical dynamics of these atoms in seven dimensional hyperspace, gives rise to the manifested forms of molecular and atomic structures which surround the central point. This is the basis of a holographic model of the physics of the human heart.

The true "substance," "atoms" or "laya centres" are *"on the seventh plane of matter counting upwards, or rather from within without. This can never be discovered on the lowest, or rather most outward and material plane."* (p. 6). Might a human being actually then have such a Monadic essence within the seven dimensional hyperspace of the Aether? This is a meaningful scientific hypothesis. Such an "I" is not simply a material composite of molecules and neurons but instead is inherently self illuminating as consciousness and the life principle within the living being.

# 7. The Kabbalist Universe & Self

"... the void of Unmanifest
Existence ... was ... the size of a
dimensionless dot in the midst of
the Absolute."
— Halevi, Kabbalist, 1977

"... the heart is truly a wonder,
for its creative action mirrors the
original act of Creation."
— *Anatomy of The Soul*,
Chaim Kramer, 1998

The teachings of Judaism and Kabbalah offer another complex mathematical and metaphysical model of the inner geometry of being and non-being, and the higher dimensional origins of consciousness within the heart Space. Although the study of Kabbalah will be progressively developed and woven into this series—into studies of physics and metaphysics, psychology and cosmology—it is valuable at this point to introduce particular aspects of Kabbalah—primarily in relation to the 'zero point hypothesis,' 'the heart doctrine' and the magical formula of 1-3-7.

The microcosm of a human being is designed on the same basic principles of creation as embodied within the macrocosm of the Universe. Hence, key Kabbalist ideas concerning the creation of the universe provide then a valuable model for the emergence of human consciousness.

## 7a. Three Realms of Negative Existence

Kabbalists describe *three Realms of Negative Existence* as underlying and sustaining the worlds. These three realms are *Ayin*, or Nothingness, *En Soph*, the Plenum or All, and *En Soph Aur*, the limitless light. These dimensions or realms are associated with the numbers of 0, 00 and 000.

To illustrate the three realms of NEGATIVE EXISTENCE, Ayin O is not depicted as it designates Nothingness and is therefore, Unspeakable; En Soph OO is completely black, containing all things within the pleroma or plenum; and En Soph Aur OOO is white, the limitless Light.

## Ayin

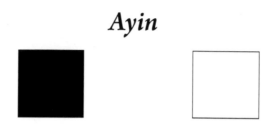

## En Soph                              En Soph Aur

Rabbi Yehuda Ashlag describes the "plenum" of the En Soph:

> The matter is as follows: all the worlds, and all that is in this world, all the creatures of the universe, in whatever age they were to exist, before they ever entered into this world, with all the souls now on earth, and those that are destined still to be created, together with their complete curve of development until the final goal of completion and perfection—all these were previously included in the world which is called "Endless," "En Soph," along with their beauty and all their fulfillments. (1984, p. 57)

The En Soph as the plenum is the root principle for the material side of nature. The En Soph includes all the varied kinds of beings and their qualities and beauties, and all the laws and forces and particles of the universe. It contains all of these things in all of their possibilities for involution and evolution, growth, change and perfection. The whole structure of the world orders on different dimensions and on different scales of existence over all times are all pre-existent in non-existence—latent within the Endlessness of the En Soph.

Kabbalist, Halevi states: *"the mystic knows that everything has its origin in Absolute Nothing and Absolute All..."*

# 7b. Supernal Points

If these two illustrations (and one non-illustration) are superimposed on one another to represent the three realm of NEGATIVE EXISTENCE, they can be depicted by an infinite number of dots distributed throughout infinity, but latent in Non-Being.

Next, take two enlargements of NEGATIVE EXISTENCE. On the left, the dots begin to emerge as discrete elements or I's, stepping out of the background of Negative Existence into Positive Existence. These dots represent infinitely small points beyond material measurement, zero points of no dimension. On the right, one dot is taken as an "I" of the Creator.

The point represents the Creator in the state called EHEIEH (ee-eye-ah), which means, *"I shall be."* Creation emerges out of NEGATIVE EXISTENCE into Positive Existence from a zero point source of unfoldment. A Macrocosm or Universe and a Microcosm, an individual human being, are described in Kabbalah as having such interior zero point origins.

Kabbalists portray the creation of the universe as emerging from a supernal point of no-dimension out of a background in NEGATIVE EXISTENCE. It is quite astonishing that this creation scenario is so similar to modern scientific accounts. In quantum physics, the quantum vacuum is regarded as a seeming void, which is paradoxically 'full'—the quantum plenum. The scientific theory of "vacuum genesis" is in fact quite consistent with the Kabbalist description of creation as emerging from within the three realms of Negative Existence— the *creation ex nihilo* of the mystics. Mystics and scientists both regard creation as emerging from point sources out of the seeming Nothingness, which is paradoxically the Plenum. A modern physicist declares, *"All of physics is in the vacuum"* and this is supportive of the Kabbalist ideas concerning the three realms of negative existence.

Kabbalists described the zero point origin of the universe well ahead of the modern scientists who imagine that they originated such a concept. In *Visions & Voices,* Jonathan Cott (1987) interviewed Rabbi Lawrence Kushner, whose writings explore the parallels between modern science and Jewish mysticism:

> *Jonathan Cott*: Cosmologists have speculated that at the first explosive moment of the birth of the universe, everything that exists—or ever will exist—was contained within a single spark of energy, smaller than an atom's nucleus and ruled by a single primordial law.
>
> *Rabbi Lawrence Kushner*: One dot—a point of light. Perhaps the fact that contemporary cosmologists talk about a dimensionless point of light from which all being sprang and that the Kabbalists long ago came up with precisely the same image (in the fourteenth century, Moses de Leon spoke of *"a hidden supernal point"* whose *"primal centre is the innermost light, of a translucence, subtlety, and purity beyond comprehension"*) means that this awareness comes from something we all carry within us. We're walking Torahs...if we could just shut up and listen to it. As Rabbi Dov Baer of Mezritch said: "I shall teach you the best way to say Torah. You must cease to be aware of yourselves. You must be nothing but an ear, which hears what the universe of the word is constantly saying within you." (p. 209)

Kabbalists and Rabbis, as well as modern scientists, suggest the zero point origins of the universe—depicting it as originating from *"a dimensionless dot in the midst of the Absolute'* (Halveri, 1977); a 'supernal point' or *'primal centre.'*

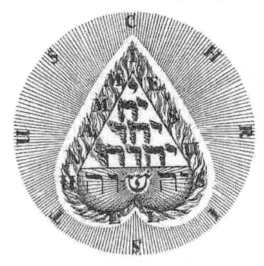

However, the Kabbalist extends this notion to apply to ourselves—as we are living Torahs with the Word and the laws of God written into our very being—in fact into the Heart. So also, we might imagine a human being as having such zero point origins in a type of ultra-physics of consciousness and the heart. This figure from mystic Jacob Boehme depicts the name of God inscribed within the heart—although a spiritual heart of flames turned upwards relative to the material heart.

Kabbalists maintain that there are such Divine source Emanations or Divine Sparks, as stars in space, points of supernal light within the higher dimensional vacated Space of the heart! Kramer describes such 'sparks of holiness' and their emergence from the primordial realm of *Adam Kadmon*:

> The consequences of Adam's fall can be compared to a beautiful and expensive piece of crystal that is dropped from a great height and shatters into thousands of tiny pieces which become scattered over a large area. Adam had contained within himself the souls of all mankind in a state of perfect unity. His fall shattered that holy unity into countless *"sparks of holiness"* which subsequently became dispersed throughout the entire world. It has since been man's mission, utilizing the spiritual inclinations incorporated within his system, to search for, find, purify and elevate these sparks, that they may return to their source. This will ... even improve upon, the vessel from which they originated—Adam. ... (p. 56)

Human beings have a remarkable nature according to Kabbalist teaching—as 'sparks of holiness.' "I" originates from within the deepest realms as an infinitesimal point source of Divine Will and Light Consciousness—"I" stands out and declares *"I AM."*

> *"...every created being cries out the name I AM*
> *as it emerges from Kether, before plunging into the Cosmic Sea below."*
> — Halevi, 1977

Kabbalist teachings certainly support the zero point hypotheses and the notion that human beings have such a 'primal centre.'

## 7c. The Zimzum & the Vacated Heart Space

A creation process described by the Kabbalists involves the withdrawal of the Infinite Light (the En Soph Aur) from around a central point—which creates an empty space or vacuum. This concept has application to understanding the mysteries of the vacated heart Space and the psychology of human beings.

Luria describes the Zimzum or Self-constriction:

BEHOLD HE THEN RESTRICTED HIMSELF, IN THE MIDDLE POINT WHICH IS IN HIM, PRECISELY IN THE MIDDLE, HE RESTRICTED THE LIGHT. AND THE LIGHT WAS WITHDRAWN TO THE SIDES AROUND THE MIDDLE POINT. AND THERE HAVE REMAINED AN EMPTY SPACE, ATMOSPHERE, AND A VACUUM SURROUNDING THE EXACT MIDDLE POINT.

God as the Creator withdrew the Limitless Light from that Space surrounding an exact middle point. This created a vacuum and empty space surrounding a middle point—a form of *'nothingness at the heart of Being.'* It is of course quite logical that the Infinite Being would have to withdraw from a space in order to allow a finite being or Universe to come into existence. Without this self-contraction, everything is swallowed up in the Infinite.

Kramer explains the *"Torah of the Vacated Space,"* known in Hebrew as the *Challal HaPanuy*:

> Prior to the Creation, there was only God. ... Since God is everywhere, there was no "room" for the Creation to come into being, no *place* which could accommodate His Infinite Light. God thus restricted His Light away from a "center point," as it were, to create the Vacated Space. In this space would be created all the supernal Universes, and also the material world ... God contracted His Light, as it were, concealing Himself from man, making it seem to man's limited vision as if there is a vacuum, a place devoid of Godliness. This is the mystery of the Tzimtzum (Self-constriction). (1998, p. 207)

Kramer explains that the action of the Heart *"mirrors the original act of Creation"* and the Heart is such a hollow Space within us. In this sense, there is a form of *"nothingness at the heart of being."* Kramer explains: *"the passion of the heart is really an infinite desire for the Ein Sof."* (p. 211)

The concept of the vacated Heart Space (of Binah) is of a profound nature and has applications to understanding creation physics and both normal and supernormal psychology. If we take the idea literally, as we should, it suggests a model of how human beings are rooted within into zero point fields with a vacated space at the heart of being, which can be illumined by the light of consciousness. All things exist within such higher dimensions, which underlie, sustain and unify them. The Heart is further the place wherein Godliness can be revealed in stages, according to the Kabbalist teaching.

# 7d. The *Tree of Life*

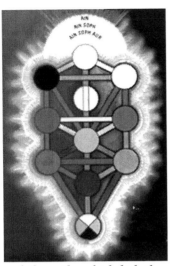

The Kabbalist *Tree of Life* is a mystical symbol depicting the higher dimensional structures of existence. It is essentially a diagram of God: a diagram of the microcosm or macrocosm and the principles of design inherent to nature. All things in creation embody the sacred principles of the Laws of Three and Seven depicted in the *Tree of Life*, through different generations of causes and effects—all worked out from *within without*. The *Tree of Life* can be used as a model for mystical states and applied to the study of physics and metaphysics, as well as to any other area of inquiry.

The *Tree of Life* is composed of 10 Sephirot and the paths which link them. The term "Sephirot" refers to "numerations," "Lights" or "aspects" of God. The Sephirot are represented as circles or spheres in diagrams of the *Tree* and are arranged on Three Pillars (also referred to as the Three Splendors). An eleventh invisible Sephira is also part of Kabbalist teaching and is located between the supernal triad of Sephirot and the seven lesser Sephirot below.

In the *Tree of Life*, the three superior Sephirot are within the *unmanifest supernal realm* and embody the three-fold nature of Negative Existence. Ayin is embodied in the first Sephira, Kether, the Crown and portrayed as a dimensionless point. Chokmah is the Divine Father, the active spiritual force and embodies the En Soph Aur—the Limitless Light. Binah is the Divine Mother and embodies En Soph, the plenum, the seven-fold Aether of Space—the roots of material nature. Binah is associated with the Heart.

> "When applied to the Act of Creation and to the Vacated Space, the Creation represents Chokhmah while the Vacated Space represents Binah. With Chokhmah alone, there would be no diversification within Creation. It is through the Vacated Space, corresponding to Binah, that the design of all the Universes comes into being." (C. Kramer, pp. 211-210)

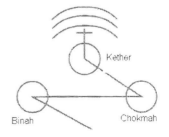

Chokhmah is assigned the attribute of Wisdom. In the Bible, it is written, *"In the*

31

*hearts of the wise, I have placed wisdom."* (Exodus 31:6). God is said to have made all things with Chokhmah or Wisdom and these take form within the heart in Binah. The heart is *"the one that gives form to this thought."* Rebbe Nachman explains: *"For the heart is the "tZuR of the worlds" (Isaiah 26: 4), meaning, tZayaR, the one that gives form to the Attributes."* The *vacated space of the heart* is a sevenfold hyperspace dimension underlying the sevenfold material realms within positive existence.

In the creation metaphysics of Kabbalah, Binah, the Divine Mother, gives birth or form to the *seven lesser Sephirot* in the Worlds below. In *The Book of Concealed Mystery* of the *Zohar*, Moses of Leon wrote:

> "And here the idea or universal form of all the shells is understood, which encompasses the seven inferior emanations of the queen." The 'Seven Inferior Emanations' of the queen are the seven lower Sephiroth..."

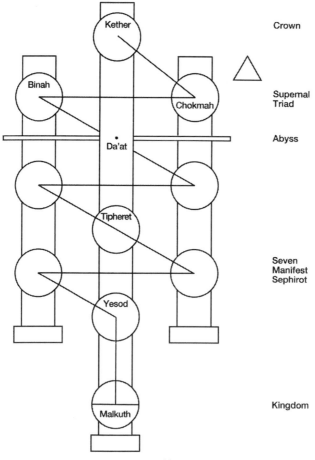

In terms of modern science, this suggests that the ultimate Aether of Space and the roots of material creation within Binah, the Divine Mother, have an inherent sevenfold nature. For Blavatsky, this is the *Seven-skinned Eternal Parent Space*. In Kabbalah, this supernal mother principle, Binah, as the Aether of Space, gives birth to seven lower Sephirot.

This model is consistent with the mystic axiom that: *God is first One, then Three and then Seven.* The division of white light by a three-sided prism to yield a spectrum of seven colours illustrates these arcane principles. Similarly in creation metaphysics, the One manifests a Triune Nature and produces seven worlds below. Furthermore, this pattern is reiterated through many generations of causes and effects. The Mind of God illuminates the Vacated Space of the Heart, as Chokmah and Binah, and the matrix of creation is set into motion through these metaphysical processes.

The conjunction of Kether, Chokmah and Binah (the supernal Father and Mother) produces the Son, Da'at—the $11^{th}$ invisible Sephira, also represented as a point within a circle. Kramer explains: *"Daat is the external manifestation of Keter, It is a quasi-sefirah that must be formed by the confluence of Chokhmah and Binah."* Further, *"Chokhmah is the male aspect that unites with Binah, the female aspect, to create Daat."* (p. 181)

Da'at is the first external manifestation of the Supernal Triad into the worlds below the abyss. Kramer thus explains that: *"Daat itself went into exile"* and further, that an individual can *"redeem Daat from its exile."* The Point that stands out and emerges from the Supernal Triad is the 'spark of holiness.' Blavatsky similarly describes the three falling into four and initiating the pilgrimage of the Son.

Chokmah is associated with Wisdom, Binah with Understanding and Da'at with Knowledge—including the Knowledge of God. Kramer explains in regards to Da'at: *"Man's goal must therefore be the pursuit of Daat, to build his personal sanctuary of spirituality, wherein Godliness can be revealed."* (p. 180)

Da'at embodies Kether as it descends the central pillar of the Tree into the sphere of Tipheret—associated with the Heart. The central pillar of the *Tree of Life* represents the pillar of light, will and consciousness, relative to the side pillars of force and form, the masculine and feminine principles and their generations. The supernal triad manifests as Da'at and this is brought down into the Heart in Tipheret. The Self is thus established within the heart.

Tipheret is associated with the Sun and with the attribute of beauty. Tipheret is the only Sephira directly connected to each of the three supernal Sephira and it is the seventh Sephira central to the other six lesser Sephirot.

However, the consciousness of most people becomes centered over the two lower spheres—of the psyche associated with the genitals and the moon over the Sephira *Yesod*; and the physical body associated with the feet and the earth, and the Sephira *Malkuth* representing material nature. The Sephirot on the central pillar (*Kether, Da'at* and *Tipheret*) represent possible higher levels of human consciousness and illumination, while most peoples' false consciousness system is centered over *Yesod* or *Malkuth*.

According to Kabbalah, creation involves the *"descent of supernal light,"* the *kav* or Ray, from above into the hollow or vacuum created through the Zimzum contraction (and the withdrawal of the Infinite Light). This leads to the sequential unfoldment of the ten Sephirot within the *Tree of Life*. Kabbalah also describes four world orders of *Emanation, Creation, Formation* and *Made*, which can be depicted on the Tree of Life, or as four *Trees of Life*, which overlap and descend from each other as one world order generates the next successive world order. The four worlds of represent the elements of fire, air, water and earth, while the fifth realm of *Adam Kadmon* is the realm of Unity within Negative Existence.

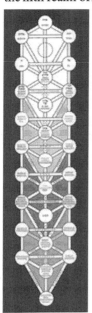

The Kabbalist model of the cosmos is most relevant to the study of a human being and the origins of consciousness and Self. Like the macrocosm, the microcosm or Self, originates as a point source of supernal light and is then conditioned by the three pillars or principles of nature and embodied within seven different world orders. Further, a human being has a physical nature in the world made, a psychical and soul nature in the world of formation, a spiritual nature in the world of creation and a divine nature in the world of Emanation. There is an entire inner physics and metaphysics of being, which serves to *clothe those material points without extension* in different interpenetrating bodies and dimensions.

The *Book of Genesis* describes the *Tree of Life* as existing within the Garden of Eden. Adam and Eve were able to eat freely of the *Tree of Life* but forbidden to eat of the *Tree of Knowledge of Good and Evil*. The eating of the apple of the latter led to the loss of Eden, human exile, the dualities of existence and the certainty of facing physical death. The mystical aim is thus to return to Eden by ascending the Central Pillar through the awakening of consciousness. The *Tree of Life* thus embodies a profound mystery teaching and a map of higher dimensional space and states of higher consciousness.

The zero point teaching in Kabbalah is also represented in the next illustration from Manly Hall's *Secret Teachings of All Ages*. There is a zero point centre surrounded by four worlds—each of which would have a supernal triad and seven planes of manifest existence. All of these dynamics are established surrounding the metaphysics of the divine element, the Monad, within the higher dimensional space of the human heart. These ideas of the

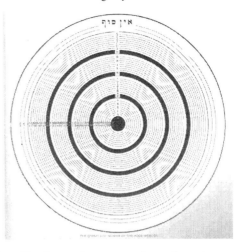

Kabbalists certainly suggest a profoundly alternative approach to the enigmas and mysteries of human consciousness and existence.

*As above, so below*: An individual human being as a microcosm of the macrocosm is designed on the same principles and patterns as are evident in the origin and creation of the universe. Thus, it makes sense to consider the possible zero point origins of human consciousness, the triune and sevenfold nature of human beings and the nature of the light and space within the inner world. Further, just as Binah represents the heart of the Universe—the Aether underlying the material worlds—so it is embodied within the heart Space of a human being. Human beings also come out of the seeming nothingness at the heart of being at the beginning of time and eventually return into the root principles of creation at the end of time. In between, there is a profound mystery play going on. We live a multi-dimensional existence with spirits and souls, and forces that scientists have only begun to imagine.

A mystical account of creation regards all cosmic manifestation as being caused by divine, spiritual, soul and material forces within nature. Subtle higher dimensional forces, intelligences and realms underlie and sustain the observable and tangible material and subtle worlds. From a mystical perspective, the world is really nothing like what the materialist scientists believe or what most people in the normal ego states of human consciousness imagine it to be. The material scientist takes only the last Sephira of the *Tree of Life* or the *Ladder of Jacob* and considers that it exists merely as a physical object and that it has no inner higher dimensional physics to it. Similarly, the heart is considered as only a physical organ and it is not imagined that there might be a higher dimensional metaphysics to the human heart.

All the external phenomena of the world are produced in a manner unspeakable—through an inner geometry involving the circulation and

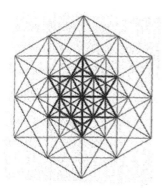

reflection of light within the vacated spaces of zero point fields. The dynamics of these subtle realms of light are governed by a complex and magnificent inner physics and metaphysics of human consciousness and the heart. Kabbalah and Judaism, like *The Secret Doctrine* of H. P. Blavatsky, offer a profound metaphysical view of the nature of the human heart and a model of the higher dimensional origins of consciousness.

Kabbalist L. Leat (1999) depicts the nature of *Da'at, the 11th invisible Sephira* the Son born of the Supernal Triad, which crosses the abyss and declares 'I Am.' The central point of Da'at is surrounded by the *"matrix of creation"*—generated as the Ladder of Jacob unfolds. A multidimensional Star of David surrounds a central point and the I is embodied within the *"matrix of creation,'* as a spider in a web spun of spirit and matter. In essence, this might be considered the "God Particle" of the Kabbalist. It embodies the Star of David pattern with a seventh central element, described by H.P. Blavatsky as *'the seventh key,'* depicted as an ankh at the centre of the *Star of David.* Within *The Secret Doctrine,* Blavatsky provides this summary of the plight of the Monad, which reinforces the system of the Kabbalist enumeration:

> … the MONAD returns into silence and Darkness as soon as it has
> evolved the *triad,* from which emanate the remaining seven numbers
> of the 10 (ten) numbers which are at the base of the manifested
> universe. (I., p. 427)

# 8. Back to the Fool

Divine sparks descend through higher space dimensions within the seven depths of the Divine Mother. The mystic poet Kabir depicts this: *"Inside this jar there are seven oceans and innumerable stars."* Such a seemingly bizarre teaching of cosmic and self-origins is articulated by H. P. Blavatsky in her magnum opus, *The Secret Doctrine* and it can be found within the Kabbalists teachings of the *Tree of Life*. Such teachings offer a profound view of the origins of life emerging "within without from zero points," all through some mysterious inner chemistry or alchemy of multi-dimensional existence.

Unfortunately, scientists have failed to explore the possibility that there are essential links between physics and the study of consciousness, or even to consider the metaphysics of existence. According to a mystical perspective, this is an error of unfathomable proportions as all cosmoses embody the same metaphysical and physical principles of creation and design: *"As above, so below."* All living cosmoses, including the microcosm of human consciousness, emerge from zero point sources and are rooted into the same subtle underlying realms. In this view, the development of a more comprehensive science demands *"a science of the soul"* and with this, a physics and metaphysics of consciousness and the Heart. In fact, the basic concepts of physics and cosmology can be applied to thinking about the origin and nature of consciousness and the heart, if we have the missing links provided by esoteric mystical doctrines.

The *Within-Without from Zero-Point* series involves a complex synthesis of ancient wisdom and modern science. The framework developed allows us to understand how human consciousness might be related to the metaphysical root principles of creation, to a spiritual and soul life, to the larger universe and ultimately to what people call God. These things can all be described in terms of a complex physics and metaphysics of consciousness, light and the heart Space.

Mystical teachings claim that in higher dimensional Space, all things are ultimately integrated into one unifying Source—God or the Absolute. In this vein, all separate individuals around us in life and we ourselves are expressions of the same Unifying Life, which lives through us all. We are all individual "eyes" or "I"s of "THAT"—the divine unity within which we live, move and have our being. Mystical experiences involve penetrating various veils of nature which allow for the realization of these higher Space dimensions and experiences of the unity of things. Human beings have long known in their hearts that such realities exist.

A mystical axiom states: *"Know thyself, and thou shalt know the Universe and the Gods."* In fact, such possibilities are suggested throughout the spiritual, religious and metaphysical teachings of the ages. God is traditionally described as omnipresent—present everywhere, omnipotent—containing all potencies; and omniscient—all knowing. Thus if God exists, then ultimately as we penetrate to the heart of being, to the heart of matter or to the heart of self, then we must arrive at this Unity. Somehow, the universe concentrates itself, as it were, into a single point.

A zero point is a source of light consciousness, life and will, established within the void/plenum, the darkness and fullness of seven dimensional cosmic Space. Every man, woman and child has such a zero point centre —the star nature—established within a higher seven dimensional space. What exactly does this mean and what are the implications and applications of such deceptively simple concepts? These are the deep mysteries to be explored by the fool at the zero point.

This introduction summarizes essential teachings of the *Within-Without from Zero Point* series—concerning the zero point hypotheses, the heart doctrine and the basic metaphysical principles concerning the triune and seven dimensional nature of creation. We turn now to a broader discussion of the issues of science and mysticism, the enigmas of consciousness and the heart, studies of creation physics and metaphysics, to gradually elaborate upon such arcane claims and ideas. Certainly, the enigmas of human consciousness are deep indeed if we consider seriously the claims and theories of the mystics, saints and alchemists.

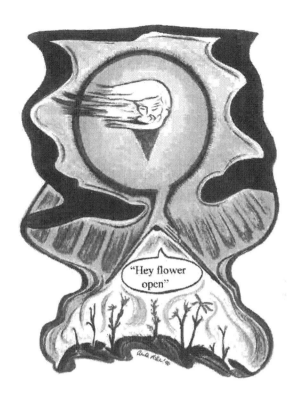

# II
# The Problem of
# God's Contracting Universe

*"As we learn more and more about the universe,*
*there seems less and less for God to do."*

—Carl Sagan

*"...our proposition is that you remain a physical*
*scientist, but you should try to explain God....*
*That is real scientific discovery—to find out God."*

—Swami Prabhupada

# 1. The Problem of God's Contracting Universe

# As posed by Dr. Carl Sagan, Paul Davies & Stephen Hawking

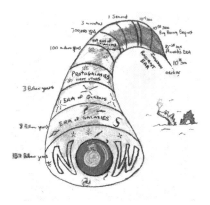

> *"As we learn more and more about the universe,*
> *there seems less and less for God to do."* Carl Sagan (1979, p. 268)

Modern science provides one set of answers to the mysteries of life. In the twentieth century, scientists have articulated an astonishing set of ideas about cosmic origins. The creation of the universe is now traced back to the first moments of existence estimated at some fifteen billion years ago. Physicists and astrophysicists describe the first instant of creation when the universe was $10^{-43}$ seconds old and less than a billion times smaller than the diameter of a proton in size, $10^{-33}$ cm! Such an infinitesimally small point source is called a singularity. Scientists propose that our vast universe had just such zero point or singularity origins.

Physicists are also seeking to unify the four fundamental laws of physics into one "superforce," "superstring" or holographic principle, which would have ruled creation at this first instant of creation before being divided into the various forces and particles of nature. Physicist Paul Davies labels this as the 'God like Superforce.' Thus, scientists trace the universe back to what can be described as a zero point wherein all of the forces of nature are unified.

Beyond the singularity, physicists are concerned with the hidden dimensions of the quantum vacuum, the underlying source of all things. Space and the quantum vacuum are not really 'nothing' as appears to physical perception, but are full of particles, energies, forces and information. One modern physicist declares: "The whole of physics is in the vacuum." The quantum vacuum is both the void and the plenum, the nothingness and its potencies. At the beginning of time, all the quanta (particles) composing material reality manifested out of the seeming nothingness of the quantum vacuum—all through a process of symmetry breaking in higher space dimensions. Physicists label this modern creation scenario 'vacuum genesis' and comment on its likeness to the creation ex nihilo of the mystical and Christian traditions.

From the first instant of creation to the world today, modern scientists have pieced together a fascinating, seemingly consistent and rational view of the origins and evolution of matter, the universe and solar system, the planets, biological life and ultimately humankind. There are theories about the origins of matter, the formation of stars, galaxies and solar systems, the origins of molecular substances and cells, and the neo-Darwinian evolution of plants, animals and human beings from lower life forms. Biologists, biochemists and medical researchers are busily unravelling the mysteries of genetics, the mechanisms of evolution and the dynamics of health and disease.

At the same time, neurologists and neuro-psychologists have explored that most complex and distinctive human organ—the brain, dissecting and mapping its structures and analysing its functions. The nature of intelligence and the capacities of thought and cognition have been subject to countless studies and experiment. In fact, philosophers, psychologists and sociologists seem to have probed every conceivable quirk and quark of the human psyche and its immensely complicated behavioural and emotional patterns.

In every department of the natural and social sciences, a massive literature, multiple theories and mini-theories and arrays of technologies have been accumulated—documenting the scientific advances made over the past century. The development of modern science is an amazing feat which contemporary science writers celebrate and praise lavishly. Clearly, modern science affords profound and penetrating insights into the nature of reality and the issues of origins. Imagine that, that the scientists trace the origin of the Universe to a point source singularity emerging out of a seeming nothingness!

\*\*\*

Dr. Carl Sagan was a celebrated American astronomer and exo-biologist, science writer, television personality and host of the highly acclaimed *Cosmos* T.V. series. Over the past thirty years, Dr. Sagan was one of the most widely read of popular science writers to represent modern scientific ideas, facts and philosophy to the general public. In that role, Dr. Sagan romantically praised the advances of modern science and spoke eloquently on the topics of the nature and philosophy of science, the pseudo-sciences, religion, environmental and cultural issues.

In his writings, Dr. Sagan covered a wide spectrum of subjects ranging from the creation of the universe to the evolution of humankind; the nature of the brain and mind; explorations of alleged paranormal phenomena; environmental and political issues; and even a discussion of the "God hypothesis." In Broca's Brain: Reflections on the Romance of Science, Dr. Sagan considered the viability of religious teachings in view of science's spectacular advances. In a chapter, A Sunday Sermon, he ventured into areas where even angels might fear to tread to address 'the God hypothesis.'

In his sermon, Dr. Sagan argues that as science advances, we are able to explain natural phenomena without recourse to supernatural explanations. As an example, he considers the opening of a morning glory flower. He suggests that at one time, people used to believe that any such event was due to *"direct microintervention by the Deity."* Thus, in order for the flower to open, *"God had to say 'Hey, flower, open.'"* Dr. Sagan then explains that scientists can now account for the opening of the morning glory because they understand phototropism and plant hormones and consequently, there is no need to refer to any sort of divine microintervention. Sagan then applies this same line of reasoning to the whole scheme of creation and evolution, and concludes: *"As we learn more and more about the universe, there seems less and less for God to do."* (1979, p. 286)

Dr. Sagan's comments pose what I call "the problem of God's contracting universe." Is it really correct to say that as science advances, there is less and less for God to do? Has science's progress really removed God from the entire skein of causality all the way back to the beginning—including the very first moment of creation? Carl Sagan expresses a sentiment common to most scientists: that science offers the only valid and comprehensive approach to understanding the nature of reality. Science involves submitting hypotheses to tests of empirical evidence, in terms of a specific set of rules and procedures, which allows one to falsify propositions. It represents a rational and objective body of knowledge, in dramatic contrast to religious teachings which Sagan portrays as only matters of dogma and belief. Dr. Sagan argues that the beauty and strength of the scientific method is that it has freed humans from the dogma and irrationality imposed by religious authority. In Sagan's view, the scrutiny of science exposes the subjectivity of religious insights and pronouncements like a 'candle in the dark.'

In this spirit, Sagan explains, scientists have come to regard all references to God as unnecessary. Sagan offers various examples of natural phenomena which were once believed to be caused by supernatural forces but which gradually 'yielded to scientific understanding.' He states that when Newton explained planetary motion in terms of the theory of gravitation, it was no longer necessary for the "angels to push and pummel the planets." Similarly, when the Marquis de Laplace offered a rational explanation of the origin of the solar system, there was then no need to invoke God to be involved in its creation. (1979, p. 286)

Of course, Dr. Sagan's stories are entertaining but was he really serious about these scientific ideas disproving God? Who exactly is it that said angels had to push and pummel the planets, or that the existence of God is negated by a theory of gravity? Did Carl Sagan really believe that God takes time out from his busy schedule to tell the morning glories, "Hey, flower, open"?

Sagan's examples are most peculiar. His representation of a religious world view is a caricature; a straw man erected in order to push and pummel it with the formidable power of pseudo-scientific thought. By casting religious views in such simplistic terms, Dr. Sagan fixes the outcome of his debate between science and religion. Why would a theory about the origin of the solar system profoundly challenge the necessity of a God being involved in the origins of things? How do these modern theories, or scientific theories in general, bear upon the issue of whether God or Gods exist? Dr. Sagan confidently dismisses the possibility that spiritual or religious perspectives might offer any legitimate scientific hypotheses and he is simply asserting his belief that all religious and spiritual world views are inferior to science—the supposed epitome of rationality and objectivity.

\*\*\*

In *The Mind of God*, Paul Davies, another popular science writer, presents a dialogue between an atheist and a theist, a scientist and a theologian, to illustrate arguments about the existence of God in light of scientific advance. Davies explains the current concept of "the God of the gaps" and discusses how God got "squeezed out" of science. Essentially, the thrust of the atheist's argument is the same as Dr. Sagan's—that as science advances, there is less and less for God to do—He gets squeezed out. Davies's atheist explains that science's capacity to do away with a God or gods now extends all the way back to the very questions of origins and interpretations of the meaning of the "big bang:"

> Atheist: At one time, gods were used as an explanation for all sorts of physical phenomenon, such as the wind and the rain and the motion of the planets. As science progressed, so supernatural agents were found to be superfluous as an explanation for natural events. Why do you insist on invoking God to explain the big bang? ... Theists have always been tempted to seize on any process that science could not at the time explain and claim that God was still needed to explain it. Then, as science progressed, God got squeezed out. You should learn the lesson that this "God of the gaps" is an unreliable hypothesis. As time goes on, there are fewer and fewer gaps for him to inhabit. I personally see no problem in science explaining all natural phenomena, including the origin of life. I concede that the origin of the universe is a tougher nut to crack. But if, as it seems, we have now reached the stage where the only remaining gap is the big bang, it is highly unsatisfying to invoke

the concept of a supernatural being who has been displaced from all else, in the "last-ditch" capacity. (1992, pp. 58-9)

The problem of the 'God of the gaps' is the same as the 'problem of God's contracting universe.' As science advances, there are fewer "gaps" in scientific theory and less reason to regard the world as having "a creator" or to be the result of supernatural or metaphysical causes. The scientists assume that life can be explained most simply in terms of purely natural material processes. The theist's view that God might somehow be involved in the mysterious nature of the big bang and the emergence of a singularity is regarded as a last ditch effort to invoke a superfluous God hypothesis. This is a common attitude expressed by those scientists enthused with modern science and technology, who believe that they are close to solving the mysteries of origins.

In *God and the New Physics*, Paul Davies warns that even when we do find some gap in scientific theory, we should be most cautious about invoking supernatural agencies or forces as causes:

> What once seemed miraculous...perhaps requiring a supernatural input at the big bang, now seems explicable on ordinary physical grounds, in the light of improved scientific understanding. However astonishing and inexplicable a particular occurrence may be, we can never be absolutely sure that at some distant time in the future a natural phenomenon will not be discovered to explain it. (1983, p. 31)

Most scientists are of the opinion that there are few remaining gaps for God to inhabit, now that we are close to understanding the ultimate issues of universal origins.

The prominent physicist and cosmologist Stephen Hawking attempts to explain creation in such a way so as to avoid the God hypothesis. In his best seller, *A Brief History of Time* (1988), Professor Hawking puts forth the view that if scientists are successful in developing a unified theory of quantum gravity, then it would do away with the necessity of a big bang singularity. Hawking explains:

> all our theories of science are formulated on the assumption that space-time is smooth and nearly flat, so they break down at the big bang singularity, where the curvature of space-time is infinite. ... predictability would break down at the big bang. ... Many people do not like the idea that time has a beginning, probably because it smacked of divine intervention. ... There were therefore a number of attempts to avoid the conclusion that there had been a big bang." (1988, pp. 46-7)

In Hawking's unified theory of quantum gravity, the mysterious singularity is simply "smeared out" according to the uncertainty principle of quantum theory. In this case, he argues, science will have arrived at a completely natural explanation of the origin of the universe and there is no need to invoke any metaphysical causes, or God, even in the beginning:

> the quantum theory of gravity has opened up a new possibility, in which there would be no boundary to space-time and so there would be no need to specify the behaviour at the boundary. There would be no singularities at which the laws of science broke down and no edge of space-time at which one would have to appeal to God or some new law to set the boundary conditions for space-time. ... The universe would be completely self-contained and not affected by anything outside itself. It would neither be created nor destroyed. It would just BE." (p. 136)

Professor Hawking portrays himself as explaining away the big bang singularity in terms of natural laws, so that there is nothing left for God to do. He extends this line of reasoning back to the beginning of time in order to argue that we do not need mysticism, religion or God, now that we have science and his promises of a quantum gravity theory. In an interview, Hawking comments: *"We still believe that the universe should be logical and beautiful. We just dropped the word 'God.'"* (In Weber, 1986, p. 212)

* * *

Of course, heaven only knows why Dr. Hawking thinks that there is nothing "mystical" about a singularity—even if it is smeared out into the unity! Of course, Hawking does not consider any of the mystical teachings about zero point origins in his account of science, mysticism and religion. Most orthodox scientists hold pejorative views of religion and mysticism, regarding them as pseudo-scientific, irrational, superstitious, vague and misty belief systems. Charles Tart (1975) once commented that *"being a mystic is considered pathological by most...One of the most deprecating remarks you could make about a scientist's work is to say that it shows signs of being 'mystical.'"* (p. 111) This attitude is evident in Hawking's comments in an interview with Rene Weber (1986):

> I very much disapprove of mysticism. ... I think it's a cop-out. If you find theoretical physics and mathematics too hard, you turn to mysticism. I think people who have this idea about mysticism in physics are people who really can't understand the mathematics. (p. 210)

Many scientists would agree with Hawking's contention, that those who turn to mysticism do so because they are incapable of meeting science's intellectual challenges. Thus, Heinz Pagels (1985a), in an otherwise marvelous book on the creation of the universe, quotes the physicist R. Feynman and draws similar conclusions:

45

If you expected science to give all the answers to the wonderful questions about what we are, where we are going, what the meaning of the universe is, and so on, then I think you could easily become disillusioned and look for some mystic answer. How a scientist can accept a mystic answer, I don't know. I can't believe the special stories that have been made up about our relationship to the universe at large because they seem to be too simple, too connected, too provincial. People ask me if science is true. I say no, we don't know what's true. We're trying to find out, and everything is possibly wrong." (Feynman, quoted p. 368) ... And where am I? I am in the present, this imperfect moment, trying to remain vulnerable to its intense specificity. There is no other time for me to be or place to go, no cosmic consciousness nor facile mysticism into which I can retreat. (p. 370)

In the views of Hawking and Feynmann, mysticism is nothing more than subjective fancy, the refuge of the intellectually challenged and emotionally self-indulgent—in contrast to the objective knowledge of science. Certainly, no one would look to mysticism for insights into the subtle dimensionality of creation or the mysteries of Space, or the issue of the origin of human consciousness.

However, it is readily apparent on reading Sagan, Pagels, Hawking and other popular science writers, who explore creation issues (i.e., Jastrow, Asimov, Davis, Gribbin, Trefil), that these scientists are completely ignorant as to what esoteric religious and mystical teachings actually entail and how they compare to modern scientific theories. They confidently dismiss mysticism as nothing but vague pseudo-sciences, yet there is no academic or scholarly consideration of mystical or esoteric doctrines. In their eagerness to deny mysticism relevance or significance in the search for understanding, scientists betray their unmistakable ignorance of these subjects.

There is, however, one type of God that scientists are willing to admit. In his Sunday Sermon, Dr. Sagan comments that he is frequently asked after his lectures if he "believes in God," and that his answer depends on what the word "God" is taken to mean. Like other scientists, Sagan is willing to accept the idea of God if we equate this concept with the sum of the natural laws of nature, but not if we identify God with some bearded patriarch sitting on a throne counting sparrows, or saying "Hey, flower, open." For Dr. Sagan, the God alternatives seem to be exclusively restricted to a choice between bearded patriarchs and natural laws. He is entirely unaware of the complex metaphysical models and systems which mystical and spiritual teachings put forth.

But clearly, a religious or spiritual person could hardly accept Sagan's identification of God as simply being a label for the sum of physical and natural laws. From a religious or mystical viewpoint, God transcends the laws of nature and is the source of these laws. This Divine Being is omnipresent (present everywhere as the source of all things), omnipotent (containing all potencies for creation and cosmic manifestation) and omniscient (all knowing). These attributes suggest that God is a form of Absolute Consciousness and Being which pervades and sustains creation, and yet is simultaneously transcendent, existing beyond the manifest Cosmos. Dr. Sagan may believe that he is appeasing devotional and religious sentiment but this God of material science—as the sum of natural laws—simply does not coincide with religious or mystical viewpoints.

Further, those who believe in God regard human beings as having a spiritual or soul nature, in addition to the life of the material body/brain. The "soul hypothesis" is a corollary of "the God hypothesis." God is said to be the source of the consciousness and life within the individual, the source of spirit and soul, and even a divine spark. From a religious and mystical viewpoint, all the laws of nature and of the psyche are ultimately of supernatural origin.

Despite his rather limited imagination on the subject of God, Carl Sagan is—excuse the expression—a brave and hearty soul. Thus, he offers some encouragement for the religiously-minded suggesting that:

> a questing, courageous and open mind seems to be the essential tool
> for narrowing the range of our collective ignorance on the subject of
> the existence of God. (1979, p. 311)

How true this is! The questions of the existence of God, spirit and soul, need to be approached with a questing, courageous and open mind, in order to overcome our ignorance about these important subjects. Unfortunately, scientists are not typically exposed to the esoteric side of religious and mystical teachings, and dismiss these possibilities without at all understanding what they entail.

Elsewhere, Dr. Sagan gets to the heart of the problem in his discussion of religion and science noting:

> it is a kindness neither to science nor religion to leave unchallenged
> inadequate arguments for the existence of God. Moreover, debates on
> such questions are good fun, and at the very least, hone the mind for
> useful work. Not much of this sort of disputation is in evidence today,
> perhaps because new arguments for the existence of God which can
> be understood at all are exceedingly rare. (1979, p. 130)

From a scientific perspective, traditional arguments for the existence of God are inadequate and superficial. They are untestable and cannot be falsified, and therefore are considered pseudo-scientific. Science meanwhile discovers natural laws and we might question how it would ever be possible to discover any God, demigods, divine beings or other supernatural forces manifesting in the phenomena of nature according to scientific principles. As Carl Sagan suggests, arguments for the existence of God which can be understood at all within a scientific perspective are exceedingly rare. The matter would seem to end here, with science and religion a world apart and irreconcilable.

Paul Davies' atheist elaborates these same arguments:

Atheist: ... unless you (the theist) have other reasons to believe in God's existence, then merely proclaiming "God created the universe" is totally ad hoc. It is no explanation at all. ... One mystery (the origin of the universe) is explained only in terms of another (God). As a scientist I appeal to Occam's razor, which then dictates that the God hypothesis be rejected as an unnecessary complication. ... the bald statement that "God created the universe" fails to provide any real explanation unless it is accompanied by a detailed mechanism. One wants to know, for example, what properties to assign this God, and precisely how he goes about creating the universe, why the universe has the form it does, and so on. In short, unless you either provide evidence in some other way that such a God exists, or else give a detailed account of how he made the universe that even an atheist like me would regard as deeper, simpler, and more satisfying, I see no reason to believe in such a being. (1992, pp. 59-60)

The *Within-Without from Zero Points* series is an attempt to take up the challenge posed by Drs. Sagan and Hawking and by Davies' atheist. The aim is to elaborate a model of how metaphysical and supernatural forces might indeed create and sustain material worlds and human consciousness, and to illustrate the applications of such a perspective. This is a model of "intelligent design" based upon the study of the esoteric metaphysics articulated within the authorative work of H. P. Blavatsky, Kabbalah and other traditions. Otherwise, if we do not have a model of Intelligent Design, no further progress can be made in the theist-atheist debate. The theist will argue that nature shows evidence of intelligent design and the atheist will argue that it doesn't—that it is just all chance and randomness, and order inherent to material reality. A substantive God theory is needed which describes the mechanisms and dynamics of divine, spiritual and psychical forces, and how these are related to material processes—hence, simplifying the known, predicting new observations and allowing for empirical tests and verification. This is exactly what is inherent and hidden within The Secret Doctrine—a model of such metaphysical dynamics.

Of course, scientists also feel awe in the face of the mysterious nature of existence and do sometimes admit to their ignorance on the ultimate unknowns. Carl Sagan exemplifies this attitude and so, at times, does Stephen Hawking. In Shirley MacLaine's (1989) popular new age book Going Within, she recounted a rather unusual and paradoxical interaction with Dr. Hawking and his then wife, Jane:

I don't remember who made the initial foray into the discussion of "truth beyond what is provable." ... In any case, Jane (Mrs. Hawking) said she was often frustrated with Stephen and his scientific approach to truth because she felt that there was an explanation for life that lay in the lap of the Gods and the heart.

"I don't like mysticism," Stephen said via his voice box computer. "But my wife and I don't always agree." He smiled at her and then at me. "But I need the heart because physics isn't everything."

He hesitated a moment and then said, "I need heart and physics, but I believe that when I die, I die, and it will be finished." (pp. 297-298)

Intuitively, Dr. Hawking feels that there might be something to the heart, something beyond his physics. On the other hand, with his mind and intelligence, Dr Hawking "believes" that when he dies, that's it. He will cease to be and there will be no simple retreat into mystical unity, God or heaven. He does not realize that his own favourite black hole physics, might apply to Self. Maybe he will prefer his nothingness for a while but eventually have time to review it all and ultimately to get it right or at least try again.

The Secret Doctrine proposed new arguments and theories concerning God and creation dynamics, which have never been understood by contemporary science or academic scholarship. This series is a serious scholarly attempt to take up these issues of metaphysics, science and religion, and to address the issues of God and the origins of both the Universe and human consciousness— in a new way, based upon the wisdom teachings of humankind.

Certainly, the God hypothesis and the soul hypothesis are not granted serious consideration by those who subscribe to Dr. Sagan's philosophical approach to universe, nor by adherents of Dr. Hawking's interpretations of quantum gravity theory. However, in the light of esoteric teachings, we can propose a physics with a heart and in fact penetrate to the heart of physics. The key to exploring the God hypothesis actually lies within the physics and metaphysics of the heart itself, the mysteries of zero points, holography and higher space dimensions.

Scientists simply do not understand what esoteric mystical teachings entail, particularly The Secret Doctrine, and how such ideas are related to scientific facts and theories. Consequently, when Dr. Sagan turns his careful thinking to spiritual realities and the existence of divinity, he ends up telling us about God talking to flowers, or angels pushing and pummelling the planets. In this rare book, I have attempted to "modernize the God hypothesis," through a comparative study of modern psychology, physics and cosmology, with the ancient wisdom and secret doctrines. This is a worthwhile endeavour even if it is only "to hone our minds for useful things." At least it can be good fun as Dr. Sagan notes and even allow us to integrate physics and the heart for Dr. Hawking.

# 2. The Problem of GCU as posed by an Indian Swami: On Spiritual Knowledge & Space Flight

The views of His Divine Grace A. C. Bhaktivedanta Swami Prabhupada (1980) provide a dramatic contrast with the materialist perspective of modern science and psychology. The Swami founded the International Society for Krishna Consciousness in America and published a profound library of books articulating the ancient Vedic teaching of India. The title swami means "who is one with Self." The Swami has apparently experienced Self-realization, enlightenment and spiritual awakening. What might the Swami think about Dr. Sagan's claim that there is less and less for God to do, now that we have material science? Whereas western science throughout the last century has denied the existence of the soul and spirit, and the possibilities of supernatural, metaphysical and spiritual realities, and ultimately even God, Swami Prabhupada regards these as the most essential and profound areas for human inquiry into the ultimate realities.

In a conversation with a modern physicist Dr. Gregory Benford, the Swami begins with a straightforward critique of materialist science:

Swami: ...Now, you are a scientist—physicist or chemist?

Scientist: Physical.

Swami: So, by your study of physical laws, if you try to prove there is God, that is your success.

Scientist: It can't be done.

Swami: Then that is your imperfection. ... When you can come to understand Krsna (God) by studying these physical laws, then your science is perfect. Because He is the ultimate source of everything, if you can come to God by studying your physical laws, that is your perfection. Therefore, our proposition is that you remain a physical scientist, but you should try to explain Krsna (God). ... That is real scientific discovery—to find out Krsna. Find out how God is working in the physical and chemical laws, how His brain is working. Everything is working by His brain. There are chemical and physical energies, but everything is going on by God's brain. These chemical and physical laws are acting in such a subtle way that we see everything as coming automatically. There are chemical and physical laws, but how these laws are working you do not know. ...

Scientist: ...you cannot find out anything about God by studying science....

Swami: There is nothing but Krsna. There is nothing else except God. (1980, pp. 15-17)

The Swami is indeed a scoundrel. He claims that all the physical and chemical laws of the universe (and he would include the biological, cosmological, and psychological laws) are operating within the mind or brain of God and that these laws must be understood in this way if we are to perfect science! Of course, modern scientist don't consider the world in this way, nor how the evidences and laws of science could be related to such a God hypothesis.

Dr. Benford assumes that "It can't be done," although he has not likely seriously considered any scientific theory from such a perspective. Dr. Benford points out to Prabhupada that scientists now understand the nature of matter—such as the make up of the grass on which they are sitting, the kinds of molecules which compose it and what forces of nature hold it together. However, the Swami is not impressed and he questions the significance of such knowledge:

> you would rather study the insignificant grass than the God who has created everything. If you could understand Him, automatically you would study the grass. But you want to separate His grass from Him, to study it separately. In this way you can compile volumes and volumes on the subject, but why waste your intelligence in that way? The branch of a tree is beautiful as long as it is attached to the main trunk, but as soon as you cut it off it will dry up. Therefore, what is the use of studying the dried up branch? It is a waste of intelligence. (p. 9)

In Prabhupada's view, the study of any part has to be taken in relationship to the whole—which ultimately is God. We should study the physical laws of nature and of life but not detach them from the main trunk, the mind/brain or being of God. Everything is working as a result of metaphysical causes and therefore science needs to approach nature in this way.

According to the Swami, the supreme knowledge is self-knowledge or "atma-jnana." At one point, he questions Dr. Benford about the scientific knowledge of the spiritual self. Benford notes that there is really *"no scientific knowledge of the spirit soul."* Prabhupada responds by stating simply that: "Therefore there is actually no advancement of scientific knowledge." The Swami explains that there are many departments of knowledge—including the biological and medical study of the body and the psychological study of the mind, but that ultimately, science has to come to study the soul and the spiritual/transcendental nature of the human being. In Prabhupada's view, the body and mind are simply coverings of the spirit soul, just as clothes which cover the material body. Knowledge of the body and the mind is compared to knowledge of an individual's garments, while knowledge of the spirit soul is knowledge of the real Self. It certainly would be silly to study a person's clothes thinking that they are what the individual is. It would be like not knowing where the mind is. Obviously, that would not constitute an advancement of knowledge.

The Swami continues in this vein and makes the wildest claims about the nature of human beings and the implications of this for science and education:

> Swami: You should try to understand this science of God consciousness. ... everyone has dormant consciousness of God. ... It simply requires proper education to awaken it. However, this education is not given in the universities. That is the defect in modern education. ... Because our government does not know that life, especially human life, is meant for understanding God, they are supporting all the departments of knowledge very nicely except the principal department, God consciousness. ... Reasons there may be many, but the principal reason is that this age is the Kali-yuga (dark age). People are not very intelligent, therefore they are trying to avoid this department of knowledge, the most important department of knowledge. ... You do not know so many things. ... (pp. 7,19)

The swami claims that we all have dormant consciousness of God, which can be awakened through education. Further, there is a "science of God consciousness," which the Vedas and other esoteric teachings elaborate. From the Swami's perspective, there is something fundamentally fraudulent about modern materialist science: scientists ignore the most important issues of self-knowledge and the spirit-soul, and study the parts taken out of relationship to the whole. Scientists study the physical laws but ignore the underlying metaphysical causes.

The Swami's comments pose many enigmas and issues, which most scientists dismiss out of hand. The scientist can point to the material benefits of modern science as evidence that at least the scientific method works, whereas the mystical or religious method seems to be simply a matter of faith or delusion. Scientists can split the atom and penetrate matter with particle accelerators, describe the origin of the universe, explore the outer cosmos with telescopes and probes, and have built space stations and landed men on the moon. How could the Swami ignore such advances of scientific knowledge and technology?

As it happens, Prabhupada claims that advanced yogis can acquire far more profound powers and abilities than offered by all of these technologies, by simply observing the practices and disciplines of the science of consciousness and through the attainment of self-knowledge. In a book *Easy Journey to Other Planets*, the Swami notes:

> Even if a materialist wants to enjoy developed material faculties, he can transfer himself to planets where he can experience material pleasures much more advanced than those available on the earth planet ... one can transfer himself to other planets in the material sky by utilizing yogic powers. The playful spaceships of the astronauts are but childish entertainments and are of no use for this purpose. ... In the higher planets of the material world, the yogis can enjoy more comfortable and more pleasant lives for hundreds of thousands of years, but life in those higher planets is not eternal. ... the gross materialists ... reside on this seventh-class planet "Earth." (1977, pp. 28/21)

Prabhupada dares to describe humans' spaceships as childish entertainments and claims that yogis can acquire more advanced mystic powers through this science of consciousness!

Not many scientists or psychologists are likely to consider such claims seriously. The easier and more reassuring course is to simply dismiss the Swami as being just another religious fanatic, like a Kabbalist who might claim to have seen angels. However, if there were any truth to the Swami's remarks, then mystical science would indeed be more advanced than modern science. We can barely reach the moon, the closest of all cosmic bodies to our planet, yet alone explore distant planets in the material or spiritual sky. Imagine being able to travel within the spaces of the larger solar system and beyond, or through other interior dimensions of being. To do this, the yogi would not blast off with rockets, polluting the Earth and costing billions of dollars. Instead, he or she achieves such a feat through knowledge of Self and awakening within other vehicles of the inner cosmos of consciousness.

Of course, it is easy to dismiss the Swami as a lunatic but perhaps he is in touch with truths that are beyond anything that scientists have yet imagined—an ancient yet secret science. In the Swami's view, God's does not have anything less to do in the universe now that we have modern science and Stephen Hawking's quantum gravity theory. Instead, the scientists simply live in "ignorance" of Self and study everything in isolation out of relationship to the whole. Furthermore, there are innumerable "gaps" in modern understanding, especially when it comes to understand the illusive nature of human consciousness.

# 3. The Common Mystics: On the Pervasiveness of Belief in Spiritual Realities

Despite sciences' advances in explaining many aspects of the mind and the physical universe, there is still widespread "belief" throughout our society in supernatural forces and phenomena. The majority of people do believe in some kind of spiritual reality or God and/or claim themselves to have had psychic, mystical and spiritual experiences. Like Mrs. Jane Hawking, the majority of the population feels that *"there is an explanation for life that lay in the lap of the Gods and the heart."* Mrs. Hawking remained unconvinced that Stephen's great intellect and science provided an exhaustive account of creation, but felt that there is something more within the heart. There is, in fact, a fundamental split between what the scientists think they know with their minds and what people intuitively feel in their hearts.

Two major surveys by sociologist Andrew Greeley demonstrate that belief in mystical, spiritual and psychic realities is indeed widespread and the norm in American society. Greeley surveyed 1467 subjects in 1973 and 1474 in 1984. Sample statistics from Greeley's 1984 study show that 67% of Americans claim to have had ESP experiences; 73% believe in life after death; 74% believe that they will be re-united with loved ones after death; and 42% claim to have had contact with the dead. Surveys by the Gallop Organization over the years are consistent with these estimates. Gallop found that 43% of subjects (in 1985) had an unusual spiritual experience; 71% believed in afterlife (in 1981); 95% believed in God or a Universal Spirit, and so on.

In Canada, similar patterns are evident: A 1984 Gallop poll reported that 87% of the Canadian population believe in the existence of God; 71% in the existence of heaven; 39% in hell; and 29% in reincarnation.(Toronto Star, 1984) A more recent VisionTV/TIME poll found that 81% of Canadians strongly (66%) or somewhat (15%) agree that they believe in God; and sixty percent believed in the existence of heaven and/or hell—other dimensions of afterlife existence. When asked whether "having an inner spiritual life" was important, 51% of the sample described this as "very important," and a further 26% as "somewhat important." (TIME, November 24, 2003)

Greeley (1987) discounts the possibility that such statistics simply reflect the prevalence of mental illness or of religious convictions among the population:

> our studies show that people who've tasted the paranormal, whether they accept it intellectually or not, are anything but religious nuts or psychiatric cases. They are, for the most part, ordinary Americans, somewhat above the norm in education and intelligence and somewhat

less than average in religious involvement. We tested people who'd had some of the deeper mystical experiences … with the Affect Balance Scale of psychological well-being, a standard measures of the healthy personality. And the mystics scored at the top. Norman Bradburn, the University of Chicago psychologist who developed the scale, said no other factor has ever been found to correlate so highly. (p. 48)

Indeed, most people in our technological culture do not accept the conclusions of Carl Sagan and Stephen Hawking, materialist science and soul-less psychology and education. Beliefs in God, psychic and spiritual realities are pervasive and in fact are on the upswing. Studies consistently show that psychical experiences and spiritual beliefs are associated with psychological and physical health, social adjustment and creativity—rather than indicating psychological difficulty, social maladjustment or intellectual naiveté.

Throughout the world, vast segments of humanity believe in God, in multiple Gods, in ghosts, afterlife, magic, religion, in psychic phenomena and the paranormal. In fact, the majority of humankind identifies with some major traditional religious teaching, or alternatively with some spiritual philosophy. Surveys demonstrate a modern diversification of religious and spiritual beliefs with increasing adherence to less traditional or orthodox religions and a widespread interest in "otherworldly" subjects—beyond the limits of scientific materialism.

The rigid rationalist and sceptical view is that these facts simply indicates people's gullibility, irrationality, dogmas and delusions. In this vein, Carl Sagan argued passionately that scientists had failed to educate the public about the methods and discoveries of science, and this is why contemporary thinking is so plagued by belief in such psychic and mystical nonsense. Sagan argues that scientists have to be more active in promoting awareness of science's methods and advances in order to combat such belief in the supernatural. Certainly, the sceptics have their work cut out for them in changing the hearts and minds of the public!

Another emerging trend is the rise of New Age philosophies: spiritually oriented but non-dogmatic philosophies with interests ranging from green environmental issues, to native teachings, holistic living, alternative medicines and spiritual growth psychologies. Shirley MacLaine is one prominent New Age spokesperson whose views have been fiercely criticized by journalists and sceptics. Although, ridiculed by some as flaky and opportunistic (Gordon, 1988), MacLaine's success points to the fact that she expresses popular public sentiments and people's spiritual yearnings.

Basic concepts of the New Age philosophy most obviously promote healthy life values and spiritual ethics. MacLaine defines the New Age movement in her book *Going Within* (1989):

the most controversial concept of the New Age philosophy (is) the belief that God lies within, and therefore we are each part of God. Since there is no separateness, we are each Godlike, and God is in each of us. We experience God and God experiences through us. (p. 100)

And all of it comes down to the belief that we each contain and hold the God-spark within us. ... If God is love and each of us possesses God within us, then all of us would be happier and more peaceful with one another, recognizing that the more we try to express as God, the more harmony there will be in the world. That is the basic principle of the New Age. (p. 108)

Certainly, these are valuable ethical and spiritual principles. Unfortunately, as MacLaine notes, there exists within academic and scientific circles a marked hostility and prejudice towards psychical and spiritual ideas. She comments: "... no one is more hidebound than your average scientist." In a similar vein, Greeley describes a "scientific iron curtain raised against serious research on these experiences." For the most part, the educational system unconsciously inculcates the biases of a materialist scientific paradigm and a soul-less psychology.

Of course, the fact that the majority of people believe in the existence of supernatural phenomena does not make them true. However, it also does not mean that they are false and it does suggest that scientists should seriously consider such areas of investigation. In fact, there are innumerable gaps in modern thinking and science left for gods or other invisible powers to inhabit, which will be amply illustrated through this WWZP series. In fact, in every department of human knowledge, there are enigmas, unexplained phenomena and unknowns. Furthermore, the most important scientific issue, the question of the origin and nature of human consciousness, constitutes the most significant unknown.

Perhaps, God and other invisible powers might fill in the gaps in our understanding of consciousness, self and space. If human beings have souls, or "God sparks" within, can live an afterlife and experience other dimensions and spiritual realities, then such significant phenomena necessitate the development of an entirely new scientific paradigm. Mystical and esoteric teachings suggest truly awesome possibilities within the inner cosmos of consciousness, which extend the meaning and significance of human existence in highly significant ways. Unfortunately, scientists and educators consistently ignore the investigation of the most fundamental and profound issues raised by mystical and spiritual teachings, and have no idea of how such teachings relate to the facts, theories and enigmas of science itself. There is considerable fear within scientific circles of mixing "real science" with spirituality or vague mystical speculations. Unfortunately, new arguments for the existence of God which can be understood are exceedingly rare.

The emphasis on the unity and wholeness of life is another central theme in both New Age and ancient mystical teachings. MacLaine notes:

> Basic to New Age subatomic discoveries is the concept that in the subatomic world—the stuff of the universe—everything, every last thing, is linked. The universe is a gigantic multi-dimensional web of influences, or information, light particles, energy patterns, and electromagnetic "fields of reality." Everything it is, everything we are, everything we do, is linked to everything else. There is no separateness. (1989, p. 100)

Various ideas have emerged within modern science to support this basic concept of the wholeness and interrelatedness of life. Holographic models of consciousness, physicist David Bohm's model of "wholeness and the implicate order," and recent ideas concerning creation physics, all illustrate these basic concepts. In addition, there are a number of serious scientists who do search for the soul. Dissatisfied with traditional scientific explanations, these scientists do seek to articulate a more comprehensive account of human nature and the universe, which includes spiritual elements and metaphysical principles.

The common mystics are the masses of people convinced as a result of personal experience and/or religious sentiment, that human beings do indeed have a spiritual or soul nature; and furthermore, that our understanding of the world will be incomplete until we can penetrate to the heart of these most essential and significant issues. They believe that God is not simply the sum of the laws of nature but a living conscious Being-omnipresent, omniscient, and omnipotent-which permeates and sustains all living things from within/without. Emerging ideas in modern science are beginning to provide a scientific basis upon which these ancient claims can be explored. Unfortunately, Carl Sagan and many other scientists, when articulating their Sunday sermons, seem strangely unaware and ill-informed of these matters which challenge the view that God has less and less to do, now that we have modern scientists.

# 4. Mysticism, Science & the Search for Truth

*"Know thyself, and thou wilt know the Universe and the Gods."*
—Ancient mystical axiom—

## 4a. Mystical Self-Knowledge and Unity

A standard dictionary provides these definitions of mysticism:

mysticism: 1. The experience of mystical union or direct communion with ultimate reality reported by mystics; 2. the belief that direct knowledge of God or of spiritual truths can be achieved by personal insight and inspiration; 3. a vague guessing or speculation; also, a belief without a sound basis: guess.

Most scientists and materialist philosophers subscribe to the pejorative view of mysticism implied in the third definition—it involves vague guessing or speculation. Mysticism is viewed as being the domain of the weird or pathological, a cop-out or pacifier for those who are incapable of understanding the mathematics of Stephen Hawking, the theological debunking of Carl Sagan, or Dawkins' selfish-genes.

However, the true meaning of mysticism suggests awesome possibilities for direct experience of the subtle dimensions of being, knowledge of cosmic and spiritual truths, and God realization. *"Know thyself, and thou wilt know the Universe and the Gods."* This ancient maxim expresses the essential mystical claim that the individual can attain supra-mundane Self-knowledge and realize deep truths about the inner nature of reality. By penetrating the veils of illusion imposed by normal waking consciousness and absorption in the subjective world of the ego, the Self reveals the hidden and subtle dimensionality of life and the universe. Mystical teachings and experience provide testimony to the existence of psychic, spiritual and transcendental realities. Self-knowledge is attained through the transformation and awakening of consciousness and the heart and experiences of varied states of mystical realization and union. This includes the direct, immediate and ineffable apprehension of the unity of self with the universe and experiences of metaphysical realities, including the transcendental void and plenum, and God. These provocative claims are made throughout the esoteric spiritual traditions. Certainly, these metaphysical teachings of the ages warrant serious scientific consideration.

In her seminal work, Evelyn Underhill defined mysticism as *"the art of union with reality"* and elaborates upon the possibilities for super-sensual experience:

> Union: the true goal of the mystic quest. In this state the Absolute Life is not merely perceived and enjoyed by the Self, as in Illumination: but is one with it. ... Union must be looked upon as the true goal of mystical growth; that permanent establishment of life upon transcendental levels of reality, of which ecstasies give a foretaste to the soul. ... The Ego is the limitation; that which opposes itself to the Infinite; the states of consciousness free from self, lost in a vaster consciousness, may become modes of the Infinite, and states of Divine Consciousness. ... the ideal ... is to become "modes of the Infinite" ... filled with an abounding sense of the Divine Life .... (1974, pp. 170 & 172)

The mystic seeks union with reality within various realms and to varying degrees, through the transformation and awakening of consciousness. There are numerous states of illumination and super-sensual knowledge and experience legitimately described as mystical.

S. Abhayananda discusses the extraordinary quality of mystical experiences of unity and their astonishing implications for understanding the universe, the Gods and ourselves:

> These assertions by the great mystics of the world were not made as mere philosophical speculations; they were based on experience—an experience so convincing, so real, that all those to whom it has occurred testify unanimously that it is the unmistakable realization of the ultimate Truth of existence. In this experience, called samadhi by the Hindus, nirvana by the Buddhists, fana by the Muslims, and "the mystic union" by the Christians, the consciousness of the individual suddenly becomes the consciousness of the entire vast universe. All previous sense of duality is swallowed up in an awareness of indivisible unity ... .
>
> Even if, before, as a soul he sought union with his God, now, there is no longer a soul/God relationship. ... For him, there is no more relationship, but only the eternal and all-inclusive I AM. Not surprisingly, this illuminating knowledge of an underlying 'I' that is the Soul of the entire universe has a profoundly transformative effect upon the mind of those who have experienced it. The sense of being bound and limited to an individual body and mind, set in time and rimmed by birth and death, is entirely displaced by the keenly experienced awareness of unlimited Being; of an infinitely larger, unqualified Self beyond birth and death. (1996, pp. 2-3)

If the mystical experiences of illumination, revelation and the unity of life are genuine, then they document the fact that there are ways of knowing reality which are totally unlike anything recognized within modern science, philosophy or psychology. Of course, this would only be true if such states are not merely a matter of delusion or intoxication, megalomania or self-indulgence—as the skeptics presume.

Mystics suggest that individual consciousness is rooted into deep levels of Self and underlying dimensions of the cosmos. Certainly, if yogis can actually travel in their subtle bodies to other planets and the Tibetan masters can know the depths of the void or cosmic unity, then mysticism, rather then being some vague pseudo-science, would be a form of *ultimate science*. If there is truth to mystical claims, then all of modern psychology and science is founded upon major misconceptions and mistaken assumptions about the nature of reality and human consciousness.

An esoteric maxim describes a human being as a *"microcosm of the macrocosm."* Thus, within one's being—in the inner universe—there exists a cosmos, which mirrors the essential structure of the external universe. There is an isomorphism, an identity of structure and functions on different scales, between a human being and the universe! A hierarchy of levels of consciousness and being within the human reflects the hierarchical structure of the universe. The mystic, G. I. Gurdjieff described human beings as such *"similitudes of the whole."*

What then is mysticism? Is it vague guessing and the speculation of the deluded and disillusioned, or is it potentially an ultimate science leading to Self-realization, objective knowledge about the mysteries of creation and states of God consciousness? These are most important questions to consider individually in our lives and scientifically, if we are to understand the mysteries of life and the enigmas of human consciousness.

# 4b. Traditions of Mysticism & Esoteric Teachings

Throughout the history of humanity, there have existed numerous mystical, spiritual and occult teachers, schools and influences. The traditions of mysticism form the esoteric or hidden side of the major world religions and include numerous lesser known teachings and philosophies. Like mysticism, the terms "esoteric" and "occult" are widely misunderstood. These terms are defined in a standard dictionary:

esoteric–1a: designed for or understood by the specially initiated alone; 1b: of or relating to knowledge that is restricted to a small group.

occult–1: not revealed: Secret 2: abstruse, mysterious 3: not able to be seen or detected: concealed 4: of or relating to supernatural agencies, their effects, and knowledge of them.

The terms esoteric and occult suggest secret and hidden teachings known only to those initiated into such traditions. In contrast to "esoteric," the term "exoteric" refers to that which is *"suitable to be imparted to the public, belonging to the outer or less initiated circle."* However, esoteric knowledge is based on the realization of higher states of consciousness rather than acquired through mere intellectual development. Its acquisition demands adherence to spiritual disciplines, processes of initiation and direct experiences of Self-realization and illumination.

While this may sound like something of a fairy tale, the fact that most people are unaware of the nature of esoteric teachings and their significance in human history attests to how well such things have been hidden. Nonetheless, for thousands of years, esoteric "schools" have existed wherein this special knowledge and its methods and disciplines have been passed on by direct instruction. Although specific schools have come and gone, and the outer forms of the teachings change, the teachings persist. As a result, these schools produce, at indefinite intervals in history, remarkable figures who introduce systems of thought, religion, philosophy or art forms, which express occult or esoteric knowledge, and which attract those who seek to know the innermost truths.

The richness of the esoteric mystical tradition is apparent when one realizes that its sources include: the Hindu, yogic and Vedic teachings of India; Tibetan mysticism, Buddhism and Taoism; Kabbalist and Jewish mysticism; the philosophies of Pythagoras, Socrates and Plato; Hermes Trismegistus and the Egyptian mystery teachings; the doctrines of the Essenes and Gnostic Christians; Sufism and Islam; and native or aboriginal spirituality. Unfortunately, the hidden mystical aspects of the major world religions are often lost amidst the diverse practices and dogmas of the varied communities of believers. Those who cling to the outer, exoteric forms of worship and belief, usually do so without any idea of their religion's esoteric origins and teachings.

There are a wide variety of both ancient and modern mystical and spiritual teachers and teachings. The eastern traditions include numerous yogis, swamis, and enlightened souls—such as Swami Vivekananda, Sri Aurobindo, the Sufis Rumi and Hazarat Inayat Khan, Paramahansa Yogananda, Swami Muktananda, Swami Rama, Swami Satchitananda, Swami Prabhupada of the Krishna consciousness movement, Ramamurti Mishra, Sri Chinmoy and Sai Baba, the miracle man of modern India. Modern western mysticism includes such psychics, mystics and seers as the alchemists and Hermetic philosophers; Jacobe Boehme; St. Francis of Assisi; Emmanuel Swedenborg; the Rosicrucians; Madame Blavatsky, A. Besant and C. Leadbeater, the teachers of Theosophy; R.

Steiner and the spiritual science of Anthroposophy; the fourth way teaching of G. I. Gurdjieff and his student P. D. Ouspensky; Aleister Crowley and the practice of Magick; Omraam Aivanhov of the Great Universal White Brotherhood; and contemporary American teacher, Adi Da Samraj, embodying the Way of the Heart; and many others.

The mystical traditions can be clearly distinguished from popular New Age philosophies; investigations of psychic phenomenon, such as studies of near death experiences, reincarnation, ghosts and mediumship, and the like; and parapsychology, a highly limited scientific approach to the investigation of such phenomena such as E S P, psycho-kinesis and remote viewing. Material from these sources, although relevant to the study and teachings of mysticism, is distinct from the deeper metaphysical philosophies and spiritual disciplines of the esoteric traditions.

***

The *Within-Without from Zero Points* series draws from a wide range of authentic mystical sources. It is foolish to think that any one teaching embodies the whole and only truth, or that all sources of mystical teachings are equally deep and penetrating. Genuine mystics and spiritual teachers claimed to have penetrated the veils of nature and achieved states of union, spiritual insight and cosmic realization. It seems obviously worthwhile from a scientific and scholarly viewpoint to explore the mystical psychologies, metaphysics and cosmologies of such supposedly enlightened individuals and traditions. What weird things do the yogis, Buddha, Christ, the saints and swamis, masters and spiritual teachers, have to say about the mystical nature of human consciousness and about the relationship of the microcosm (the individual) to the macrocosm (the universe), and to God? What possibilities exist for the awakening of human consciousness, both within life and/or after death? Further, how do the ideas of the mystics compare with those of contemporary psychology and science?

Carl Sagan suggests that debates on the existence of God can at least help to *"hone the mind for useful work."* Unfortunately, he fails to mention the esoteric mystical and spiritual traditions when he hones his mind and dismisses the God hypothesis and the soul hypothesis, with a hop, a skip and a jump. Perhaps the *Within/Without from Zero Points* series can fill the void left by the pronouncements of materialist science philosophers, through a comparative analysis of mystical teachings and modern psychology and science. Esoteric and occult teachings certainly raise fundamental questions about the limitations of modern scientific thought and methods, and offer a radically different approach to understanding the mysteries of human consciousness, cosmic origins, and even God.

# 4c. Illusions of Self-Knowledge: On the Psychopathological and Sleepwalking State of Humanity

If a man could understand all the horror of the lives of ordinary people who are turning round in a circle of insignificant interests and insignificant aims, if he could understand what they are losing, he would understand that there can be only one thing that is serious for him-to escape from the general law, to be free. What can be serious for a man in prison who is condemned to death? Only one thing: How to save himself, how to escape: nothing else is serious. (Gurdjieff, in Ouspensky, 1949, p.364)

Most people think that they already know themselves and there does not seem to be anything mystical or special about that knowledge. An article from the *Toronto Sun* (1984) illustrates this: Five individuals responded to the question: *"How well do you know yourself?"* Jeanine, Gary, Carol, Brian and Anne responded:

"I know myself *very well* because I was able to grow up being myself and that helps a lot. I usually know why I do things and I think friends see me as I see myself. I've met a lot of people who have no idea about what they are all about."

"I know myself *pretty well*. I know my limits in food and drink and I know my capabilities and how far I can go in my job. Psychologically, I'm pretty level. I'd say I am an easy-going, likeable guy who enjoys people and enjoys life."

"*Pretty well.* You get to know yourself by the reactions you get from others in things you do over the years. I analyze everything that happens to make it come together. What I don't know is why I'm 15 minutes late for everything."

"I know myself *pretty well.* It's really important if you want to be happy in life. You can tell just by knowing if you're happy with your life and your job. It's important to know what your capabilities are and what you want out of life."

"Yes, *pretty well.* I started to get to know myself well about a year ago when I started working full time. A lot of it has to do with communicating with other people. It feels good, because you understand why you do some of the things you do." (Emphasis added)

People typically think that they already know themselves *"pretty well"* or *"very well."* They believe that knowing oneself involves knowing your name and personal history, your traits and characteristics, likes and dislikes, ambitions and fears, habits and peculiarities, and the like. However, all of these things constitute people's personalities and personal identities—the egos, masks or personas, which obscure the essential dimensions of a human being.

Even if we were to ask these individuals such grand questions as to the nature of the universe and the Gods, they would undoubtedly be full of many attitudes, opinions and beliefs about those matters as well. Most people have an egocentric attitude, thinking that they are in the know and understand themselves, life and the issues of God—at least as well as anyone else does. As such, they are satisfied to repeat superficial pronouncements and parrot acquired explanations about life gained through the so-called 'education' offered in modern times. Generally, people in life unconsciously gloss over the awesome mysteries posed by the very facts of existence and the extraordinary nature of the world and universe.

Mystics are clearly not referring to ordinary self-knowledge when they speak of knowing the Self, the universe and the Gods. Instead, they are suggesting the existence of a hidden, mysterious Self, which the individual ordinarily does not realize—a Hidden Self. To the mystic, the familiar self is illusory, a persona, mask or veil, a false ego which obscures the true nature of Self. Thus, the mystic's quest is to penetrate the surface personality in order to attain different levels of Self-realization through the process of awakening and psycho-spiritual transformation.

The claim—that human beings in the normal waking state live under a spell of illusion about themselves and the nature of reality—is an ancient theme. In the fourth century B.C., Plato depicted the state of humankind as being that of prisoners chained within an underground den. This is a classic portrait of the sleepwalking and pathological state of humanity:

they see only their own shadows, or the shadows of one another, which the fire throws on the opposite wall of the cave. ... the truth would be to them just nothing but the shadows of the images. ... At first, when any one of them is liberated and compelled suddenly to go up and turn his neck around and walk and look at the light, he will suffer sharp pains; the glare will distress him and he will be unable to see the realities of which in his former state he had seen the shadows; ... what he saw before was an illusion. ... And if he is compelled to look at the light, will he not have a pain in his eyes which will make him turn away? ... And suppose once more, that he is reluctantly dragged up a steep and rugged ascent, and held fast until he is forced into the presence of the sun himself, do you not think that he will be pained and irritated ... He will require to get accustomed to the sight of the upper worlds. ... at last he will be able to see the sun, and not mere reflections of him in the water, but he will see him as he is in his own proper place, and not in another .... (Republic, VII)

Humans take the shadows to be the truth and are incapable of looking into the light of true existence, especially to gaze into the sun or spiritual realms. An individual must *"grow accustomed to the sight of the upper worlds."*

In reality, people are imprisoned by their conditioning and attachments, by a false sense of self, by imaginary fears and concerns. Human beings are like puppets, controlled by invisible strings and hypnotized by the play of shadows. It is only with great difficulty and struggle that an individual can turn around, see the light and know the truth of existence. Plato offers a powerful image of humanity living in ignorance of the light. These themes recur throughout the mystical and spiritual literature.

In the Gnostic *Gospel of Truth*, the nightmare parable depicts the condition of humankind:

Thus they were ignorant of the Father, he being the one whom they did not see. Since it was terror and disturbance and instability and doubt and division, there were many illusions at work by means of these, and there were empty fictions, as if they were sunk in sleep and found themselves in disturbing dreams. Either (there is) a place to which they are fleeing, or without strength, they come from having chased after others, or they are involved in striking blows, or they are receiving blows themselves, or they have fallen from high places, or they take off into the air though they do not even have wings. ... When those who are going through all these things wake up, they see nothing, they who were in the midst of all these disturbances, for they are nothing. Such is the way of those who have cast ignorance aside from them like sleep ... they leave them behind like a dream in the night ... And this is the way he has come to knowledge, as if he had awakened. (Robinson, 1981, p. 43)

The themes of living in darkness, illusion and confusion are central to mystical teachings about the sleepwalking condition of humankind. The *Gnostic Gospels* depict people as *"having no root"* in themselves and as experiencing *"terror and confusion, instability, doubt and division."* We are the lost souls, oblivious to the light and the true nature of Self, shackled by ignorance and preoccupied by the illusory play of shadows.

G. I. Gurdjieff, a twentieth century master and mystic, provides a sophisticated approach to understanding consciousness and the psychopathology of humankind. Whereas an individual can know four levels of consciousness, most people know only the lower two, the *sleep* and *waking sleep* levels. Although people think that they know the next level of *'self consciousness,'* and that they know themselves 'pretty well' or 'very well,' Gurdjieff explains that this is their principle mistake. The effects of education, the media and life experiences are to create a 'false consciousness system' and 'false personality' centred in the intellectual centre and the individual's essential consciousness passes into their so-called 'subconscious.' The masses of people do not attain to the third state of *self consciousness,* nor that of *objective consciousness*. In the normal state, humans are like sleepwalkers in a sleeping world—machines or automatons to whom everything happens and who can "do" nothing. A person is completely controlled by the past conditioning of their mind and emotions, and a false consciousness system replaces their essential consciousness. Gurdjieff states that a human's normal consciousness is an automated state of "waking sleep" wherein the individual no longer *"instinctually senses reality"* or *"remembers himself."*

Replying to a pupil's protest that psychologists, scientists and philosophers regard "consciousness" as being indefinable, Gurdjieff scoffed that this is: *"all rubbish—the usual scientific sophistry."* Gurdjieff explains that we can know consciousness in ourselves, but only when we have it. Unfortunately, humans do not generally attain real I and the state of true Self-consciousness. And so, consciousness is not understood because we are not properly conscious.

The primary mistake, according to Mr. G., consists in thinking that consciousness is always present or that it is never present. In reality, there are different degrees and different levels of consciousness, which can be understood in one's self by "sensation"—by inner taste. No definitions are possible so long as one does not experience directly what we want to define. Consciousness must be distinguished from the *"possibility of consciousness."* Humans have the possibility of consciousness but only rare flashes of deeper consciousness of self. *"Therefore we cannot define what consciousness is."*

Consciousness is a highly variable and dynamic property. Most frequently, a person is embedded or absorbed in the shifting complex of habitual thoughts, feelings and actions, which dominate attention. To realize this in a concrete and practical way is only possible if we systematically attempt to remember to be aware of ourselves in day-to-day, moment-to-moment activity. According to Gurdjieff, it is absolutely useless to attempt to convince an individual through argument, that he or she is not properly conscious. Instead, it is necessary for the individual to make the conscious effort to self-remember to uncover such secrets.

The practices of "self-observation" and "self-remembering" are the main methods within Gurdjieff's approach to self-study. Self-observation is a process of observing, without analysis or judgment, various aspects of one's functioning whether physical, emotional or intellectual. The practice of self-remembering is a method of developing self-awareness by which one attempts to remember to be more fully conscious of one's presence in the here and now. To the extent that one is aware of oneself *being here now*, maintaining one's wakefullness, one is closer to "self-consciousness." Self-observation provides evidence that moments of consciousness are brief and are separated by long intervals of unconscious, mechanical working of "the machine" and the habitual turning of the mind.

By attempting to self-remember, one seeks to become increasingly self-consciously aware and awaken from the state of waking sleep—of always being lost to ourselves. Through repeated attempts to remember oneself, an individual is capable of becoming present in an increasingly deepened state of self-consciousness. Gurdjieff explains also that the true state of self consciousness involves the awakening of the 'higher emotional centre,' associated with the heart and the deep experience that *"I AM."* The distinction between "self-consciousness" and the "waking sleep" of humankind is critical to understanding the personal and scientific illusions about the nature of consciousness, and the difference between the lesser ego and the hidden Self.

Another of humans' most significant and cherished illusions is the belief that we are unified beings and that we know real "I." In reality, a person's presence is fragmented into many little i's, each of which is a partial aspect of the whole, conditioned to internal and external stimuli. Gurdjieff characterizes the common disunity and fragmentation of the sleepwalking state:

> One of man's most important mistakes,…one which must be remembered, is his illusion in regard to his I. … Man has no permanent and unchangeable I. Every thought, every mood, every desire, every sensation, says 'I,' and in each case it seems to be taken for granted that this I belongs to the Whole, to the whole man, and that a thought, a desire, or an aversion is expressed by this Whole. In actual fact there is no foundation whatever for this assumption. Man's every thought and desire appears and lives quite separately and independently of the Whole. And the Whole never expresses itself … Man has no individual

I. But there are, instead, hundreds and thousand of separate small I's, very often entirely unknown to one another, never coming into contact, or, on the contrary, hostile to each other, mutually exclusive and incompatible. Each minute, each moment, man is saying or thinking 'I.' And each time his I is different. ... Man is a plurality. Man's name is legion. (1949, pp. 59-60)

A human being can attain a permanent, unified "I," in the state of true self-consciousness. At a deeper level of oneself, such already exists. However, to awaken to this and then to abide within the state is a process that demands persistent work. Unfortunately, people imagine that they already possess self-consciousness, an unchangeable "I" and the ability "to do," and hence are unwilling to strive in this direction. Thus, humans lose themselves in circles of insignificant interests and insignificant aims, which Gurdjieff describes as the *"horror of the lives of ordinary people."*

For the individual, who does make the effort to study himself or herself, the question of our psychological illusions grows in complexity and significance. He or she realizes the necessity and the importance of being free from the imprisonment of negative emotions, selfishness, attachments and identifications, imaginations and daydreams. These shocking discoveries shatter illusions about who and what we are. As Gurdjieff explains:

self-study and self-observation, if rightly conducted, bring man to the realization of the fact that something is wrong with his machine.... because he is asleep ... he lives and works in a small part of himself. ... the vast majority of his possibilities remain unrealized, the vast majority of his powers are left unused. ... And in observing himself a man notices that self-observation itself brings about certain changes in his inner processes. He begins to understand that self-observation is an instrument of self-change, a means of awakening. By observing himself he throws, as it were, a ray of light onto his inner processes, which have hitherto worked in complete darkness. And under the influence of this light the processes themselves begin to change. There are a great many chemical processes that can take place only in the absence of light. Exactly in the same way many psychic processes can take place only in the dark. Even a feeble light of consciousness is enough to change completely the character of a process, while it makes many of them altogether impossible. Our inner psychic processes (our inner alchemy) have much in common with those chemical processes in which light changes the character of the process and they are subject to analogous laws. (Ouspensky, 1949, pp. 145-6)

The possibility of escaping the sleeping world lies in the persistent effort to cultivate self-awareness and increase the light of consciousness, knowing oneself more fully and deeply at subtle levels and eventually to awaken within one's higher emotional centre. Awakening is associated with the light of consciousness and states of enlightenment. Maurice Nicoll, one of Gurdjieff's pupils, explains:

> what we seek above all things is Light—and Light means consciousness. We seek to live more consciously and to become more conscious. We live in darkness owing to lack of light—the light of consciousness— and we seek in this work light on ourselves. ... And it is very strange this light. ... In the deep sleep we live in, in the light of the Kingdom of Heaven, we are all utterly insane and do not know what we are doing. (1975, pp. 35-6)

By working to awaken, consciousness can be brought to bear within the inner world to dissolve the dreams and sleepwalking state.

Human beings' illusions about themselves are so entrenched and pervasive that they pose almost insurmountable obstacles to the goal of awakening. In order to consciously evolve, the individual must realize in a practical and direct way how infrequently he or she is properly conscious and what powerful forces govern the sleepwalking state. Ouspensky explains:

> When we realize that we are asleep we will see that all history is made by people who are asleep. Sleeping people fight, make laws; sleeping people obey or disobey them. The worst of our illusions are the wrong ideas among which we live and which govern our lives. If we could change our attitude towards these wrong ideas and understand what they are, this in itself would be a great change and would immediately change other things. (1957, p. 29)

The process of awakening dissolves the false ego, which obscures the essence of a human's being. As a rich man cannot enter into the Kingdom of Heaven, so too, the individual conditioned by false ego, cannot enter into the light kingdom and know the truth of existence.

P. D. Ouspensky explains that we cannot understand supernormal psychology because we do not know enough about ordinary psychology and our ordinary state. In this view, esoteric or real psychology deals with the *psychology of a human's possible evolution:* that is how we can evolve in terms of the development of consciousness and being. In contrast, Ouspensky regards modern psychologists as studying man as *"they imagine him to be."* He likens this approach to that of attempting to understand real flowers by studying artificial flowers. (Or, this might be likened to studying a person's clothes, while thinking that they are the person, as in Prabhupada's analogy.)

Western scientists approach the study of consciousness from neurological, biological and philosophical perspectives, from cultural and experimental perspectives, but they neglect the most obvious and important approach of self-study—through self-observation and self-remembering, or through related meditation practices within other teachings. Of course, we can only know consciousness within ourselves, as we can never observe anyone else's inner states. Therefore, psychology cannot be approached solely on an intellectual basis but rather requires the awakening of consciousness within oneself. Most importantly, we have to develop an understanding of humans' normal pathological state, which we do through self-remembering. Ouspensky writes:

> So, at the same time as self-observing, we try to be aware of ourselves by holding the sensation of "I am here"—nothing more. And this is the fact that all Western psychology, without the smallest exception, has missed. Although many people came very near to it, they did not realize the importance of this fact and did not realize that the state of man as he is can be changed—that man can remember himself, if he tries for a long time. (1957, p. 5)

Self-remembering is a method of studying consciousness by making efforts to develop the inner quality of the "I experience." Ouspensky argues: *"... psychology begins at this point ... man does not remember himself but could remember himself if he made sufficient effort. Without self-remembering there can be no study, no psychology."* (1957, p. 120) The most crippling illusion in modern materialist science is the belief that consciousness can be understood outside of oneself—without self-study, self-remembering or a systematic struggle to awaken.

Awakening and self-realization involve the emergence of a hidden order of "I," the basis for the mystical declaration that "I AM." Real I is of divine and spiritual origin and involves the experience of pure light consciousness and inherent blissfulness. This "I"—the I of mystical union—is centered within the metaphysical dimensions of the heart, rather than being produced by the material processes of the brain. The wisdom of the heart and the mystical realizations of "I AM" are the basis for states of mystical union and objective knowledge of the universe and the Gods.

# 4d. Science, Mysticism and the Search for Unity

The scientist and the mystic are both concerned with the search for truth and with the search for unity. The scientist strives from the particulars to the universal, attempting to explain the laws of nature in terms of fewer and fewer fundamental principles. Thus, physicists explain the laws of chemistry in terms of a limited number of atomic elements, which are then reduced to a smaller number of elementary particles that constitute atoms, then further reduced to the subatomic realms of quarks, and finally to higher dimensional superstrings or M-branes. Physicists have also reduced all the phenomena of material nature to four fundamental laws and are striving to describe these as variations of one fundamental superforce. Similarly, astrophysicists trace the creation of the vast universe back to a singularity at the beginning of time—that is, to an original unity. The major quest—the Holy Grail—of modern science is to unify the laws of physics in order to account for the original creation events.

On the other hand, occult science approaches the question of unity from above rather than below. The occultist or mystic regards all phenomena as manifestations of One Life and seeks to derive the many from the One. Prabhupada demonstrates this attitude by assuming that the grass and all the laws of nature are manifestations of the mind/brain of God or Krishna. The Swami encourages us to remain scientists but to explain how the myriad of cosmic phenomenon is derived from the One—how the Universe, as it were, concentrates itself into a point or a particle.

However, there are also fundamental differences between science and mysticism. Rene Weber, (1986), in *Dialogues with Scientists and Sages: The Search for Unity*, explains:

> The drive for unification is a further link between the aims of science and mysticism. ... Despite these similarities, science cannot and should not be conflated with mysticism. The domain and style of science are the cognitive and, unlike mysticism, science asks its questions mainly with the mind. ... if the search for unity is intrinsic to science, an unsettling possibility suggests itself. By the criterion of unity, science may be less "scientific" than mysticism, which aims at a more comprehensive unification. It is mysticism, not science, which pursues the Grand Unified Theory with ruthless logic—the one that includes the questioner within its answer. Although the scientist wants to unify everything in one ultimate equation, he does not want to unify consistently, since he wants to leave himself outside of that equation. ... Of the mystic, more is required. He is engaged in deconstructing and reconstructing not some neutral external reality, but himself. ...
>
> By analogy with the physicist's splitting of the atom, the mystic is engaged in splitting his self-centered ego and the three dimensional thinker that sustains it. ... in his altered state of consciousness, the mystic has learned to harmonize his awareness with the sub-atomic matter of which he is composed. In this process, he aligns himself with the deep structure of nature. ... The mystic, a true alchemist, brings micro-level and macro-level together.

A parallel principle drives both science and mysticism—the assumption that unity lies at the heart of our world and that it can be discovered and experienced by man. ... All mystics seek the depths ... . (pp. 6-16)

The mystical quest is to directly experience unity and not simply to know it with the mind as an intellectual abstraction. Hence, the mystic includes him/herself in the equation as he/she attempts to penetrate to the heart of being.

The mystical search for unity thus involves a struggle to attain more subtle states of unified consciousness. Rodney Collin (1980) vividly portrays the dilemma of searching for unity in a fragmentary state:

> In every age men have tried to assemble all the knowledge and experience of their day into a single whole, which would explain their relation to the universe and their possibilities in it. In the ordinary way they could never succeed. For the unity of things is not realizable by the ordinary mind, in an ordinary state of consciousness. The ordinary mind, refracted by the countless and contradictory promptings of different sides of human nature, must reflect the world as manifold and confused as is man himself. A unity, a pattern, an all-embracing meaning—if it exists—could be discerned or experienced by a different kind of mind, in a different state of consciousness. It would be realizable by a mind, which had itself become unified. What unity, for example, could be perceived by even the most brilliant physicist, philosopher or theologian, while he still trips absent-mindedly over a stool, becomes angry at being short-changed, fails to notice when he irritates his wife, and in general remains subject to the daily trivial blindness of the ordinary mind, working with its customary absence of awareness? Any unity he reaches in such a state can exist only in his imagination. Thus the attempt to gather all knowledge into a whole has always been connected with the search for a new state of consciousness. And it is meaningless and futile apart from such a search. (p. xi)

Herein lies a profound idea, which raises fundamental epistemological and ontological issues. Humans' knowledge and understanding of life and the universe are limited by the development of their own consciousness and being. Ordinary science is conducted primarily in the waking sleep state of normal consciousness, relying on the faculties of the senses and the cognitive functions of the mind. Might it indeed be possible in more refined states of consciousness to experience reality in direct and deeper ways through states of unity, enlightenment and cosmic/spiritual realization?

If consciousness is rooted into subtle, hidden dimensions of space/time, then expanded states of awareness could reveal truths of a different order than those apprehended by normal waking consciousness, conditioned by the material senses and desires. Certainly, normal waking consciousness allows for a more objective knowledge of life and the universe than the illusory world of dream states. In the same way, mystics repeatedly claim that there are more advanced states, which are to normal consciousness what the normal state is to the dream state.

In their consideration of consciousness, modern scientists and psychologists tend to subscribe to a simple dichotomy: human beings are asleep or awake, conscious or unconscious, aware or unaware. In the *Scientific American* article on consciousness, Roth had a continuum with 'vigilance' as one endpoint and 'coma' as the other. And while many scientists and psychologists may obliquely acknowledge the phenomenon of higher states of consciousness, there is, in effect, practically no recognition of the theoretical implications of this possibility and, hence, no admission of the need to consider a hierarchy of consciousness states and the higher-dimensional nature of human existence. Conventional thinking does not allow for the idea of higher understanding or wisdom of self, reality, or the universe.

By limiting its application to the material world and normal consciousness, science's quest for an objective understanding of the universe is a grand illusion. Science fails to understand that higher metaphysical dimensions not only exist, but inform and direct all manifestation of matter and energy within the time and space of the physical universe. By ignoring methods of developing higher states of consciousness, science commits itself to a method which in its quest for a comprehensive explanation of the universe is fundamentally flawed. The scientist is left out of the equation.

Mystical and esoteric teachings assert that the level of one's knowledge is dependent upon the level of one's being. As Rodney Collin points out, the attempt to gather all knowledge into a whole must be *"connected with the search for a new state of consciousness."* Further, this new state of consciousness is dependent upon the processes of psycho-spiritual transformation.

According to Hindu and Buddhist teachings, normal waking consciousness and the level of physical reality which it apprehends are ruled by *maya* or illusion. The terms illusion or maya do not mean that the world is not real or has no existence. Lama Govinda, a twentieth century Tibetan Buddhist teacher and commentator, identifies the strict sense in which *maya* means illusion:

> If we call maya a reality of a lower degree, we do this because illusion rests on the wrong interpretation of a partial aspect of reality. Compared with the highest or 'absolute' reality, all forms, in which this reality appears to us, are illusory, because they are only partial

aspects, and as such incomplete, torn out of their organic connections and deprived of their universal relationship. The only reality, which we could call 'absolute,' is that of the all-embracing whole. Each partial aspect must therefore constitute a lesser degree of reality—the less universal, the more illusory and impermanent. (1962, p. 217)

The study of any partial aspect of reality deprived of its universal relationship can only result in knowledge which is incomplete and misleading. We take the shadows as reality and ignore the underlying causes. Ultimately, everything must be understood in relationship to the all-embracing unity, in order to properly understand any of its partial aspects.

Judging the validity of these claims is a very difficult and exacting task. As Renee Weber says, the mystic *"is engaged in splitting his self-centered ego and the three dimensional thinker that sustains it... ."* It is this Herculean labor, which one must undertake in order to properly assess mystical knowledge. For anyone who makes even the most rudimentary efforts to study himself, it becomes evident early on that this task demands discipline, effort and commitment, and then grace. In contrast to the pejorative views of mysticism suggested by Stephen Hawking, Carl Sagan, and thinkers of their ilk, the mystic quest to include consciousness and knowing Self in the equation is most profound.

Of course, there is nothing new in this idea that mystical knowledge may be more comprehensive and unified than scientific knowledge. In this vein, Ouspensky (1922) stated: *"science must come to mysticism, because in mysticism there is a new method—and then to the study of different forms of consciousness, i.e., forms of receptivity different from our own."* Ouspensky claimed that science should throw off almost everything old and start afresh with a new theory of knowledge based on understanding levels of consciousness.

Some fifty years later, with the publication of *The Tao of Physics* (1975), Fritjof Capra revitalized interest in the significance of mystical teachings for modern thought. He detailed similarities between the world-views put forth by mystics and modern physicists. Capra noted that science historically has been based on Descartes' dictum, *"I think, therefore I am,"* which encouraged western philosophers to equate their identity with the mind and the ego isolated within the body. In contrast, Capra noted that eastern spiritual teachings emphasize the basic unity of the universe and that the highest mystical aim is to experience the interrelatedness of all things. In this case, the isolated individual ego is transcended and one might experience deeper realities in states of enlightenment. Capra recounted his personal experiences which led to the writing of *The Tao of Physics*:

Five years ago, I had a beautiful experience... I was sitting by the ocean one late summer afternoon, watching the waves rolling in and feeling the rhythm of my breathing, when I suddenly became aware of my whole environment as being engaged in a gigantic cosmic dance. Being a physicist, I knew that the sand, rocks, water and air around me were made of vibrating molecules and atoms, and that these consisted of particles which interacted with one another by creating and destroying other particles. I knew also that the Earth's atmosphere was continually bombarded by showers of 'cosmic rays,' particles of high energy undergoing multiple collisions as they penetrated the air. All this was familiar to me from my research in high-energy physics, but until that moment I had only experienced it through graphs, diagrams and mathematical theories. As I sat on that beach my former experiences came to life; … I 'saw' the atoms of the elements and those of my body participating in this cosmic dance of energy; I felt its rhythm and I 'heard' its sound, and at that moment I knew that this was the Dance of Shiva, the Lord of Dancers worshiped by the Hindus. (1976, p. 9)

Whereas Capra had intellectually known the theories about the underlying quantum world, he then had this remarkable experience and directly apprehended the vibratory quantum reality. Capra was not in a state of Absolute Union, knowing the universe and the Gods, but he did experience a state of union on a lower order of scale in relation to his immediate environment. The Hindu mystics would describe this as one of varied states of samadhi.

Capra's extraordinary experience illustrates the differences between scientific and mystical knowledge. While most scientists confidently dismiss mysticism, their attitudes are really nothing more than the product of their conditioning, exposure to materialist science philosophy, and studies of isolated phenomena taken out of relation to the whole. Scientists generally do not know themselves or have informed opinions on mystical teachings and claims, or the issues of consciousness. Perhaps enlightened or awakened states of consciousness do allow for the penetration of the cosmic mysteries and the direct realization of ultimate realities. A flash of such awareness appears to have happened to Capra, as to many others, who are then convinced that there is something far deeper to reality than ordinarily meets the senses, or engages the minds of skeptics and material scientists.

Shiva stands upon the Dwarf of Ignorance, detailed here. The Dwarf of Ignorance represents the masses of humankind who live in ignorance of Self. Shiva, in the dance of ecstasy, portrays the transcendence of this ignorance within ourselves and realization of the inner life of ecstasy. Humans live in a state of forgetfulness, like the Dwarf of Ignorance, but the possibility exists to remember one's true nature. Mystical and spiritual teachings set forth different emphases and assume different orientations to transformation and awakening, but all speak of the possibilities  for enlightenment and supernatural modes of experience and existence. In fact, all of life is miraculous and it is only we, in our state of sleep, who are ignorant about the essential nature of reality and self. All of material nature exists in relationship to deeper dimensions of existence and being, and all physics must ultimately lead to metaphysics.

***

To return to *the problem of God's contracting universe:* we certainly have two diametrically opposed viewpoints and approaches to explore. On the one hand, the natural scientists, represented by Drs. Sagan and Hawking, maintain *"as science advances, there is less and less for God to do."* This line of reasoning is applied to everything—indeed to the very creation of the universe from a singularity! On the other hand, we have a little Indian swami who claims that all the laws of nature are operating within the mind/brain of the Supreme Krishna (or God), and that we all have dormant consciousness of God, which can be realized if we attain true self-knowledge. Is there really less and less for God to do, if we can smear out the big bang singularity and arrive at a quantum gravity theory to unify the laws of physics? Or, are the materialist scientists simply sleepwalkers, conditioned and limited by normal egoistic consciousness and lacking the true wisdom and understanding of self?

There is one major fly in the ointment for modern scientists, who so readily and eagerly dismiss God, the mystical and the paranormal. This fly—this issue—concerns the nature and origin of human consciousness. The issue of consciousness is the major enigma or unsolved mystery within the domain of modern psychology and science, and no account of creation and evolution will be complete until it is resolved. Perhaps the problem for the materialist scientist is simply that s/he has not shattered the self-centered ego and explored the depths of consciousness, thereby penetrating to the mystical heart of being. Furthermore, a new model and understanding of consciousness raises all kinds of issues in other areas and disciplines—in physics, cosmology, evolutionary theory, in the life and social sciences.

In the spirit of the scientific endeavor, it is important to consider seriously such states of expanded and enlightened consciousness, and how such things might be possible. Carl Sagan and Stephen Hawking may dismiss God and mysticism with a hop, skip and a jump, but are themselves only human, failing to know when they irritate their wives and feeling annoyed when they are short-changed. Mrs. Hawking might know, in her heart, something which Stephen's great ego and intellect will never penetrate. Nevertheless, we need a model and theory which does not simply assert that God exists, but which also explains the mechanisms, dynamics and implications of such supernatural causes and processes. As it happens, esoteric teachings do just this and provide a complex and detailed perspective on the origins and nature of human consciousness, and of the physics and metaphysics of life and the cosmos. Indeed, the sophisticated metaphysical views of the mystics are highly relevant to the solution of the enigmas and mysteries of modern science.

# 5. The Occult Side of Nature

In 1888, Blavatsky published *The Secret Doctrine*, a massive, seemingly incomprehensible manuscript detailing mystical and esoteric views of *Cosmogenesis*, the creation of the universe or cosmos, and *Anthropogenesis*, the origins or genesis of humankind.

One of Blavatsky's stated aims, in *The Secret Doctrine*, was to demonstrate that *"the occult side of Nature has never been approached by the science of modern civilization."* Despite the fact that a few scientists search for the soul or explore mysticism and the new physics, scientists have hardly begun to scratch the surface of the ancient wisdom teachings. This is largely because scientists do not know of or understand the occult teachings. Beyond this pervasive ignorance, there is a more fundamental fear of mystical teachings: scientists do not want to see their so-called *real science* mixed up with mystical nonsense, vague metaphysical speculation or superstition. However, Blavatsky regarded scientists' attitudes towards mysticism as being indefensible. She bluntly accused them of being irrationally close-minded, noting that, *"...in our days, Scientists are more self-opinionated and bigoted than even the clergy."* (p. 509)

Madame Blavatsky did not regard science and occultism as incompatible. Rather, her view was that as science advanced, it *must* come to validate mystical teachings:

> There can be no possible conflict between the teachings of occult and so-called exact Science, where the conclusions of the latter are grounded on a substratum of unassailable fact. ... Science can, it is true, collect, classify, and generalize upon phenomena; but the occultist, arguing from admitted metaphysical data, declares that the daring explorer, who would probe the inmost secrets of Nature, must transcend the narrow limitations of sense, and transfer his consciousness into the region of noumena and the sphere of primal causes. (1888, p. 477)

Blavatsky explains that when so-called exact science really achieves a correct understanding of the nature of life, it will confirm the claims of mystic seers who directly apprehend the underlying or innermost side of creation.

Although Madame Blavatsky was very outspoken in her attacks on the scientific opinion of her day, she was not motivated by disrespect for scientists' aims. Rather, she sought the advancement of science and in *The Secret Doctrine* she goes to great lengths to demonstrate the relationships between the ancient teachings and the prevailing scientific views of her time. She notes:

> the Secret teachings ... must be contrasted with the speculations of modern science. Archaic axioms must be placed side by side with

modern hypotheses and comparison left to the sagacious reader. (1888, p. 480)

According to Blavatsky, scientific theories are inadequate because they base their level of causal explanation on material processes alone and settle for a partial apprehension of the whole. Scientists deal only with the observable side of phenomena rather than the underlying noumena or causes, because they exclude consideration of the spiritual and metaphysical side of life:

> To make of Science an integral *whole* necessitates, indeed, the study of spiritual and psychic, as well as physical Nature. ... Without metaphysics ... real science is inadmissible. (p. 588)

All science must ultimately lead to metaphysics and supernatural causes, because these dimensions and forces exist and underlie all things!

In this view, scientists should give special consideration to the ancient wisdom in four major areas of inquiry: 1) cosmogenesis, the genesis or creation of the cosmos or universe; 2) the relationship of the laws of physics to ancient metaphysics, to explain the ultimate nature of matter, energy, time and space, and the mechanisms of the laws of nature; 3) evolution, which needs to be considered from a spiritual and metaphysical perspective, in addition to the material and biological; and, 4) human consciousness and existence, which involve a soul and spiritual life, and are rooted into deep metaphysical realities. An occult perspective requires the inclusion of spiritual and metaphysical explanations in all four areas. As Madame Blavatsky states, "*Without metaphysics ... real science is inadmissible.*" (p. 588)

It is over a hundred years since the publication of *The Secret Doctrine* but there has been little change in the dominance of materialism and reductionism within modern science despite the multiple enigmas posed by the new physics. It is unfortunate that scientists tend to equate belief in the spiritual nature of life, or in mysticism and ancient wisdom, with the belief in an old, bearded man who sits up in heaven counting sparrows or talking to flowers. These scientists have no idea of the profound metaphysical philosophies and scientific viewpoints embodied within the ancient wisdom teachings.

The views of consciousness and metaphysics of the mystical tradition are most worth of scholarly and scientific investigation. Kabbalah provides a remarkable teaching, as does *The Secret Doctrine*, the Vedas, and such. The *Within-Without from Zero Points* series will elaborate upon the astonishing convergence of ancient wisdom and the most recent ideas in modern physics and cosmology in understanding creation events and the holographic physics of life. We need to lay the viewpoints side by side, with the head doctrine compared to the heart doctrine and modern physics compared to ancient metaphysics. However, it is the study of consciousness that provides the key to penetrating the deeper cosmic mysteries and resolving the problem of God's contracting universe.

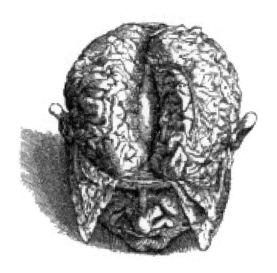

# III

# THE HEAD DOCTRINE
## Modern Views of the Origin and Nature of Human Consciousness

"The cerebral cortex is where matter (is) transformed into consciousness."

—Carl Sagan, 1980

"I don't see any way for consciousness to emerge or be generated apart from a functioning brain." —Roger Sperry, 1984

"The molecules of my body, after my conception, added other molecules and arranged the whole into more and more complex form, and in a unique fashion, not quite like the arrangement in any other living thing that ever lived. In the process, I developed, little by little, into a conscious something I call "I" that exists only as the arrangement. When the arrangement is lost forever, as it will be when I die, the 'I' will be lost forever, too."

—Isaac Asimov, 1981

# 1. Modern Definitions of Psychology

The original Greek meaning of the term psychology suggested a science or knowledge (logos) of the soul (psyche). However, with the advent of modern psychology, this definition effectively disappeared. At the turn of the last century, Darwin's theory of natural selection offered an explanation for the evolution of humankind in terms of natural laws, rather than by invoking supernatural agencies or forces. As a result, psychologists, who wished to establish their fledgling discipline as a legitimate science, were freed from religious dogma and sought to develop natural scientific explanations of human nature. They did away with the concept of *soul* and the term *psyche* was reinterpreted to mean *mind*. Human beings came to be regarded as essentially material biological organisms with a mind and a body. Under this theoretical imperative, the early introspectionists, behaviourists, psychoanalysts and empirical philosophers all rejected any consideration of the human soul or spirit, and regarded such concepts as unscientific, superstitious and simply religious dogmas.

In 1879, Wilhelm Wundt established the first modern psychological laboratory, earning him the title of the father of experimental psychology. As an introspectionist, Wundt held that the major task of psychology was to analyze the contents of consciousness in order to determine the structure of the mind. Accordingly, he had subjects introspect upon the processes of sensation, perception, discrimination, thinking, imaging and so on, in order to describe them in standardized laboratory settings. Analyzing subjects' introspections, Wundt concluded that awareness of the self or ego was nothing more than awareness of thoughts, feelings and sensations. He asserted that careful introspection failed to reveal anything in the nature of a soul over and above these processes of the mind.

However, it was the behaviourists who were most instrumental in leading modern psychology to abandon not only the study of psyche, but even the study of consciousness and mind. In 1913, John Watson defined psychology as the "science of behaviour," which was to exert a major influence on the course of western psychology over the next seventy years. Behaviourism was to be a purely objective, experimental natural science with the theoretical goal of predicting and controlling behaviour. Watson declared: *"The time seems to have come when psychology must discard all references to consciousness."* (1913, p. 163)

Watson disposed of the spirit or soul as easily and arbitrarily as he disposed of all mental constructs. He linked the idea of a soul to that of a *"substantive consciousness;"* a consciousness which is some thing, having some form of substance, matter or energy, and which exists in its own right. Watson (1924) rejected both:

> 'consciousness' is neither a definable nor a usable concept; that it is
> merely another word for the 'soul' of more ancient times. ... No one

has ever touched a soul or seen one in a test tube. Consciousness is just as unprovable, as unapproachable as the old concept of the soul. The behaviourists reached the conclusion that they could no longer be content to work with intangibles and unapproachables.

By declaring consciousness to be as unapproachable and unprovable as the existence of the soul, Watson's behavioural manifesto largely banished the concepts of consciousness from modern academic psychology for the next fifty years.

In contrast to the behaviourists, Sigmund Freud, regarded as the father of modern theories of personality and psychopathology, was primarily interested in the workings of the psyche, which he took to involve three levels of the conscious, preconscious and unconscious mind. However, Freud regarded consciousness and the psyche as the product of purely material forces and the biological transformation of energies. Freudian psychology acknowledged the utility of such concepts as consciousness and the mind, but in keeping with the intellectual spirit of the times, all references to the soul or spirit were omitted. At times, Freud expressed interest in paranormal phenomena but for the most part he dismissed religious ideas of the soul and God as simply being expressions of infantile conflicts and needs. Religion was rooted in *primary process* and magical thinking, rather than in the rational *secondary process* thinking of the conscious ego. For Freud, the idea of God arose with the formation of the superego during the Oedipal period of psychosexual development. Similarly, he regarded religious aspirations and beliefs as nothing more than a means of dealing with unacceptable sexual and aggressive impulses towards one's father and mother. The *"oceanic feelings"* of oneness reported by mystics were interpreted by Freud as expressing a desire to return to the tensionless conditions of the womb and pre-birth existence.

Freud provided explanations for religious and spiritual phenomena in terms of organismic energies, primitive psychic functioning and pathological psychodynamics. In this reductionism, there could be little future for religious belief. In 1914, in *The Future of an Illusion*, he wrote:

> The scientific spirit engenders a particular attitude to the problems of this world; before the problems of religion it halts for a while, then waivers, and finally here steps over the threshold. In this process there is no stopping. The more the fruits of knowledge are accessible to men, the more widespread is the decline of religious belief... .(p. 48)

Thus, Freud anticipated modern attitudes in suggesting that there would be less and less for God to do with the advancement of science.

In twentieth century philosophy, the logical positivist perspective also served to discredit beliefs in metaphysics and the soul. In his book, *The Concept of the Mind*, the Oxford philosopher, Gilbert Ryle (1949) argued that the idea of a soul, or of some immaterial mind over and above the activities of the body/brain, was simply a *"category mistake:"* that is, an error in logic and language. Ryle reasoned that the mind or spirit is not a thing, which can be separated from a person's thoughts, feelings and actions. There is no "I" or self apart from the sum total of the activities of the material brain. He attacked the *"dogma of the ghost in the machine:"* the belief that there is some immaterial soul or mind, which could exist and function independently of the organism's biological makeup.

Modern psychology thus assumes that in studying human behaviour and experience, there is no need to consider the existence of a soul–or any other divine or spiritual principles within human beings. Psychologists assume a purely materialist approach to the nature of the brain, the mind and self. There is no "I" or self apart from the sum of the person's psychological functions (of thinking, feeling, sensation, and so on)—all of which are the end products of processes within the physical brain. The opening quotation from Isaac Asimov illustrates this principle. Asimov describes his "I" as having developed directly from the molecular arrangements of his physical body and he argues that when the body/ brain disintegrates and the arrangement is lost at death, then *"the 'I' will be lost forever, too."* (1981) Similarly, Paul Davies states that: *"There seems to be no scientific evidence for any special divine quality in man... ."* (1983, p. 96) The vast majority of psychologists, philosophers and scientists accept such a viewpoint, at least as a working assumption. There is no ghost in the machine.

In introductory textbooks, psychology is today most widely defined as *the science of human behaviour and mind.* The strict behaviourist influence has waned to some extent and theoretical approaches emphasizing mental and cognitive processes have become increasingly prominent in recent years. However, mainstream psychology has yet to reconsider the possibility of a science of the soul. Thus, psychologists subscribe to the predominant scientific paradigm in which human life and consciousness are viewed as having emerged in accordance with natural laws from non-sentient matter, in a god-less universe, governed by chance and the random processes of natural selection. Accordingly, human beings are *nothing but* biological organisms—higher primates—pursuing pleasure and avoiding pain, trying to reproduce their genes, searching for meaning and selfhood within complex material and social environments, all between the poles of existence, birth and death. When the arrangement of molecules is lost, the "I" is believed to disappear.

Of course, some psychological theorists and modern thinkers do explore the significance of such distinctly human attributes as the capacities for abstract thought and cognition, the use of language, altruism and subtle emotions, intuitions and inspirations, self awareness or self consciousness. Others even explore the peak experiences of ecstasy and insight, and altered states of consciousness related to such things as hypnosis, drug use, meditation and psychiatric conditions. Nevertheless, despite these inquiries, the mainstream of modern, so-called exact psychology and science still rejects the possibility of psychology as a science of soul.

# 2. William James on the Most Mysterious Thing in the World

William James, the early 20th century American philosopher and psychologist, has been one of the most influential figures in promoting western approaches to the study of consciousness and mind. This was evident in the frequency with which James was cited as an authority during the 1970's and 1980's when the topic of consciousness re-emerged in psychology.

James' early *Principles of Psychology* (1890) began with this definition of psychology: *"Psychology is the Science of Mental Life, both its phenomena and their conditions."* (p. 1) In the 1892, abridged version of the *Principles*, this definition is changed to: *"... the description and explanation of states of consciousness as such."* (p. 15) Psychology was, according to James, most essentially concerned with the mental life and consciousness. Although James modified his views of the nature of consciousness and mind through his life, a number of his early descriptions of consciousness are widely quoted in contemporary psychology:

> By states of consciousness are meant such things as sensations, desires, emotions, cognitions, reasonings, decisions, volitions, and the like. (p. 1)

> The first and foremost concrete fact which every one will affirm to belong to his inner experience is the fact that *consciousness of some sort goes on. 'States of mind' succeed each other in him.* ... we must simply say that *thought goes on.* (p. 167)

Consciousness is identified in a general way with the stream of psychological processes which go on within the mind. Hence, it is equated with the flow of sensations, desires, emotions and cognition, the *"stream of subjective life"* or the *"stream of thought."* James even suggested the site which he thought was most likely basis of these states of consciousness: *"The immediate condition of a state of consciousness is an activity of some sort in the cerebral hemispheres."* (1892, p. 18)

In modern consciousness studies, Strange (1978), in *The Stream of Consciousness*, describes James as a prominent influence:

> James contributes the basic definition of consciousness to the mainstream of American, functional, cognitive psychology–consciousness is thought, which includes all the mental activities, such as feeling, imagining, reasoning, knowing, perceiving, conceiving, remembering, and all the rest. Consciousness, according to him, is not a substance, nor a place, nor any *thing*, except a stream of thought that results from pure experiencing. (p. 15)

Strange's comments identify two definitive elements in the modern approach to the study of consciousness. Firstly, it is equated generally with the stream of thought, minding activity or of subjective life. Experimental approaches to consciousness are then based upon subjects' reports of *the contents* of their inner experiences. Hence, researchers sample different thoughts and daydreams over time and describe this as a study of the "stream of consciousness."

The equation of consciousness with thinking, or cognition, became quite prominent within the minds of most psychologists. Ey (1978) comments:

> It is common knowledge (psychologists have all noted—and it is not an original discovery to repeat it) that to be conscious is to know one's experience, and that all experience insofar as it is 'known' by the subject is discursive. ... Consciousness lies in the verbalization of the phenomena, which unfold in consciousness. ... to be conscious is to be capable of grasping one's knowledge in the categories of verbal communication. ... Language is thus a structural quality of consciousness. (p. 16)

Certainly not all psychologists have taken language to be a structural quality of consciousness, but nonetheless this is a definitive feature of cognitive theories.

Secondly, as Strange notes, consciousness is defined as "a stream of thought that results from pure experiencing." Thus, consciousness has two defining features: a pure experiencing or awareness component, which exists in relation to the particular contents of experience (the thoughts, feelings, sensations and the like.) Whereas experimental approaches to consciousness focus on the contents of consciousness, philosophical approaches often refer to this abstract, subjective side. Significantly, most psychologists simply equate consciousness with thinking and cognitive processes and ignore the trickier issues concerning the nature of the pure experiencing element. It is simply assumed that the stream of consciousness is equivalent to the stream of thought and neurological processes occurring within the brain. The scientific approach emphasizes the object side of consciousness and politely ignores its subjective aspect. Scientists do not regard the subjective side of consciousness as being anything substantive in itself apart from the contents of the mind. William James described this dualistic nature of the self:

> Whatever I may be thinking of, I am always at the same time more or less aware of *myself*, of my *personal existence*. At the same time it is I who am aware; so that the total self of me, being as it were duplex, partly known and partly knower, partly object and partly subject, must have two aspects discriminated in it ... the *Me* and ... the *I*. (1892, p. 189)

For practical purposes, psychologists do not explore the "I" aspect of self–the pure experiencing component–but focus on the "me" aspect. Thus, consciousness is equated with the general stream of inner thoughts, images, feelings and all the rest. The empiricist skirts around a host of extremely tricky and perplexing issues in this way.

Later in his life, William James, after years of investigating consciousness and the possibility of survival after death, came to regard consciousness as being most elusive. Nevertheless, he concluded that it was *not substantive*. Natsoulas (1978) explains:

> In time, consciousness came to be a theoretical nonentity. Nonentity was James's (1904) word in "Does Consciousness Exist?" where he inveighed ... against the existence of consciousness qua substance or entity. James considered consciousness the most mysterious thing in the world. But he was sure it was *no actual thing*, that it was a *non*-entity. Those psychologists who would cling to a substantive consciousness were said to be clinging "to a mere echo, the faint rumour left behind by the disappearing 'soul' upon the air of philosophy." (James, 1904, p. 477) ...Rather, James considered consciousness to be a "function," specifically the function of knowing. (p. 906)

Once again, the idea of a *substantive consciousness* is linked to the idea of a soul—some immaterial thing connected to the material body/brain—and both such possibilities are discounted.

In the *American Psychologist* (1978), Natsoulas noted that psychologists needed to readdress the issues of consciousness:

> We should not quickly decide, for example, that consciousness is no more or less than James's function of knowing and proceed to study merely that. At this point in the *history* of scientific understanding, an effort at comprehensiveness surely seems called for. ... (However, I) ... predict that psychology will not define consciousness as a substance or as an entity again. Note that this prediction refers to the scientific discipline and not to individual scientists. ... Scientific knowledge has not yet rendered consciousness as a distinct entity unthinkable. (p. 907)

The nature of consciousness, that *"most mysterious thing in the world,"* remains a profound enigma within modern science. Science has not disproved the possibility that consciousness might be substantive. Likewise, it has not produced any evidence which would deny the existence of an immaterial mind, spirit or soul. Instead, psychologists ignore these tricky issues of consciousness and simply equate consciousness with thinking, reasoning and all the other mental processes. Unfortunately, scientists who regard these issues as having been resolved ignore the fact that they have been determined by fiat and methodological considerations, rather than on the basis of scientific evidence.

Despite this wilful ignorance and oversimplification, many psychologists are aware on some level that the question of consciousness remains an extraordinary mystery and a fundamental enigma within the discipline. This is evident when one realizes how often psychologists cite the following quotation from William James in the contemporary literature on consciousness and "altered states:"

> our normal waking consciousness, rational consciousness as we call it, is but one special type of consciousness, whilst all about it, parted from it by the filmiest of screens, there lie potential forms of consciousness entirely different. … No account of the universe in its totality can be final which leaves these other forms of consciousness quite disregarded. How to regard them is the question—for they are so discontinuous with ordinary consciousness. … At any rate, they forbid a premature closing of our accounts with reality. (1958, p. 298)

Although scientists are content to simply explain altered states of consciousness as being the result of altered neurological or biological processes within the brain, James remained intrigued by glimpses into other experiential states and realms. Further, many psychologists acknowledge James' contention that the existence of these states of consciousness does need to be explained in order to provide *"an account of the universe."* We cannot leave ourselves out of the equation. Unfortunately, the mainstream view does not consider that there might a 'substantive' consciousness or 'I principle.'

# 3. The Head Doctrine

"The cerebral cortex (is) where matter is transformed into consciousness ...." —Carl Sagan, *Cosmos*, 1980

In western thought and mainstream science, it is generally assumed that the neurological activities within the brain generate human consciousness and the mind. Further, it is assumed that consciousness and the mind disappear with the disintegration of the brain. This is the essence of the head doctrine.

Kenneth Pelletier, in *Towards a Science of Consciousness* (1978), labels this as *"the under the hat theory of consciousness."* He writes:

> Our present science and common sense support the concept that awareness resides predominantly at a point behind the eyes, between the ears, and above the neck. (p. 22)

Pelletier considers alternative views but begins by establishing this basic assumption underlying consciousness research and theory. This seems quite reasonable. Roger Sperry, a prominent neuroscientist, voices the widespread assumption: *"I don't see any way for consciousness to emerge or be generated apart from a functioning brain."*

The head doctrine assumes that the origins of consciousness are in matter, produced by neurological activity within the brain; and not in spirit, soul or anything immaterial beyond the physical realm. The mind and brain provide the foundation for experience, self or "I," for human intelligence and self-consciousness. Carl Sagan embraces this basic assumption regarding the nature of human consciousness and mind. In *The Dragons of Eden*, he explicitly stated:

> My fundamental premise about the brain is that its workings–what we sometimes call 'mind'—are a consequence of its anatomy and physiology, and nothing more. ... because of the clear trend in the recent history of biology and because there is not a shred of evidence to support it, I will not in these pages entertain any hypotheses on what used to be called the mind-body dualism, the idea that inhabiting the matter of the body is something made of quite different stuff, called mind. (1977, p. 7)

Contemporary scientists take human beings to be higher primates that have evolved through random genetic changes and the process of natural selection. There is no immaterial mind, spirit or soul, and the highest or most noble human faculties are regarded as being dependent upon the cerebral cortex. These themes run through Sagan's writings:

> The cerebral cortex (is) where matter is transformed into consciousness .... . The cortex regulates our conscious lives. It is the distinction

of our species, the seat of our humanity. Civilization is a product of the cerebral cortex. ... What distinguishes our species is thought. The cerebral cortex is liberation. We need no longer be trapped in the genetically inherited behaviour patterns of lizards and baboons. (*Cosmos*, 1980, pp. 277-8)

Thinking and reasoning, language faculties and various other cognitive abilities can be localized within various areas of the cerebral cortex. Further, neurologists have identified the sensory-motor strip of the cortex as a site of bodily sensation and control; while emotions, drives and passions are related to the limbic system and mid-brain structures. All such findings suggest the general notion that consciousness and mental states are dependent upon the brain, particularly the cortex, which is so richly developed in the higher primates. Cortical areas are required for abstract thought and language faculties and hence are regarded by Sagan as the *"seat of our humanity."*

Nevertheless, Dr. Sagan steps out on a limb in declaring that *"the cerebral cortex is where matter is transformed into consciousness ... ."* (p. 277) He does not define consciousness, nor elaborate what it is, nor where and how it is *transformed out of matter*. This is simply a declarations unsubstantiated by evidence. There is something fundamental missing in these accounts from a scientific perspective.

In 1995, Dr. Sagan continued to maintain this same basic position. In an interview in *Psychology Today*, he comments:

the mind is merely what the brain does. There's nothing else, there's no soul or psyche that's not made out of matter, that isn't a function of 10 to the 14$^{th}$ synapses in the brain. (p. 65)

There are other diverse views within mainstream psychology as to what consciousness entails and how it is produced or localized within the brain. Sometimes, different states of consciousness are identified with different divisions of the brains, as for example, with the left and right hemispheres, or with MacLean's triune brain model (i.e., the reptilian, old mammalian and new mammalian brains). Sagan discusses MacLean's work in *The Dragons of Eden* (1977) and addresses different faculties and levels of the mind. However, he most clearly relates consciousness to the cortical areas in the "new mammalian brain."

Other theorists regard the sub-cortical areas as more directly involved in generating consciousness, particularly the reticular activating system and the brain stem. These structures are involved in mediating arousal, wakefulness and the control of attention. Thus, while scientists put forth various possibilities concerning the generation and localization of consciousness, they share the basic assumption that consciousness and the mind are centred exclusively in the brain.

Nobel laureate, Francis Crick, is another prominent theorist who articulates the head doctrine. Given the conventional viewpoint that he espouses, the title of Crick's recent work *The Astonishing Hypothesis: The Scientific Search for the*

*Soul* (1995) is quite misleading. His "astonishing hypothesis" is anything but "astonishing." Crick merely restates the common belief, or assumption, held within psychology and science for the past century:

> The Astonishing Hypothesis is that "You," your joys and your sorrows, your memories and your ambitions, your sense of personal identity and free will, are in fact no more than the behaviour of a vast assemble of nerve cells and their associated molecules. As Lewis Carroll's Alice might have phrased it: *"You're nothing but a pack of neurons."* This hypothesis is so alien to the ideas of most people alive today that it can truly be called astonishing. (p. 3)

Crick's point is that this hypothesis is astonishing when contrasted with the popular belief in spirit and the existence of the soul. The subtitle of Crick's book is misleading however, in that he makes no effort to review the scientific work of scientists who do search for the soul or who explore alternate views of consciousness. Instead, Crick deals exclusively with attempts to explain how consciousness might be generated by neurons within the brain. How astonishing!

Although Crick suggests the need for a broader investigation of the nature of human consciousness, he focuses exclusively on trying to understand visual awareness. He explains that the neural substrate of visual awareness involves various cortical areas (layers 4, 5 and 6), which sub-serve visual analysis in association with activity in the thalamus. Crick regards consciousness as *"involving some form of memory"* and as *"closely associated with attention."* The thalamus participates in both of these processes, involving the control of attention and the establishment of reverberating circuits for short-term memory. Crick regards the cortical layers 5 and 6 as most critical to visual awareness since these layers express the results of computations taking place in the primary cortical layers. Reverberating circuits are established connecting cortical layer 6 to the thalamus and back again to cortical layers 4 and 6. Crick proposes that synchronized rhythmic firing in the 40 Hertz range binds these processes into a seemingly unified state of visual awareness.

In summarizing his work, Crick expresses a number of reservations:

> So much for a plausible model. I hope nobody will call it the Crick Theory of Consciousness. While writing it down, my mind was constantly assailed by reservations and qualifications. If anyone else produced it, I would unhesitatingly condemn it as a house of cards. Touch it, and it collapses. This is because it has been carpentered together, with not enough crucial experimental evidence to support its various parts. Its only virtue is that it may prod scientists and philosophers to think about these problems in neural terms, and so accelerate the experimental attack on consciousness. (p. 252)

What is most contrived about Crick's model of consciousness is that it is based exclusively on an analysis of visual awareness processes and leaves aside all of the other psychological processes which are subjectively experienced–such as thoughts, emotions, sensations, desires, self awareness, digestive problems, sexual arousal and so on.

Crick himself recognizes the tentative and incomplete nature of his model and his main aim is to encourage scientists to focus their efforts on this *"mystery of consciousness."* He notes that the issue of consciousness has been widely ignored by both psychologists and neuroscientists and yet it constitutes the fundamental enigma within the life sciences.

Crick notes that *"this book has very little to do with the human soul as they (readers) understand it."* Certainly, this is true, as he never gives the soul hypothesis any serious attention. Most importantly, Crick recognizes that the issue of the existence of the soul is intimately tied to the issue of the nature of human consciousness and that it is time that scientists face this critical issue. Further, he recognizes that his theory is simply a "hypothesis," which is "plausible," but not established with any certainty. In fact, it may be little more than a *"house of cards"* ready to collapse with the slightest breeze. Crick portrays the mystery of consciousness as a central problem in science, which must be addressed, yet he *assumes* from the outset that the question to be answered is simply *which neurons in the brain* produce consciousness. Crick's theory has no substantive basis in experimental fact and is simply another fiction of cognitive science.

David Chalmers, of the philosophy department at the University of Arizona, is another prominent mainstream consciousness theorist. Chalmers suggests that the search for the neural correlates of consciousness (or NCCs) is *"the cornerstone in the recent resurgence of the science of consciousness."* (2000, p. 1) He defines a neural correlate of consciousness as a neural state that directly correlates with a conscious state or which directly generates consciousness. In a paper on NCCs, Chalmers lists a number of proposals which have been forwarded to explain the nature and location of consciousness. These include:

40-hertz oscillations in the cerebral cortex
Intra-laminar nuclei in the thalamus
Re-entrant loops in thalamocortical systems
40-hertz rhythmic activity in thalamocortical systems
Extended reticular-thalamic activation system
Neural assemblies bound by NMDA
Certain neurochemical levels of activation
Certain neurons in inferior temporal cortex
Neurons in extrastriate visual cortex projecting to prefrontal areas
Visual processing within the ventral system (2000, p. 1)

All of these suggestions or hypotheses are variants of the head doctrine and localize consciousness within one or more areas of the brain. Each is derived from research investigating the neurological basis of particular mental or perceptual processes and none really deals with the issue of the substance of consciousness, or with its subjective nature. Although many researchers recognize the enigmas and mysteries of consciousness, the possibility that consciousness might exist apart from the neurological activity of the head brain is never given any consideration. The head doctrine is the fundamental assumption underlying most modern consciousness research and speculation and it blinds scientists to a whole array of alternative ideas and theories.

Theorist John Searle (2003) writes about *"The Problem of Consciousness,"* at his website, www.ecs.soton.ac.uk; and his comments again illustrate the *assumptive basis* of the head doctrine:

> The most important scientific discovery of the present era will come when someone–or some group–discovers the answer to the following question: How exactly do neurobiological processes in the brain cause consciousness? This is the most important question facing us in the biological sciences.... By 'consciousness' I simply mean those subjective states of sentience or awareness.... Above all, consciousness is a biological phenomenon. ... Conscious states are caused by lower level neurobiological processes in the brain and are themselves a higher level feature of the brain. ... the critical functional elements are neurons and synapses. ... we simply know as a matter of fact that brain processes cause conscious states. We don't know the details about how it works and it may well be a long time before we understand the details involved. ... Given our present explanatory apparatus, it is not at all obvious how, within the apparatus, we can account for the causal character of the relation between neuron firings and conscious states. But, at present, from the fact that we do not know *how* it occurs, it does not follow that we do not know *that* it occurs. Many people, who object to my solution of the mind-body problem, object on the grounds that we have no idea how neurobiological processes could cause conscious phenomena. But that does not seem to me a conceptual or logical problem. That is an empirical/theoretical issue for the biological sciences. The problem is to figure out exactly how the system works to produce consciousness, and since we know that in fact it does produce consciousness, we have good reason to suppose that there are specific neurological mechanisms by way of which it works."

Searle's comments illustrate the assumptive basis of the head doctrine and how assumptions end up being taken as 'facts.' At one point, Searle admits that we have no idea how neurobiological processes produce consciousness but a moment earlier he has just stated: *"… we simply know as a matter of fact that brain processes cause conscious states."* The facts seem to have disappeared from Searle's account and it is instead plagued with assumptions. Searle has "promissory science" to offer us—promising in the future to fill in the gaps in the mysteries of consciousness. Certainly Searle would not consider a need to entertain any type of metaphysical considerations or even any physics of consciousness. Instead, Searle assumes that consciousness is simply a biological phenomenon.

A last illustration of the head doctrine and its assumptive basis is provided by Roth's recent *Scientific American* article, "The Quest to Find Consciousness." Roth maintains that: *"Individuals consciously perceive only that information processed in the associative regions of the cerebral cortex. But many regions that operate on a subconscious level participate in the various states of consciousness."* (2004, p. 35) Under the title of *"The Seat of Consciousness,"* Roth offers a picture of the cerebral cortex, which shows its various lobes, responsible for varied mental functions. At the same time, Roth does admit that there *is "no consensus"* as to how consciousness arises and as to what it consists of. All the while, he *assumes* it is simply a matter of figuring out *which* of the brain's interactive processes produce it. Roth also ends on a promissory note:

> For now, no definite explanations exist, but that is not likely to remain true forever. Consciousness has a rather unique character, but at least some of the mysteries that surround it should nonetheless—eventually—fall away in the face of persistent scientific inquiry. (p. 39)

Scientists thus promise to fill in the gaps in the head doctrine and certainly few consider that there might be any gaps left for God, spirits or souls to fill in.

# 4. Roger Sperry's Mental-Consciousness Revolution

In 1981, Richard Sperry received the Nobel Prize for his pioneering split-brain research. A prominent psychobiologist and neuroscientist, Dr. Sperry later turned his attention to more philosophical concerns. On the one hand, his work was at the forefront in defining the changing paradigm in psychology, which he alternately refers to as the *"consciousness revolution"* and the *"mental/cognitive revolution."* (*Structure and Significance of the Consciousness Revolution*, 1988.) On the other hand, Sperry is interested in critical social and philosophical issues related to the roles of science and religion in determining human values. (*Science and Moral Priority*, 1983) We will consider Dr. Sperry's *emergent views of human consciousness* and how he attempts to relate these to human values.

While Dr. Sperry is one of the pioneering figures in the consciousness revolution, his writings are notably lacking when he attempts to define consciousness. Basically, he follows the lead of William James and modern cognitive psychologists and equates consciousness most generally with mental or cognitive processes. He explains that the *revolution*, which has allegedly occurred in modern psychology, involves the acceptance of a more subjective, cognitive or mentalist paradigm: wherein subjective phenomena, including mental images, feelings, and so on, are again considered as legitimate explanatory constructs.

In explaining the *"new legitimacy of the subjective,"* Sperry outlines his emergent views of consciousness and the mind and contrasts them with the materialist reductionist philosophy. According to the materialist paradigm, consciousness and mental experience are epiphenomenona—nothing more than by-products of the brain's physical and chemical activities—and therefore play no causal role in determining neurological events. In contrast, in Sperry's emergent view, the whole is regarded as more than simply the sum of the parts and this emergent consciousness can have a causal role within neural networks. New features of the mental life and human consciousness emerge with the increasingly complex levels of hierarchical ordering within the brain and cannot simply be reduced to the simplest subatomic or neurological processes.

> The key realization was that the higher levels in brain activity control the lower. The higher cerebral properties of mind and consciousness are in command. They call the plays, exerting downwards control over the march of nerve-impulse traffic. (1984, p. 194)

Sperry points out that his views do not suggest anything mystical or supernatural, as they do not allow for consciousness or mental processes to exist in any way independently of the brain:

94

The mental qualities used to be conceived in non-physical or supernatural terms, but we now view them as emergent properties of brain processes. ... We wholly reject anything supernatural, mystical, or occult in favour of the kind of reality validated by science ... I don't see any way for consciousness to emerge or be generated apart from a functioning brain. Everything indicates that the human mind and consciousness are inseparable attributes of an evolving, self-creating cerebral system. Some people have used the new mentalist concepts to bolster mystical and supernatural belief, including those of parapsychology. Actually, under the new model, mental telepathy, psychokinesis, precognition, and other so-called psi phenomena become even less likely than before. (1984, pp. 195 & 199)

Although consciousness, mind and human values are regarded as emergent phenomena or *"higher cerebral properties,"* and not totally reducible to physiology, Sperry still regards them as dependent upon the material, neurological processes of the brain. In essence, this is a neo-reductionism and neo-materialist viewpoint.

Sperry rejects anything that smacks of vitalism: the view that there is some immaterial life principle which animates the body or brain. He explains that biologists hunted for a vital principle but *"failed to find anything"* and that, *"The longer, the harder, and deeper they looked, the more convincing it appeared that there are no such things."* (1984, p. 199) However, Sperry argues that biologists are wrong to conclude that, *"all living things are nothing but physical and chemical processes."* In his modified view, he states that these *"emergent, holistic properties"* are similar, but that: *"This doesn't mean they're in any way supernatural or mystical. ... My colleagues shudder (at the idea of vitalism) ... because of the mystic connotations the word has."* (p. 200) Certainly, Sperry does not support any notions of a substantive consciousness principle. There is no glimmering of a soul, a vital principle, or ghost within the machine.

When it comes to the issue of values and religion, Dr. Sperry maintains that in the emergent views of consciousness lay the seed of a new ethic and natural theology, which allows for both religion and science. However, the kind of religion Dr. Sperry has in mind is a very strange one, to say the least:

*Omni Interviewer*: But wouldn't a merger with science demand excessive restraints on religious doctrines?

*Sperry*: In the past, perhaps, under the materialist philosophy. Past efforts have been very one-sided, asking, in effect, that religion mend its ways in order to conform with the facts of science, but with no similar request the other way around. On our present terms, however, it becomes a two-way compromise. Religion gives up dependence on mystical concepts, whereas science gives up much of its traditional materialist legacy. ... Everything considered, it would seem safer for our children's children if we don't continue to gamble the world's destiny on conflicting mystical answers anymore—or on outmoded materialist ideology. (1984, pp. 203 & 207)

Sperry sounds as if he really expects that such a compromise between religion and science can be reached on his terms. All religion has to do is give up God, spirit and soul, vitalism, immaterial mind, and anything supernatural, metaphysical and mystical! On the other hand, scientists must abandon a completely reductionist view, in which consciousness and human values are solely the result of material processes, and accept a neo-reductionist view, that consciousness, while an emergent phenomenon with a causative role in the material world, is still ultimately dependent on material processes of the brain considered as a whole.

In fact, there is no point for unification or reconciliation in Dr. Sperry's proposals. Of course, he wants to keep some aspects of religion because he believes in the importance of ethical and moral values in society. However, he believes that *"spiritual like values"* need to be based, not on religion, but on a modified version of scientific materialism that allows consciousness and mental processes to exert a causative role in the functioning of the head brain. In Sperry's new theology, we will simply worship the wonderful emergent properties of the cerebral cortex.

Dr. Sperry has no need for mysticism or God. But is he correct? Is consciousness simply an emergent property of hierarchical brain functions? What is this consciousness, which emerges? How does it emerge and from what? What are the mechanisms and processes by which consciousness plays a causal role and how does it function? Unfortunately, Dr. Sperry is silent on all of these critical scientific issues and his work fails completely to address the complexities of consciousness. He leaves us still with huge *gaps* in his explanatory schemes.

In fact, Dr. Sperry's so-called *"consciousness revolution"* is simply the outcome of his *speculations* about these perplexing mysteries. Although he presents his views as representing the most advanced findings of real science, his model of consciousness is based on assumptions, prejudices and beliefs. There is not one iota of evidence to support his *revolutionary perspective*. And yet, Dr. Sperry unabashedly proffers his insights as a basis for reconciling science and religion!

Imagine Dr. Sperry expecting religion to give up God and soul in order to embrace a cerebral cortex manufacturing consciousness out of material processes! How could religion accept the idea that there is nothing supernatural or mystical about the nature of consciousness and why would it wish to do so? And why do scientists *"shudder"* when they hear the words vitalism or mysticism?

# 5. Neurological Enigmas

... although the content of consciousness depends in large measure
on neuronal activity, awareness itself does not.
(Wilder Penfield, 1977, p. 55)

Mind-scientists and philosophers cannot even agree on what
consciousness is, let alone how it should be explained.
(John Horgan, 1999, p. 228)

Many scientists like Sagan, Crick and Sperry, assume that the cerebral cortex (and/or subcortical areas) produce consciousness and the mind. However, when it comes to specifying exactly what this consciousness is and by what mechanisms it is produced, the so-called exact scientists are strangely vague. Talbot (1987) writes:

> Most neurologists remain convinced that consciousness is a consequence of the anatomy and physiology of the cerebral cortex, and though a great deal is known about the biological workings of the brain, when backed into a corner, most scientists are forced to admit that no one really has any idea how the brain contrives to produce consciousness. (p. 89)

Scientists assume that neurological processes within the brain produce consciousness but what and where this consciousness is, remains a fundamental enigma.

Stanislav Grof MD (1993) notes that mental functions are obviously linked to biological processes in the brain but that this does not necessarily support the metaphysical conclusions which are usually drawn from these facts. A wealth of clinical and experimental work establishes relationships between states of intoxication, trauma, tumours and other brain pathologies to loss of cognitive and mental functions and to dramatic changes in conscious states. Grof notes, however, that this does not necessarily mean that consciousness originates in or is produced by the brain—a conclusion that is a metaphysical assumption, rather than a scientific fact. Grof states, "... the assumption that consciousness is a by-product of material processes occurring in the brain has become one of the most important metaphysical tenets of the Western worldview." (p. 5)

Wilder Penfield, a prominent Canadian neurophysiologist, argued that the brain couldn't yet account for consciousness and the mind. In his pioneering efforts to treat epilepsy, Penfield developed methods of electrically stimulating the cerebral cortex of conscious subjects. Using these methods, he was able to map how different functions of the mind are located in specific areas of the cortex.

However, in *The Mystery of the Mind,* Penfield (1977) explained that the results of his investigations led him to the conviction that there is some form of "mind" which cannot simply be accounted for in terms of brain mechanisms. Penfield notes that electrical stimulation of the cortex can cause subjects to experience crude sensations, or perform simple movements, or have vivid recollections of the past, yet the subjects always *"remains aloof"* like spectators observing and passing judgments on what is happening. The subjects realize that it is the experimenter causing the experiences. Thus, the electrical stimulation produced various contents of conscious experience (sensations, perceptions, actions, feelings, thoughts and memories), but the subjects' consciousness and mind were somehow separate from the electrical activity stimulated. The "I" was present to the various sensations, memories, etc., but not completely determined by them. Penfield argued that the patient's mind, observing this situation in an unattached manner, has to be something other than the neurological action itself. He concludes: *"... although the content of consciousness depends in large measure on neuronal activity, awareness itself does not."* (p. 55)

This is not what Penfield had expected to find. To the contrary, he notes that throughout his career he had attempted to explain the mind in terms of the brain's activity. However, in light of his shocking findings, he was forced to grant serious consideration to the idea that there could be some form of independent mind which interacts with the material brain. Penfield's comments are a long way from those of Carl Sagan, who suggests that: *"there is not a shred of evidence to support ... any ... mind-body dualism."* The esteemed Dr. Penfield argues that there was no evidence to support the reduction of the mind to the cerebral cortex and cognitive functions, which Sagan and Sperry embrace as an article of faith:

> In 1936 ... I presented the obvious conclusion that had been forced upon me in the first years of neuro-surgical practice ... that the integration within the central nervous system, which makes consciousness possible, did not take place in the cerebral cortex. ... to expect the highest brain mechanism ... however complicated, to carry out what the mind does ... is quite absurd. ... the mind seems to act independently of the brain in the same sense that a programmer acts independently of his computer .... (Penfield, 1977, pp. 111-2 & 79)

Unfortunately, Penfield offers no arguments as to what this other mind or awareness might be, nor how it interacts with the material brain. Nevertheless, Penfield's research had a profound philosophical effect upon him, as he concluded: *"... the scientist, too, can legitimately believe in the existence of the spirit!"* (p. 85)

Penfield's final conclusions are a leap of faith beyond that supported by his data. He does not prove the existence of spirit or the *substance* of consciousness or mind. However, he did realize that the existence of spirit is not inconsistent with what has been scientifically established about the nature of the mind, brain and consciousness. In fact, materialist scientists make such leaps of faith in assuming that the material brain can account for consciousness. Really, there is no evidence to support that conclusion. Whether one is a dualist, believing in the existence of both matter and spirit, or a strict materialist, subscribing to the view that matter alone is sufficient to account for reality, the question is moot from a scientific viewpoint,. Neither position has been proven.

Sir John Eccles, another prominent neuroscientist, assessed his discipline's enigmas and anomalies and concluded that: " ... *consciousness is a nonmaterial something that does indeed exist apart from our biological selves and causally determines which of our neurons fire and which do not.*" (Talbot, 1987, p. 103) Eccles regards the supplementary motor area of the cortex—the SMA—as a site at which mind and matter interact. He reached this conclusion as a result of the experimental work of neurophysiologists R. Porter and C. Brinkman. These researchers implanted electrodes in the SMA of a monkey and found that 1/100th of a second before the monkey pulled a lever to obtain a reward, the cells in the SMA began to fire; that is, the cells in the SMA fired *before* cells in related parts of the brain were activated. Eccles interprets this to mean that the SMA is a site where *"mental intentions"* occur as precursors to physical movement. Hence, he believes that this is a site where mind might influence matter.

Eccles concluded: *"It is important to recognize that this burst of discharge of the observed SMA cells was not triggered by some other nerve cell of the SMA or elsewhere in the brain. ... So we have here an irrefutable demonstration that a mental act of intention initiates the burst of discharges of a nerve cell."* He goes on to argue that mental intentions can initiate different patterns of neural discharge in the SMA, and that somehow *"the nonphysical mind is actually 'playing' the 50 million or so neurons in the SMA region as if they were the keys to some sort of piano."* (Talbot, p. 107)[1]

1    Similarly, Eccles regards the work of Lassen and Roland (1980) as providing biochemical evidence of the interaction between the brain and a non-physical consciousness. They investigated the activity of the SMA by monitoring blood flow. Blood flow to different parts of the nervous system is delicately controlled by the vascular system. Brain activity consumes energy and oxygen in the same way that muscle activity and organ activity do. Hence, when different parts of the brain are activated for different tasks, there is increased blood flow to those regions. By the injection of a radioactive sub¬stance into the blood, researchers monitor brain activity using radiation detectors. This technology allows one to graphically see which parts of the brain are busy during various mental activities.

Using this technology, Lassen and Roland found that a fraction of a second before a movement is initiated, there is an increased blood flow to the SMA and the motor areas of the brain. Further, if a subject performed an activity mentally with no physical movement, then blood flow increased to the SMA but not to the motor cortex. They also determined that if a movement was repeated until it became habitual and could occur without conscious attention, the anticipatory activity of the SMA also disappeared.

Eccles' views raise some of the neurological enigmas associated with attempts to identify and understand the nature of *'the mind.'* What is known of neurophysiology does not allow us to explain consciousness and the mind. It is reasonable then to consider the idea that there is some form of immaterial mind or substantive consciousness. Could consciousness and mind be something separate from the brain, and if so, how it is related to the material neurological processes of the brain? Eccles maintains a dualistic view of immaterial mind and material body and assumes that the interaction of the mind with body has its focus in the brain.

John Lorber, a British neurologist, is another researcher whose work highlights the significance of neurological enigmas. In a controversial article, published in *Science* (1980), he dared to ask the question: *"Is the Brain really necessary?"* In the mid 1960's, Lorber discovered two very young hydrocephalic children who appeared to show normal mental development—despite their apparent lack of a cerebral cortex! (Hydrocephalus is a condition in which an abnormal accumulation of cerebrospinal fluid fills the brain cavity and the cortex does not fully develop.) Although his two patients died at an early age, Lorber regarded their unexpected mental capacities as comprising an intriguing and provocative conundrum. If consciousness and intelligence are products of the brain (particularly, the cerebral cortex), then how was it possible that these children were not severely mentally impaired when their cerebral cortex was barely existent?

One patient, a student with an IQ of 126 and an honours degree in mathematics, posed a particularly puzzling case. When he was referred to Lorber because of a slightly larger than normal head, Lorber ran a CAT scan (measuring brain densities), only to discover that the patient had *"virtually no brain."* Instead, his skull was lined with a thin layer of brain cells, a millimetre or so thick and the rest of his cranium was filled with cerebrospinal fluid. Apparently, this boy *"continues to live his life normally except for the fact that he is now aware that he possesses no brain."* (Talbot, 1987, p. 87)

Lorber continued to turn up cases of individuals who functioned normally despite highly reduced brain development. The *Science* article described a study sample of some 600 hydrocephalic patients. In the worst of four conditions—in which the subjects had cerebral fluid filling 95% of the cranium—half of the subjects were severely mentally disabled but the remainder possessed IQs greater than 100! Surprisingly, Lorber's findings are not unprecedented. In fact P. Wall, a professor of anatomy, states that: *"Scores of similar accounts litter medical literature, and they go back a long way."* (Talbot, 1987, p. 88) These cases suggest that neurologists face an utterly mysterious and profound task in their efforts to

---

Eccles appears to ignore the role played by increased blood flow as related to the consciousness of neural activity.

explain the existence of consciousness, mind and intelligence, strictly in terms of the cerebral cortex.

In the last decade, *Scientific American* published two articles on the study of consciousness—a first for this prestigious, yet conservative magazine. In one, David Chalmers addresses "The Puzzle of Conscious Experience." (December 1995) He describes consciousness as being paradoxically, *"the most familiar thing in the world and the most mysterious,"* and he notes a *"tangle of diverse and conflicting theories"* existing within the field. According to Chalmers, the *"easy problems of consciousness"* concern the mechanisms of various forms of cognition, while the *"hard problems"* concern *"how the physical processes in the brain give rise to subjective experience."* The basic facts of the subjective side of consciousness simply cannot be deduced from physical facts about the brain's functioning. He notes that we have no idea how the subjective experiences arise from neurological processes. Between the physiological processes and the subjective experience, there is, in scientific terms, *an explanatory gap.*

Chalmers' solution is to suggest that consciousness is perhaps a *"fundamental feature of the world,"* irreducible to anything else. He compares this to basic physical concepts such as space-time, mass, charge and so on, which are regarded as fundamental properties, unexplained in terms of lower order phenomena. Chalmers notes that the physicist John Wheeler argued that *"information"* is fundamental to the physics of the universe, and so Chalmers suggests that consciousness might be the *"subjective side"* of information. In this case, information has a dual nature as physical and experiential, objective and subjective. Thus, a model of consciousness might require a set of fundamental laws unique to the description of consciousness, analogous to the laws of physics used to describe the physical world. This is a new form of dualism–not of mind and matter–but of the subjective and objective sides of information. It also brings us back to the possibility of a substantive consciousness, which is *some thing*--whatever that might be. Ideas about the substance of consciousness are emerging again in a contemporary form. Basically, we still have not solved the problem of the 'I' and the 'me.'

In a second *Scientific American* article, "Can Science Explain Consciousness?" (July 1994), John Horgan reviewed the diversity of theories presented at a scientific conference on consciousness. Horgan clearly acknowledges the profound mysteries of consciousness:

> a growing number of scientists have dared to address what is simultaneously the most elusive and inescapable of all phenomena: consciousness, our immediate, subjective awareness of the world and of ourselves. (p. 88)

Although he focuses on Crick's work, Horgan surveys a broader range of ideas from the conventional to those bordering on the mystical. Despite the narrowness of the conventional scientific thinking at the interdisciplinary conference,, there remains a diversity of views and approaches to consciousness. For example, Brian Josephson, a Nobel laureate in physics, called for the development of a unified theory of consciousness which would allow for the existence of mystical and psychic experiences. Another speaker described thoughts as *"quantum fluctuations of the vacuum energy of the universe–which is really God."* Still, other theorists—most notably, Roger Penrose—suggest that consciousness might be the result of quantum effects at the levels of microtubules, which are protein bodies within cells that perform quantum based computations. Horgan does not elaborate upon the complexities of these viewpoints but gives a flavour of the diversity of modern theories and the lack of scientific consensus concerning the enigmas of consciousness.

In his book *The Undiscovered Mind* (1999), John Horgan elaborates further upon the enigmas facing researchers trying to understand consciousness and the mind. The most evident theme is again the mysterious and unknown nature of consciousness. Horgan writes: *"Mind-scientists and philosophers cannot even agree on what consciousness is, let alone how it should be explained."* (p. 228) The major assumption underlying most of the theories reviewed by Horgan is that somehow the neurological processes of the brain produce consciousness and that it is centred in the head. However, there is never any substantive evidence to support these conclusions.

Interestingly, Horgan quotes Harvard psychologist, Howard Gardner, who suggests that someone may find *"deep and fruitful commonalities between Western views of the mind and those incorporated into the philosophy and religion of the Far East."* Gardner suggests that a fundamentally new insight is necessary, although unfortunately, *"we can't anticipate the extraordinary mind because it comes from a funny place that puts things together in a funny kind of way."* (p. 260) These comments ironic indeed, as there is such a fundamental difference between western so-called scientific views of the mind and the spiritual teachings of both the eastern and western traditions. Understanding this difference between the *head doctrine* and the *heart doctrine* provides just such a novel perspective on the issues of consciousness and does put things together in a *"funny kind of way."*

In summary, these articles underline the fact that while the problem of consciousness gives rise to a great diversity of ideas and theories, it remains the most paradoxical, unexplained mystery within science today. Generally, theorists talk over consciousness, around it, under it, about it, but have few substantive ideas which do more than scratch the surface of this profound mystery. In this critical area, science is almost purely speculative. Most of the recent theoretical perspectives subscribe to the common *assumption* that the brain produces consciousness and the mind, but the details of this magical transformation are lacking. When we look more closely at scientific explanations of what consciousness is, and *how* and *where* it is produced by the brain, they are based on mainly on speculation and hunches–a house of cards, as Crick admits may be true of his own theory.

If there is an immaterial mind, spirit and soul, or some form of irreducible consciousness, what are these things and how do they relate to the physically body and brain, and heart? There are many issues to be resolved and all the doors should be kept open in trying to understand these mysteries. The idea, that a human being has a spirit, soul or divine spark, has not been disproved, as indeed the issues of human consciousness continue to pose profound unresolved enigmas. Scientists only *assume* that the brain's neurology processes produce consciousness and they simply gloss over the gaps in science.

# 6. Enigmas of the Heart

"If the 20th century has been, so to speak, the Century of the Brain,
then the 21st century should be the Century of the Heart."
(Schwartz and Russe, in Pearsall, 1998 p. xiii)

If we turn to contemporary science to shed light on the nature of the heart,
we find another series of interesting enigmas. Although humankind has long ascribed emotional and feeling states to the heart, modern psychologists typically
identify the brain's limbic system as the centre for emotional reactions. Since
consciousness and the mind are taken to exist within the head, it seems natural
to assume that the brain is the site where we experience emotions and feelings.
Scientists seldom consider that consciousness and emotions exist physically
in relationship to the heart, the autonomic nervous system, or through other
parts of the body. Nevertheless, the enigmas of the heart are intimately tied to
the issues not only of feelings and emotions but also to those issues of human
consciousness and soul.

The heart has traditionally been regarded as the basic symbol of life.
From four weeks after conception when it begins to beat until death, the heart
maintains life within the material body. The heart's regular contractions pump
de-oxygenated blood to the lungs, where it is oxygenated, and returned to the
heart, to be pumped out through the network of arteries which interpenetrate
the body and brain. Oxygenated blood is red in colour and travels through the
body in arteries and capillaries; while the blue, de-oxygenated blood returns to
the heart through the veins. The blood is the *river of life* maintaining all the cells
and organs through the transport of oxygen and other nutrients. Oxygen is the
fuel of life required for all vital and metabolic processes within the body/mind.

Modern science regards the heart as essentially a mechanical pump composed of soft muscle tissue. Nevertheless, the scientific knowledge of the heart is
far from complete and there are a number of major enigmas regarding its nature.
The most notable of these enigmas is the long-standing mystery of the heart's
pacemaker. The pacemaker is identified with the sinoatrial node (SA Node),
situated near the top of the right atrium. This body of cells produces the basic
life impulse–the spark of life–that propagates through the heart in three phases,
causing the contraction and relaxation of the various heart chambers. What produces the basic life spark within the SA Node? In a *Scientific American* article,
Adolph addressed this issue:

> How does the pacemaker work? On this central question there are,
> unfortunately, very few clues so far. ... Indeed no model yet suggested
> has given us much enlightenment on how the pacemaker translates

metabolic energy into its rhythmic beat, how it synchronizes the discharges of its many cells or how it changes the tempo of its beat as it ages. ... To sum up, it appears that when the heart of the embryo begins to beat, it functions as an independent organ, driven only by its own inherent pacemaker. (1967)

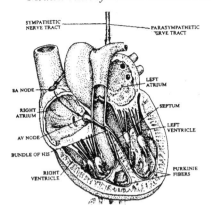

Fifteen years later, an article from *Science Digest* informs us that the issues of the pacemaker remain unsolved:

> About 70 times each minute, more than 2.5 billion times in a lifetime, the heart beats on. What keeps it going? The heart, it seems, has a life of its own. The muscle fibres that make it up differ from those elsewhere in the body in that some of them generate their own electricity without receiving signals from the brain. In fact, the foetal heart begins beating *before* it has even formed nerve connections. The heart's pacemaker is a group of self-triggering cells called the sinoatrial (SA) node. ... What initiates the current in the SA node remains unknown, but its cells behave more like neurons than muscle fibres. (1984, Aug., p. 90)

The cells of the SA Node are permeated with sodium and potassium ions which create a polarized environment: in which the inside of the cell is negatively charged and the outside is positively charged. At regular intervals, the cell membranes leak and cause the cell to depolarize. As a result, the cells contract and an electric impulse is generated bringing life into the heart. The mystery of how these impulses originate has yet to be fully explained in terms of biochemical and metabolic processes.

Psychologist Barbara Brown (1974) comments upon the enigma of the heartbeat:

> The genesis of the heartbeat is as unknown as the genesis of man, and equally a miracle. A squib of tissue so small and so well camouflaged as to be unseen by the naked eye is the progenitor of beats. By some unknown ultrachemistry, this squib of tissues generates a flow of electric impulses, bip-bip-bip, one after the other with bewildering unmatched regularity. ... The generator is inborn, inherent. (pp. 227-8)

Like Adolph, Brown assumes that this generator is programmed by metabolic energy. Certainly, it is reasonable for a scientist to seek a material cause in attempting to resolve the mysterious generation of the heartbeat. Nevertheless, Brown's comments are most appropriate: *"The genesis of the heartbeat is as unknown as the genesis of man … ."*

The role which most people attribute to the heart, as the center of the emotional life, is another intriguing paradox associated with this mysterious organ. The heart is the most powerful symbol of human emotions: We talk of "loving with our hearts," of being "heartbroken," of having "a heavy heart," of knowing compassion and caring "with the heart," or of experiencing excitement and anxiety, when "the heart skips a beat." When we see cruelty, we wonder how someone can be so "heartless," so selfish and contracted about themselves, so cold-blooded. We talk of "hearty" welcomes, if our "hearts are in it;" of "losing heart" and giving up hope and knowing "heartache," with the loss of love.

Certainly, one would be wary of someone who claimed to love you with "all of their head," instead of "all of their heart"! If someone proclaimed to love you with all of their limbic system or their cerebral cortex, you might want to refer them to a psychiatrist, or to Drs. Sagan, Crick or Chalmers. The literary, poetic and musical dimensions of human life attest to the life, loves and sufferings of the heart. The heart is regarded as a mind of its own, one which can function quite independently of the brain. The heart is regarded as being the core of our being, the deeper self. We speak of getting to the heart of a matter when we attempt to penetrate to the core of something, or to its essence. Are these and other expressions simply metaphors, or do they indicate that life, human emotions and intuitive wisdom, are directly experienced in relationship to the heart?

In *New Mind, New Body*, Barbara Brown provides fascinating insights into the enigmas of the heart. The heart plays a role in the experiencing of emotions and feeling, in willing, in having a mind of its own, in learning and knowing, and in healing. She describes the heart as having a secret life intricately connected to the thoughts, feelings and desires of the individual. Brown explains how in different experiments the heart can learn without "the conscious mind" knowing; how the heart is the most sensitive of the organs to emotional states; and how the heart rate increases or decreases with the shifting of attention and awareness.

Studies of biofeedback training and the skills of yogis have demonstrated that the heart can be brought under various forms of self-control. Brown describes how some yogis can radically lower their heart rate or even stop their hearts for brief periods. Others exercise control over their vascular systems, altering blood flow to particular parts of the body in very specific ways. The experimental evidence suggests that changes in the heart rate can be brought about through "intention," as though the heart has its own "will." Brown concludes that a very strong feedback mechanism exists between the brain and the heart, which somehow involves the control and awareness of emotions.

These observations represent a major enigma: Is there a consciousness of the heart, or are we conscious of feelings and emotions in the heads alone?

Human experience suggests that consciousness is not confined to the cerebral cortex and limbic system, but can be experienced throughout the body. Brown comments:

> Perhaps the confusion related to the heart's learning lies in the researcher's head. There seems to be an unending war between the mind of the heart and the ideas of the researcher. (1974, p. 258)

Indeed, the central tenet of the head doctrine—that consciousness is produced within the brain—may well be the result of confusion in the researcher's head.

In *Towards a Science of Consciousness*, Kenneth Pelletier (1978) argued for an expanded view of the possible nature of consciousness. Pelletier questioned the validity of the head doctrine which he labelled as the *"under the hat theory of consciousness:"*

> In contrast to this naive belief (of the under the hat theory of consciousness) stands a vast array of information, ranging from Vedantic texts to laboratory research results, that supports the concept that the entire body is an instrument of consciousness. One particular component of awareness resides in the brain, while other physiological systems of the body seem more attuned to other aspects of awareness. Thus, our language is laden with expressions indicating that the seat of the emotions lies within the heart and cardiovascular system…. According to their tradition, the Hopi 'knew' that consciousness resided in the heart and they thought white men were foolish because they believed that they thought with their heads. Were a Hopi researcher approaching the problem of the neurophysiological basis of consciousness, he would elect to make a detailed analysis of the electrical activity of the heart rather than the brain. (pp. 23 & 22)

Quite simply, there is absolutely no reason to assume that consciousness is located exclusively within the head. In fact, the entire body, including the heart and the cardiovascular system, could be construed as being an instrument or vehicle for consciousness. Even if we accept the idea that consciousness is produced by neurological activity, then we must recognize the electromagnetic and neurological fields generated by and within the heart itself. The heart has its own neurological system, including the SA Node, which is independent of the brain. In addition, the autonomic nervous system exists outside of the central nervous system and effects many organs and glands related to emotional and instinctual states. Neurological activity is not simply confined to the brain but extends throughout the body and scientists have done nothing to demonstrate why only the brain's neural activity would produce consciousness, but not other centres of electromagnetic and neurological activity. It seems entirely reasonable to suppose that the heart's neural activity might also be linked with the experience of consciousness and of the 'I' experience.

In *The Heart's Code*, psychologist Paul Pearsall (1998) maintains that, energetically speaking, the heart–rather than the brain—is clearly the centre of the psychological universe:

> The heart's EMF (electro-magnetic field) is five thousand times more powerful than the electromagnetic field created by the brain and, in addition to its immense power, has subtle, non-local effects that travel within these forms of energy. ... the heart generates over fifty thousand femtoteslas (a measure of EMF) compared to less than ten femtoteslas recorded from the brain. (p. 55)

The profound significance of these facts leads Gary Schwartz and Linda Russe, in the forward of Pearsall's book, to comment:

> *The Heart's Code* points the way to a new revolution in our thinking. Metaphorically, the heart is the sun, the pulsing, energetic center of our biophysical "solar" system, and the brain is the earth, one of the most important planets in our biophysical system. One implication of the energy cardiology/cardio-energetic revolution is the radical (meaning "root") idea that energetically, the brain revolves around the heart, not the other way around. (1998, p. xii)

The heart is the largest source of biophysical energy in the body and within our psychological life. In Pearsall's view, the heart involves energy and information that comprises the essence or soul of who we are.

The idea that the heart is the center of the psychology of the individual, instead of the brain, would indeed revolutionize our understanding of normal and supernormal psychology. Adopting this view would be analogous to the Copernican revolution, wherein scientists realized that the Earth, rather than being the centre of the universe, travelled around the sun within the solar system. The egocentric attitude of humans was shattered. Likewise, the acceptance of a deeper conceptualization of the heart, consciousness and the nature of Self, would similarly constitute a revolutionary development in modern psychology, philosophy and the life sciences.

In 1996, Drs. R. Allan and S. Scheidt proposed that modern psychology should include a field of "cardiac psychology" as a branch of health psychology. Cardiac psychologists have generally focussed on identifying the psychological, social and environmental risk factors for heart disease, and the psychological repercussions of heart attacks and other cardiac illness. However, Pearsall, Schwartz and Russek, and others propose a broader definition of cardiac psychology: one in which the heart is regarded as a thinking, feeling, and willing organ, with profound energetic influences on humans' psychological, emotional and physical life.

The heart has its own form of intelligence, independent of the brain. It can perceive internal and external stimuli and react on its own to the outside world. It communicates *"an info-energetic code"* which is conveyed through tens of thousands of miles of vessels and 75 trillion cells of the heart and circulatory system. In addition, neurotransmitters, which are found in the brain, have also been discovered in the heart. The heart produces the hormone and neuro-peptide, Atrial Naturetic Factor (ANF), which communicates with the brain, particularly the limbic system and hypothalymus, which mediate emotions, and the pineal gland which regulates sleep/waking cycles, aging processes and activity levels. The activities of the heart are also recognized to have effects on the immune system and physical health. Pearsall notes:

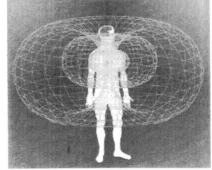

> As research from neurocardiology continues, it is becoming clearer that the central role of the heart in our consciousness is much more than metaphor and that, as happened with the brain, continuing research will reveal complexities of a conscious heart that our brain cannot yet imagine. (1998, p. 69)

Pearsall states that we have been too "brain focussed" in the search for mind and that instead of thinking in terms of a dual mind and body, a more rewarding and appropriate approach would be to adopt a triune model: that is of a thinking brain, the material body and the energetic and emotional heart. The heart is the primary energy centre within the individual and in Pearsall's terms *"conveys the code that represents the soul."*

Pearsall explores the nature of cellular memory, *life fields* and non-local information fields, in an attempt to account for various clinical and psychological evidences that are emerging about the mysterious qualities of the human heart. In fact, Pearsall argues that through the psychology of the heart, modern psychology is *"beginning to make its first tentative contacts with the soul."* (p. 6)

The remarkable stories of heart transplant recipients bear testimony to the secrets of the heart. Pearsall recounts an incident which happened to him after he had presented a lecture on the heart's role in humans' psychological and spiritual life. A member of the audience, a psychiatrist, was moved to tears as she recounted a dramatic story about an eight year old girl who had been the recipient of a heart transplant. The heart donor, a ten-year-old girl, had been murdered. After the transplant, the recipient suffered nightmares about the man who had killed the donor and was able to describe the time, weapon, and place, the man's appearance, what the little girl had said to her assailant, and so on. The police were able to identify and prosecute the murder based on her evidence! Somehow the recipient had access to the memories, information and emotional terror, and the soul influences of the donor!

Although his evidence is anecdotal, Pearsall cites several cases in which those who have received transplanted hearts are profoundly affected by the donors' personalities, proclivities and life histories. It seems that in receiving another's heart, the recipients establish a connection with their donors, as this organ of 'the soul' maintains some connection to the donor's life energies and memories–in ways that defy and confound current scientific understanding.

In *A Change Of Heart* (1997), Claire Sylvia, the recipient of a heart-transplant, recounts her remarkable experiences. She describes how the energies, emotions, and soul life of the donor seemed to become intertwined with her own. Thus, she experienced an extraordinary metamorphosis after her transplant. She acquired her donor's food and beverage preferences, his conflicted feelings towards his father, his sexual attractions and impulses, and other energetic dynamics! Her dreams of the donor enabled her to establish who he had been and to meet his family, with whom she felt immediately connected. Apparently, heart-transplant recipients frequently report such astonishing experiences. Nevertheless, doctors, scientists and other professionals either dismiss or politely ignore these intriguing phenomena.

In another somewhat bizarre case, Sonny Graham, a seemingly happily married 69-year-old man living in the U.S. state of Georgia, shot himself without warning. Sonny had received a transplanted heart from a man who had also shot himself in identical circumstances. After receiving a heart transplant, Sonny tracked down the wife of the donor and fell instantly in love with her. *"When I first met her,"* Sonny told a local newspaper, *"I just stared. I felt like I had known her for years. I couldn't keep my eyes off her."* He spoke of a deep and profound love for her. It was instant and it was passionate and they quickly wed. The tragedy of Sonny Graham will, no doubt, be written off as mere coincidence.

Perhaps the twenty first century will indeed be the century of the heart as its mysteries are revealed.

# 7. The Dualities of Formatory Mind & Formatory Science

*"...in order to comprehend the world of many dimensions, (we) must renounce the idol of duality."* (Ouspensky, 1922, p. 239)

While those sceptics who dismiss mysticism take delight in ridiculing any discussion of sacred numbers or numerology, the importance of such concerns becomes apparent when one considers the extent to which *"thinking in twos"* dominates modern thinking. Dualistic thinking is an unconscious and unrecognized self-element which pervades modern philosophy, psychology, science and common language and thought. It is as if scientists and philosophers always think that everything or anything has only two parts to it or exists simply in two states or in two conditions. The tendency towards dualistic thinking is a "self-element" in science: a personal element unconsciously projected onto all sorts of subject matters. Unfortunately, people do not realize that dualistic thinking is a hidden, unconscious pattern, which limits understanding and shows one to be *'third force blind.'*

Certainly, life seems to be pervaded by opposites: male and female, good and bad, positive and negative, up and down ... with love and hate, pain and pleasure, the conscious and unconscious, the rational and the emotional, the mind and the body ... all between life and death. If that is not enough, we have the left brain and the right brain, science and pseudo-science, cause and effect, action and reaction, stimulus and response, input and output ... in the binary age of 0 and 1, with subjects and objects, black and white, night and day, hot and cold, in and out, off and on, in the past and into the future ... all made of matter and energy, trapped within time and space, between being and non-being, on heaven and on earth ... with spirit and matter, God and the Devil. Life is full of opposites or at least this is how people tend to conceptualize it.

A Yin/Yang play of opposing forces seems to dominate existence and humans' patterns of thinking about that existence. Whenever people consider any subject of human discourse or academic science, they tend to uncritically embrace dualistic thinking. In modern psychology, discussions of human nature, consciousness, mind, personality and the self are hopelessly dualistic. Thus, we find that almost all of psychologists' considerations of human nature are framed in terms of dualistic principles: there are two states of consciousness, two types of mind and two dimensions to the self. The central duality of modern psychology is the view that human beings consist of two primary parts: a mind and a body.

Psychology itself is most frequently defined as the science of behaviour and mind, and philosophers debate endlessly the mind/body duality, the division between the psyche (mind) and the soma (body). Even when we are so bold as to ask if there is anything beyond the physical or the material realm, we assume that it must consist simply of the opposite—the metaphysical or immaterial realm. The automatic assumption is that if something can't be fit into one category, it must somehow fall into the opposite. In this vein, Carl Sagan applies his cerebral cortex to the mystery of consciousness and assumes that there is no immaterial mind connected to the material body.

With reference to consciousness, the most common dualities are between the conscious and the unconscious, waking and sleeping, being aware or unaware. Alternatively, other theorists discuss the differences between consciousness and awareness, or consciousness and self-consciousness. At one symposium on consciousness, the duality was drawn between Consciousness I and Consciousness II, to differentiate the basic consciousness shared with other living organisms from the kind of self-consciousness which humans are thought to have.

These dualities are also tied into the dualities of the mind and self. Based upon a hundred years of psychological and philosophical inquiry, decades of split-brain research and equally enduring simplistic patterns of thinking, psychologists usually distinguish between two modes of mental functioning. There are two modes of knowing, two types of intelligence, two types of information processing, two types of mind and even two cerebral hemispheres. In 1966, Ulrich Neisser, a major figure in the re-emergence of cognitive study in psychology, commented:

> Historically, psychology has long recognized the existence of two different forms of mental organization. The distinction has been given many names: "rational" vs. "intuitive," "constrained" vs. "creative," "logical" vs. "pre-logical," "realistic" vs. "autistic," "secondary process" vs. "primary process." To list them together casually may be misleading … nevertheless, a common thread runs through all of the dichotomies. (p. 297)

This historic tendency to conceptualize dual mental principles received a major boost with advances in split-brain research. Neurologists since H. Jackson (1864) have taken the left hemisphere to be the centre for the faculty of expression as required for the analysis of language and speech formation. Indeed, Carl Sagan's book, *Broca's Brain*, refers to Paul Broca, the scientist who isolated the area in the left temporal lobe responsible for speech and language synthesis, which bears his name: Broca's area. In contrast to the left hemisphere's role in verbal expression, Jackson noted that a patient with a right hemisphere tumour *"did not know objects, persons and places."* Since Jackson, many neurophysiologists have confirmed the cerebral localization of mental faculties. The left hemisphere is concerned with the processing of language, while the right hemisphere is more prominent in the cognition of forms and sequences–as required for instance in music, facial and pattern recognition, and so on.

In modern split-brain research, the corpus callosum which connects the right and left hemispheres is surgically severed. This work pioneered by Richard Sperry fuelled the imagination of three decades of dualistic psychologists and consciousness researchers. At last there seemed to be hard evidence to support the traditional dualities of mind. In this vein, Bakan (1978) explained:

> The left hemisphere mode is described as symbolic, abstract, linear, rational, focal, conceptual, propositional, secondary process, digital, logical, active, and analytic. The right hemisphere mode is described as iconic, concrete, diffuse, perceptual, pre-propositional, primary process, analogue, passive and holistic ... The two modes are antagonistic and complementary, suggesting that a unity and struggle of opposites is characteristic of mental functioning. (p. 163)

So many philosophers and psychologists have formed their own favourite dualities of the mind that it was only a matter of time before all of these dualities were taken to refer to the same fundamental dualistic truth of dualistic reality.

In 1972, Robert Ornstein published a popular and influential book entitled *The Psychology of Consciousness*. One of Ornstein's central themes was the duality of human consciousness and the differences between the hemispheres of the cerebral cortex:

> The recognition that we possess two cerebral hemispheres, which are specialized to operate in different modes, may allow us to understand much about the fundamental duality of our consciousness. This duality has been reflected in classical as well as modern literature as between reason and passion, or between mind and intuition. Perhaps the most famous of these dichotomies in psychology is that proposed by Sigmund Freud, of the split between the 'conscious' mind and the 'unconscious.' The workings of the 'conscious' mind are held to be accessible to language and to rational discourse and alteration; the 'unconscious' is much less accessible to reason or to the verbal analysis. ... There are moments ... when our verbal intellect suggests one course and our "heart" or intuition another. (pp. 74-75)

Dichotomania is a term coined by neuroscientist, M. Kinsbourne, to describe this unthinking tendency to construe all phenomena in dualistic terms and then to superficially equate all these dualities. Dichotomania leads to confusion and babble. Is the heart really in the right hemisphere–along with passion, intuition and the unconscious? Certainly a long list of philosophers and psychologists take a dualistic approach to the mind sciences and to consciousness studies.

Unfortunately, this dualism reflects theorists' limited thinking patterns–rather than representing the dichotomous nature of reality.

Ornstein goes further to relate these dualities of consciousness and the mind to dualities in the world and to the basic Yin and Yang poles of existence. He produces the following table of correspondences ranging across psychology, philosophy and dimensions of science (1972, p. 83):

## THE TWO MODES OF CONSCIOUSNESS:
### A Tentative Dichotomy

Who Proposed it?

| | | |
|---|---|---|
| Many sources | Day | Night |
| Blackburn | Intellectual | Sensuous |
| Oppenheimer | Time, History | Eternity, Timelessness |
| Deikman | Active | Receptive |
| Polanyi | Explicit | Tacit |
| Levy, Sperry | Analytic | Gestalt |
| Domhoff | Right (side of body) | Left (side of body) |
| Many sources | Left hemisphere | Right hemisphere |
| Bogen | Propositional | Appositional |
| Lee | Lineal | Nonlineal |
| Luria | Sequential | Simultaneous |
| Semmes | Focal | Diffuse |
| I Ching | The Creative: heaven masculine, Yang | The Receptive: earth feminine, Yin |
| I Ching | Light | Dark |
| I Ching | Time | Space |
| Many Sources | Verbal | Spacial |
| Many Sources | Intellectual | Intuitive |
| Vedanta | Buddhi | Manas |
| Jung | Causal | Acausal |
| Bacon | Argument | Experience |

Are the mind and the world really so pervaded by these contrasting principles or forces?

Scientists also find dualities in studies of the natural laws. In fact, all the apparent laws of physics seem to deal with two fundamental dualities. Astronomer and science philosopher, H. Shapley (1967) described the basic elements of the universe and laws of physics:

> The basic entities (of physics and astronomy) are commonly recognized to be space, time, matter, and energy; the first two can be linked together as space-time, and the last two as mass-energy. It is

difficult to isolate any universal quality that is not a variation on these four. Speed, weight, light, distance, momentum, and the like are all derivatives of the four, or combinations ... . (pp. 111-2)

The basic quadrant of elements in classical physics concerns two fundamental dualities: matter/energy manifesting within time/space. Is there anything beyond this–anything at the heart of being?

There are, of course, numerous other dualistic distinctions in physics: waves and particles, the observer and the observed, positive and negative charges, bosons and fermions, left-turning particles and right-turning particles, electric and magnetic forces, matter and anti-matter, and all forms of being manifested out of non-being. No doubt, there is something important to be grasped in understanding the role of dualistic forces and principles throughout nature, the physical as well as the psychological.

The mystic philosopher, P. D. Ouspensky (1957) described dualistic thinking as a *"self-element"* in science, an example of *"formatory thinking."* In the fourth way teaching of Gurdjieff and Ouspensky, the mechanical portion of the intellectual centre is referred to as the *"formatory apparatus."* Formatory thinking is intellectual activity which involves the least amount of effort and awareness, such as the memorizing and rote repetition of information. Ouspensky explains:

> 'Formation' is a conclusion arrived at by the way of least resistance, avoiding difficulty. It is easier because it makes itself–ready-made phrases, ready-made opinions, like a stamp. It is generally defective with the exception of the simplest cases. (p. 65)

Unfortunately, for most people, the formatory apparatus dominates their thinking and they simply parrot attitudes, opinions and beliefs acquired through conditioning, imitation and socialization. Ouspensky describes another limitation of the formatory apparatus:

> One of its peculiarities is that it compares only two things, as though in any particular line only two things existed. ... Another of its peculiarities is immediately to look for the opposite.

Formatory thinking is a pervasive element within the "waking sleep" state—as a source of unconsciousness, confusion and misunderstanding. Dualistic thinking is a lazy mental habit which blinds us to the full spectrum of existence—as we automatically look only for two elements, two principles, two components or two aspects in all and everything.

From a mystical perspective, Yogananda (1972) suggests that dualities only dominate the world of appearances but that at a deeper level of understanding, there exist more subtle forces and intelligences, that transcend the apparent worlds of opposites:

> The Vedic scriptures declare that the physical world operates under one fundamental law of maya, the principle of relativity and duality. ... The entire phenomenal world is under the inexorable sway of polarity; no law of physics, chemistry, or any other science is ever found free from inherent opposite or contrasted principles. (p. 310)

In Vedic teachings, the physical world is regarded as illusory, not because it is unreal, but because the appearances are only shadows of deeper underlying causes and dimensions. Hence, the phenomenal world might appear dualistic but if we penetrate further into the nominal realm, which underlies and informs it, then additional forces provide the medium for manifestation and bring about the reconciliation of the opposing forces. Ruled by maya—by surface appearances—humans construe cosmic phenomena in terms of dualities, as if every whole consisted of only two parts. Ouspensky (1922) explains: "... *in order to comprehend the world of many dimensions, (we) must renounce the idol of duality."* (p. 239)

It is hard for dualistic thinkers to appreciate the multi-dimensional heuristic of the *Tree of Life*, based on the Laws of Three and Seven, through four worlds and many generations of causes and effects. Modern philosophers and scientists are more comfortable with a dualistic approach to the mysteries.

# 8. The Accidental and Random Universe & Evolution

"The evidence for random universes is precisely zero."
—Haisch (2006)

Scientists ascribe a peculiar role to accidental and random factors in the creation and design of the universe and the evolution of humankind. Whereas a religious view suggests that a divine Being or Intelligence created the world, life and human consciousness, scientists resort to *accident theory* to explain the mysteries. A critical analysis of twentieth century science with its materialist philosophy cannot avoid this puzzling feature–evident within Dr. Sagan's writings, as well as in numerous other popular accounts of creation, physics and evolution. Modern scientists regard many key creation and evolutionary processes as essentially the outcome of random or arbitrary processes, nothing more than fortunate and lucky coincidences within the stream of time which gave rise to human life on planet earth.

What happened in the beginning? The most recent scientific creation scenario is that of vacuum genesis and the emergence of the universe from a singularity point out of the quantum vacuum at the first instant of time. According to the uncertainty principle of quantum theory, the vacuum energy is continually fluctuating randomly, and on one occasion, this fluctuation *happened* to be strong enough to instigate the process of universal creation. Overbye (1983) depicts the creation scenario: *"(The Universe) ballooned accidentally out of the endless void of eternity ... tiny bubbles of ordinary space appear randomly, and expand into separate bubble universes. ... space-time itself can arise from random fluctuations in a primordial nothingness."* (1983, pp. 93 & 99) In this view, the first cause of creation is a *random* quantum event.

Astronomer Robert Jastrow, author of *God and the Astronomers* (1978) and *Genesis Revealed* (1979/1980), describes subsequent stages of the evolution of the universe. In reference to the formation of the stars and the solar system, he writes:

> These pockets of gas that evolve into stars are formed *by accident,* in the random motions of the clouds that surge and eddy through the Universe. (1977, p. 38)

> Nearly five billion years ago, in one of the spiral arms of the Milky Way Galaxy, a cloud of gaseous matter formed *by accident* out of the swirling tendrils of the primal mist. (1979, p. 38)

Jastrow attributes the evolution of the stars and solar system to accident and the force of gravity. He then moves on to the formation of the planets, where according to exact science:

> While the Sun was forming, smaller condensations appeared in the outer regions of the cloud. These condensations, appearing *by accident*, were also held together by gravity, as the Sun had been. The smaller knots of matter became the planets. (1980, p. 69)

Included among the accidentally formed planets was Earth. Jastrow continues:

> How our planet accumulated out of that halo of tiny, orbiting grains is one of the minor mysteries of science. Probably the accumulation resulted from random collisions occurring now and then between neighbouring particles in the course of their circling motion. (p. 42)

After evolving the stars, the solar system, the sun, planets and moon, and the earth—*all by accident* and the law of gravity—Jastrow moves on to describe the origins of life on earth through the theory of neo-Darwinian evolution:

> during the course of a billion years, every conceivable size and shape of molecule is created by random collisions. ... (p. 47) Eventually, after countless millions of chance encounters, a molecule is formed that has the magical ability to produce copies of itself. (p. 48) Nature required several hundred million years of ceaseless, random experimentation to discover the chemical pathways to life on the earth .... (p. 51) ... nature uses random accidents as the means of improving the design of living organisms. (p. 58) ... accidental variations from one individual to another provide the raw ingredients for evolution. (1977, p. 6)

Not surprisingly, Carl Sagan was thoroughly enamoured with accident theory. In *The Dragons of Eden* (1977) and *Cosmos* (1980), he continually emphasized the randomness of evolutionary processes. Natural selection is the preferential survival of organisms which *by accident* are better adapted to their environment. Sagan explains: *"Biology is more like history than it is like physics; the accidents and errors and lucky happenstances of the past powerfully prefigure the present."* (1977, pp. 5-6) In regards to the most essential aspects of human beings, including consciousness, Sagan writes: *"all of these are, at least in part, the result of apparently minor accidents in our immensely long evolutionary history."* (1980, p. 282)

These passages represent the philosophical underpinning of a particular approach to science and the idea of evolution. Whereas the ancients attributed the origin and evolution of life to God, Yahweh, Lord Krishna, Divine Mind and Spiritual Intelligences, modern science suggests that the evolution of the universe and life on planet earth proceeded by random fluctuations and colli-sions, happenstance and circumstance, accidental mutations, stray cosmic rays, magical abilities, and *"a little bit of luck"*! And this accidental, random *stuff* is called scientific!

In *Shadows Of Forgotten Ancestors* (1992), Carl Sagan and Anne Druyan in-voke the randomness feature of evolutionary theory to argue against the general concept of supernatural causes: *"It does not seem to be how a Deity intent on special creation would do it. The mutations have no plan, no direction behind them; their randomness seems chilling ... ."* (p. 84) In Sagan's view, consciousness itself is just another evolutionary feature which happened to evolve by chance, rather than being an intrinsic aspect of creation. Whenever so-called exact science reaches a certain limitation or boundary condition–that is, the limits of what it can plaus-ibly explain–scientists reflexively and automatically invoke happenings, random processes and fortunate accidents as the supposed causal principles or agents.

Steven Weinberg, a well-known physicist and cosmologist, is the author of *The First Three Minutes* (1979), which chronicles the physics of the early uni-verse. After providing a fascinating account of the origin and evolution of matter and energy in the early universe following the Big Bang, Dr. Weinberg concludes with these philosophical ruminations:

> It is almost irresistible for humans to believe that we have some special relation to the universe, that human life is not just a more-or-less farcical outcome of a chain of accidents reaching back to the first three minutes, but that we were somehow built in from the beginning .... But if there is no solace in the fruits of our research, there is at least some consolation in the research itself. Men and women are not content to comfort themselves with tales of gods and giants, or to confine their thoughts to the daily affairs of life; they also build telescopes and satellites and accelerators, and sit at their desks for endless hours working out the meaning of the data they gather. (pp. 143-4)

In Dr. Weinberg's view, to engage in *tales of gods and giants* or to feel that human life has some *"special relation to the universe"* is nothing more than a source of self-consolation and self deception. Such ideas, he believes, have nothing to do with the nature of reality discovered by science. Instead, he suggests that human life is more like a *"farcical outcome of a chain of accidents."* Humanity's saving grace consists of those scientists who struggle so valiantly to collect data and solve the mysteries of life and the universe—all while sitting at their desks. It seems quite evident to Drs. Weinberg, Jastrow, Sagan and Hawking, that there is less and less for God to do, now that we have real science with its accident theory.

Nevertheless, it certainly seems that scientists have merely substituted one unsubstantiated solution for another. The miracle of divine creation has been re-placed by science's lucky happenstance, the random mutations of evolution and the uncertainties of quantum physics. However, as a theory or model, Dr. Sagan does not *prove* the accidental nature of any specific creation or evolutionary process. In fact, his claim is not even likely *falsifiable*. Traditionally, scientists have accepted the idea that, in order for a theory to be considered scientific, it should be capable of being falsified and hence subject to experimental testing, verification or disputation. In fact, accident theory itself cannot be disproved in terms of scientific criterion. Paradoxically, scientists criticize theologians for invoking a God of the gaps but then invoke their own accidental and random scheme to plug up the many gaps in evolutionary and physical theories.

There are numerous remarkable coincidences in modern science having to do with the manner in which the constants of nature are precisely fine-tuned to give rise to the structures of the physical universe and to life on planet earth. One of those life forms, human beings, then by chance, acquires the faculties of mind and intellect necessary to study the laws of science and creation and to question the origin and nature of their own consciousness and that of the whole universe. Surely there have been some remarkably fortunate occurrences!

In *The Mind of God* (1992), scientist Paul Davies discusses the interpretation of the many coincidences in science and life:

> The apparent "fine-tuning" of the laws of nature necessary if conscious life is to evolve in the universe then carries the clear implication that God has designed the universe so as to permit such life and consciousness to emerge. It would mean that our own existence in the universe formed a central part of God's plan. (p. 213)

The universe looks *as if* it unfolds according to some plan or blueprint—with certain essential conditions and laws initially set. In this case, the evolution of the universe and human consciousness have not been simply the result of a series of fortunate and arbitrary events, but are somehow "built in" from the beginning and derive from metaphysical dimensions. Davies explains:

> There is no doubt that many scientists are opposed temperamentally to any form of metaphysical, yet alone mystical arguments. They are scornful of the notion that there might exist a God, or even an impersonal creative principle or ground of being that would underpin reality and render its contingent aspects less starkly arbitrary. Personally, I do not share their scorn. ... We have cracked part of the cosmic code. Why this should be, just why *Homo sapiens* should carry the spark of rationality that provides the key to the universe, is a deep enigma. We, who are children of the universe—animated stardust— can nevertheless reflect on the nature of that same universe. ... How we have become linked into this cosmic dimension is a mystery. Yet the linkage cannot be denied. ... I cannot believe that our existence in

this universe is a mere quirk of fate, an accident of history, an incidental blip in the great cosmic drama…. Through conscious beings the universe has generated self-awareness. This can be no trivial detail, no minor by-product of mindless, purposeless forces. We are truly meant to be here. (pp. 231-232)

For the most part, scientists simply disregard the larger philosophical issues of science and focus on the reductionist program of explaining the mechanisms of particular life processes. Modern science is a *little bit science*, in the sense that the world is divided up into smaller and smaller and more varied bits. Scientists study these bits in all their different aspects but divorce them from understanding the underlying whole which sustains them. Perhaps evolutionary events are seen as random and arbitrary precisely because they are considered solely in terms of physical forces acting on blind matter. If the same events were studied in terms of a model which recognizes metaphysical forces, then the random and arbitrary properties might be revealed to be as illusory as the shadow play in Plato's cave.

Swami Prabhupada, a mystic sage, advised Dr. Benford, a physicist, to study the laws of nature but to understand them as manifestations of the Mind of God. Human consciousness and mind particularly need to be understood in this way—that is, as being rooted into the metaphysical nature of life. Maya is a world of illusion, not because it is unreal but because it does not contain its causes within itself. Anything in the material realm—whether a microbe, tree, cow, planet or a galaxy–is created and sustained by subtle, metaphysical dimensions and processes. The attempt to formulate a comprehensive explanation of the natural laws responsible for life, without referring to these metaphysical dimensions and their operative principles, is thus ultimately futile, as all things eventually lead back to the Divine Grounds of Being—to Lord Krishna, Brahman, the Tao, Void, God, or, what Blavatsky labels as simply THAT. From a mystical perspective, all manifest things embody deep inner forces, intelligences and laws. In this view, randomness is an illusion, which arises when bits are isolated and interpreted without reference to the whole.

We should not readily dismiss the intricacies of nature and creation by attributing them to random and accidental forces and thereby neglect to look for conscious design or higher intelligence, whatever that might be. H. P. Blavatsky provided the gems of wisdoms necessary to lead to reinterpret many facts, theories and enigmas of modern science. Scientists should remain open to the possibility that order arises out of chaos, not accidentally and randomly, but as a consequence of underlying forces and laws, spiritual intelligences and even Divine Beings, manifesting through zero point dynamics. Scientists seldom consider such ideas because they subscribe so unconsciously to a materialistic and reductionist philosophy with its denial of spirit and soul.

When it comes to the matter of attaining ultimate knowledge, Paul Davies is surprisingly open to the idea that a transformation of consciousness and the experience of mystical states might allow science to penetrate further into the cosmic mysteries. He concludes: *"It seems at least worth trying to construct a metaphysical theory that reduces some of the arbitrariness of the world. ... Possibly the mystical path ... (may) provide the only route beyond the limits to which science and philosophy can take us, the only possible path to the Ultimate."* (pp. 231-2) These comments are similar to those of Rene Weber, who suggests that mystics may ultimately be more scientific than the so-called objective scientists, because they include self-knowledge as *the key* to understanding the deeper nature of reality; thereby including themselves in the equations.

Mystical teachings maintain that the processes of creation and evolution embody metaphysical principles and dimensions within the material forms. The causes of things visible are invisible because they manifest from "within/without" from zero point sources rooted into an alternate interior Space. Maya, as the world illusion, arises as the mind apprehends only the surface appearances, studies everything in a dualistic way and fails to consider phenomena in relationship to underlying causes and dimensions. Materialist scientists regard any explanation which invokes divine intelligence as being superstitious, yet explanations of life and consciousness which invoke accidents, happenstance, random processes and a little bit of luck, are celebrated as being scientific!

What is lacking in the debate between science and mysticism is a deeper appreciation of the substantive metaphysical views elaborated within occult and esoteric sources—particularly *The Secret Doctrine* and the teachings of occult scholar H. P. Blavatsky. Such teachings include profoundly different views of the nature of human consciousness and mind, and of the nature of multidimensional existence and the principles of creation.

How then could we look for God in the laws of nature or in the processes of the psyche or mind? We may not see angels pushing planets around or God talking to the morning glory plant, but we may find other more subtle forms of *"micro-intervention."* Mystical and metaphysical ideas can indeed be brought into the domain of rational science and they do offer hypotheses which could be falsified. They also allow for the reinterpretation of other facts and theories. In fact, mystical ideas are extraordinarily rational, intelligible and comprehensive, although they seem somehow to have almost completely eluded the accident theorists. On the other hand, what could be more irrational and ad hoc than accident theory?

# 9. The Fool's Enigmas: On the Assumptive Basis of Modern Psychology and Science

> "If in reality we were to collect these system-destroying facts they
> would be so numerous in every department of knowledge as to exceed
> those upon which existing systems are founded. The systematization
> of that which we do not know may yield us more for the true
> understanding of the world and the self than the systematization of
> that which in the opinion of "exact science" we do know."
> (Ouspensky, 1922, pp. 16-17)

To a fool, who knows nothing, the materialist paradigm which dominates modern psychology and science is a highly questionable framework of assumptions and speculations. The biases of theorists and researchers, the multitude of things unknown and enigmatic, and the incompleteness of our understanding of life, all point to fundamental mistakes in modern psychology, philosophy and science. Unconscious self-elements colour and determine much of contemporary science philosophy and psychology, and the puzzles of consciousness are only beginning to be addressed more earnestly.

In *The Structure Of Scientific Revolutions* (1962), Thomas Kuhn popularized the concept of a *scientific paradigm* and explained the means by which scientific revolutions come about. A paradigm is a way of approaching and thinking about some area of scientific inquiry. It involves a "tacit infrastructure of ideas," or assumptions, which guide scientific inquiry. These assumptions are hidden or implicit, rather than obvious and explicit, unconscious rather than conscious. A paradigm determines the types of questions asked, the methods used and the manner in which data are interpreted within a theoretical framework. A paradigm acts like a set of lenses or spectacles, which bring into focus certain types of empirical and theoretical issues and determines what questions and issues are given priority. However, at the same time, a paradigm can blind us to other issues.

Kuhn explains that during periods of regular science, research is conducted and knowledge accumulated within the context of the dominant paradigm. In this way, modern psychology has made significant strides in understanding such complex matters as the anatomy and physiology of the brain, the functions and capacities of the mind, and the complex of personality and social variables that determine human behaviour. There are extensive psychological and scientific literatures on these subjects that are derived from a particular framework of ideas and assumptions regarding human nature and material reality. Further, these ideas have positive but limited applications to understanding how the mind functions, the nature of personality and interpersonal dynamics, and the application of psychology in clinical and counselling work, forensics, organizational psychology, and the like.

Within this framework of assumptions, scientists follow Dr. Sagan's advice and do not consider one iota of evidence for the existence of some kind of immaterial mind, soul or substantive consciousness. The issues concerning the ultimate nature of consciousness, mind, spirit and soul, simply do not seem relevant for such applied purposes. However, scientists forget that they are wearing only one set of glasses and think that they are wearing the only possible glasses, or at least the most important glasses. In reality, psychologists ignore the most essential questions of the science of psychology and opt instead for a reductionist, little-bit science. While this approach may be applied to the study of the various quirks and quarks of human behaviour, it ignores the deepest issues as to the spiritual dimensions of life and the ultimate nature of self. Materialist assumptions are unthinkingly regarded as truths and there is a widespread belief that psychology is progressing when in fact fundamental errors colour everything. If the science of psychology is based upon a faulty set of assumptions, then we have constructed an imaginary bridge to nowhere with no solid foundation.

A *scientific revolution* involves a paradigm shift and the emergence of a new understanding, which leads to new applications and poses new theories and hypotheses. Kuhn argues that such revolutions are foreshadowed by an accumulation of unsolved problems, enigmas, paradoxes and unexplained observations that are inconsistent with the assumptions of the predominant paradigm. Eventually, scientists or philosophers propose radically different ideas that challenge the foundation of the existing paradigm and result in a revolutionary shift of understanding. Consequently, a quantum leap—a discontinuous jump or transformation—occurs in theorists' understanding. In such cases, innovative ideas, theories or assumptions allow a reinterpretation of earlier theories and data, while raising new questions and leading to new approaches and methods. According to Kuhn, the progress of science is marked by such discontinuous quantum leaps in thought and the emergence of a new paradigm, which in turn results in a period of normal science based on these new assumptions.

In psychology, many researchers regard the so-called "consciousness" or "cognitive revolution" as having overturned behaviourism, and as such constituting a paradigm shift. Whereas the behaviourist focussed exclusively on observable behaviour and ignored the study of subjective experience, thought, cognition and consciousness, the cognitive theorists now consider mental processes as legitimate areas of psychological inquiry! Wow, what progress! Really, the most essential and difficult questions concerning consciousness, mind and self remain. How does consciousness originate within us? This is the intergalactic, super-bowl mystery of consciousness, which psychologists, scientists and philosophers have been unable to decipher.

To modern psychologists, the "cognitive revolution" may seem to constitute a great scientific advance, but it seems like little more than a change in direction created by one group of sleepwalkers overtaking another. What is so startling or revolutionary in Roger Sperry's work? He uses the word consciousness which is a step up from the behaviourists, but he is not referring to a substantive consciousness. Dr. Sperry regards consciousness as an "emergent property" but he gives no account of what it is or where it emerges. He assumes that it is produced within the brain in the head:

> The mental qualities used to be conceived in non-physical or supernatural terms, but we now view them as emergent properties of brain processes. ... We wholly reject anything supernatural, mystical, or occult in favour of the kind of reality validated by science. ... I don't see any way for consciousness to emerge or be generated apart from a functioning brain. (Sperry, 1984, pp. 195 & 199)

The problem is that Dr. Sperry imagines that some "kind of reality" has been "validated by science." This simply is not so, as science has not validated the reality of what consciousness is or is not. Further, it is presumptuous to *"wholly reject anything supernatural, mystical and occult,"* when science itself is at an impasse in understanding the ultimate issues of consciousness and self. Furthermore, Dr. Sperry is ill informed regarding the substance of mystical, occult and spiritual teachings, as is evident in his glib dismissal of these traditions.

Most of modern consciousness and cognitive theory is based on the same tacit infrastructure of ideas as behaviourism and the natural sciences, assuming that human beings are the mere by-product of material biophysical evolution and that they have no immaterial nature–spirit, soul or substantive consciousness. Of course, Sperry and Sagan do not know what consciousness is, but *they do assume what it must be*, and they present their beliefs as if they were scientific findings. This is the great lie of modern science—one which obscures the gaps in contemporary understanding. Commenting on this issue, Moffatt (2002) argues that the ascendancy of scientific materialism, rather than being the triumph of evidence and fact over superstition and dogma, simply replaced one set of arbitrary assumptions with another: *"Science did not disprove mystical, religious and animistic views of the universe; it banished them."* (p. 316)

P. D. Ouspensky (1922) explained the value of seeking out the mysteries and enigmas, or *"system destroying facts"* as a route to understanding the limitations of contemporary knowledge:

> In general, to a disinterested observer, the state of our contemporary science should be of great psychological interest. In all branches of scientific knowledge we are absorbing an enormous number of facts destructive of the harmony of existing systems. And these systems can maintain themselves only by reason of the heroic attempts of scientific men who are trying to close their eyes to a long series of new facts which threatens to submerge everything in an irresistible stream. If in reality we were to collect these system-destroying facts they would

be so numerous in every department of knowledge as to exceed those upon which existing systems are founded. The systematization of that which we do not know may yield us more for the true understanding of the world and the self than the systematization of that which in the opinion of "exact science" we do know. (pp. 16-17)

System destroying facts are the enigmas, paradoxes and unknown elements which haunt psychologists and material scientists. Modern science is riddled with these enigmas, mysteries and paradoxes. In fact, there are fundamental issues yet to be resolved in every department of modern scientific study–within both the social and natural sciences, and massive evidence for a wide range of paranormal phenomena. Taken together, these enigmas suggest that there is something fundamentally lacking in the predominant materialist paradigm of twentieth century science. Although modern science has made great strides in understanding the material aspect of life and brought us powerful technologies, there remain profound mysteries, enigmas and "gaps" which reveal the limits of the materialist approach.

\*\*\*

In psychology there are unresolved issues surrounding virtually every essential topic which confronts the discipline: we do not know what consciousness is, whether or not it is substantive, or where it originates. Similarly, we do not understand the nature of the mind or the self; nor even if these things are anything at all. We do not know how thoughts occur and influence the material body or brain; or what emotions entail; or where memories are stored; or how the integration and coordination of information takes place within the nervous system that enables conscious experience and the sense of personal and individual identity.

Next, there are innumerable enigmas raised by the vast literature, anecdotal and scientific, attesting to the psychic and paranormal nature of life. This includes anecdotal, experimental and scientific evidence for extra-sensory perception, psychokinesis, clairvoyance, meaningful patterns of coincidence, out-of-body-experiences, after-life states, ghosts and poltergeists, psychic and spiritual healing, reincarnation, remote viewing, and much more. Although Carl Sagan and Roger Sperry argue that there is not one iota of evidence for such inexplicable phenomena, their views reflect their prejudices and assumptions, rather than being based on a careful assessment of the evidences or the process of self study. In fact, there is overwhelming evidence for the legitimacy of paranormal phenomena, and these are all topics which should be approached with an open-mind and a sense of humility about the limits of what we know and do not know.[2]

---

2    Dean Radin, in his recent work (1997), *The Conscious Universe: the Scientific Truth of Psychic Phenomena* debunks the sceptics' claim that there is no scientific evidence for so-called paranormal phenomena. In a comprehensive review of scientific studies, Radin argues that a proper statistical analysis reveals that evidence for the reality of psychic

The unknown origin and history of humankind poses a multitude of other issues for our study. There are questions about the origins of life, the evolution of human beings, human history, the cycles of civilizations and lost civilizations, mystery schools, UFOs and alien beings, and the future prospects of human beings. There are innumerable unknowns within all of these areas, which cannot be simply dismissed by an impartial investigator.

The existence of mystical and spiritual teachers and teachings pose another set of enigmas. The most influential figures in modern religions have been mystics, saints and seers–who have supposedly realized the deepest origins of self, the existence of spiritual and divine principles and forces in life, or, who have realized oneness with God and the Universe. There are known and unknown histories of the lives of such enlightened and self-realized individuals, who are the source of different mystical traditions and teachings. Masters are said to manifest in various supernatural ways and to have super mundane experiences and realizations. It is foolish and arrogant to dismiss such possibilities out of hand, and state that there is not "one iota" of evidence for the existence of an immaterial something to connect to the material—as does Dr. Sagan.

Instead of being irrational and misty ideas, idle speculations or fancy, mystical and spiritual teachings are extraordinarily rational, intelligible and lucid. Taken as a whole, they provide the basis for an entirely novel paradigm in psychology and science, and speak to the most essential questions raised by the gaps within modern science. The gaps concern the ultimate issues of consciousness and mind, the nature of the heart, the origin of the universe, the nature of matter/ energy, space/time, and the mysteries of evolution. The physics, metaphysics, cosmologies and evolutionary views of the mystics and occultists are unquestionably relevant to the enigmas faced within the material sciences–just as mystical psychologies are relevant to the deepest enigmas in modern psychology.

Of course, psychology's assumptive framework is but one part of the broader materialist perspective which dominates modern science. Scientists are not only opposed to considering the possibility that human beings might possess a soul or embody a spirit, but also to the idea that the universe embodies divine or spiritual laws and intelligence. Scientists do not know how to consider such ideas and even fear and loathe such questions. Thus, biologists shudder at the thought of vital principles, just as psychologists cringe at talk of the soul, and physicists scoff at the mention of metaphysics in relation to physics. When scientists put on their philosophical hats, they do not realize how their attitudes simply express their presumptions and prejudices.

---

phenomena is overwhelming! Moreover, the preponderance of anecdotal evidence for various classes of paranormal phenomena should also give any open-minded investigator reason to wonder about what these phenomena involve, rather than whether or not they are real. Of course, many people already accept the existence of such supernormal possibilities because of personal experiences. However, there is certainly a massive anecdotal and scientific literature, which documents the existence of such phenomena.

Just as there are major enigmas in psychology, so also, they exist in every area of the natural sciences. A few of these enigmas can be listed here and elaborated in detail throughout the *Within-Without from Zero-Points* series.

\*\*\*

In physics, fundamental enigmas include the paradoxes of the uncertainty principle, the wave/particle nature of matter/energy, the probabilistic nature of quantum processes, the mysteries of quantum interconnectedness (as suggested by the E.P.R. paradox, Bell's inequality and the evidence for non-local effects), the difficulties faced in unifying the laws of physics in higher space dimensions, the nature of gravity and light, and the most recent views of the universe as a hologram. Physicists also face enigmas in the description of elementary particles/quanta, the mysterious nature of the quantum vacuum–the primordial nothingness, which is the root principle of creation, problems with infinities and the renormalization of quantum field equations, the emerging idea of "Phase III science" (which regards information/mind as a third force in relationship to matter/energy), the role of consciousness and the observer in determining physical reality, models of higher and hidden dimensions of space/time, the dynamics superstrings and M-branes, and David Bohm's model of wholeness and the implicate orders. As science has advanced, it has yielded more and more mysteries as to the ultimate nature of things, not fewer.

\*\*\*

In cosmology, basic enigmas are raised by the most recent *vacuum genesis* scenario, problems with singularities at the beginning and end of time, notions about hyperspace or superspace dimensions, issues concerning the origins of galaxies and large scale structures of the universe, questions raised by the formation of the solar system, the origins of the sun, the planets and moon, enigmas concerning the permanence or impermanence of matter, questions about the fate of the universe, and paradoxes raised by the anthropic principle, dealing with the relationships of mind to matter and the cosmos. Why would scientists assume that there is nothing mysterious about the origin of the universe from a zero point source out of the nothingness of the quantum vacuum and higher space dimensions? While such ideas and theories may solve some mysteries, they certainly pose new ones and can be interpreted in various ways—even as supportive of mystical doctrines.

\*\*\*

In biology and medicine, there are fundamental enigmas concerning the origins of biological life, how order arises out of disorder or chaos, morphogenesis (how life forms are created and maintained), by evidence for the discontinuous nature of evolutionary change and for subtle body fields and life fields. Sheldrake's *"new science of life"* suggests unknown fields and forces effecting and interconnecting species and the "Gaia hypothesis" views the earth as a living entity. Holistic medicine and science further suggest all kinds of enigmas about subtle energies in the life of humans, hidden factors in health and disease, and the role of the psyche and spirit in matters of life and death.

The existence of enigmas and anomalies in all areas of science and human inquiry reveal the limits of the materialist/reductionist paradigm and suggest the need for a more comprehensive alternative. A new model of life and creation must address all the *"system-destroying facts"* and the gaps within science itself. Instead of thinking that the *"end of science"* is near, as suggested by various popular writers such as Sagan, Hawking and Smolin, the signs of the times point to an emerging paradigm shift. Various facets of such a new paradigm have been accumulating over the past twenty years within alternate psychologies, holistic medicine, eastern practices and sciences, holographic theories, the understanding of higher space dimensions, investigations of quantum vacuum and the Aether, and emerging views of a substantive consciousness.

Thus, in contrast to Carl Sagan's contention, that as scientific advances there is *"less and less for God to do,"* we can stand this proposition on its head. In fact, the opposite is true--as we learn more and more about life and the universe, we discover ever more mysteries, enigmas, paradoxes and uncertainties as we come to address the ultimate issues. The accumulation of system-destroying facts suggests that the materialist and reductionist perspective embodies some very basic misunderstandings about the nature of Self and reality. When confronted by the most essential issues, we know nothing and are like fools before the mysteries.

The *Within-Without from Zero Points* series explores all of these enigmas while elaborating an alternate mystical-spiritual model of consciousness and creation. Such teachings actually provide a most profound challenge to modern science. H. P. Blavatsky remarked: *"...the occult side of Nature has never been approached by the Science of modern civilization."* (1888, p. viii) In the ensuing century, little has changed. In fact, the materialists' dominance of modern thought has exacerbated the failings that Blavatsky described. Thus, we have formatory psychology and science, dominated by the spells of dualistic thinking, materialist dogma, accident theory and the head doctrine.

The issues of human consciousness pose the most profound mysteries and enigmas for those who seek to understand the nature of self and the deep roots and origins of their being. The God hypothesis is certainly tied to the soul hypothesis and to many other "gaps" in scientific and modern understanding. The essence of what it is to be human is far more mysterious than what materialists and reductionists imagine, or what is assumed by the head doctrine theories.

Rassouli, *Veiling of the Soul*, www.Rassouli.com

# I V

# THE HEART DOCTRINE
## Esoteric Views of the Origin and Nature of Human Consciousness

*" ... THE SONS EXPAND AND CONTRACT*
*THROUGH THEIR OWN SELVES AND HEARTS;*
*THEY EMBRACE INFINITUDE."*
—Stanzas of Dzyan, Blavatsky, 1888

*" ... dive deep within, even to the lotus of the heart,*
*where dwells the Lord ... . so all beings live every moment*
*in the city of Brahman (God), yet never find him,*
*because of the veil of illusion ... ."*
—Chandogya Upanishad

*" ... in the inmost recesses of his heart is his real "I," his God.*
*... God is an infinite Consciousness. He is also the self-illumining Light.*
*There is no human being who does not have within him*
*this infinite Consciousness and this self-illuminating Light."*
—Sri Chinmoy, 1970

# 1. Consciousness, Mind and the Diagnosis of Modern Psychology

In order to approach the issue of what consciousness is, it is also necessary to define what it *is not*. From a mystical perspective, modern thought has been dominated by major mistakes and misconceptions, which has led to confusion and babble within the consciousness literature and common thought. Recall Guru Bawa observations of western psychology and its misunderstandings of Self: *"Psychologists don't know where the mind is ... the mind is in the heart, and that is what psychologists do not know. Unless the heart opens, you will be driven crazy by the monkeys of the mind."*(1976) If this is true, modern psychology and science are in a sad state of affairs and labour under major illusions about the nature of consciousness, the mind and the self.

In 1922, the mystic philosopher, P. D. Ouspensky, drew a clear distinction between consciousness and the psychic or psychological functions. He contrasted his views with those in the psychology of his era, including William James. Ouspensky notes that even in psychology *"purporting to be scientific,"* the term consciousness is used for *"the designation of a complex of all psychic functions in general, or for their separate manifestation."* Ouspensky notes that Professor William James defined thought as *"a moment of consciousness."* From Ouspensky's standpoint, it is necessary to regard consciousness as distinct from the commonly understood psychic functions: including thought, feeling and sensation. He describes consciousness as having definable forms or phases, in which thoughts, feelings and sensations can function. Thus consciousness is described as *"a background upon which thoughts, feelings and sensations reveal themselves."* Further, Ouspensky notes that this background can be more or less bright—as consciousness is equated with light, which can vary in terms of its intensity and degree of illumination. However, as a starting point, Ouspensky stresses: *"It is important only to establish the fact that thoughts, feelings and sensations, i.e., psychic functions, are not consciousness ... ."* (1922, pp. xiii-xiv)

Within the fourth way teaching, Gurdjieff and Ouspensky do not equate consciousness loosely with the stream of subjective life (thoughts, feelings, sensations and all the rest), as does William James. In fact, the continual stream of associative thought and the habitual activities of the mind are regarded as major obstacles to the awakening of consciousness. A student of the fourth way explains:

> 'Thinking' is one thing and 'consciousness' is an entirely different thing. ... There can be thinking without any awareness of thinking, and still more important, there can be consciousness devoid of any

thought. The latter is what happens in higher states of consciousness. ... the associative thinking, which goes on all the time by itself, is the chief obstacle to our attainment of any higher level of consciousness. (Walker, 1965, p. 45)

The continual state of absorption by mental and egoic activities prevents the individual from awakening to the true source and nature of consciousness and Self.

Psychological processes, neurological and biological activities can all provide possible contents of conscious experience, but they do not constitute the consciousness itself. Instead, consciousness is a more primary ground of the "I existence." It is the presence of this self illuminating consciousness that allows for awareness of thoughts, feelings and sensations.

Thinking that consciousness consists of thinking is a problem that arises when an investigator thinks about what consciousness might be and then concludes that it is the thought process itself. Vaysse (1979) makes these points in his critical account of the type of "self-analysis" and "introspection" used in modern psychology:

(A) very bad effect of this analytic method is that it makes for arbitrary divisions of the functions of the man who studies himself in this way; whichever function is predominant (almost always the intellectual) stands apart from all the other functions and looks at them in its own way, and often evaluates or judges all of them as though it understood them. Such an attitude can but increase the predominance of one function over the others ... No observation has any real value for self-knowledge unless it is looked at in relation to the whole structure of the observer.... (pp. 20)

Thought has to be understood in relation to the whole structure of the observer. Otherwise, the researcher ends up identifying mental processes as constituting consciousness, instead of being simply one class of the contents of experience.

Yogananda (1972) defines yoga as the *"science of mental control"* and explains that the attainment of higher consciousness involves the *"suspension or neutralization of the incessant waves of thoughts and emotions that arise and subsist in consciousness."* Yogis refer to this constant involuntary stream of thoughts as the *"turning of the mind"* and the *"monkeys of the mind."* These are obstacles to the development of consciousness and self-realization. In a similar vein, Madame Blavatsky explains that: *"The Mind is the great Slayer of the Real. Let the Disciple slay the Slayer."* (1889, p. 1) According to the esoteric mystical teachings, consciousness exists beyond the level of thoughts, feelings, sensations and desires. It is of a more subtle inner nature and the means by which these psychological (or psychic) processes are illuminated and known in awareness.

These themes are depicted throughout the ancient Upanishad of India:

> He who dwells in the mind, but is separate from the mind, whom the mind does not know, whose body the mind is, and who controls the mind from within—he, the Self, is the Inner Ruler, the Immortal.

> Unseen, but the seer; unheard, but the hearer; unthinkable, but the thinker; unknown, but the knower—there is no seer but he, there is no hearer but he, there is no other but he, there is no knower but he. He, the Self, is the Inner Ruler, the Immortal. Anything that is not the Self perishes. (*Brihadaranyaka Upanishad* Prabhavananda, Manchester, 1957, p. 96)

Whereas thoughts, feelings and sensations are constantly changing, the Self is the permanent principle which transcends the psychological processes of the mind and personal identity. At the same time, the presence of Self—of this illuminating consciousness—enables seeing, hearing, knowing and so on, to be experienced. Therefore, it is most important to regard consciousness as being distinct from the psychological functions of the mind, but as both illuminating and witnessing the phenomena of mind. The mind is a vehicle of Self but the roots of Self are deeper within the Heart.

Ramana Maharshi, another Eastern sage, similarly describes the Self as being related to the mysterious heart centre. Consciousness, the mind and the breath, are all described as arising from the same source in the heart—*"the center of the self-luminous Self."* In fact, the goal of yoga is defined as the *"dissolution of the mind in the Heart lotus."*

> Where the 'I' thought has vanished, there the true Self shines as 'I.' 'I' in the heart. ... The 'I,' the Self, alone is real. As there is no other consciousness to know it, it is consciousness. (1977, pp. 90-1)

Sri Ramana prescribes the path of *Vichara* or Self-Enquiry as a route towards self-realization and discernment of the true Self. He elaborates this essential practice most simply:

> sit in meditation, concentrating on the spiritual heart, the supreme center of Consciousness and at the same time, concentrating on the question "Who am I." One should try such a course and not merely argue, so as to have real experience. With continuous and sufficient practices, this meditation would awaken a current of Awareness, discarding the Ego-sense, but rousing a feeling of the essential 'I'— The Universal Self. (Padmanabhan, 1980, pp. 10-11)

The aspirant to spiritual knowledge attempts to merge the mind into the heart, dissolving the inquiring mind and false ego—through the control of the breath and the process of self-inquiry. Ramana describes the process of self-realization as entailing: *"... not a new acquisition but only a removal of the clouds that hide the Reality that we always are by the extinction of the super-imposed non-real ego, that makes us see and experience diversity in the one Universal Self... ."* (Subbaramayya, 1967, pp. viii) In this view, cognitive scientists are making a fundamental mistake in considering their thoughts and mental activities to constitute consciousness! In fact, all these minding process obscure the light of the self-luminous I within the Heart.

It is this experience of Self within the heart which is the source of the cryptic mystical declaration that "I AM." The quest is to know the origin and nature of consciousness within oneself through such direct inner experiences of Self-realization. Sri Chinmoy simply explains the results of the search for Self: *"What he sees in the inmost recesses of his heart is his real 'I,' his God."* (1970, p. 16)

This mysterious Self is connected inwardly to the larger universe, to spiritual and divine realities, and even to God. Certainly these are wonderful possibilities, which provide a viewpoint profoundly contrary to that espoused in so-called exact science. If we speak off the tops of our heads, we will identify consciousness and mind with the head brain; but if we penetrate to the heart of being, we might indeed become *"knowers of Self."*

# 2. Consciousness: Light of the Self

Mystical and spiritual teachings equate consciousness most directly with light. The light of consciousness illuminates the psyche and the activities of the mind/body complex, allowing awareness of psychological processes within one's inner experience. The Self—the spiritual soul—is inherently self-luminous, an element of pure light consciousness. In this vein, Ramana Maharshi refers to the *"self-luminous Self"* and notes, *"I in the heart, it is consciousness."* Similarly, Swami Prabhupada explains, this *"soul is consciousness and conscious."*

These themes are found throughout the mystical literature. Sri Chinmoy explains:

> God is an infinite Consciousness. He is also the self-illumining Light. There is no human being who does not have within him this infinite Consciousness and this self-illumining Light. ... in the inmost recesses of his heart is his real 'I,' his God. ... In the spiritual life, the thing that is most needed is the awareness of consciousness. Without it, everything is a barren desert. ... It is our consciousness that is self-revealing in everything. (1970, pp. 15, 16 & 19)

Just as we can be aware of things in the outer world when light illuminates the objects of perception, so also there is an inner light source which allows consciousness of the objects of inner experience. Ouspensky (1957) explains this in a practical way:

> It must be clearly understood that consciousness and (psychological) functions are quite different things. To move, to think, to feel, to have sensations—these are functions; they can work quite independently of whether or not we are conscious or not; in other words, they can work mechanically. To be conscious is something quite different. ... Functions can be compared to machines working in varying degrees of light. These machines are such that they are able to work better with light than in darkness; every moment there is more light the machines work better. Consciousness is light and machines are functions. (p. 55)

The activities of thinking, feeling and sensation provide the contents for conscious experience, but do not constitute consciousness itself. Consciousness is a substantive light principle, which inwardly illuminates the psychological processes.

A verse of the ancient Brihadaranyaka Upanishad states:

> The self-luminous being who dwells within the lotus of the heart, surrounded by the senses and sense organs, and who is the light of the intellect, is that Self. (p. 104)

Mystics relate the Self to the sun and the mind to the moon. The moon has no light of its own but simply reflects the light of the Sun. Similarly the mind has no consciousness or light of its own but reflects the light originating from the self-luminous element within the lotus of the heart.

The Sufi poet, Rumi, describes the mysteries of light within the external and inner worlds:

> Outward colors arise from the light of sun and stars,
> And inward colors from the Light on high.
> The light that lights the eye is also the heart's Light;
> The eye's light proceeds from the Light of the heart.
> But the light that lights the heart is the Light of God.
>
> (Whinfield, 1979, p. 23)

The ultimate source of Light—spelled with a capital L—is of God. External colors are described as being manifestations of light with a small l. The eyes' light (with a small l) is reflected light, which proceeds from the Light of the Heart. The heart's Light is also capitalized as it originates from the Light of God.

This teaching contrasts sharply with the western convention of regarding consciousness as not being substantive. Instead, mystical teachings associate consciousness with a very substantive light—both supernal (metaphysical) light and natural light. Unfortunately, as semi-conscious, sleepwalking human beings, we do not typically appreciate the nature of light, especially the light within. Instead, humans live in darkness and in ignorance of their true nature. The consciousness of the Self is pure Light but it is obscured by our typical attachments, desires, fantasies, suffering and conditioning. The Light of Self is beyond thought, beyond the mind/body complex, beyond the patterns of conditioning and attachment to material nature—although it is the means by which these are known. Mystical self-knowledge, like spiritual teachings, involves awakening to the Light within the heart, which can then illuminate the mind. Both ancient and contemporary mystical teachings reflect these themes.

The equation of consciousness with light must be understood in a practical way through self-study and awakening. Recall Nicoll's comments, explaining the fourth way psychology:

> what we seek above all things is *Light*—and Light means *consciousness*. We seek to live more consciously and to become more conscious. We live in darkness owing to lack of light—the light of consciousness— and we seek in this work light on ourselves. ... And it is very strange this *light*. ... In the deep sleep we live in, in the light of the Kingdom of Heaven, we are all utterly insane and do not know what we are doing. (1975, pp. 35-6)

The individual can learn to live more consciously in the light, less conditioned by the modes of nature, less attached to mundane thoughts and feelings, sensations and desires. Humankind lives in outer darkness, hypnotized by shadows and illusions. Paradoxically, the dramas of our lives are always sustained from within/without by an underlying realm of Ineffable Light. These profound claims about the nature of consciousness as light are repeated throughout the mystical and esoteric literature.

Unfortunately, scientists consider such ideas to be merely metaphors for the poets of the heart and soul, and do not regard them as posing serious scientific hypotheses. Instead of believing in a self-luminous divine or spiritual spark or Self within the heart, scientists imagine that the cerebral cortex magically manufactures consciousness out of material processes.

In the *Upanishads*, the ancient esoteric Hindu scriptures, there are numerous references to the light of the Self and the self-luminous nature of Brahman. Brahman is the *"light of lights,"* the supreme principle embodied within the *"bright throne"* of the heart. The Self is described as being self-luminous and qualitatively of the same stuff as Brahman, God or the Absolute:

> The light that shines above the heavens and above this world, the light that shines in the highest world, beyond which there are no others—that is the light that shines in the heart of men. —Chandogya Upanishad (p. 64)

> Unite the light within you with the light of Brahman. Thus will the source of ignorance be destroyed, and you will rise above karma. ... The yogi experiences directly the truth of Brahma by realizing the light of the Self within. He is freed from all impurities—he is pure, the birthless, the bright. ... He is within all persons as the Inner Self, facing in all directions. —Svetasvatara Upanishad (p. 121)

The mystic goal is to *"unite the light within the Self with the light of Brahman."* The yogi realizes the light of Self—beyond life and death, pain and suffering, beyond the intellect—as being the Inner Self facing in all directions and rooted into the heart of being.

In the *Bhagavad Gita*, a verse depicts the self luminous nature of the individual Self: *"... as the sun alone illuminates all this universe, so does the living entity, one within the body, illuminate the entire body by consciousness."* (13, 34) Swami Prabhupada explains these basic Vedic principles: *"... a small particle of spirit soul, although situated in the heart of this body, is illuminating the whole body by consciousness. ... consciousness is ... the symptom of the living entity."* (1972b, p. 659) The individual soul, the jivatma, is qualitatively one with the supreme self or the Atman. Thus, the Supersoul and the individual soul both inhabit the body and are associated with the heart—as the "sun" of the body. The spirit soul is self-illuminating and its light is an expression of the infinite light of That Self, the Supersoul.

Another authority on Yogic and Vedic metaphysical philosophy, R. Mishra,

M.D., explains the distinction between the nature of "Purusa" (the Self) and "Prakriti" (material nature):

> In Samkhya (philosophy), the technical name of Self is *Purusa*. *Purusa* is identical with the *Atman* of the Upanishads; it is independent of matter and the material universe. ... *Purusa* is one side which is purely subjective, and *prakriti* is the other side which is purely objective. ... The very name *Purusa* means the Principle, which uses matter as its bed (*puru*, matter + *sha*, sleeper). ... This material body with its perceptual mechanism is for the sake of Self. ... Consciousness is not a creation of material elements because it is characteristically different from them. ... Consolidation of experience as subjective consciousness is due to the presence of *Purusha*. ... *Purusha* is Pure Consciousness, changeless, ever-present behind all these states. It is the Light by which matter and material objects are perceived. It is Self-luminous and It illuminates *prakriti* and its manifestations (the seen and known). (1973, pp. 33-7)

The light of the Self and the greater Self are present within ourselves as the light of consciousness. The *purusa* is the source of 'I,' whereas prakriti is the source of the 'me'—the spiritual as opposed to the material. In this way, the spirit soul is embodied and said to fall asleep in matter, conditioned by the modes of material nature.

Mishra provides profound depictions of the dynamics of consciousness:

> Knowledge-stuff is illumined by the Principle of Consciousness. As dust particles shine in light and indicate the path of light although the real nature of light is unknown, so each particle of knowledge-stuff carries its own manifestation and awakening in the light of Consciousness. (1971, p. 37)

Neurological process in the brain produce varied contents for conscious experience but they do not constitute consciousness itself, nor do they produce it. It is the presence of the illuminating Self within the heart which allows the contents of the mind to be illuminated, as dust particles in light. In a state of yoga, or union with the Self, the yogi no longer identifies with the thought waves (vritti) of the mind, and instead experiences the Atman or Self shining forth in its true nature as pure consciousness and supernal light.

In part, the light of Self is light as we ordinarily consider light. However, light must also be understood in its higher nature and "supernal" forms. The term "supernal" is defined as: "... *pertaining to things above, celestial, heavenly, exalted*" (Webster). The light of the Self is of an exalted celestial nature but is reflected in the material world as the light of individual consciousness, which illuminates the heart, mind and body. The aim, in mystical union, is to unite the light and consciousness of self with the light and consciousness of the greater Self.

The Gnostics and early sects of Jewish and Christian mystics emphasized that to know oneself at the deepest level was simultaneously to know God within oneself as the origin of pure light consciousness. The Gnostic *Gospel of Thomas* relates a story of the disciples asking Jesus where they should go and Christ replies:

> There is light, within a man of light, and he (or it) lights up the whole world. If he (or: it) does not shine, he (or: it) is darkness. ... Jesus said, "If they say to you, 'Where did you come from?' say to them, 'We came from the light, the place where the light came into being on its own accord and established itself and became manifest through their image.'" ... The images are manifest to man, but the light in them remains concealed in the image of the light of the Father. (Robinson, 1981, pp. 121-3, 127)

The phrase, *"We came from the light,"* suggests that "I" originates, emerges or emanates from within a realm of supernal light.

Other Gnostic gospels similarly encourage the disciples to gain the light that is within, as opposed to living in outer darkness. In the *Dialogue of the Saviour*, Christ says:

> "The lamp of the body is the mind; as long as you are upright of heart ... then your bodies are lights. As long as your mind is darkness, your light which you wait for will not be." ... The Lord said, "... when you remove envy from you, then you will clothe yourself with the light, and enter into the bridal chamber." (Robinson, 1981, pp. 231-235)

We have to be *"upright of heart"* for our bodies to be filled with light. In various Christian writings, this light is described as the light of the Sun, as the light of the Son (Jesus Christ), and as the Light of the Father. One Gnostic gospel declares: *"Search ever and cease not till ye find the mysteries of the Light, which will lead you into the Light Kingdom."* (Cohen, Phipps, 1979, p. 235) Recall also the words of Christ from the *Gospel of Truth*, suggesting that those of *"interior knowledge"* know that, *"in you dwells the light that does not fail ... the light which is perfect and filled with the seed of the Father, and which is in his heart, and in the pleroma."* This verse suggests the mystical and metaphysical origins of the light of consciousness and Self.

Another Gnostic text, *Pistis Sophia*, also presents the teachings of the light and the light kingdoms. Christ instructs his disciples:

> seek ye all the Light, that the power of the stars which is in you, may live. ... For God shall save their soul from all matters, and a city shall be prepared in the Light, and all the souls who are saved, will dwell in that city and will inherit it. (Mead, 1974, p. 41)

*Pistis Sophia* elaborates upon the possibilities for super-sensuous knowledge and realization for those souls who enter into the Ineffable Light, into the dimensions of Higher Space and the Light Kingdoms.

Baha'u'llah, the prophet of the Baha'i religion, similarly portrays the relationship of the light within the soul of a human being to the light of the *"King of Oneness:"*

> Whensoever the light of Manifestation of the King of Oneness settleth upon the throne of the heart and soul, His shining becometh visible in every limb and member. ... all the pillars of the dwelling are ashine with His light. And the action and effect of the light are from the Light-Giver; so it is that all move through Him and arise by His will. ... And the splendour of that light is in the hearts ... when thou strippest the wrapping of illusion from off thine heart, the lights of oneness will be made manifest. (1945, pp. 22-24)

> "Knowledge is a light which God casteth into the heart of whomsoever He willeth." (p. 54)

Consciousness or the I AM principle is sometimes described as ultimately emerging from a point source, from a spiritual or divine spark. There is a point source of Light within the heart, which is of the Supreme Self and the Infinite Light. The contemporary heart master, Adi Da writes:

> the Divine Soul is Original White Light. All phenomena are thus a Play of the Original Light, or Unqualified Bliss, of God. And all souls, or all living beings (human or otherwise), are points or atoms of the Original Light or Radiant Bright Consciousness of God. (1978, p. 492)

This point source of light emerges from a realm of infinite light—that is supernal, divine, ineffable Light. The Self illuminates the inner world through the interior dimensions of a human being, emerging through and within the life of the heart, but then allowing for the illumination and knowing of the mind and body.

This point source of pure light is enthroned within the *Bliss Sheath* of the Heart—the *Anandamaya Kosha* of yogic teachings, or the *"causal body"* of theosophy. Saraswati (1987, p. 112) describes this as *"an oval mass of unemergent light,"* approximately the size of a baby's thumb or a small grape. This *"unemergent light"* does not radiate away from its source but is contained within a volume of space. (Similar methods are being developed in fibre optics to contain light within a volume of space.)

The nature of consciousness, light and space are all profound mysteries. While scientists usually consider the equation of consciousness with light as simply being a metaphor, mystical teachings consistently associate the *substance* of consciousness with light. In the same manner, modern thinkers are likely to consider that the idea of the Self as being related to the heart is nothing more than a metaphor. Can we really love with the heart or know God through the heart? Or "see the light," "know the light within ourselves," or "be enlightened"? Perhaps these expressions and concepts, so ingrained in our language and in religious maxims, have a very concrete reality. Can we really become knowers of Self and become enlightened, or are we too caught up with the monkeys of the mind, full of ourselves and self-satisfied with the dogma of the head doctrine? Could the poets of the heart and soul truly know awesome possibilities, beyond anything that the scientists, philosophers and pundits imagine? From a mystical perspective, western conceptualizations of consciousness are fundamentally flawed, the result of too much head-learning and too little soul wisdom.

# 3. The Life of the Heart, the Blood & Transformation

The physical heart and physical consciousness are related. In the same way, the spiritual heart and spiritual consciousness are related. ... Life and consciousness are byproducts of the heart. ... Biological heart and consciousness are physical in nature and they depend on the metaphysical heart and consciousness. In reality, consciousness is not created but manifested and this manifestation depends on the evolution of the nervous system ... and blood .... Your principle aim is to reach the spiritual heart and spiritual consciousness by means of the physical heart and physical consciousness.

(Mishra, 1969, pp.139-40)

## 3a. The Vital Life Principle

The heart is a sacred place wherein divine and spiritual forces act within the psychological and material world to ensoul the human being, bringing vitality and consciousness into the mind/brain complex. Swami Prabhupada provides an overview of the principles by which the Self *ensouls* the body:

> the individual particle of spirit soul is a spiritual atom smaller than the material atoms ... This very small spiritual spark is the basic principle of the material body, and the influence of such a spiritual spark is spread all over the body as the influence of the active principle ... thus all the energies of bodily movement are emanating from this part of the body. The corpuscles which carry the oxygen from the lungs gather energy from the soul. (1972, pp .95-6)

Just as the sun is the source of light and life in the outer world, so the Self within the heart is the light and life source within the body. The heart and blood are related to the electric and vital energies emerging from within the mysterious heart space.

The material body is thus ensouled through the breath and through the circulation of blood (and through subtle energies and influences within the subtle bodies). The relationship of the breath to the soul of a human being is referenced in the book of Genesis (2, 7): where the Lord God breaths into man *"the breath of life"* and *"man became a living soul."* The life of the breath is intimately tied into the life of the heart and soul.[1]

---

1    "There is a great secret to the breath. You have a built-in ability to calm the mind, heal the body, and energize the whole system in minutes, simply with the breath." (Sri Ravi Shankar, Tone, 2004)

After his illumination, Jacob Boehme, a 17th century Christian mystic, espoused such a view of the heart as a sacred place embodying the life principle. Hartmann (1954) describes Boehme as having *"acquired the capacity to see henceforth with the eyes of the soul into the heart of all things,"* and as, *"recognizing the divine order of nature."* In his discourses, Boehme expounded these claims concerning the interaction of the soul with the heart:

> Why will you let the Anti-Christ befool you with his laws and his talk? Why will you seek for God in the depths above the stars? You will not find Him there. Seek Him within your own heart, in His own dwelling; in the generation of your own life. (*Three Principles*, p. 313)

> The heart is the true origin of the soul, and in the interior blood of the heart is the soul, the fire, while in the *tincture* the soul is its spirit (its light); the spirit floats above the heart, and communicates itself to the body and to all of its organs. ... the spirit moveth upon the heart in the bosom of the heart. (*Forty Questions*, p. 200)

The spirit moves within the bosom of the heart space and ensouled the body through the interior blood of the heart.

One intriguing piece of evidence indicates that the seat of the soul is intuitively felt and located in the heart center. In a simple pointing exercise, a person is asked to point to various objects within the environment or to various parts of the body. Lastly, the person is asked to point to "yourself." Having conducted this experiment with thousands of people through talks and lectures, I have found that the vast majority of people intuitively point towards the center of the chest to locate "I." Far fewer think about the question for a few moments and point more to the throat area—as if confused about choosing between the heart and the head. However, it is extremely rare that people point to their heads to indicate 'I'—as one might imagine they would do given that scientists localize the mind, consciousness and the self there. Most frequently, individuals spontaneously indicate the center of the chest as the center of self. It seems that, as mystics claim, humans have intuitive knowledge, feeling and recollection of the Self—the hidden self originating from within the mysterious heart space.[2]

The enlightenment of the heart and then of the higher faculties of the mind allow for states of samadhi or enlightenment, and for varied psychical experience. In life, an individual may simply experiences flashes or glimpses of such

---

2    "Sri Bhagayan observed that by His own experience He first knew the spiritual Heart to be in the right side of the chest. ... "Why, even a child," added Sri Bhagavan,, "when he affirms 'I,' points his finger always to the same place on the right side of his chest and never to his physical heart or between his eye-brows or to his head." (Subbaramayya, 1967, p. 6) Although the mass of the heart is to the left of the body centerline, seldom do people point to the left. Varied authors depict the spiritual heart as shifted to the right relative to the physical heart. The electrical SA node is more centrally located.

elevated states, or as Dr. Mishra suggests, one can learn to live consciously in the awareness of the heart:

> The heart is the doorway of spiritual illumination. ... The important work of the aspirant is to impress this heart memory upon the brain mind. Man must learn to think with his heart. (Heline, 1937, p. 152)

As noted by Dr. Mishra, the physical heart plays a role in determining physical life and consciousness, just as the spiritual heart is critical to the awakening of spiritual consciousness. Unfortunately, modern psychology is only beginning to understand how there might be a *psychology of the heart* and have yet to relate this to the *psychology of consciousness*. Scientists do not imagine that the dimensions of the heart might be related to the soul or to spiritual and divine forces within the life of a human being. These forces are "metaphysical"—in contrast to what materialist scientists naively assume to be purely "physical" processes.

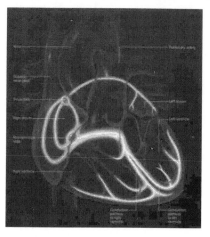

"A natural pacemaker sends the spark that starts a heartbeat."
(*The Incredible Machine*, National Geographic Society, 1992)

## 3b. Generation of the Heart Beat

The heart contracts and beats rhythmically as a result of action potentials that it generates by itself—a property referred to as auto-rhythmicity.[3] Three specialized regions of cardiac cells display such auto-rhythmicity. These include the sinoatrial node (the SA node), the atrioventricular node (or AV node) and the Bundle of Hiss (the atrioventricular bundles). The cardiac auto-rhythmic cells all display pacemaker activity and do not have resting potentials. Their mem-

3 Sherwood (1989), in Human Physiology, defines an action potential as, "brief reversals of membrane potential brought about by rapid changes in membrane permeability." (p. 94)

brane potentials constantly depolarize or drift between action potentials, until a threshold is reached and they discharge. Sherwood explains: *"Through repeated cycles of drift and fire, these auto-rhythmic cells cyclically initiate action potentials, which then spread throughout the heart to trigger rhythmic beating without any nervous stimulation."* (1989, p. 267) The auto-rhythmicity of these cells produces the basic pulse of the heart.

The heart cells with the fastest inherent rate of action-potential initiation are localized in the SA node—which bundle is usually referred to as the "pacemaker" of the heart. However, the other two auto-rhythmic bundles are also latent pacemakers, and if not driven by the SA node, they can take over in initiating the heart beat. The AV node and the Bundle of Hiss have inherently lower rates of activity. The normal rate of 70-80 action potentials/minute is inherent to the SA node, while the AN node might display an auto-rhythmic rate of 50 action potentials, and the Bundle of Hiss and its branches have an inherent rate of 30. Normally, the SA node's rhythm is dominant and the other auto-rhythmic cells do not assume their naturally slower rates.

Scientists do not understand the reason why these cells have this strange auto-rhythmicity. Generally, they assume that there are sufficient physical and biochemical explanations, yet the mysteries of the generation of the physical heart beat continue to elude understanding. Recall B. Brown's most apt comment: *"The genesis of the heartbeat is as unknown as the genesis of man, and equally a miracle."* (1974, p. 68) The generation of life within the heart poses a profound enigmas within science—a gap or puzzle which certainly leaves room for the existence of a life generating, self-illuminating, spiritual spark or "mass of unemergent light" at the heart of being. From an occult or mystical view, the physical pulses of the heart must be related to metaphysical causes, because the physical heart is rooted into the metaphysical spiritual and divine heart, which are the deeper source of life and consciousness.

The claim that the soul or Self are tied to the generation of the heart beat can be found in the ancient Upanishads and it is articulated by other swamis and masters who have mystically examined the interior dimensions of the heart. In the *Mundaka Upanishad*, the Self is related to the heartbeat and to enlightened consciousness.

> The subtle Self within the living and breathing body is realized in that pure consciousness wherein is no duality—that consciousness by which the heart beats and the senses perform their office. (Prabhavanada & Manchester, 1957, pp. 47)

Swami Yogeshwaranand Sarawati, in explaining the science of yoga, relates the jivatma—the spiritual or divine spark—to the generation of life within the interior dimensions of the heart:

In the middle of the heart is a small etheric cavity called the cave of heart, the size of the thumb of a baby or a white grape; it is not part of the physical organ. In this inner cave of the heart is the abode of Chitta (mind stuff) in the form of an oval mass of unemergent light; this Chitta is the abode of Jivatmam. The modern experts of surgery have also seen a small hole-like part close to the blood repository in the heart which is a bit raised and which has a constant vibration on it. They have named it Auriculo-ventricular Bundle of Hiss. ... The effects of Chitta and Atman is observed at this point first of all and causes the working of the heart whereby the activity is sent forward to the entire physical body ... . (1987, p. 112)

Somehow, the jivatma or spiritual soul brings life into the heart through these subtle dimensions—giving rise to the heartbeat, as well as to the circulation of energies through the blood, distributing soul and vital life influences throughout the body/mind. The heart center, or Heart Chakra—*Anahata*, is identified with mass of unemergent light within the subtle space underlying the physical dimensions of the heart.

Heart Master Adi Da, outlines such dynamics, based upon his studies and experiences of enlightenment:

The true Self is Awake in your own heart. ... The region of the heart, which is the seat of the soul and the doorway to the true Self, is one of the primary areas of the body-mind traditionally inspected by mystical vision. ... The true center of the heart is intuitively felt. It is not objective to the soul. It is not seen by the soul. It is the soul. ... The heart-root is prior to the physical and subtle structures of the body-mind. ... It is prior to all energies and forms in the Realm of Nature. (1978, pp. 387-90)

The Self is prior to the physical and subtle dimensions of the heart. Adi Da provides specific descriptions of the initiation of the heartbeat:

The bulk of the physical heart is in the left of the center of the chest, but the "pacemaker" of the heartbeat is located in the right atrium, or upper right chamber of the heart. It is here that the Radiant Transcendental Consciousness is continually associated with the impulse of Life in the individual body-mind. The nerve impulses are sent from the sinoatrial node (the "pacemaker" in the upper wall of the right atrium) to the distribution point or atrioventricular node just below, and the space between them is the true heartbeat, the area we intuitively identify as the Life-Center, or the "seat of the soul." ... the primal activity of the pacemaker is native to the pacemaker itself. It works on its own, in direct association with the Transcendental Force of Life, independent of the brain and all other extended functions of the body-mind. (1978, p. 401)

Individual consciousness arises as a result of a primary contraction out of infinite consciousness within the subtle dimensions and Aether of the heart space. This contraction initiates the action potentials and the firing of cells within the SA node and the other auto-rhythmic areas, and generates an active electric energy, which is distributed through the heart and blood. The heartbeat is dependent upon spiritual forces and dimensions acting within the spiritual and physical heart space. Adi Da explains that in the process of spiritual awakening, one transcends the death of the egoic psyche by *"awakening at the heart in the disposition that is prior to the heartbeat itself."* By this passage, the peripheral personality yields to the central consciousness of being!

Although the actions of the spiritual spark and its orbits of influence are responsible for the generation of the heartbeat, they are not simply identified with physical structures. Saraswati explains that the real heart center is a mass of *unemergent light* within the subtle dimensions. This is certainly not going to be observed by material scientists, although its presence might be inferred from its effects or it might be apprehended directly through mystical awareness. Recall that the electromagnetic volume of the heart is estimated to be five thousand times that of the brain. (Pearsall, 1998, p. 55) Thus, a human being, as a quantum system, clearly has its center of electromagnetic being within the heart area.[4]

---

4    The *Science News, www.ScientificAmerican.com,* reports that: *"Electrical Signals key to culturing heart tissue."* (December 14, 2004) Conventional culture methods for growing tissues apparently do not usually work for heart cells as they do for other cells. However, a team of researchers report applying electrical signals designed to mimic a beating heart to the cells and this allowed for the transformation of the cells into functional heart tissue. We might similarly conceive of there being an underlying physics to the heart which provides such electrical impulses and guides the formation of the heart tissues and the heart's activities.

# 3c. Consciousness, Vitality & Blood Flow

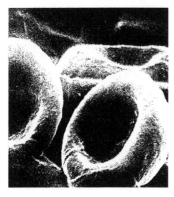

Image 1: Red blood cells magnified 20,000 times. They have a diameter of .007 to .008 mm. And are 60% water. The cells contain Hemoglobin, and iron element, which binds oxygen and transports it throughout the body.

The influence of the Self within the heart is linked to the circulation of blood and vital energies throughout the body/mind. The body is ensouled through the breath and the process of oxygenation. Prabhupada states: *"... the corpuscles which carry oxygen from the lungs gather energy from the soul."* The hemoglobin molecules in the blood include iron atoms, which bind the oxygen supplied by the breath and transport it through the circulation. From a mystical perspective, these basic physiological processes serve the life of the soul in spreading its influence and vitality throughout the body.[5]

Corinne Heline (1937), in *Occult Anatomy and the Bible*, draws descriptions of the heart and blood from a variety of mystical and occult sources:

"The Ego controls the dense body by means of the blood, which is its particular vehicle." —Max Heindel

"... the blood is the medium through which the inner man—the Ego, the I-dentity—rules his body in our present state of evolution."
—Heline (p. 224)

"The human blood contains an airy, fiery spirit, and this spirit has its center in the heart, where it is most condensed and from which it radiates, and the radiating rays return to the heart." —Paracelsus

"The circulation of Life, Prana, through the body is by way of the blood. It is the vital principle in us ... its red corpuscles are drops of electrical fluid." —M. Blavatsky

"... The life of the flesh is in the blood." —Moses

The I-principle is enthroned within the heart as the centre or Sun of the human microcosm. The blood and other vital energies are the agents for the inner

---

5    It is interesting to note that the hemoglobin molecules are the only cells of the body, which do not contain the genetic materials. It is as if they represent a more universalized medium rather than individualized medium for consciousness.

circulation of consciousness, vitality and the influences of the soul.

Swami Saraswati describes the role of the heart:

> The heart is the center of blood purification; it attracts gross or impure blood, purifies it and infuses pure blood throughout the body. With the circulation of the blood, the functions of knowledge and action also pervade the entire body. (p. 202)

Saraswati describes the jivatma as underlying the generation of the heartbeat and as spreading its influences through the purification of the blood. He also suggests that the jivatma spreads it influences through the veins drawing the impure blood to it for purification.

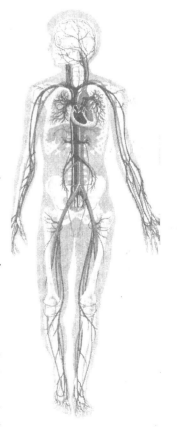

The idea that consciousness and vitality are related to blood circulation provides an interesting alternative perspective on physiology and the mechanisms of one's psychological and psychic life. A mystical perspective suggests that consciousness originates through the metaphysical and physical heart and circulates with the blood throughout the body and mind. In this case, the whole body and mind are potential vehicles for consciousness experience. Through self-awareness, one can experience the inner distribution of blood flow and consciousness through the body and mind.

A variety of observations and research findings illustrate these concepts. Scientists use imaging technologies to show different activities of the brain but these techniques actually monitor the flow of radioactive substances through the blood circulation. Imaging techniques demonstrate which parts of the brain are most active during various mental activities. Brain activity consumes energy and oxygen, as does muscular activity or any cellular activity, and so the activation of particular portions of the brain or body requires an increased blood flow. If a particular portion of the cortex is activated by an intellectual, motor, imagining or sensory task, then there is increased blood flow to that area. In this way, the researcher can see what portions of the brain are active when a person reads a book, looks at a picture or solves a mathematical problem. Increased oxygenation and blood flow accompanies neurological, muscular and cellular activity.

Scientists usually assume that the increased blood flow is secondary to the increased neurological activity. However, an occult viewpoint suggests that activities within the brain and body are influenced and even controlled through the blood. Further, this is related to the directing of attention and the presence of consciousness. In fact, blood flow continually changes as people engage in varied activities involving different parts of the body, mind and emotions. Cognitive scientists and psychologists make a fundamental mistake in assuming that consciousness is localized only within the brain or head and not throughout our selves.

These ideas drawn from a mystical perspective are congruent with our everyday experience. Different feeling states and physical activities do seem inwardly to centre consciousness within different bodily areas in keeping with blood circulation. Hence after a big meal, one will experience the heaviness of a full stomach—as there is increased blood flow to the digestive system. Can our consciousness not be in the stomach and abdomen area? Although scientists consider that consciousness cannot be centered within the abdomen, that view is quite inconsistent with immediate self awareness. Similarly, sexual arousal concentrates blood and awareness in the genitals. Physical activity, such as jogging, enhances physical consciousness, as there is greater blood flow to the major muscle groups. Blood flow throughout the body is continually affected by an individual's psychological and physical states and activities. Consciousness and vitality are distributed and experienced in accordance with the flow of blood. Thus, if the circulation is cut off to any part of the body, a person will lose consciousness and sensation in that area. If a modern researcher wants to study the distribution of consciousness, she or he should consider monitoring blood flow throughout the organism.

Another simple experiment illustrates these concepts. Put your hands together and view the relative sizes of the hands and fingers. Usually, people's hands are about the same size. Now, separate your hands and bring your awareness as fully as possible into one of your hands, while ignoring the other. Maintain this for thirty seconds or so and then place the hands together again to judge their relative sizes. For a good portion of subjects, the hand, which you brought your consciousness to bear upon, will be approximately a quarter of an inch larger than the neglected hand. This indicates that as the awareness or consciousness of one's hand is enhanced, there is increased blood flow to the hand which slightly enlarges it.

Esoteric principles suggest that scientists have fallen prey to major illusions about the functioning of the mind and brain, and the nature of consciousness. The study of circulatory patterns and electrical activity throughout the whole material body/brain (not just within the head) is an area of inquiry most worthy of scientific consideration.

Heline suggests that the "I-principle" controls the body through the blood and that blood flow can be withheld from some areas of the brain and body, and intentionally enhanced to other areas. She notes that the direction of the blood to particular areas *"now generally dormant"* will confer *"esoteric powers"* upon the initiate. From an occult view, there are dimensions to the heart and blood far more mysterious than brain scientists imagine.

Heline foresees the basis for future understanding of the life sciences as being dependent upon our penetrating the enigmas of the heart and blood:

> The illumined healer of the future will study circulatory rhythms of the blood relative to the soul growth and the moral and spiritual development of the patient. Initial soul rhythms which govern blood circulation, have their origin in the heart, and this organ will ultimately become the chief light of the body, both physically and spiritually. (1937, p. 231)

The idea, that the heart and blood are related to the soul life and the inner circulation of consciousness, provides an alternate perspective on datum and enigmas of modern consciousness research. Perhaps, some day people might come to understand such a provocative teaching as that articulated in the Gnostic Christian Gospels—wherein the Lord explains:

> "... the physicians of the world heal what belongs to the world.
> The physicians of souls, however, heal the Heart."
> (Robinson, Ed., 1978, p. 270)

# 3d. The Alchemy of the Blood

Whereas scientists conceive of blood simply in material terms, mystics assert that all things have a subtle nature related to the subtle planes, energies and matters. Thus, in addition to material blood, there are various subtle bloods (or vital energies) related to the subtle bodies. In this view, the alchemy and spiritualization of the blood involves not only the purification of the physical body, but also the refinement of subtle life energies within the subtle bodies.

Gurdjieff describes humans as *"three-brained beings,"* who function physically, emotionally and mentally. The centers of these activities are interconnected through the blood of the physical body, as well as the blood energies of the subtle bodies:

> the body is connected to the feeling organization by the blood, and the feeling-organization is connected to the organization actualizing the functioning of mentation or consciousness by what is called Hanbledzoin (the blood of the astral/or Kesdjan body). (1950, p. 1200)

The body and emotions are connected through the physical blood, while the mind is dependent upon the more subtle energies of the astral blood.

Gurdjieff explains that the substances in the blood required for the physical body are primarily related to the transformation of the *"first being food,"* material food and drink. The substances required for the astral (or Kesdjan/emotional) body are obtained from the *air*, the *"second being food,"* through breathing and through the pores of the skin. The blood of the astral body (which Gurdjieff refers to as Handblezoin) is related to elements of the earth's atmosphere, as well as to energies from the planets and the sun which flow through the atmospheres. Thirdly, Gurdjieff states that, *"that part of the being-blood ... which ... serves the highest part of the being called the soul, is formed from the direct emanations of our Most Holy Sun Absolute."* (p. 569). In this view, various refined subtle energies and influences of the larger cosmos circulate through the blood of the physical, astral and spiritual/mental bodies.

Ouspensky (1949) recalls Gurdjieff's explanations of the alchemical processes, which occur if certain "hydrogens" (elements of different *matter/energy and intelligence* densities) are accumulated within a human being:

> The work of the (human) factory consists in transforming one kind of matter into another, namely, the coarser matters, in the cosmic sense, into finer ones. The factory receives, as raw material from the outer world, a number of coarse 'hydrogens' and transforms them into finer hydrogens by means of a whole series of complicated *alchemical* processes. But in the ordinary conditions of life the production of the human factory of the finer 'hydrogen' ... is insufficient ... If we could succeed in bringing the production up to its possible maximum we should then begin to save the fine 'hydrogens.' Then the whole of the body, all the tissues, all the cells, would become saturated with these fine 'hydrogens' which would gradually settle in them, crystallizing in a special way. This crystallization of the fine 'hydrogens' would gradually bring the whole organism onto a higher level, onto a higher plane of being. ... *'Learn to separate the fine from the coarse'*—this principle from the 'Emerald Tablets of Hermes Trismegistus' ... creates ... the possibility of an inner growth ... the growth of the inner bodies of man, the astral, the mental, and so on, is a material process completely analogous to the growth of the physical body. (1949, pp. 179-80)

In Gurdjieff's fourth way teaching, the student struggles with negative emotions, self-love and mechanical thought, while cultivating self-remembering (or self-conscious awareness) by being- here-now. Through this process, physical, emotional and mental energies, as well as the energies of consciousness, are accumulated instead of being continually wasted and drained. This promotes the development and refinement of the astral and mental bodies—the *"higher being bodies*" in Gurdjieff's terminology. This is a valuable perspective on the alchemy of the blood and how psychological processes affect the energy dynamics of the higher being-bodies.

Gurdjieff explains that the individual attains the state of self-consciousness through the balanced development of the three lower centers and the awakening of the higher emotional center, associated with the heart. Self-consciousness involves the realization of Real "I," based upon a development of the essence. Real I exists beyond the level of the many small i's—states of identification and attachment—which dominate ordinary waking consciousness. A further state of mystical awareness is labeled "objective consciousness," described as yielding objective knowledge of the universe, its mysteries and dimensions. The higher states of consciousness are dependent upon the accumulation of subtle energies and the refinement of the blood life and the psychic life. These psychological processes all affect the makeup of the blood:

> the quality of the composition of the blood in the three-brained beings...depends on the number of the being-bodies already 'completely formed.' (Gurdjieff, 1950, p. 569)

The accumulation of rarified "hydrogens" allows for the growth of the subtle being-bodies and changes the alchemy of the blood. For Gurdjieff, the objective of awakening involves the accumulation of finer energies (or hydrogens) within the blood of the various "higher being bodies," enabling an individual to actually become *"immortal within the limits of the Solar System."*

The Sufi master, Hazrat I. Khan, (1960) similarly describes an alchemical process, which can change the composition of the blood into divine blood. In this case:

> If the divine blood begins to circulate through the veins of a person, this body is no longer a heavy body; it becomes as light as vapour. It is heavy when the weight of the earth has fallen upon it, but when the weight of the earth is taken away from it, it is lighter than the air. (1960, p. 192)

Heline (1917) provides a similar perspective on the spiritualization of the blood and the alchemy of transformation. The blood does not simply contain material elements but other more subtle life energies:

> When studied clairvoyantly within the body, etheric blood [i.e., the subtle energies within the blood] is seen as a refined, vibrating light essence. The higher the attainment of the individual, the more rarefied and luminous becomes his blood. Early church legends about saints whose blood became white refer to this high state of spirituality, wherein the body becomes radiant by reason of this effulgence. Every aspirant to inner knowledge must begin his work by purification

of the blood. ... He guards his every thought, work and deed, for he learns that his life and environment are pictured in his blood, and that his life is fashioned subconsciously in accordance with these pictures. The misuse of the creative force within man's body, his use of improper foods, and impurity in thought and speech tend to thicken the blood. ... the blood assists in the alchemy of spiritualization and, together with the desire body, in the process of re-creation. (pp. 224-5)

Only by high thinking and pure living may an aspirant to the holy Mysteries come to understand the process of changing blood *heat* into blood *light*. This, the Christ taught ... when the blood has been transmuted into golden light essence, oxygen will be superseded by another and more rarefied Sun element. (pp. 237-8)

In contrast to science's strictly material explanations and accounts, mystics assert that the influence of the life principle or spiritual soul is distributed through the blood circulation, as well as through subtle energy channels and centers. An inner circulation of light and finer vital elements is established within the subtle dimensions of human beings. The transformation of consciousness is linked to the alchemical refinement of the blood and the accumulation of more rarefied Sun elements.

The object of self-transformation is to separate the *"fine from the coarse,"* and accumulate more of the subtle energies of the subtle bodies. Gurdjieff describes this process as *"coating"* the *"higher being bodies"* for the life of the soul. According to Gurdjieff, even *"the emanations of our Most Holy Sun Absolute,"* influence the composition of the blood of the spiritual dimensions of a human being.[6]

---

6    The nature of the *higher being bodies* described by Gurdjieff, the subtle bodies described by the theosophists and others, and the various "sheaths" described in yogic literature, will be elaborated in Book III of the *Within-Without from Zero Points* series.

# 4. Science of Soul

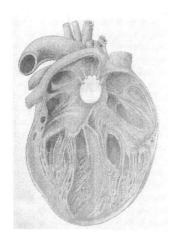

"... it is instinctually recognized that
Jivatman denoted by the pure form of "I"
has its abode in the heart, and in Samadhi
there is direct realization of this."
(Yogeshwaranand Saraswati, 1987, p. 69)

Swami Yogeshwaranand Saraswati in his text
*Science of Soul: A treatise on Higher Yoga* (1987)
provides one of the most thorough and comprehensive accounts of the nature of the soul and its
relationship to the physical and subtle bodies.
The science of soul is based upon Saraswati's
studies of the Upanishads, the Vedas, the yogic
aphorisms of Patanjali and most importantly, upon his own attainments through
meditation, raja yoga and the direct experiences of levels of "samadhi"—enlightened states of super-consciousness.

Saraswati elaborates *Atma Vijnana*, the science of soul. The term *Atma* is defined as the soul, while the term *Vijnana* refers to knowledge or science. The term
*jiva* is also defined as soul and as a being having life. The combined term, jivatma
thus refers to the individualized or embodied soul. In contrast, the Paramatman
refers to the Supreme God or Over-Soul. Whereas Paramatman is infinite, the
jivatma is infinitesimal. Both are depicted as enthroned within the palace of the
heart and to be known through awakening within the heart. Sarawati quotes the
*Upanishads*:

"Jivatma (the Individual Self), that is subtle and minute,
and Ishwara (or Paramatman, the Supreme Self) who is greatest of all,
both dwell in the cave of the heart." (p. 13)

According to the science of soul, the gross material and subtle worlds are
created for the enjoyment and eventual release of the jivatma (the individual
spirit-soul), the immortal Son of the unborn. The Lord or Father of the universe
created a beautiful temple within the heart similar to His own illimitable divine abode and installed the individual soul there. The consciousness principle,
Purusa, lies down within material nature, Prakriti—the feminine principle and
goddess. The three modes of nature produce different substances, elements and
realms which can be experienced by the jivatma. The jivatma can also be liberated or released from the three modes of nature, so as to recover the experience
of its essential nature. Of course, the jivatma always exists within its essential
nature but the nature of consciousness becomes obscured by the veils of nature,

the sheaths and bodies, and all of the activities therein. Thus, humankind lives in a state of forgetfulness and ignorance of this Self.

The seat of the individual soul is in the heart. The jivatma is likened to *"an infinitesimal poppy seed,"* which has no form or colour. This atomic or indivisible entity is embodied in *"a hollow the size of a small thumb in the heart."* (p. 36) Saraswati describes the Bliss Sheath:

> the golden sheath of the divine city ... which is a mass of light filled with bliss, has its abode in the subtle area of grape-sized hollow of this physical heart, the repository of blood. It is in the castle of this causal sheath that the immortal individual soul abides with its supreme protectos, all-powerful, omniscient, adorable father — God. The temple of a yogi is inside the heart alone. There ... the vision of Divinity ... the nectar of bliss ... the Bliss Sheath (or Anandamaya Kosha). (p. 37)

The Bliss Sheath is a *"mass of light filled with bliss"*! This is the ensouled jivatma, which is also referred to as the causal body. In Figure 1, the Bliss Sheath is the egg shaped sphere within the heart, shown as emanating or radiating five luminous white rays. These rays are those of the subtle Pranas, which irradiate life and vitality throughout the individual human being.

The science of soul and of yoga is extremely subtle and complex. The Jivatman—the Purusha principle of pure spirit and consciousness—is embodied within Prakriti or nature, composed of the three gunas or "modes of nature." The three modes of nature—sattva, rajas and tamas—represent the triune *intelligence, energy* and *matter.* These principles are related to the mental, astral and physical bodies; or to the body, mind and soul of Christian teachings. The jivatma itself has a threefold nature as 'sat, chit, ananda' —or being, consciousness and bliss—which embodies the three gunas.[7]

Saraswati describes various orbits of influence within the heart, in addition to seven chakras, three bodies and five sheaths, all of which compose the subtle anatomy of a human being. The jivatma is embodied through these elements, sheaths and bodies in a complex manner, which can be understood through meditation and the consequent attainment of discriminative knowledge and self-realization.

The jivatma (or spiritual soul) is conscious and abides within the heart, which is likened to both a cave (the Cave of Brahman) and to a castle. The jivatma is the Lord of the castle and is embodied in complex ways through the

---

7    Whereas modern physics considers primarily a duality of matter and energy, mystical teachings suggest that spiritual intelligence and Divine mind are the third force inherent everywhere within the medium of space. Everything in nature is a product of the joint interactions of the three gunas, and never simply two, within the seven dimensions or realms of Maya.

differentiation of the elements. Saraswati describes the human being as having three bodies (the physical, the astral and the causal), composed of five different sheaths. The *causal body* is the Bliss Sheath, or *Anandamaya Kosha*. The astral body is composed of the mind sheath, or the *Manomaya Kosha*, and the intellect sheath, the *Vijnanamaya Kosha*. The physical body is composed of the food sheath, the *Anandamaya Kosha*, and the vital air sheath, the *Pranamaya Kosha*.

**Figure 2** The Bliss Sheath depicted as five orbits of influence surrounding the jivatma as a point within the centre.

Within the Bliss Sheath, there are orbits of different principles, which mediate the interface between the divine atom, or jivatma, at the center, and the dimensions of the sheaths and bodies. Through yogic practices and austerities, consciousness can be freed from the outer sheaths and abide again in the bliss sheath—in its essential nature. As these processes of liberation occur, varied states of super-consciousness and realization (or *samadhis*) are experienced. There are subtle distinctions to be made between experiences of self, cosmic and divine realization, which can be attained through the awakening within the heart.

In Figure 2, the Bliss Sheath appears as an oval mass of light composed of five orbits of influence surrounding the jivatma at the center. The two outer orbits are the most inclusive—those of Brahman (or Purusha) and undifferentiated Prakriti (the womb of material creation). The orb of Brahman is omnipotent, the substratum of an eternal, omnipresent, all pervading consciousness. The orb of Prakriti is a non-manifest Aether, the root principle of material creation, which maintains the other orbits in its womb. In the orbit of undifferentiated Prakriti, the three modes of nature are in perfect symmetry and hence unmanifest, or *signless*. The orb of Prakriti is the ultimate Aether of the heart. Saraswati explains that this *"... ether of the heart is the mirror for the vision of Brahman."* The two outermost orbits of Purusha and Prakriti are the ultimate substratum of spirit/consciousness and matter.

The Atman (the divine spark) is within the center of the Bliss sheath. Saraswati describes it as *"an extremely subtle point or dot,"* most similar to Brahman in its subtlety. The Atman is then surrounded by three orbits—of *Chitta* (Mind Stuff), Ahamkar (the Ego principle) and *Subtle Prana* (vital energy). The jivatma within the heart has these three servants: mind stuff, the ego principle and subtle prana/vital energy.

The orb of Chitta in the Bliss Sheath is the deepest level of the mind-stuff and there are usually constant ripples of thought, or *Vrittis*, occurring there like waves on an ocean. The Chitta is the *"revealer of the consciousness of the soul … as it is in this cave of the heart that Atman abides."* (p. 208) The orbit of Ahamkar, the Egoic principle, is a grosser form of Asmita (the principle of 'I'-ness), inherent to the Jivatma. Thirdly, the orbit of subtle vital energies or Prana is described as a luminous vapor, which plays a role in infusing consciousness and life throughout the subtle and material bodies. These five orbs—two of the underlying cosmic

Figure 3 The three servants of the jivatma.

principles and three modifications of individual existence—exist as an aggregate in the region of the heart and together appear as a *"mass of light,"* the *Bliss Sheath.* This is the true heart center—the metaphysical substrates of a human being, from which consciousness and the life principle emerge.

Saraswati explains how the rays emanating from the Bliss Sheath illuminate and enliven the other sheaths and bodies. Whereas the Bliss Sheath within the heart is the size of a small seedless grape, the sheath of the mind (Manas) is the size of a peacock egg centered within the skull, in the middle of the brain (Figure 4). The Intellect, or Buddhi—Lord of the mind—is the smaller white sphere on the top of the peacock egg. Buddhi, as the intellectual and reasoning faculty, is the master of the mind and senses. The smaller spheres located in the band across the mind sheath represent different sensory and motor nuclei present to the mind. However, the true mind and intellect are actually "subtle senses" which underlie the material sensory nuclei.

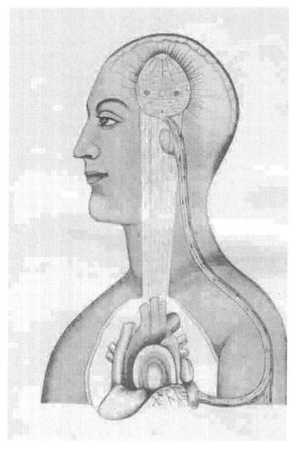

Saraswati describes the mind as *"ever engaged in bringing knowledge and action as perceived by the senses,"* which it offers to Buddhi, the intellect, *"like a servant to his mistress."* The mind functions to carry out the instructions of the intellect. Both the mental and astral bodies have knowledge and action principles enabling experience within the subtle realms. The third force is filled by the subtle Pranas (vital energies), which pervade the mental, astral and physical bodies, and are related to the blood and breath.[8]

Generally, this model of the heart and mind enables us to link the origin of consciousness within the heart to the dynamics of consciousness within the head. Saraswati's explanations are quite in keeping with modern attempts to depict the neural correlates of consciousness and the mind within the brain but these dynamics are regarded as secondary to the illumination of light from the Bliss Sheath. There certainly is consciousness and light within the brain but material neurological processes do not generate it. Rather, it originates from the deeper heart centre. The Heart is the Sun of the human cosmos, the inherent self-illuminating principle; while the mind, like the Moon, reflects the light of the Sun. These descriptions link the heart to the head brain and mind through the circulation of light within the subtle dimensions.

There is an inner circulation of consciousness, light and sentience, which originates from within the Bliss sheath of the heart and is distributed from various centers throughout the bodies and sheaths. Sarasvati depicts the complexity of the inner circulations of light and subtle forces:

> Luminous rays emanate from the senses, subtle organs of action, mind, intellect and other orbs also. These rays are of different kinds and they are seen to perform different functions. ... Mind Sheath—Intellect Sheath and the orb of five Tanmatras (or subtle senses) ... and the luminous orb or mass belonging to the Bliss Sheath—all these are light, (weightless) like wind waves, short and light as fire, transparent as the sky, shining like lightening ... very charming and beautiful, full of consciousness and the wonder and grandeur of life, pleasing.... They are ever in movement. (p. 146)

---

8    Saraswati explains that the jivatma has a fourfold "organ," the *Antahkarana Chatustaya*, formed from the first modifications of Prakriti (material nature). This organ is composed of two substances of the Bliss Sheath of the heart and two substances within the subtle centers of the head. The fourfold organ of the jivatma allows the functions of the causal body associated with the Bliss Sheath to be embodied within the astral and physical bodies, as vehicles for knowledge and action. The two principles within the heart are Chitta, the mind stuff of memory and emotion, and ahamkara, the sense of individuality or egoism. The two principles within the head are the intellectual sheath, Buddhi, the faculty of reasoning and leader of the mind, and Manas, the mental faculty, lord of the senses and organs of action. Chitta is the mirror, which reflects the light and qualities of the Soul, and it underlies Buddhi; while Ahamkara, the sense of individuality underlies Manas. Chitta and Buddhi are "knowledge predominating principles," while Ahamkara and Manas are "action predominating principles."

Sarasvati's science of the soul depicts a variety of subtle substances, light and vital principles, which allow for the embodiment of the Jivatma and the circulation of consciousness within the inner cosmos. In this teaching, consciousness and life originate within-without from a zero point jivatma, rooted into Brahman and subtle Prakriti within the mysterious Bliss Sheath of the heart center.

It is most difficult to grasp all the details of Saraswati's model of consciousness. However, it is obvious that, rather than being "vague" or "non-substantive," these mystical explanations provide sophisticated and detailed alternative views of the dynamics of consciousness. Such an elaborate perspective reveals how thoroughly uninformed scientists are when they routinely dismiss mysticism as the refuge for the intellectually challenged, wishful thinkers or the hopelessly gullible. Saraswati's explanations provide a foundation for a science of the soul and for "the soul hypothesis," which deserves to be considered seriously—especially, given the many enigmas concerning the fundamental issue as to the origin and nature of human consciousness and the I experience. Perhaps, an individual can *"instinctually recognize"* that, *"... I' has its abode the heart,"* as Yogeshwaranand suggests.

# 5. Eastern Sources of the Heart Doctrine

The heart doctrine is elaborated throughout eastern and western mystical teachings of both ancient and modern times. Drawing from eastern traditions, the themes of the heart doctrine are evident within a) the Upanishads, the sacred Hindu texts are dated to centuries and millennium B.C.; b) the Bhagavad Gita, described as the *"Bible of the east"* and the *"cream of the Vedas;"* and c) Sufism and Islamic mysticism, as well as the writings of other mid-eastern poets of the heart and soul.

## 5a. The Upanishads: The Cave of Brahman

The term Upanishad means *"at the feet of the master."* The Upanishads are lyrical and cryptic accounts of mystical revelation and experience recorded by early East Indian seers. These sacred verses repeatedly refer to the Self within the *"lotus"* (flower) of the heart and the *"cave of Brahman"* (God). The Self is beyond the material body and world, and yet the source of light, consciousness and individual identity:

> Self-luminous is Brahman (God), ever present in the hearts of all. He is the refuge of all, he is the supreme goal. In him exists all that moves and breathes. In him exist all that is. He is both that which is gross and that which is subtle. ... Beyond the ken of the senses is he. Supreme is he. Attain thou him!
>
> Within the lotus of the heart he dwells, where, like the spokes of a wheel in its hub, the nerves meet. ... This Self, who understands all, who knows all, and whose glory is manifest in the universe, lives within the lotus of the heart, the bright throne of Brahman.
>
> Self-luminous is that Being, and formless. He dwells within all and without all. He is unborn, pure, greater than the greatest, without breath, without mind. ...
>
> By the pure of heart is he known. The Self exists in man, within the lotus of the heart, and is the master of his life and of his body. ... The knot of the heart, which is ignorance, is loosed, all doubts are dissolved, all evil effects of deeds are destroyed, when he who is both personal and impersonal is realized. In the effulgent lotus of the heart dwells Brahman who is the passionless and indivisible. He is pure, he is the light of lights. Him the knowers of the Self attain. Mundaka Upanishad (Prabhavanada & Manchester, 1957, pp. 45-6)

There are a number of very significant points being made here about the nature and origin of Self. First, the Self exists within the heart or the *"lotus of the heart,"* where the nerves meet—in a particular area. Secondly, the Self is of the same being, of the same 'stuff,' as Brahman, the Lord or God. Thirdly, the Self is the life principle and spiritual element within and behind the mind and the material body—*"the master of his life and of his body."* Fourthly, the Self is self-luminous, possessing an inherent light nature and dwelling in the bright throne of Brahman. Fifthly, the Self is described as usually obscured by "ignorance" and the "knots of the heart." Lastly, the Self is the supreme goal of the seeker. Thus, a guru or yogi is one who knows Self and experiences "I Am" within the heart. The experience of Self Realization can then lead to the individual self merging with the supreme Self in experiences of God realization. The knowers of Self attain the pure light of lights within the lotus of the heart.

The themes are similarly presented in the *Chandogya Upanishad.* Brahman and Self exist within the heart, hidden and obscured by illusion, yet the greatest of all treasures:

> lo, all shall be ours if we but dive deep within, even to the lotus of the heart, where dwells the Lord. Yea, the object of every right desire is within our reach, though unseen, concealed by a veil of illusion. As one not knowing that a golden treasure lies buried beneath his feet, may walk over it again and again, yet never find it, so all beings live every moment in the city of Brahman, yet never find him, because of the veil of illusion by which he is concealed.
>
> The Self resides within the lotus of the heart. Knowing this, devoted to the Self, the sage enters daily that holy sanctuary.
>
> Absorbed in the Self, the sage is freed from identity with the body and lives in blissful consciousness. The Self is the immortal, the fearless; the Self is Brahman. This Brahman is eternal Truth.
>
> The Self within the heart is like a boundary, which divides the world from THAT. Day and night cross not that boundary, nor old age, nor death; neither grief nor pleasure, neither good nor evil deeds. (Prabhavanada & Manchester, 1957, pp. 75-6)

This is the Self we must know in order to be 'knowers of Self' and further to realize the Lord or God. Self originates from a metaphysical realm beyond matter and energy, time and space, beyond the dualities of existence. It originates from within the realm of the formless Brahman, the realm of the Light of lights. The Self within the heart is a boundary point dividing this world of material creation from "THAT"—the formless realm of Brahman which underlies and sustains all things.

The *Upanishads* attribute the most paradoxical dimensions to Self:

*162*

Smaller than a grain of rice is the Self; smaller than a grain of barley, smaller than a mustard seed, smaller than a canary seed, yea, smaller even than the kernel of a canary seed. Yet again is that Self, within the lotus of my heart, greater than the earth, greater than the heavens, yea, greater than all the worlds. (*Chandogya*, ibid, p. 65)

The Self is infinitesimally small—a zero point—smaller than anything we know outwardly. Yet at the same time, this element is related to the dimensions of the larger world or universe and the Supreme Self, which permeates all and everything.

All things exist within the lotus of heart. The following verse depicts these mystical dimensions of the heart, as a microcosm of the macrocosm, holographically reflecting the universe:

As large as the universe outside, even so large is the universe within the lotus of the heart. Within it are heaven and earth, the sun, the moon, the lightning, and all the stars. What is in the macrocosm is in this microcosm ... All things that exist ... are in the city of Brahman. (*Chandogya*, ibid, 1957, pp. 74)

These are the mystical dimensions of the heart, the metaphysical realities, which link individual consciousness to realms of the cosmic or Supreme Consciousness. Thus, a human being can potentially experience consciousness of the larger cosmos and realms of spiritual and divine being. In fact, a human being can come to *"know the universe and the Gods."* To realize such dimensions of Self is the supreme life adventure and quest, yet requires overcoming ignorance, undoing the knots of the heart and lifting the veils of illusion. The usual sense of personal and individual consciousness arises from the identification of the Self, through ignorance, with the elements in which it is embodied. Rising above the elements, the individual self merges into the deeper Self. *"Brahman is the soul in each; he indeed is the Self in all."* (*Brihadaranyaka*, ibid, p. 89)

# 5b. The BHAGAVAD GITA;
# Lord Krishna on the Spirit Soul

The Supreme Lord is situated in everyone's heart, O Arjuna, and is
directing the wanderings of all living entities, who are seated as on a
machine made of material energy.

(18, 61) (Prabhupada, 1972)

The *Bhagavad Gita* is a classic text of Indian spiritual knowledge described
as *"the cream of the Vedas."* Within the *Gita*, Lord Krishna, the Personality of the
Godhead, elaborates upon the nature of the Self and the process of attaining self-
knowledge. The *Gita* includes materials on the ensnarement of the individual
soul within the three modes of material nature, the cycles of life and death, the
relationship of the individual Self to the Supreme Self or Lord, and the science
of self-realization. The realization of Self—*"mukti"*—entails the liberation of
the soul from material nature and the cycles of life and death. According to the
Bhagavad Gita, both the Supreme Lord (the Supersoul or Paramatma) and the
individual spirit soul (the jivatma) are associated with the heart:

> The physical nature is known to be endlessly mutable. The universe is
> the cosmic form of the Supreme Lord, and I am that Lord represented
> as the Supersoul, dwelling in the heart of every embodied being. (8, 4)

> Out of compassion for them, I, dwelling in their hearts, destroy with
> the shining lamp of knowledge the darkness born of ignorance. (10, 11)

> I am the Self, O conqueror of sleep, seated in the hearts of all creatures.
> I am the beginning, the middle and the end of all beings. (10, 20)

> One who sees the Supersoul accompanying the individual soul in all

bodies and understands that neither the soul nor the Supersoul is ever destroyed, actually sees. (13, 28)

The two souls, the Supersoul and the individual soul, are compared to two birds sitting together on the branch of a tree. The individual soul is captivated by the fruits of the tree which represent material desires, while the Super Soul is a silent witness. To attain liberation, the individual spirit soul must overcome patterns of attachment to pleasurable experiences, desires and the fruits of action, and surrender to the larger Self of the Lord. Self-realization, or union with the Lord, comes through awakening to the eternal principle within the sacred temple of the heart.

The story of the *Gita* is set on a battlefield and involves a dialogue between Lord Krishna and Arjuna, a warrior and student. Arjuna is lamenting the reality of a impending major battle about to be fought between two warring families. He is full of compassion and grief, knowing that death and destruction is inevitable for both families which include friends and warriors on each side. At one point, Arjuna sets aside his bow and arrows, unable to fight. He surrenders in despair to Lord Krishna. Krishna then undertakes the task of enlightening Arjuna—as to the nature of the Self, the situation of the conditioned soul, the modes of nature, and the teachings of yoga, or union.

Lord Krishna explains to Arjuna that he should not lament over life or death, because the essential Self is not dependent upon the body or mind, and does not terminate with material death. Instead, the Self has an inward connection to the greater life of the Supreme Lord. As to the true nature of the soul, Lord Krishna instructs Arjuna:

> While speaking learned words you (Arjuna) are mourning for what is not worthy of grief. Those who are wise lament neither for the living nor the dead. (2, 11)

> Never was there a time when I did not exist, nor you, nor all these kings; nor in the future shall any of us cease to be. (2, 12)

> As the embodied soul continually passes, in the body, from boyhood to youth, and then to old age, the soul similarly passes into another body at death. The self-realized soul is not bewildered by such a change. (2, 13)

> That which pervades the entire body is indestructible. No one is able to destroy the imperishable soul. (2, 17)

> For the soul there is never birth nor death. Nor, having once been, does he ever cease to be. He is unborn, eternal, ever-existing, undying and primeval. He is not slain when the body is slain. (2, 20)

> As a person puts on new garments, giving up old ones, similarly, the soul accepts new material bodies, giving up the old and useless ones. (2, 22)

> The soul can never be cut in pieces by any weapon, nor can he be burned by fire, nor moistened by water, nor withered by the wind. (2, 23)

> This individual soul is unbreakable and insoluble and can be neither burned nor dried. He is everlasting, all pervading, unchangeable, immovable and eternally the same. (2, 24)

> It is said that the soul is invisible, inconceivable, immutable and unchangeable. Knowing this, you should not grieve for the body. (2, 25)

> All created beings are unmanifest in their beginning, manifest in their interim state, and unmanifest again when they are annihilated. So what need is there for lamentation? (2, 28) (1972)

Lord Krishna explains to Arjuna that he should not grieve over death as the soul is everlasting and passes into other bodies with the dissolution of the physical body. The soul exists beyond the elements of material nature (any physical weapon, fire, water and wind/air), and hence is indestructible. It assumes various bodies (or garments) during life—from conception, through infancy to old age—and after death, as it passes into subtle dimensions of being in afterlife worlds.

The individual spirit soul will experience innumerable incarnations (or reincarnations) until it attains liberation and self-knowledge. The living entity in the body, the jivatma or individual spirit soul, and the Supersoul are both of a transcendental nature, but the individual becomes conditioned by the three modes of nature, the three gunas, and loses awareness of the true nature of Self. Lord Krishna explains:

> The Vedas mainly deal with the subject of the three modes of material nature. Rise above these modes, O Arjuna. Be transcendental to all of them. Be free from all dualities and from all anxieties for gain and safety, and be established in the self. (Ch. 2, V. 45)

According to the Vedic teaching, the three gunas compose the spiritual, psychic and physical materials within all manifest planes of being. These three gunas are headed by the demi-gods: Brahma, the creator; Vishnu, the preserver; and Shiva, the destroyer—and their bodies compose the Universe. Whereas western scientists distinguish between matter and energy, the Vedic distinguish between a threefold material, energetic and mind/intelligence principle within all things. The three modes of nature are referred to as tamas, rajas and sattva, and as the modes of ignorance, passion and goodness.

In the *Gita*, Lord Krishna explains, *"I am the seed giving father"* (Ch. 14, V. 4) and He impregnates the mother, or material nature. The spiritual spark, or jivatma, is thus embodied within the three modes of nature and conditioned by them. The mode of sattva, or goodness, is purer than the others and related to intelligence, illumination and mind. Individuals under the influence of sattva become conditioned by the concepts of happiness and goodness. In the mode of rajas, the soul becomes conditioned by passion, attachments, desires and long-ings, as characterized by the sexual attraction between men and women. Lastly, the mode of tamas, of mass, inertia, and ignorance, causes *"the delusion of all living entities."* (Gita, Ch. 14, 8) Tamas is related to sleep, indolence and foolishness, and manifests in depression, laziness, addictions and false knowledge. The Dwarf of Ignorance is a manifestation of the mode of Tamas.

The three modes of nature are intertwined in all things but one or another will dominate in different manifestations and people. Lord Krishna explains:

Sometimes the mode of passion becomes predominant, defeating the mode of goodness ... and sometimes the mode of goodness defeats passion. Again, sometimes the mode of ignorance defeats goodness and passion. In this way, there is ever a competition for supremacy. (Ch. 14, 10)

Swami Prabhupada explains, *"the mode of goodness is the purest form of exist-ence in the material world."* (1972b, p. 677) Thus the yogi, or spiritual aspirant, would make efforts to cultivate sattvic properties.

The afterlife state and fate is determined by which mode of nature predomin-ates within a person's life. If situated in the mode of goodness at death, the spirit-ual soul passes upwards to the *"higher planets;"* an individual conditioned by the mode of passion will be attracted to the *"earthly planets;"* and one conditioned by the mode of ignorance will *"go down to the hellish worlds."* (Prabhupada, 1972, p. 681) The yogi, who is one with Self, transcends the modes of nature and can escape from the cycles of life and death to share in the Eternal Life:

When the embodied being is able to transcend these three qualities, he can become free from birth, death, old age and their distresses and can enjoy nectar even in this life. (Ch. 14, 20)

From the viewpoint of the *Gita*, modern psychology and science are ruled by the *"mode of ignorance"*—foolishness and false knowledge, wherein the centre of self is imagined to be in the mind, material nature is taken to be the cause of living entities, and the "seed" of the Godhead is ignored. The individual spiritual soul, in realizing the deeper Self, is freed from this delusion and from material entanglement.

The nature of human consciousness must be understood as originating from the jivatma or the individual spiritual soul within the heart. According to this formulation, consciousness is related to the light of the spiritual soul. The jivatma is inherently self-illuminating:

> as the sun alone illuminates all this universe, so does the living entity, one within the body, illuminate the entire body by consciousness. (Ch. 13, V. 34)

Swami Prabhupada elaborates upon the meaning of this sacred text:

> As the sun is situated in one place, but is illuminating the whole universe, so a small particle of spirit soul, although situated in the heart of this body, is illuminating the whole body by consciousness. Thus consciousness is the proof of the presence of the soul, as sunshine or light is the proof of the presence of the sun. ... consciousness is not a production of the combination of matter. It is the symptom of the living entity. The consciousness of the living entity, although qualitatively one with the supreme consciousness, is not supreme because the consciousness of one particular body does not share that of another body. But the Supersoul, which is situated in all bodies as the friend of the individual soul, is conscious of all bodies. That is the difference between supreme consciousness and individual consciousness. (1972b, pp. 659-660)

A small particle of spirit soul (the spiritual spark) inhabits the material heart as the "sun" of the body. The spirit soul is self-illuminating and its light is an expression of the infinite light of That Self, the Supersoul. The substance of consciousness is light, and ultimately, this light originates from a realm of supernal Light.

The knowledge of Self and of Krishna, the Supersoul, enlightens the individual and destroys the illusions of the false ego:

> When, however, one is enlightened with the knowledge by which nescience (ignorance) is destroyed, then his knowledge reveals everything, as the sun lights up everything in the daytime. (Ch. 5, V. 16)

Ordinary consciousness, so-called waking consciousness, is conditioned by the material realm, by the senses and desires of the body, and by the psychological needs of the ego. A false ego forms as a product of conditioning and assumes a bodily conception of consciousness. Liberation requires a freedom of consciousness from material nature and a realization of pure spiritual consciousness. This liberation of the spirit soul is called enlightenment or "mukti." This is the way of Arjuna the spiritual warrior.

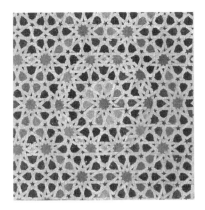

# 5c. From Islam & Sufism to Bhagavan Sri Ramana, Gibran & Baha'u'llah

"I who cannot be fit into universes
upon universes, fit into the heart of
the sincere believer."

"Everything needs a kind of polish
to cleanse it, and the polish for the
Heart is the remembrance of God."
—Muhammad

"The heart is the treasury in which God's mysteries are stored;
Seek the purpose of both the worlds through the heart, for
that is the point of it." —Sufi poet, Lahiji

"God placed a divine spark into every human being.
And that divine spark is the secret of secrets."
(Robert Frager/Sheikh Ragip, 2005)

In Islam, it is most important to have a benevolent heart—rather than a harsh heart. The heart holds either your belief or kufr (disbelief); dedication or indolence and hypocrisy; your praise of Allah or your forgetfulness of Him; your happiness or misery; purity or insolence and sin; mercy or inhumanity and heartlessness; knowledge/wisdom or ignorance; courage or cowardice; love or hate; decency or impropriety; chivalry or discourtesy; envy or jealousy and enmity; courage or cowardice; and decency or impropriety. There is a whole psychology to the heart and it determines the quality of a human being. The greatest of gifts of Allah is the possibilities of a loving and enlightened heart, and the Islamic religion teaches practical ways to cure a heart's harshness. Especially this involves baring or uncovering one's heart and the experience of remorse for wickedness and selfishness. To work on your heart requires inner struggle and learning to remember Allah and live by His moral teachings. Upon death, an individual is judged and punished according to the qualities of the heart.

The celebrated Sufi poet, Rumi, was born in Afghanistan in 1207 and died in 1273 in Turkey. Rumi is associated with the Whirling Dervishes, a mystical order which pursues spiritual realization through experiences of dancing, ecstasy and divine love. Sufism is a form of esoteric or mystical Islam. Rumi depicts the plight of the lost soul searching for God and Self in the outer world:

> Cross and Christians, end to end, I examined. He was not on the
> Cross. I went to the Hindu temple, to the ancient pagoda. In none

of them was there any sign. To the uplands of Herat I went, and to Kandahar, I looked. He was not on the heights or in the lowlands. ... I went to the Kaaba of Mecca. He was not there. ... I asked about him from Avicenna ... . (finally) I looked into my own heart. In that, his place, I saw him. He was in no other place. (In Shah, 1968, p. 105)

For humankind asleep, it is natural to look outwardly to find God—to go searching for God or spiritual experience. However, people seldom experience the light, love and life within themselves awakened in the bliss of the heart. Neither the soul nor God exist as objects for consciousness, as they are the source of light consciousness within Space itself, which emerge from within the depths of one's heart.

The Self within the heart is the subtlest of hidden treasures, the source of that consciousness and life which turn outwards in search of self or happiness.

> "There is a Soul inside of your Soul,
> Search that Soul.
> There is a jewel in the mountain of body.
> Look for the mine of that jewel.
> Oh, Sufi, passing,
> Search inside if you can, not outside."
> Jalal al-Din Rumi

The image of the jewel reminds us of the bliss sheath within the heart, described as *'the size of a small grape.'*

In the *Masnavi*, Rumi's greatest work composed over a forty-year period, he often refers to those *"men of heart,"* who glimpse the hidden mysteries. Rumi explains:

> The knowledge of men of heart bears them up,
> The knowledge of men of the body weighs them down.
> When 'tis knowledge of the heart, it is a friend;
>
> When knowledge of the body, it is a burden. ...
> Yea, see in your heart the knowledge of the Prophet.
> (In Whinfield, 1979, pp. 52-3)

Of course, Rumi notes, *"The people of the world lie unconscious, with veils drawn over their faces, and asleep;"* (p. 56) and are ruled by *"the sickness of your heart."*

In *Sufism: The Alchemy of the Heart*, Muhammad, Isa Waley explains that the Sufi's goal is to attain Divine Grace, a love and a certainty which spring from direct knowledge and experience of God. The Sufi thus invokes and remembers the Name of the Lord. It is through the remembrance of God that the inner being becomes increasingly illumined and achieves detachment from the world of illusion. With the selfless remembrance of God, attention to the egoistic self falls away and the heart and soul are transformed by the divine attributes. *"Recline on the throne of the heart, and with purity in manner be a sufi."* (Sa'di) The Sufi master is described as a *"physician and trainer of hearts and souls"*—the alchemist who brings about the transformation and illumination of the heart.

> What is false is that which is veiled by the veil of the ego and what is true by the veil of the Heart. The veil of the ego is a dark, earthly veil, while the veil of the Heart is a radiant, heavenly veil. (Umar al-Suhrawardi, in Waley, 1993, p. 33)

The power of love and of invocation and remembrance can open the heart to direct experiencing of the unseen—the world beyond within. The prophet Muhammad explained: *"Everything needs a kind of polish to cleanse it, and the polish for the Heart is the remembrance of God."* (Waley, p. 48) The heart is a mirror created by God and capable of reflecting the light and attributes of God.

Another Sufi master, Hazrat Inayat Khan explains the nature of one who lives *"the inner life:"*

> The exact meaning of the inner life is not only to live in the body, but to live in the heart, to live in the soul. Why, then, does not the average man live an inner life when he too has a heart and a soul? It is because he has a heart, and yet is not conscious of it; he has a soul, and knows not what it is. ... All this experience obtained by the outer senses is limited. When man lives in this limitation he does not know that another part of his being exists, which is much higher, more wonderful, more living, and more exalted. Once he begins to know this, then the body becomes his tool, for he lives in his heart. And then later he passes on and lives in his soul. ... When once he begins to realize life in his heart and in his soul, then he looks upon his body as a coat. (1960, pp. 79-80)

> Many seem wide awake to the life without, but asleep to the life within; and though the chamber of their heart is continually visited by the hosts of heaven, they do not know their own heart; they are not there. (p. 123)

Sufis suggest that humans are generally not awake to the inner life of the heart. They are turned towards the external senses and dramas of life, and do not remember. The greatest treasure is to live fully within the life of the heart and thereby, increasingly within the life of the soul. Even the hosts of heaven visit the dimensions of the Heart!

Robert Frager, by his Sufi name—Sheikh Ragip, is an American psychologist and Sufi teacher. Frager provides lucid descriptions of essential Sufi practices and teachings:

> The secret of secrets is the divine spark within each of us. Remembrance is remembering that which we already know. It is to get in touch with

that divine spark that God has placed within each human being. In the Koran it says that God breathed from the divine soul into Adam; another way of translating that would be that God placed a divine spark into every human being. And that divine spark is the secret of secrets. My master put it this way: That spark in us could set the whole universe on fire. It's greater than the universe itself because it's a spark of what is infinite. And it's within every one of us. Who we are is far more than who we think we are. (2005)

A divine spark is a zero point source emanating out the infinite realm within. This spark is beyond the level of physical differentiation in terms of the Planckian units of physics, beyond which we cannot measure. A divine spark does not 'have extension,' as judged from the external viewpoint. Recall Blavatsky described *"material points without extension"* as the basis upon which the God's and other invisible powers clothe themselves in bodies. Human consciousness is due to such a metaphysical process, which brings the light of consciousness and the life principle into the heart. The divine spark exists always at the centre of our being at zero point levels, and through the breath and blood, consciousness and life are infused into a living, breathing human being. Remembrance is recalling and living in this inner experience, which had strangely been forgotten, as the light had been veiled.

In *Revelation*, Bhagavan Sri Ramana writes:

Unto that transcendental Being, the unborn (Self) shining in the Heart, in every creature, as the limitless I, the Guru of all gurus, my real Self and Lord ... The Sun of Pure Consciousness ... is most excellent. Verse 1 & 3

Since that (Reality) dwells, thought-free, in the Heart; how can It,—Itself named the Heart,—be meditated on? And who is there, distinct from It, to meditate on It, the Self whose nature is Reality Consciousness? Know that to meditate on It is just to be at one with It within the Heart. Verse 4

When the mind, introverted by being engaged in the Quest of 'Who am I,' is lost in the Heart, and the ego bows his head in shame, there shines by Its own light a Pure Consciousness as the limitless Light; that (Consciousness) is not the spurious ego; It is the Transcendental, Infinite Reality: It is the blissful Real Self. Verse 35 (Sarma, 1980)

In these beautiful verses, Bhagavan depicts the subtlest of ideas so simply. To meditate on the Self *"is to just be at one with It within the Heart"*!

Elsewhere, in Kahil Gibran's classic work, *The Prophet*, a man from the village approaches the Prophet and asks him to:

172

"Speak to us of Self-Knowledge."

And he (the prophet) answered, saying: "Your hearts know in silence the secrets of the days and the nights. But your ears thirst for the sound of your heart's knowledge. You would know in words that which you have always known in thought.... the treasure of your infinite depths would be revealed to your eyes. But let there be no scales to weight your unknown treasure; ... For self is a sea boundless and measureless. ... The soul unfolds itself, like a lotus of countless pearls." (1968, pp. 54-55)

Gibran contrasts the thoughts of the mind and ego with the secret self within the heart. Whereas the mind is full of chatter, the Self within the heart is known in silence. Again, the heart center is compared with a flower, a lotus unfolding from within-without.

Baha'u'llah, the prophet of the Baha'i religion, also elaborates upon the inner mysteries of the heart:

How often hath the human heart, which is the recipient of the light of God and the seat of the revelation of the All-Merciful, erred from Him Who is the Source of that light and the Wellspring of that revelation. It is the waywardness of the heart that removeth it far from God, and condemneth it to remoteness from Him.

Baha'u'llah depicts the Self as a light source—recipient of the light of God—within the heart. Further, he asserts that it is the false or unnatural condition of the heart in its waywardness, which obscures the deeper spiritual or divine realization of God.

Baha'u'llah (1945) depicts the divine treasures hidden within the dimensions of the heart. In *The Seven Valleys and the Four Valleys*, Baha'u'llah explains:

He hath most excellent names in the hearts of those who know. ... there shall appear upon the tablet of thine heart a writing of the subtle mysteries ... and the bird of thy soul shall recall the holy sanctuaries of preexistence ... cleanse the heart—which is the wellspring of divine treasures ... .(pp. 2-5)

With inward and outward eyes he witnesseth the mysteries of resurrection in the realms of creation and the souls of men, and with a pure heart apprehendeth the divine wisdom in the endless Manifestations of God. In the ocean he findeth a drop, in a drop he beholdeth the secrets of the sea. Split the atom's heart, and lo! Within it thou wilt find a sun. (p. 12)

...the grades of knowledge relate to the knowledge of the Manifestations of that Sun of Reality, which casteth Its light upon the Mirrors. And the splendour of that light is in the hearts, yet it is hidden under the veilings of sense and the conditions of this earth, even as a candle within a lantern of iron, and only when the lantern is removed doth the light of the candle shine out. In like manner, when thou strippest the wrappings of illusion from off thine heart, the lights of oneness will be made manifest. (pp. 23-4)

Knowledge is a light which God casteth into the heart of whomsoever He willeth. (p. 54)

*"Split the atom's heart, and lo! Within it thou will find a sun."* These mystical verses suggest the deep origins of consciousness and life within inner dimensions of the heart, the mirror of the *Sun of Reality*. The wisdom of the heart reveals and illuminates the mysteries of self and God.

Eastern and mid-eastern spiritual teachings provide profound poetic and lyrical descriptions of the Self. Mystics repeatedly identify the Self with the heart and relate it to the Supreme Self, or God. Like the sun, the Self is self-luminous, a light emerging out of infinite light, a point source of consciousness reflecting a Supreme Consciousness. The Self is also described as having a zero point source of origin—as a *'divine spark,'* or *'the secret of secrets.'* The Self and the Heart are mysteriously related to the larger universe, to the unity of life, to the experience of higher love and ultimate realities. To gain the understanding and wisdom of the Heart and of Self is the primary goal of spiritual realization.

# 5d. The Dalai Lama's Teachings of Tibetan Buddhism

## *On the Indestructible Drop within the Heart, Consciousness as the Mind of Clear Light & the Empty Space Particles*

*In Buddhism, since the definition of "living" refers to sentient beings, consciousness is the primary characteristic of "life."* (2005, p. 106)

The Dalai Lama explains Tibetan Buddhist views of the nature of human consciousness and describes some of the subtle anatomic processes which underlie life and death. The following notes draw from the Dalai Lama's book *Advice on Dying, and Living a Better Life* (2002) his dialogues with Renee Weber and David Bohm in *Dialogues with Scientists and Sages* (1986) and *The Universe in a Single Atom* (2005). We will explore the Dalai Lama's teaching as most pertain to the investigation of the heart doctrine, the nature of human consciousness as light and the concept of zero point origins.

The Dalai Lama states that after conception the psyche and body grow from that which forms into the heart. He describes three major channels interconnecting seven major "channel-wheels" or centres within the subtle anatomy as the basis for consciousness and mind within the body—supported by various *'winds,'* as the medium for mind. He also describes various *'knots'* or constrictions established at the heart centre, as well as at the other six centres:

> In the body there are at least seventy-two thousand channels—arteries, veins, ducts, nerves, and manifest and unmanifest pathways—which start growing at what will be the heart soon after conception. ... (There are) three most important channels ... At vital places in these three channels are seven channel-wheels, with differing numbers of spokes, or channel-petals. ... The wheel of phenomena is found at the heart ... the residence of the very subtle wind and mind that are themselves the root of all phenomena. At the heart, the left and right channels wrap around the central channel three times (each channel also looping over itself), and then proceed downwards. This results in a six-fold constriction at the heart, which prevents

the passage of wind in the central channel. At each of the (other six) centres ... the right and left channels wrap around the central channel once each (each channel also looping over itself), thereby making two constrictions. The right and left channels are inflated with wind and constrict the central channel such that the wind cannot move in it; these constrictions are called "knots." (pp. 138-9)

All the channels, arteries and such, grow out from that which forms into the heart. The inner circulation of the 'winds' which support consciousness and mind, is then distributed through three major channels and seven centres—in the pattern of 1-3-7 as befits the description of light. Just as white light divided by a prism yields a spectrum of seven colours, so also there is an inner circulation of consciousness and vitality through the inner human being—through the subtle 'winds' which are the basis for mind and conscious experience. The 'knots' within the heart restrict the winds in the central channel, as do the knots at other centres. At death, these knots are loosened and the winds move again within the side channels and then withdraw into the central channel and finally return to the heart. Although the 'winds' do not ordinarily move in the central channel, yogic techniques can enable this, which leads to the *"more profound states of mind ... ."*

The Dalai Lama explains some of the dynamics of death and dying:

During the last four phases of dying, the winds that serve as the foundations of consciousness enter into the right and left channels and dissolve there. In turn, the winds in the right and left channels enter into and dissolve in the central channel. The deflation of the right and left channels loosens the constrictions at the channel knots: When the right and left channels become deflated, the central channel is freed, thereby allowing movement of wind inside it. This movement induces the manifestation of subtle minds, which yogis of Highest Yoga Tantra seek to use in the spiritual path; the winds on which a deeply blissful mind rides are intensely withdrawn from moving to objects, and such a mind is particularly powerful in realizing reality. (p. 143)

The Dalai Lama describes the *"indestructible drop"* within the heart and how there are *"essential fluids"* in each of the centres. In another profound passage, he explains esoteric physiology within Tibetan Buddhism:

At the center of the channel-wheels are drops, white on the top and red on the bottom, upon which physical and mental health are based.

At the top of the head, the white element predominates, whereas at the solar plexus the red element predominates. These drops originate from the most basic drop at the heart, which is the size of a large mustard seed or small pea, and, like the others, has a white top and red bottom. Since it lasts until death, this drop at the heart is called the "indestructible drop." The very subtle life-bearing wind dwells inside this drop; at death, all winds ultimately dissolve into it, at which point the clear light of death dawns. (p. 145)

The indestructible drop within the Heart is the origin of life and consciousness within the body. As a person dies, the vital energies and consciousness withdraw through the channels and gather at the heart before the soul leaves the body. As this happens, as the life principles resolve back into the underlying metaphysical realms of being, the heart essentially functions as a black-hole computer. All of the information of a persons' life is available as consciousness resolves back to zero point levels and the patterns of life are illuminated by a consciousness reflecting the Mind of Clear Light.

The Dalai Lama offers profound teachings on the nature of the human subtle anatomy and the physiology of life and death. Such concepts represent a coherent proposal and model of the psyche, a worthy hypothesis for scientific inquiry. Such a view of an indestructible drop within the heart provides an alternative perspective to "the head doctrine" of modern science—the belief or assumption that material-energetic processes of the brain produce consciousness.

In *The Universe in a Single* Atom (2005), the Dalai Lama discusses the issues of consciousness and provides a valuable critique of the head doctrine and its assumptive basis:

Until there is a credible understanding of the nature and origin of consciousness, the scientific story of the origins of life and the cosmos will not be complete. (p. 115)

Western philosophy and science have, on the whole, attempted to understand consciousness solely in terms of the functions of the brain ... Many scientists, especially those in the discipline of neurobiology, assume consciousness is a special kind of physical process that arises through the structure and dynamics of the brain. (p. 127)

Despite the tremendous success in observing close correlations between parts of the brain and mental states, I do not think current neuroscience has any real explanation of consciousness itself. (p. 130)

The view that all mental processes are necessarily physical processes is a metaphysical assumption, not a scientific fact. I feel that, in the spirit of scientific inquiry, it is critical that we allow the question to remain open, and not conflate our assumptions with empirical fact. ... At

*177*

least in my view, so long as the subjective experience of consciousness cannot be fully accounted for, the explanatory gap between the physical processes that occur in the brain and the processes of consciousness will remain as wide as ever. (pp. 128-129)

The Dalai Lama notes that in Buddhist epistemology, *"there was no clear recognition of the role of the brain as the core organizing structure within the body ... ."* (p. 170) The Dalai Lama's teaching about the indestructible drop within the heart, the chakras and channels, winds and knots, represent the more complex esoteric view concerning the origins of consciousness and life.

Whereas modern psychology and science have considered consciousness to be non-substantive, nothing in itself, the Dalai Lama most clearly equates consciousness with light. He describes consciousness as inner illumination or light which reflects the deeper Mind of Clear Light:

Consciousness is defined as that which is luminous and knowing. It is luminous in the double sense that its nature is clear and that it illuminates, or reveals, like a lamp that dispels darkness so that objects may be seen. ... Consciousness is composed of moments, instead of cells, atoms, or particles. In this way consciousness and matter have different natures, and therefore, they have different substantive causes. (2002, p. 129)

Consciousness is light which illuminates the objects of human experience—the material side of nature. Again, we find the distinction between the 'I' and the 'me,' the Purusa and Prakriti. The Dalai Lama states simply: *"Matter cannot make consciousness."* (1986, p. 236)

The Dalai Lama explains that to understand human consciousness, we have to distinguish between matter and consciousness. "Space particles" (space quanta) are the basis for matter, while the *"mind of clear light"* is the basis for consciousness:

In Buddhism, there are levels of coarseness and subtlety of particles, and the most subtle of all particles would be the particles of space. These serve as the basis for all of the particles ... The particles of space remain forever. ... When you go back and back, researching what the substantial causes are, you will eventually get back to the particles of space. ... new worlds will form physically on the basis of the empty space-particles. (In Weber, 1986, pp. 235-6)

prior to its formation, any particular universe remains in the state of emptiness, where all its material elements exist in the form of potentiality as "space particles." (2005, p. 89)

According to the Dalai Lama, *"... new worlds will form physically on the basis of the empty space-particles."*

This is a remarkable teaching and concept and is consistent with Blavatsky's Secret Doctrine and the teachings of Kabbalah. H. P. Blavatsky describes the Gods and other invisible powers clothing themselves in bodies based such zero point foundations—like empty space particles. Further, she described the 'laya state' or 'laya centre' where an element is in a state of unmanifest potentiality. So also, Kabbalah describes the supernal infinitesimal point origination of a Cosmos and the Zimzum contraction creating an empty space within the Plenum—as an empty space particle at the heart of being and of ourselves.

The Dalai Lama explains that the conjunction of Light and the empty Space Particles is the basis for human experience:

> In the field of matter, that is the space-particles; in the field of consciousness, it is the clear light. These two are something like permanent, as far as continuity is concerned. ... The clear light ... is like the basic substance that can turn into a consciousness that knows everything. All of our other (kinds of) consciousnesses—sense consciousness and so on—arise in dependence on this mind of clear light. (Weber, 1986, p. 237)

Space particles are the foundation for the material realm and the contents of consciousness, while consciousness is a reflection of the mind of clear light and illuminates the material or subtle world orders. Individualized consciousness, or the I-experience, depends upon the conjunction of these elements. Certainly, if science wants a model of holography in order to understand a human being within a multi-dimensional Universe, then elements of such are provided by the Dalai Lama as by other esoteric sources. A coherent supernal light source illuminates material objects of perception and mind. What we normally consider our conscious experience is the conjunctions of these elements—the Space Particles upon which new worlds are built and the Consciousness or Mind of Clear Light, which illuminates them.

The Dalai Lama explains that there is a close association between the consciousness/mind and the 'winds,' which support it. He states:

> the wind on which consciousness is mounted, like a rider on a horse, is a physical entity that supports consciousness. Although consciousness can separate from the physical body, as it does when we pass from one lifetime to another, consciousness can never separate from the subtlest level of mind. (p. 132)

The subtle winds support the movements of subtle mind and are *"beyond physical particles,"* although substantive in their own nature. Tibetan Buddhism suggests that 'consciousness' is able to exist in relationship to seven dimensions or planes of being, each of which has a further seven fold division. Thus, esoteric Buddhism suggests seven degrees of Maya or material creation and 49 planes of existence—all of which could conceivably be illumined by the "Mind of Clear Light."

The Tibetan Buddhist description of the life review process which occurs at death is also consistent with the idea of the heart functioning as a black hole computer: As the vital winds withdraw into the heart at death, all the quantum information of one's life may become available within the subtle dimensions of being. Indeed, the Universe is a Hologram, illuminated by the mind of clear light and all new worlds are established on minute, empty space particles. Modern science has brought us to the time where we can actually relate such concepts as the Dalai Lama proposes to the hard sciences in the areas of physics, information theory, cosmology and medicine.

Meanwhile, the dogma of the head doctrine remains the most serious impediment to the progress of psychology and science, the awakening of humanity to the mysteries of the Heart, and the next step in the evolution or unfoldment of human consciousness. And who is really so enlightened as to the nature of Self and consciousness—the head brain theorists of modern psychology and science or the Dalai Lama and the other mystic explorers of consciousness?

*David Bohm and the Dalai Lama*

# 6. Western Sources of the Heart Doctrine

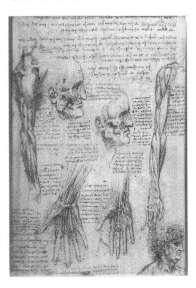

## 6a. Kabbalah and Judaism

### *i. Anatomy of the Soul*

Herein lies the mystery of the relationship
between the Holy Temple and the human body.
Each is a microcosm of the entire system designed
to help man draw down greater and greater revelations
of God's Light into the darkness of the world."
—Kramer, 1998, p. 33

In *Anatomy of the Soul*, author Chaim Kramer (1998) provides a profound account of Judaic and Kabbalist ideas about the nature of soul and human anatomy; published by the Breslov Research Institute of Jerusalem and New York. The book *"explores the Bible's depiction of man as having been created in a Godly image"* (p. v) and regards the body as *"a temple for the soul."* The work is based upon the teaching of the great Chassidic master Rebbe Nachman of Breslov (1772-1810), whose *Magnus opus* is the *Likutey Moharan*, a series of discourses on a spectrum of Torah literature. Kramer provides interesting discussions of the inherent spiritual nature of each organ and bodily system—including the heart and relates this to the various Sephirot on the *Tree of Life* and to creation dynamics.

"In the *Zohar*, the soul is said to tower so high above the body, that the body is called a "shoe" relative to the soul. Only the lowest extremity of the soul "fits" into the body. Through our desire to come close to God, through our thoughts, emotions, speech and actions, we can bring down greater and greater illumination of our own souls. In this manner, anyone has the ability to make his physical body a chariot or a temple for the highest part of the soul ... ." (Kramer, p. 7)

According to Kramer's account, there are five levels to the universe and to the soul. These begin with Adam Kadmon (Primordial Man) and then the four realms of *emanation, creation, formation* and the *world made* (or of Action/Completion, in Kramer's account.)

| Hebrew Name | Level of Soul | World Order |
|---|---|---|
| Yechidah | unique essence | *Adam Kadmon* |
| Chayah | living essence | emanation - *Atzilut* |
| Neshamah | divine soul | creation/*Beriyah* |
| Rauch | spirit | formation/*Yetzirah* |
| Nefesh | indwelling soul | world made/*Asiyah* |

Kramer provides this remarkable image of the realm of Adam Kadmon and the origin and plights of the *'sparks of holiness:'*

The consequences of Adam's fall can be compared to a beautiful and expensive piece of crystal that is dropped from a great height and shatters into thousands of tiny pieces which become scattered over a large area. Adam had contained within himself the souls of all mankind in a state of perfect unity. His fall shattered that holy unity into countless *"sparks of holiness"* which subsequently became dispersed throughout the entire world. It has since been man's mission, utilizing the spiritual inclinations incorporated within his system, to search for, find, purify and elevate these sparks, that they may return to their source. This will ... even improve upon, the vessel from which they originated—Adam. ... (p. 56)

In keeping with the soul's pursuit of perfection, all the fallen and lost sparks of holiness—shattered and dispersed by Adam's original sin—must be retrieved in order to build man's original spiritual *tzurah* (form). Man must now shift through his material surroundings in his search for the spiritual. (p. 58)

So also, there is such a *"spark of holiness"* within a human being—a zero point element beyond the levels of physical differentiation at the inner most core of being. These emerge out of the Unity of *Adam Kadmon.*

The living essence in the world of Emanation is the emergence of such div-ine sparks, which then acquire a spiritual essence in the worlds of creation, are ensouled in the world of formation and then embodied in the physical body of the world made. The inner ladder of the *Tree of Life* portrays the descent of such divine source emanations through the four world orders, finally to be manifest in the material body in the world made. The material body is the resultant of all of the processes occurring within the interior dimensions of the individual being. Life comes from Above, not from below, as the materialist view of modern science suggests. Alternatively, we might describe life as originating from within/ without from zero points.

The lowest level of the soul within the body is *Nefesh*, the *'indwelling soul.'* Deuteronomy 12:23 states: *"The blood is the nefesh (soul)."* The blood is the life-stream, transporting oxygen, nutrients and life force, to all the cells of the body. The blood stream also carries basic desires, lusts and impurities. The Talmud reads: *"I, blood, am the primary cause of illness."* (Bava Batra 58b) Rebbe Nachman states: *"For most people ... the evil inclination is actually their own polluted blood. It causes them to act foolishly and to sin.'* (p. 66) To cleanse the blood and maintain a pure bloodstream requires efforts on the physical, psychological and spiritual levels. Kramer explains that not only evil inclinations are concealed within the blood, but also a holy presence (EHYeH). In fact, *"hidden within a person's blood-stream is God Himself."* There is an inner alchemy to the blood which determines one's ascent of the spiritual ladder.

On the level of *Nefesh*, a person can gain awareness of the body as *"a recep-tacle for the spiritual."* However, this requires *"a quieting down of the awareness of the physical in order to cultivate awareness of the spiritual."* The term Nefesh means literally *"resting soul"* and the *Nefesh* is *"essentially passive."* Thus in order to experi-ence Nefesh, it is necessary to cultivate an inner emptiness, stilling the mind and calming personal emotional concerns and associative thought. Kramer explains: *"All static must be tuned out"* in order to cultivate awareness of this lowest level of the soul life.

Kramer defines the second level of the soul, *"Ruach, the "wind" blowing down to us from God's breath"* (p. 30). Rabbi Kaplan (in Kramer) describes experiences on this second rung of the ladder of the soul life:

> At this level, a person goes beyond the quiet spirituality of Nefesh and feels a completely different kind of motion. In this state of consciousness, information can be communicated, one can see visions, hear things and become conscious of higher levels of spirituality. Reaching the level of Ruach, one feels a moving spirit rather than a quieting one. At the highest levels, this becomes the experience of Ruach HaKodesh (Divine Inspiration.) This is the prophetic state in

which a person feels himself completely elevated and transformed by God's spirit. (p. 31)

The third level of Neshamah is described as the level where *"you would experience Divine breath... On this level, you not only become aware of spirituality, but also of its Source."* (p. 31) In the *Book of Genesis*, verse 2:7, states: *"And God breathed into his nostrils a soul-breath of life."* Kramer explains: *"Man's soul is thus regarded as an extension of God's breath, and as directly connected to Him,"* and further, *"God is said to breathe our divine soul into us just as He breathed into Adam."* At this level of the soul life, the individual experiences *"a level of very close intimacy with God,"* and the breath yields to the divine breath within. The soul life is intimately tied to the breath on various levels.

The fourth level of Chayah, the *"living essence,"* refers to the *"life force"* of the Creator embodied within the Divine Breath. Consciousness at this level involves *"actually the experience of being within the realm of the Divine."* (Kramer, p. 31)

The fifth level of Yechidah is that of the unique essence—"the innermost will" and "uniqueness." This would be the "sparks of holiness" pre-existent in Negative existence but still in a state of unity in *Adam Kadmon*. A divine source emanation emerges through the abyss and declares, "I AM." Rabbi Kaplan states: *"Beyond that, you are in the realm of the unimaginable."*

Certainly, this fivefold analysis of the soul is quite profound and provides a model of the vehicles for conscious experience within different realms of being. According to Kramer, *"the root and source of all complexity is in the Infinite Being Himself Who created and continues to sustain the entire interdimensional hologram we call "The Universe."* (p. 15) The ladder of creation—depicted in *Jacob's Ladder* and the *Tree of Life*—work their magic from within-without from zero point sources rooted into the Infinite! The Breath of the Divine Soul brings life, vitality and awareness into the vehicles or bodies within different interpenetrating planes of being. The universe is a living Hologram and the inner cosmos of consciousness ultimately has such zero point origins as *"sparks of holiness."* What a remarkable conception of human nature to compare and contrast to modern soul-less psychology and science!

## ii. The Life of the Heart

"God is always extremely near, for God resides within one's heart—
within one's 'vacated space.'" (Kramer, p. 218)

"The power of joy is so intense that it can bring one to a
revelation of Godliness within one's heart.
... the Divine Presence corresponds to the joy of the heart.
... One's burning desire for Torah and spirituality enables one to
draw from

the spirituality of the Supernal Heart (Binah).
(Likutey Morharan I, 42)" (Kramer, pp. 231-2)

In Judaism and Kabbalah, the heart is the seat of personal emotions and of the religious emotions of love and fear (awe) of God. It is also intertwined with the mystical dimensions of human consciousness and the soul at its varied levels.

Kramer outlines varied Judaic teachings and lore about the heart. King Solomon wrote, in Ecclesiastes 10:2, *"The wise man's heart is to his right; the fool's is to his left."* Throughout Talmud, the right side is taken to represent good and the left side, foolishness or evil. The left ventricle needs to work hardest because it has to pump blood throughout the body. Kramer explains: *"The spiritual draw-back of this system is that it is on the left side, the side of "the fool." Therefore, whatever blood is pumped into the system flows together with one's evil desires. ... the stronger a person's desire for materialism, the stronger will be the influence of the evil inclination over his "blood supply."* (p. 65)[9]

The blood transports the influences, lusts and desires that must be over-come in order to cultivate the spiritual aspect of one's existence. The three primary lusts are for wealth, sexual pleasure and food. When such lusts and desires dominate the psyche, the heart space becomes increasing cluttered and knotted and the natural light of the resting soul, the passive Nefesh, is obscured. Rebbe Nachman provides a profound description of spiritual practices and how these serve to cleanse the heart:

> The main thing is to nullify every one of your personality traits. You should strive to do so until the ego is obliterated, rendered into nothingness before God. Begin with one trait, transmute it, and then work on a second one. As each trait is thus transmuted, God's glory will begin to shine through and be revealed to you.
>
> ... God's glory is like light. ... The material obstructs the spiritual and casts shadows over it. The denser the object, the darker the shadow.
>
> When one is bound to a particular emotion or desire, God's glory is obstructed and a shadow is cast. God's light is then hidden. As one transmutes one's negative desires and emotions, the shadow is gradually removed. As the shadow departs, Godliness is revealed. Then, "The earth (one's materialism) is alight with His glory (for the spiritual is no longer concealed.)" (Kramer, pp. 41-2)

If the personality traits, addictions, desires and lusts are transmuted and the blood purified, then the ego is obliterated—rendered into nothingness be-

---

9    The spiritual heart is described as shifted to the right of the material heart, or at least, it is associated more with the centre or right side of the chest. It is within the right atrium, that the SA Node and AN Node are located, and the heartbeat is produced. The lower left ventricle at the bottom of the heart is thus furthest from the life impulse.

fore God. As this happens, the light of the soul is no longer obscured and one can *"ascend the spiritual ladder, summoning forth the beauty found within the soul."* (Kramer, p. 42)[10]

In a chapter entitled *The Paradox of Body and Soul*, Kramer writes:

Considering the ethereal composition of the soul vis-à-vis the denseness of the physical body, it is indeed a wonder that the two are able to remain together. The soul is always drawn to its sublime source, God, while the body always seeks material gratification. ...

"The soul of man is God's candle, searching all the innards of the belly." (Proverbs 20:27). Our Sages explain that God implanted within the soul a never-ending quest for perfection. The soul is forever curious: it searches and pursues—always looking for a new experience. One can find satisfaction, whether one seeks it on a spiritual or physical level. The difference between the two is that spiritual satisfaction lingers on, since the soul is eternal, whereas physical satisfaction can be only momentary, and is soon forgotten. One whose soul searches through all his innards and seeks the spirituality of life is indeed fortunate. (p. 43)

The soul longs for En Soph, the fullness of the Infinite, having deep memory of this higher dimensional realm—within the Garden of Eden. The soul is described as in exile, seeking to find its way home.

Reb Noson, in Kramer, has comments on the soul and the idea of 'gravity:'

Every person should be aware that all the obstacles and difficulties he faces in life stem from the "repellent" force, from materialism. The "attracting" force, the tzaddik, is more powerful than the repellent force, since the power of gravity ultimately prevails. ... The nature of the soul is to draw itself to its Source, to Godliness, to the true power of "gravity." (Likutey Halakhot)

This is an interesting use of the term 'gravity,' as a 'spiritual force of gravity'—as science usually regards gravity as due to mass or matter. In this view, although the centre of gravity of the material body is within the material world, the centre of gravity for the soul is within its Source—within the En Soph, the eternal parent Space of Binah and the supernal realms. The soul contains within itself the properties of Godliness and is drawn back to its source, just as the body returns to the earth—to the elements *"whence it was derived."* This gravitation of the Soul to its Source can be considered in terms of zero point dynamics, as the

---

10    The Sephira of Tipheret on the Tree of Life is associated with the perfections of "beauty," related to the Sun and to the Self within the Heart. As the ego is obliterated, the light of Self shines through.

life and consciousness principle are drawn back into the heart, on the psychical and spiritual levels, towards its zero point origins.

## iii. The Central Pillar Da'at & Tipheret

The Sephirot on the Middle Pillar ...
represent levels of consciousness
and the planes on which they operate.
Malkuth is sensory consciousness.
Yesod is astral psychism;
Tipheret, is illuminated
consciousness ...
The Middle Pillar rises through Daath,
the Invisible Sephira ...
At the head of this Pillar is Kether,
the Crown, the Root of all Being.
(Fortune, *The Mystical Qabalah*, 1935,
p. 18)

The *Tree of Life* actually provides a model of how a *'spark of holiness'* is brought down through varied interior dimensions of being and abides within the Heart of a human being. "I" originates from within the deepest realms of the Absolute, as an infinitesimal point source of Divine Will and Light Consciousness established within a seven dimensional Space of the Heart of Binah. Furthermore, a false vacuum has been created around a central point, wherein the light of the En Soph Aur has been withdrawn. There is thus a certain emptiness or nothingness at the heart of being—like an empty space particle.

The primordial realm of *Adam Kadmon* is one of Unity, like the crystal piece before it falls and shatters into the pieces—the sparks of holiness. The 'I' steps out of the realm of Negative Existence into Positive Existence and is embodied in four worlds below—representing the elements of fire, air, water and earth. The realm of *Adam Kadmon* is the fifth realm, the Aether, relative to the four material worlds. A human being similarly has a five-fold nature—within the original Unity, as a 'divine source Emanation,' as a spiritual being within the world of Creation, a psychic and soul level related to the world of Formation, and a material body within the World Made. A human being has these interpenetrating bodies and dimensions surrounding the inner most Self and vacated heart space.

The three supernal Sephirot act as a prism to define the Divine Light of Will and to bring it into manifestation within the seven worlds below, crossing the abyss at the invisible 11th Sephirot of *Da'at* as the Son. Da'at is the zero point source of light consciousness within a human being and it is associated with the Heart Space of the Divine Mother, Binah. "I AM" is represented in Da'at as the product of Kether, Chockmah and Binah--a zero point source of illumination, divine will and emanation established within the Heart Space of Binah. I descends into seven worlds below where it is established in Tipheret—as the spiritual essence within the heart. Self-realization involves the awakening to the spiritual Self within the spiritual heart and experiencing its inherent light and bliss.

Da'at is the I AM—the Son of the Supernal Triad. Da'at is on the *"the Great Vertical Line of Light (or Will)"*—of consciousness. Da'at manifests the same quality as Kether but as defined by the influences of the supernal father and mother, the spiritual and material principles. The term Da'at means "knowledge" and this Sephira is associated with the experience of divine illumination and realization. Halevi explains the nature of Da'at:

> To penetrate beyond this veil of the Holy of Holies is to see the Face of God before passing out of Manifest Existence. (p. 21)

Another Kabbalist describes the nature of the divine light, as a form of omniscience:

> According to a Biblical legend, the Light that was called forth on the first Day of Creation and is found in the seventh Heaven is of an order that enables a man to see from one end of the World to the other. Such a Divine luminosity is perceived only by those pure spirits who have made contact with the highest level of Creation after death or during a profound moment of illumination during life. This is the state and condition of the seventh Heaven that all mystics seek. (p. 50)

The seventh heaven is a world of divine luminosity–of an omnipresent unified light, the Mind of Clear Light described by the Dalai Lama. Mystics do indeed claim that consciousness can be experienced within such heavenly and divine realms of being.

Da'at is a zero point element, a level at which something disappears from existence from the perspective of the lower plane of being but which is rooted inwardly to the divine realm of emanation, omniscient light, a nothingness and plenum. As consciousness penetrates the veils of nature, it passes through zero point dynamics into the divine world. Halevi explains:

> Above Tepheret (Tipheret) on the axis of consciousness lies the invisible Sephira of Da'at, or Knowledge. Placed below the Crown, it represents in man the point where he does not just know of, but is. It is in this instant that his individuality vanishes and he may experience— or non-experience—union with the Divine Kether. ... One vanishes into ... nothing—or No-thing. A man who attains this state might well

*188*

describe a void—an abyss in which the ego dies. ... Da'at is the veil, beyond which lies knowledge and being of the Objective Universe. (1972, p. 42)

On the central pillar of consciousness, Da'at is the transition point between spiritual consciousness represented by Tipheret and God Consciousness represented in Kether.

The central pillar of the Tree of Life is referred to as the *"Great Vertical Line of Light"* (or Will). It is in equilibrium relative to the side pillars of the active and passive, masculine and feminine, energetic and material processes, Force (masculine) and Form (feminine). The vertical line of light manifests on various levels—beginning at Kether as an infinitesimal supernal point source, then at the hidden Sephira of (Da'at), also represented by the symbol of a circle with a central point and then within Tipheret, Yesod and Malkuth. Each level represents a possible level of human consciousness within this higher dimensional evolutionary model.

Da'at is the Divine Spark and Tipheret represents the Spiritual Spark. The heart is the abode of the light of spiritual consciousness within the world of creation. Just as Binah is associated with the Heart, the Divine Heart, so Tipheret is associated with the Spiritual Heart. Tipheret is the only Sephira on the Tree of Life, which has paths from each of the supernal triad. Tipheret thus embodies the triune Kether, Chokmah and Binah (or Ayin, En Soph, and En Soph Aur,) at the centre of the seven worlds below.

Tipheret is associated with the Sun, with the attribute of beauty and with the Self—or the true Ego. It is the Self relative to the personality, the outward mask that is put on in Yesod and the body that is put on in Malkuth. The symbol of the Sun in astrology is indeed a point within a circle, the same image used to depict the supernal point established in Kether and as emerging through Da'at.

In this view, the material heart exists in relationship to a deeper psychic heart, a spiritual heart, and ultimately, to a divine source element—the 'I,' within a vacated Space of the Heart of the Divine Mother! Ultimately, the spark of holiness is within the realm of Unity. These levels and processes are all operative within the higher dimensional physics of the human heart occurring within the sacred vacated Heart Space of Binah.

According to Kabbalah, ordinary ego consciousness and mind are centered on Yesod and Malkuth, conditioned by the broken symmetries of the Pillars of Force and Form. The mystical aim is to ascend the central pillar of consciousness through the reconciliation of the opposing principles and forces. Freed from the egoic psyche, one can awaken to the spiritual dimension of consciousness and the heart within Tipheret. Beyond Tipheret, the spiritual consciousness can merge with divine consciousness, through Da'at and Kether.

L. Leat (1999), in her text *The Secret Doctrine of the Kabbalah: Recovering the Key to Hebraic Sacred Science*, provides this illustration of sacred geometry most relevant to our study. In this diagram, a 'zero point' source is

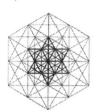

established within the center of the matrix and represents the *Da'at* Sephira in the *Tree of Creation*–the divine spark within realm of Beriah. The geometric pattern established around the central point represents the forces latent within *"matrix of creation,"* established as one descends the Ladder of Jacob.

Leat's diagram depicts a zero point centre within a *Star of David* or *Seal of Solomon*, of intertwined triangles, representing the elements of fire and water, with a zero point center. This diagram illustrates the dynamics governing the Kabbalist's *'god-particle'* (or 'superstring/or membrane' element). Leat's illustration depicts the forces and geometry by which a matrix of creation is established surrounding the zero point source, the Da'at, or divine source emanation within the heart Space of Tipheret and Binah.

The "I AM" is embodied into a structure of four world orders. These can be represented on one *Tree of Life* or as on four successive or overlapping Trees. The Malkuth of the *World of Emanations* becomes the *Da'at* in the *World of Creation*. A *'matrix of creation'* is then established surrounding this vacated space and illuminating supernal light. The illumination of Tipheret allows consciousness within the seven possible worlds below—all surrounding the zero point centre. [11]

Humankind from this perspective has an eternal life in the unity, a divine life, a spiritual life, a soul life and a material body—*in the worlds emanated, created, formed and made*. These dimensions interpenetrate and sustain one another. Human consciousness emerges within/without through these complex metaphysical dimensions and is embodied within the varied world orders. These metaphysical realities sustain physical reality and constitute the inner dimensions

---

11          As it happens, the Kabbalist diagram representing the first point of creation and the geometry of its embodiment in the "matrix of creation" is astonishingly similar to this image used by modern physicists Greene and Atkins. This is a depiction of the superstring/or membrane element of a seven dimensional "Calabi-Yau space," which in the most advanced model of physics is said to exist at every point underlying the four dimensional space-time continuum!

Similarly, we might conceive of an individual human being as having such a matrix of being or creation surrounding a divine source emanation within the vacated Space of the Heart. The teachings of the Kabbalah bear profound and complex relationships to ideas in modern science and provide a 'model' of metaphysical and physical processes which underlie and sustain all things.

of the microcosm of a human being. There is a higher dimensional holographic physics to the human heart which embodies these principles.

In the *Book of Genesis*, the *Tree of Life* is made by God to grow in the middle of the Garden of Eden, as well as the *Tree of Knowledge of Good and Evil*. Adam and Eve were forbidden to eat of the *Tree of Knowledge of Good and Evil*, *"for on the day you eat from it, you will surely die."* The tasting of the apple from this Tree was the original sin causing the loss of Eden and exile into a strange land. Humankind was born into the physical world in bodies of flesh and hence *"surely dying."* Whereas the Tree of Knowledge of Good and Evil is dualistic, the Tree of Life embodies the design of 1 divided by three to yield seven, a 1-3-7 pattern as befits the circulation of light and the patterns of creation.

Kramer explains that the *Tree of Life* is hidden inside the *Tree of Knowledge of Good and Evil* and that the *Tree of Knowledge of Good and Evil* could *"be elevated"* back into its source in the *Tree of Life*. The *Tree of Life* corresponds to the soul life, to spirituality. The *Tree of Knowledge of Good and Evil* corresponds to the body; specifically to the body potential either to reveal the soul and radiate its holiness, or to conceal and smother the soul. Adam's mission was to transform the *Tree of Knowledge* into the *Tree of Life* and to irradiate the body with the *or* (Aur, light) of the soul. Instead, he caused the soul to be obscured by the skin of the body. (p. 8)

It is most important to note how the *Tree of Knowledge of Good and Evil* is dualistic, whereas the *Tree of Life* embodies the Sacred Laws of Three and Seven. Modern scientists consider only the first tree of dualistic knowledge, but do not imagine that hidden there is a deeper *Tree of Life*, depicting the stairway to heaven, the dimensions of the soul and levels of higher dimensional consciousness.

In Kabbalah, there is a higher dimensional metaphysics to the inner levels of creation, to the human heart and to human consciousness. Awareness is never simply produced by non-sentient physical matter, as modern scientists assume. Life comes from above, rather than being created from below; or from within rather than from without.

# 6b. Mystical Christianity

"Jesus reveals the existence of this Central Point in His mustard seed parable. ... He is referring to the smallest of all things—the infinitesimally—small Center Point." (Francis, 1998, pp. 14-5)

Mainstream Christian churches and evangelical groups emphasize the worship of Christ as an external historical person and as a living being who overcame death through resurrection. In contrast, a central mystical Christian teaching is that *"the kingdom of heaven is within"* and that a state of Christ Consciousness involves the mystical awakening of the heart. This teaching is suggested within the *Old* and *New Testament* and numerous Christian writings, hymns and church doctrine. Generally, this teaching is not understood in its significance as a principle of psychology—as a science of the soul.

In the *New Testament*, the heart is depicted as an organ of thinking, reasoning and feeling, with the potential for harbouring evil or loving thoughts and feelings. Christ could perceive in spirit what was within peoples' hearts:

But when Jesus perceived their thought, he answering said unto them:

"What think ye evil in your hearts?" —Matthew 9:4

Jesus perceived in his spirit that they so reasoned within themselves,
he said unto them, "Why reason ye these things in your hearts?"
—Mark 2:8

O generation of vipers, how can ye, being evil, speak good things?
For out of the abundance of the heart the mouth speaketh.
A good man out of the good treasure of the heart bringeth
forth good things: and an evil man out of the evil treasure
bringeth forth evil things. —Matthew 12:34-35

Christ was a reader of hearts, intuitively knowing or perceiving in spirit what was within the hearts of the disbelievers, the hypocrites and scribes. Although scientists consider telepathy a mind—to—mind process, spiritual teachings regard emotional, intuitive and spiritual knowledge as being related to the dynamics of the heart. Christian teachings describe the heart as a deeper level of mind and related to the life of the soul, to Christ and to God. Satan and egoistic self—will can control the heart or it can be surrendered to the Lord:

> For where your treasure is, there will your heart be also.
> —Luke 12:34

> The sower soweth the word. And these are they by the wayside,
> where the word is sown; but when they have heard, Satan cometh
> immediately, and taketh away the word that was sown in their hearts.
> —Mark 4:14-15

> This people honoureth me with their lips, but their heart is far from me.
> —Mark 7:6

> For the people's heart is waxed gross, and their ears are dull of
> hearing, and their eyes they have closed; lest at any time they should
> see with their eyes, and hear with their ears, and should understand
> with their heart, and should be converted, and I should heal them.
> —Matthew 13:15

> Blessed are the pure in heart: for they shall see God.
> —Matthew 5:8

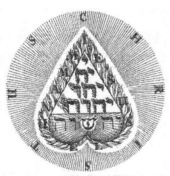

From Böhme's *Libri Apologetici.*

THE TETRAGRAMMATON IN THE HUMAN HEART.

*The Tetragrammaton, or four-lettered Name of God, is here arranged as a tetractys within the inverted human heart. Beneath, the name Jehovah is shown transformed into Jehoshua by the interpolation of the radiant Hebrew letter ש, Shin. The drawing as a whole represents the throne of God and His hierarchies within the heart of man. In the first book of his Libri Apologetici, Jakob Böhme thus describes the meaning of the symbol: "For we men have one book in common which points to God. Each has it within himself, which is the priceless Name of God. Its letters are the flames of His love, which He out of His heart in the priceless Name of Jesus has revealed in us. Read these letters in your hearts and spirits and you have books enough. All the writings of the children of God direct you unto that one book, for therein lie all the treasures of wisdom. * * * This book is Christ in you."*

Christ's message entails the healing and awakening of the heart in order that we might know and love God, and our neighbours—attaining wisdom and understanding with the heart. The deepest desire of the heart is to know God but our hearts are far from the Lord and instead filled with innumerable personal desires, lusts and ill feelings.

The verse above from Mark 4:15 suggests that the 'word' was sown in their hearts. The image here is from the mystic Jacobe Boehme and depicts the *Word*, the Hebrew four—letter name of God, as sown within the Heart. Further, *Christus* is inscribed in the outer circle surrounding the heart. This illustration is from Manly Hall's *The Secret*

*Teachings of All Ages.* The spiritual heart is turned upright relative to the material heart.

Saint John Eudes, a mystical Christian of the fifteenth century, explains that the heart has varied meanings in sacred scripture. In *The Admirable Heart of Mary*, the Saint elaborates upon these mysteries:

> The word "heart," first of all, signifies the material and corporeal heart which beats within our breast, the noblest part of the human body. It is the principle of life, the first organ to begin to live and the last to be stilled in death; it is the seat of love, hatred, joy, sadness, fear and every passion of the soul. ... The word "heart" [also] expresses the free will of the superior and rational part of the soul, the queen of the other faculties, the root of good and evil, and the mother of virtue and vice. ... We must also understand by the word "heart" that highest part of the soul which theologians call the point of the spirit ... . The word "heart" can also signify the Holy Spirit, the veritable Heart of the Father and the Son, Whom They desire to give us for our own mind and heart." And I will give you a new heart, and put a new spirit within you." ... Jesus, who is the heart of His Father, and the Holy Ghost, who is the heart of the Father and the Son, were given to Mary to be the soul of her soul and the heart of her heart. (1680, pp. 8-10)

Within Christian mysticism and scripture, the Heart is a sacred space. St. Eudes distinguishes three major hearts within the individual: firstly, the heart of flesh, the mechanical pump which empowers and enlivens the body; secondly, the spiritual heart related to the higher faculties of the soul and spirit; and lastly, the divine heart, "the point of the spirit," the most interior source of consciousness within the mystical dimensions of the heart.

The *Aquarian Gospel of Jesus the Christ* (Levi, 1907) elaborates upon the mysteries of the heart in verses attributed to Christ. Levi was an American preacher who maintained that these verses were read from the Akashic record—a realm retaining cosmic or universal memory–in which all of human history and experience is recorded. Some verses of the *Aquarian Gospel* are very close to the standard *New Testament*, while other verses recount more of Christ's esoteric teachings:

> God's meeting place with man is in the heart, and in a still small voice he speaks; and he who hears is still. (26, 7)

> And Jesus said, this kingdom is not far away, but man with mortal eyes can see it not; it is within the heart. (29, 19)

> I tell you, nay; we all are kin, each one a part of the great human heart. (51,17)

The greatest mystery of all times is the way that Christ lives in the heart. (59,10)

Give unto Caesar what belongs to him; give unto God the treasures of your heart. (73, 28)

The hour has come when men must worship God within the temple of the heart; for God is not within Jerusalem, nor in your holy mount in any way that he is not in every heart. (81, 26)

The light of life cannot shine through the murky veil that you have drawn about your hearts. You do not know the Christ and if the Christ be not within the heart there is no light. (135, 13/14)

The light of life is obscured by the murky veils of the heart–that is by the impurities of false ego, selfishness and ignorance. Christ is within the heart and this is the human meeting place with God—the inner temple of the Lord of life.

Early sects of the Gnostic Christians taught that to know oneself at the deepest level was simultaneously to know God or the Father as the source of the divine, spiritual and soul life within. This is evident when one examines the Gospels of the *Nag Hammadi Library*—manuscripts discovered in Egypt in 1945–which provide a rich source of esoteric Christian teachings. In the *Gospel of Truth*, Christ encourages the disciples to gain the light which is within them, instead of living in outer darkness; and to *"proclaim the things that are in the heart of the Father in order to teach those who will receive teaching."* The roots of the Self are within the heart of the Father and within the pleroma:

> you ... of interior knowledge ... Say, then, from the heart that you are the perfect day and in you dwells the light that does not fail. ... They are the ones who appear in truth since they exist in true and eternal life and speak of the light which is perfect and filled with the seed of the Father, and which is in his heart and in the pleroma, while his Spirit rejoices in it and glorifies the one in whom it existed. ... (Robinson, 1981, p. 44 & 49)

Those of *"interior knowledge"* have realized their spiritual nature and know of the perfect light within the heart. The "seeds of the Father" are within the "pleroma" of the divine mother. The term pleroma, like that of the divine plenum, refers to the fullness of things, or the infinite potential latent within God as the En Soph. The "point of the spirit" exists within the sacred space of the Pleroma–that is, within the mystical depths of the heart and the underlying plenum. The conjunction of the spiritual Father and the heart space of the Divine Mother is the marriage of the divine/spiritual and material principles, heaven and earth with a human being.

In the Gnostic gospel of *The Acts of Peter and the Twelve Apostles*, the disciple explains, "*the physicians of this world heal what belongs to the world. The physicians of the soul, however, heal the heart.*" (Robinson, 1981, p. 170) Mystical Christian literature depicts the heart as the bridal chamber, wherein the soul is healed and then wedded to the Lord, and an individual might attain to Christ consciousness.

> The inner process of entering the Center Point of the soul is like threading the eye of the needle. Jesus also referred to this as "entering the Kingdom of God." It requires steadiness of attention and acute perception. ... in our discussion of soul anatomy, the Centre Point of the soul is surrounded by a small shell forming what mystics call the "cave of the heart." (Francis, 1998, p. 46)

Christian mystic John Francis, author of *The Mystic Way of Radiant Love: Alchemy for a New Creation*, (Heart Blossom Books, Los Altos, California, 1998) writes, "*My mission is to help uncover the forgotten, deep heart teachings of Jesus.*" Francis explains, "*... the mystical parables and sayings of Jesus have either been ignored or given superficial interpretations that miss the original deeper, intent.*" (p. 6) Francis provides a valuable perspective on the anatomy of the soul as suggested by an esoteric interpretation of key Christian scriptures. Christ states, "*the Kingdom of God is within you*" (Luke 17:21) and further, that "*the kingdom of God is like a mustard seed.*" Francis explains that the "mustard seed" is an ancient metaphor for the Center Point of the soul. He writes:

> Mystics down through the ages have dived deeply into the soul and have made a common discovery. The soul has a Center a sacred point of contact where the human and the Divine meet in sublime communion. ... Furthermore, mystics through the ages have described God as a circle whose centre is everywhere and whose circumference is nowhere. If we think of ordinary human awareness as the circumference of a circle then its center is a point. ... Saint Francis de Sales referred to the Center as the "fine point of the soul." Father Louis Massignon of France called the spiritual Center of the soul "Le point vierge"—the virgin point. ... Father Merton in turn wrote of the little "'point' or virgin eye by which we know Him! (Christ). Jesus reveals the existence of this Central Point in His mustard seed parable. ... He is referring to the smallest of all things—the infinitesimally—small Center Point. (pp. 14-5)

Frances explains that even the word 'meditation' translated from the Latin "*mediari*" literally means, "*being returned to the center.*"

Francis draws upon other sacred verses to illustrate the heart doctrine and zero point teaching inherent to Christianity: *The Kingdom of Heaven is like a treasure hid in a field,*" which leads the man to "*sell all that he had to attain it.*"

(Matthew 13:44) This treasure is a priceless thing within a large expanse of space and Francis suggests that similarly we *"must go beneath the surface of our field of awareness to discover the soul's buried treasure."* In the next verses of Matthew, the kingdom of heaven is compared to *"a pearl of great price"* and the merchant sells off everything he has to attain this pearl. Christ then compares the Kingdom of heaven to 'leaven,' as the living substance, which is *'hid in three measures of meal,'* —suggesting that the life principles is mixed into the three modes of nature— the mental, emotional and physical lives of human beings and hidden there.

Francis quotes Matthew 6:22, Luke 11:34: *"The light of the body is the eye: if therefore thine eye be single, thy whole body shall be full of light."* Francis notes that Jesus did not say the plural "eyes" because this eye is not in the usual mode "as a perceptual receptor" but rather it *is "a point source of light."* (p. 16) St John of the Cross described the *Ascent of Mount Carmel: "With no other light or guide, than the one which burns in my heart."*

Francis notes that other Christian saints have referred to *"this interior star"*—as *"the star of love,"* the star *"that nourishes and heals"* and *"expands."* He concludes:

> "one pearl," the "single eye," and the "star" in the heart are all metaphors that can be used to represent the Center Point of the soul. Each one reveals a different attribute of this wondrous point. (p. 17)

The I—existence originates from a point source as a seed of the Father within the cave of the heart. The significance of the esoteric teaching is hidden within the parables and Church literature. Even the word meditation refers to finding one's centre within such a single I—the magical 'star' nature and being able to experience the light and love of God within oneself. The Kingdom of God is within you, Christ states; so perhaps we might wonder where and what is the significance of this within our lives, as well as for psychology and science.

Christ states in the parables that, *"It is easier for a camel to go through the eye of a needle, than for a rich man to enter into the Kingdom of God."* (Matthew 19, Mark 10, or Luke 18) Francis interprets this passage:

> The innermost anatomy of the soul can be compared to a needle's eye because the Center Point is enclosed in what could be called a shell, which creates an exceedingly small and deeply interior sacred hollow. (p. 17)

Francis explains that "this holy sanctuary" of the heart is referred to meta-phorically as a "cave," and that the mystical path is one of *"entering the Cave of the Heart."*

Christian mystics describe varied 'shells' or 'layers' which surround the div-ine spark, such that *"the inner spark of the soul is trapped in these concentric shells."*

Meister Eckhart thus wrote: *"A man has many skins in himself covering the depths of his heart,"* and Teilhard de Chardin spoke of the *"incandescence of the inward layers of being."* Francis writes:

> parables speak of the shell that encloses the inner eye of the soul ... the "three measures of flour" that hide the leaven suggest that this shell has multiple layers. Moving inward toward the Center we must pass through the physical, then the emotional and finally through the mental layer of being before entering the silent cave of the heart. (p. 21) "The inner process of entering the Center Point of the soul is like threading the eye of a needle." (p. 46)

Threading the eye of the needle is passing through and transcending these veils, sheaths, layers or bodies, which bind the soul, like the rich man, to the external phenomena of life.

Francis also provides some interesting comments on the "Inner Tree of Life:"

> In the *Book of Genesis* ... by eating of the Tree of Life humans can live forever. ... this Tree is a metaphor for an inner structure within the soul. This inner tree is "rooted and grounded in Love" (Ephesians 3:17) this is also expressed by Jesus in the parable of the greatest tree in the garden which grows from the tiniest seed. ...

> When we allow the Center Point to expand in meditation, God's Grace flows into the soul mysteriously like "living water" and vitalizes the tree of life and it grows so that its branches reach upward to the heavens. This tree then becomes a living "Jacob's Ladder."

> The roots and branches of this inner tree can be likened to the subtle nervous system of the soul. It is represented as the seven—candled menorah, which is the ancient symbol of Judaism. These seven candles have deep mystical significance. ... (pp. 26—7)

According to esoteric Judaism and Kabbalah, the *Tree of Life* is indeed a metaphor for the inner structure of the soul. Our roots are from above or within heaven and we are embodied below within seven worlds. There is a central Point at the heart of being surrounded by shells or veils or knots. Mystical Christianity certainly supports the essential teachings of the heart doctrine and the zero point hypotheses.

# 6c. H. P. Blavatsky's *The Voice of the Silence* & *The Secret Doctrine*

Helena Petrovna Blavatsky was born in Russia in 1831 and died in 1891. Blavatsky travelled widely around the world throughout her extraordinary life, involving herself in various paranormal investigations and studying eastern and western mystical, occult and spiritual teachings. She established the Theosophical Society in New York City in 1875 and then in India and wrote extensively of her studies and research. Madame Blavatsky is regarded as the grandmother of modern western occultism: a unique synthesizer of the ancient wisdom teachings and a dramatic individualist who challenged the materialist and mechanist science philosophy of the day. Her work introduced eastern mystical teachings to western audiences and encouraged the study of early western esoteric traditions.

*The Voice of the Silence* (1889) is Blavatsky's lyrical account of the nature of the soul and the processes of spiritual attainment as depicted within the occult science and the ancient wisdom teachings. These sample verses depict aspects of the plight of the soul and the necessity of overcoming the illusions of the mind:

> The Mind is the great Slayer of the Real. Let the Disciple slay the Slayer. (p. 1)

> When he has ceased to hear the many, he may discern the ONE—the inner sound which kills the outer. Then only, not till then, shall he forsake the region of *Asat*, the false, to come to the realm of *Sat*, the true. (p. 2)

> When waxing stronger, thy Soul glides forth from her secure retreat: and breaking loose from the protecting shrine, extends her silver thread and rushes onward; when beholding her image on the waves of Space she whispers, "This is I,"—declare, O Disciple, that thy soul is caught in the webs of delusion. This Earth, Disciple, is the Hall of Sorrow, wherein are set along the Path of dire probations, traps to ensnare they EGO by the delusion called "Great Heresy." (p. 4)

> Saith the Great Law: "In order to become the KNOWER of ALL SELF thou hast first of SELF to be the knower." To reach the knowledge of that SELF, thou hast to give up *Self* to Non-Self, Being to Non-Being, and then thou canst repose between the wings of the GREAT BIRD. Aye, sweet is rest between the wings of that which is not born, nor dies, but is the AUM (fundamental sound vibration) throughout eternal ages. ... Give up thy life, if thou would'st live. ... (p. 5)

Let not thy "Heaven-born," merged in the sea of Maya, break from the Universal Parent (SOUL), but let the fiery power retire into the inmost chamber, the chamber of the Heart and the abode of the World's Mother. Then from the heart that Power shall rise into the sixth, the middle region, the place between thine eyes, when it becomes the breath of the ONE-SOUL, the voice that filleth all, thy Master's voice. 'Tis only then thou canst become a "Walker of the Sky" who treads the winds above the waters, whose step touches not the waters. ... thou hast to hear the voice of thy *inner* GOD in seven manners. (p. 9)

Before that path is entered, thou must destroy thy lunar body, cleanse thy mind-body and make clean thy heart. (p. 11)

But, O Disciple, unless the flesh is passive, head cool, the soul as firm and pure as flaming diamond, the radiance will not reach the *chamber*, its sunlight will not warm the heart, nor will the mystic sounds of the Akasic heights reach the ear ... . (p. 18)

And now thy *Self* is lost in SELF, *thyself* unto THYSELF, merged in THAT SELF from which thou didst first radiate. Where is thy individuality ... ? It is the spark lost in the fire, the drop within the ocean, the ever—present Ray becomes the all and the eternal radiance. (p. 20)

Thou art THYSELF the object of thy search: the VOICE unbroken, that resounds throughout eternities, exempt from change, from sin exempt, the seven sounds in one, the VOICE OF THE SILENCE. (pp. 21-2)

Search for the Paths. But, O Lanoo, be of clean heart before thou startest on thy journey. Before thou takest thy first step learn to discern the real from the false, the ever—fleeting from the everlasting. Learn above all to separate Head-learning from Soul-Wisdom, the "Eye" from the "Heart" doctrine. (p. 25)

But even ignorance is better than Head—learning with no Soul—wisdom to illuminate and guide it. The seeds of Wisdom cannot sprout and grow in airless space. To live and reap experience the mind needs breadth and depth and points to draw it towards the Diamond Soul. ... For mind is like a mirror; it gathers dust while it reflects. It needs the gentle breezes of Soul—Wisdom to brush away the dust of our illusions. Seek O Beginner, to blend thy Mind and Soul. (pp. 25-26)

The "Doctrine of the Eye" is for the crowd, the "Doctrine of the Heart," for the elect. ... "Great Sifter" is the name of the "Heart Doctrine," O disciple. ... The wheel of the good LAW moves slowly on. ... The hand of Karma guides the wheel; the revolutions mark the beatings of the Karmic heart. (p. 27)

The Dharma of the "Eye" is the embodiment of the external, and the non-existing. The Dharma of the "Heart" is the embodiment of Bodhi, the Permanent and Everlasting. (p. 29)

Have patience, Candidate, as one who fears no failure, courts no success. Fix thy Soul's gaze upon the star whose ray thou art, the flaming star that shines within the lightless depths of ever-being, the boundless fields of the Unknown. (p. 31)

'Tis from the bud of Renunciation of the Self, that springeth the sweat fruit of final Liberation. (p. 35)

Thou shalt not separate thy being from BEING, and the rest, but merge the Ocean in the drop, the drop within the Ocean. (p. 49)

The path that leadeth on, is lighted by one fire—the light of daring, burning in the heart. The more one dares, the more he shall obtain. (p. 54)

Thou hast to study the voidness of the seeming full, the fullness of the seeming void. O fearless Aspirant, look deep within the well of thine own heart, and answer. Knowest thou of Self the powers, O thou perceiver of external shadows? If thou dost not—then art thou lost. (pp. 55-6)

All is impermanent in man—except the pure bright essence of Alaya. Man is its crystal ray; a beam of light immaculate within, a form of clay material upon the lower surface. (p. 57)

These verses on the nature of Self depict its intimate connection to the heart; its relatedness to the greater Self; its uncreated, Eternal nature; its nature as self-illuminating light; and its origin as rooted within the plenum (the fullness of the seeming void).

The Self is "heaven-born" but is submerged in the sea of Maya (the world of illusion). The Self emanates from the Universal Parent and descends into the World Mother, *"the waves of Space"* and *"the sea of Maya,"* or the chaos of modern science. The heart is *"the abode of the World Mother,"* the secret chamber wherein thy Self merges with That Self.

Blavatsky compares the "soul wisdom" to "head-learning," noting, *"the mind is the great slayer of the real."* Certainly, Blavatsky's views would suggest that: consciousness is not manufactured out of the cerebral cortex; nor is it the product of matter and neurological activity; nor does it simply dissipate at death. Instead, consciousness and Self have some mystical supernatural origin emerging from within divine and metaphysical dimensions of Being and Non-Being. The Self is most inwardly connected to the material body within the chambers of the heart.

Blavatsky challenges every basic assumption of modern scientists and intellectuals as to the nature and origin of human consciousness and Self. Rather than emerging through random evolutionary processes out of non-sentient matter, the Self is heaven born and descends into the chamber of the heart, the abode of the World Mother.

*The Secret Doctrine* depicts any cosmos as a "Son," a *"wink of the Eye of Self-Existence"* and *"a spark of eternity."* An ancient *Stanza of Dzyan* reads:

THE SONS EXPAND AND CONTRACT THROUGH THEIR OWN SELVES AND HEARTS; THEY EMBRACE INFINI-TUDE. ... EACH IS A PART OF THE WEB. REFLECTING THE "SELF-EXISTENT LORD" LIKE A MIRROR, EACH BECOMES IN TURN A WORLD. (III, 11-12)

The Sons expand and contract through their *"own selves and hearts."* This principle applies equally to the macroscopic universe and to the living entities, the quanta of consciousness, the divine sparks or Monads. Any living Cosmos, including human beings, are *"worked and guided from within outward"* from such metaphysical sources and dimensions. Further, the processes of creation and dissolution, involution and evolution, contraction and expansion, are most intimately associated with the mysterious heart center.

*The Secret Doctrine* depicts any manifest element, Son or Monad as an emanation from within the deep substrates of existence. All things emerge within/without at the beginning of time from zero point *"laya centres,"* which exist prior to physical manifestation. Further, all living cosmoses ultimately resolve back without/within to zero point laya centres and the Unity at the end of time. Blavatsky describes the journey of *"the pilgrim-soul"* as occurring through *"various states of not only matter but Self-consciousness and self-perception ... ."* (Vol. II, pp. 185-6) The Monad is a *"drop out of the shoreless Ocean beyond"* and *"(a) ray from that one universal absolute Principle."* (p. 167).

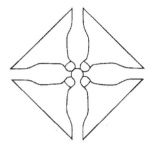

# 6d. The Impersonal Life

... [the] human brain ... acted as a veil to your Soul Consciousness ...
(Benner, 1988, p. 126)

The book, *The Impersonal Life*, was initially published in 1941 and has since been reissued numerous times. The publisher describes the author, Joseph S. Benner, as *"the Beloved Soul whose human instrument was the channel through which this inspired Message was given to the world."* In the manuscript, *The Impersonal Life*, the teaching is spoken directly to the reader from the perspective of *"the Father within Whose Voice has spoken ... and Whose Message has awakened them to a knowledge of their True Selves."* *The Impersonal Life* is the source of the individual consciousness and life within us all. This is a profound teaching about the origins of consciousness within ourselves. The individual soul consciousness is a focalized center within the Impersonal Life. Once again, the Impersonal Life and the Father are associated most intimately within the heart:

I am enabled to awaken their Soul consciousness to a real comprehension of Me, the Impersonal One, seated within–in the very midst of All, in the heart of each. (p. 186)

In the heart of each I dwell; in the heart of the human, in the heart of the animal, in the heart of the flower, in the heart of a stone. In the heart of each I live and move and have My Being, and from out the heart of each I send forth that phase of Me I desire to express, and which manifests in the outer world as a stone, a flower, an animal, a man. (p. 45)

bring about My Purpose in your heart and life and in the hearts and lives of My and Your other Selves. (p. 154)

Not until the *heart* has been quickened and has opened wide to contain Me can man, with his mortal mind and intellect, consciously comprehend My Meaning ... . (p. 177)

203

Whereas modern New Age philosophy encourages people to imagine, create and project their own intentions, desires and ambitions through the activities of the mind, the *Impersonal Life* suggests that it is the desires of the heart which create realities:

> This Key is "To THINK is to CREATE," or "As you THINK in your HEART, so is it with you." (p. 63) ... every desire of your heart comes from Me.

The Impersonal Life within the heart is prior to the functions of the mind and body and the source of consciousness and life. The mind obscures the essential nature of our being:

> That transcendental, innermost part of you ... I your *Divine* SELF. I, the I AM of you, bring to you this My Message ... I AM *not* your human mind, nor its child, the intellect. ... they are but phases of your human personality, as You are a phase of My Divine Impersonality. ... I AM come now to your Soul consciousness ... you have almost come to believe You are your intellect and body, and you have consequently nearly forgotten Me, your Divine Self. ... You must *feel* Me *within,* before you can *know* I AM there. (pp. 22, 24, 30)

> I AM that which animates your body, which causes your mind to think, your heart to beat. I AM the Innermost, the Spirit, the animating Cause of your being, of all life, of all living things, both visible and invisible. There is nothing dead, for I, the Impersonal ONE, AM *all* that there is. (p. 44)

> I AM You, the Real Self of you. All that you *really* are. That which you think you are, you are *not.* That is only an illusion, a shadow of the *Real* You, which is I, your Immortal, Divine Self. I AM that point of consciousness focalized in your human mind, which calls itself "I." I AM that "I," but that which you call your consciousness is in reality My Consciousness ... you are nothing—being only a focal center of *My* Consciousness. (pp. 49-50)

Human consciousness is derived from a deeper divine Consciousness focussed within the individual heart and which illuminates the mind and the inner being. Most simply, we are instructed, *"Be still, and know, I AM, God:"*

> I AM *you,* that part of you who IS and KNOWS; WHO KNOWS ALL THINGS. *And always knew, and always was.* Yes, I AM You, Your SELF; that part of you who says I AM; and *is* I AM. (pp. 21-2)

> "Be *still!*—and KNOW—I AM—GOD." *Without thinking,* allow this, *My Divine Command,* to penetrate deep into your Soul. ... when you have *felt* Me thus in such moments within, when you have tasted of My

Power, hearkened to My Wisdom, and know the ecstasy of My all—embracing Love—no disease can touch, no circumstance can weaken, no enemy can conquer you. For now you KNOW I AM *within*.... (pp. 31-4)

I AM the Eternal and fill all space. ... I have been leading you all the time. ... Yes, I have been within always, deep within your heart. (pp. 41-2)

Some have become so at One with Me that they no longer are separated in consciousness from Me, and in Them I live and move and express My Spiritual Nature. ... I enable the Soul consciousness to gain such glimpses of Me as each is capable of comprehending. (pp. 183 & 185)

enter into your Christ Consciousness, My Consciousness within you and within Him. (p. 203)

The Impersonal Life sustains all life within/without from the heart of being. The brain acts as a vehicle for the deeper soul consciousness and as a veil which obscures the essential nature of Self. The I AM—the Impersonal One—is the animating cause behind the body, mind and heart. This teaching can be known in any moment, here and now, simply by awakening to Self. Be still and know—I AM.

# 7. Love, Ecstasy & the Bliss of the Heart

"… the secrets of earth and heaven are revealed to the possessor of
the loving heart …"
(Sufi, Hazrat Inayat Khan,1960, p. 19)

"I will show you the immensity of love. You all live in this ocean
of love, sympathy, of understanding. Whatever befalls you, love is
underneath, around, and above you, suffering with you, carrying the
burden and sharing the joy. So linked are we that, of a great truth, all
that you experience reflects on and finds response instantly in Me."
(Anon, in Crookall, 1969, p. 85)

Accounts of awakening and self-realization depict states of bliss and ecstasy, unbounded joyousness, feelings of illumination and insight, and an ineffable love of God, one's fellow human beings and life itself. Unfortunately, what is ordinarily considered as love is, from an enlightened perspective, seldom more than self-centered feeling based on personal pleasures, attachment, insecurities and desires. This pathological condition results from the chronic contraction about the heart, the absorption in egoism and selfishness, and the avoidance of feeling relationships. Humans' hearts become conditioned by material nature and are *"far from the Lord,"* or at least they appear to be.

The experiences of love and ecstasy accompany the opening of the heart. Various individuals recount such experiences of transformation:

We get the element of love only in proportion as we have it in us. We can only draw this element from the Supreme Being. We draw in proportion as we admire every expression of the Infinite, be that expression tree or shrub or insect or bird, etc. The more of these things we really love, the more of the element of love flows to us. That element is as real as the tree itself. (Mulford, in Crookall, 1969, p. 28)

In the Divine Mind an unchanging perception of bliss is everpresent. … Suddenly I became filled with a deep sense of joy. I looked around in wonderment. The car in which I was sitting was filled with joy … The trees were filled with joy … Thoughts such as the following drifted through my mind—"God is joy. God is bliss. God is love. Only

God is real ... Spend your days in seeking Me. Love, joy, peace, bliss. This, this only, hold on to this" ... For more than two hours I sat in the Brahmic bliss, at one with God, immersed in joy. (Wilson, in Crookall, 1969, p. 27)

From a mystical perspective, love is not simply a biochemical or physio-logical process within the material brain and body, but a divine, spiritual and cosmic energy, which permeates reality and involves different possible levels of heart dynamics. Varied types of psychical, spiritual and divine love can be experi-enced with the awakening of consciousness and the opening of the heart. Love is a real and substantive energy, which permeates and interpenetrates all things. The love of God is present everywhere, although humans, in their typical state of waking sleep, are ignorant of its presence. The spiritual teachers of humanity declare: "God is love." Love is the basis of spiritual life, the fire that burns away the residues of coldness and selfishness, and which provides experiences of the deeper dimensions of the human heart. Love emerges with the experience of the unity and the interrelatedness of all things.

The Sufi, Hazrat Inayat Khan writes:

there is one stream that is the source of all (morality), and that is love. ... All deeds of kindness and beneficence take root in the soil of a loving heart. ... The great, rare and chosen beings, who for ages have been looked up to as ideal in the world, are the possessors of hearts kindled with love. All evil and sin come from the lack of love. ... the secrets of earth and heaven are revealed to the possessor of the loving heart... (1960, p. 19)

Mystical states involve a radical shift from personal emotions to profound and ecstatic realizations of love, joy and blissfulness. The problem is that humans asleep are deadened to such inner ecstatic states of the soul and such higher love and instead live in forgetfulness. Yet, the inherent bliss and love within the heart are human beings' natural birthright and primary condition. To be out of love is to be out of the Being of God and to have lost the experience of oneself rooted within the Divine Life.

The mystic philosopher P. D. Ouspensky quotes M. Lodizhensky from a text *Superconsciousness and the Paths to its Attainment*. A simple analogy is used to depict the mysteries of love, space and the unity of life:

Imagine a circle ... and in the middle of it a center; and from this center going forth radii-rays. The farther these radii go from the center, the more divergent and remote from one another they become; conversely, the nearer they approach to the center, the more they come together among themselves. Now suppose that this circle is the world: the very middle of it, God; and the straight lines (radii) going from the center to the circumference, or from the circumference to the center, are the paths of life of men. And in this case also, to the extent that the saints approach the middle of the circle, desiring to approach God, do they come nearer to God and to one another. ... Reason similarly with regard to their withdrawing from God ... they withdraw also from one another, and by so much as they withdraw from one another do they withdraw from God. Such is the attribute of love: to the extent that we are distant from God and do not love Him, each of us is far from his neighbour also. If we love God, then to the extent that we approach to Him through love of Him, do we unite in love with our neighbours; and the closer our union with them, the closer is our union with God also. (1970, p. 259)

A circle is a two dimensional image and we can imagine a sphere in the third dimension to extend this analogy. If we were to then consider the sphere in seven higher dimensions, then we would approach closer to mystical conceptions of love and higher space dimensions. All things are ultimately unified into the One in higher dimensions, and Love is ultimately the binding force of the Divine Mother, which holds it all together, and ingathers the 'sons' to her Bosom at the end of time.

H. I. Khan explains that the heart is a mirror capable of reflecting the multiplicity of life around one and that as the heart expands, so does this reflection:

In this lies the mystery of the spiritual hierarchy; it is only the expansion of the heart. Do we not see in our everyday life one person who says, "Yes, I can love one person, whom I love; but then I cannot stand the others?" It is only the limitation of the heart. ... And in proportion as the heart becomes more free of this limitation, naturally it becomes larger; because the length of the heart ... is unimaginably great. ... if the heart of man were expanded, it would accommodate the whole universe, just like a drop in the ocean. The heart can be so large that it can hold the whole universe, all. (1982, p. 71)

Love is a cosmic energy and phenomena: a mystery of life which the individual confined within the narrow boundaries of the ego, or those scientists who speak off the top of their heads, cannot imagine. Love, ecstasy and bliss are experienced with the awakening of consciousness and the realization of Self within the Heart.

The mystic Meher Baba regarded gravitational attraction itself as a basic form of love! Like gravity, love binds things together into larger wholes and unitive states. Higher forms of love build on a hierarchy from gravity, through human love and finally to God's love. The evolution of consciousness consists of striving to realize the underlying unity and the inter-relatedness of all things within the Divine Life. (Jones, 1996) Mystical teachings do not regard love as simply a material, biophysical or neurological process within brain structures, a fortunate byproduct of accidental and random mutations, but rather as a cosmic energy and Divine Law, which binds all things into a living Unity.

In *The Impersonal Life*, these teachings are directed from the I AM presence, in lucid and profound verses:

> You heretofore have not known the meaning of the Impersonal Life, hence you could not know the meaning of Impersonal Love. Love to you ... has always been a human emotion or expression; and you have been unable to conceive of a love devoid of or unattached to some human or personal interest. Now, as you begin to feel Me within your heart and open it wide to contain Me, will I fill you with a wondrous strange new feeling, which will quicken every fibre of your being with the creative instinct, and be to you a veritable Elixir of Life. For in the outer expression of *that* feeling, when I thus, through you, pour it forth into the world, will you taste of the unutterable sweetness of My Holy *Impersonal* Love, with Its accompanying illumination of mind and consciousness of unlimited Power; and It will make you a wholly self—less and therefore perfect channel for the Impersonal Expression of My Divine Idea. (pp. 211-2)

*The Impersonal Life* depicts Impersonal Love as one of the "*Holy Three-in-One*" of "*Love-Wisdom-Power*," the divine attributes inherent to reality. In Kabbalah, we would identify these with Binah-Chokmah and Kether, on the Three Pillars of the Tree of Life. Love is not produced by the limbic system of the head brain, nor in the hormones and the autonomic nervous system, nor in the sexual center. Instead, love has to do with the mystical dimensions of the heart and the deeper soul life, and it originates from within spiritual and divine realities established within higher space dimensions. Love is one aspect of the trinity of Self, the I AM presence.

M. Aivanhov (1976) portrays the nature of love as a cosmic energy which sustains life in nature and which ultimately derives from the divine life:

> Love is divine life that has come down into the lower regions to take over, to spray love around, to bring all to life. It is manifest everywhere without humans realizing that it is always the same force, the same cosmic energy that has all kinds of aspects. Humans do nothing but waste this energy thinking that it is only an instinct, a moment of pleasure, and a means to propagate the species. Initiates who have risen above to study the divine power of love, tell us that it is the same energy that comes from the sun, the same light, the same warmth, the same life, but that in coming down to us, like a river, it assumes

the impurities of the regions it has to go through. But this doesn't mean that it didn't spring forth pure and crystal clear at the top of the mountain. This energy which we call love comes from heavenly regions, exactly like the rays and heat of the sun, but it has become unrecognizable because of its descent into the lower layers, among human beings. ... we must realize that there are thousands of degrees of love .... In the future you will learn to love as the sun loves, as the angels love, as the great Masters love, without stealing, without taking, simply by giving. (pp. 108-110)

Human beings seek love, as they subconsciously remember the beatific feelings inherent within their essential nature. Unfortunately, the energies of love are colored and conditioned by attachments and possessiveness, selfishness and impurities, sensation and desires. The opening of the heart to spiritual and divine life allows the individual to know deep truths about the mysteries of love and higher space, and experience varied levels of the interrelatedness and unity of life. Baha'u'llah explains that there is actually a *"science of the love of God,"* as love and light dwell within the heart and allow for direct experiences of spiritual and divine realities. The deeper the love, the closer the individual is to the center.

In the Vedic teaching, the original nature of the spiritual soul is described as "sat, chit, ananda"—Being, Consciousness and Bliss. Awakening to Self within the Anandamaya Kosha, or bliss sheath, naturally awakens one to the ecstasies of the Soul. In fact, all pure feelings such as faith, devotion, trust, fearlessness and love *"abide in subtle impressions"* within the heart. Various samadhis are experienced as the jivatma is freed from entanglement with the ego principle, the subtle pranas and the Chitta within the orbits of the heart center. As the individual dissociates from the mental waves, the chitta or mind stuff becomes pure and calmed, and Atman is experienced as within the infinite ocean of the bliss of Brahman. Saraswati states: *"in the state of Samadhi, having attained identity with Brahman, the soul enjoys the infinite bliss ... ."* (1979, p. 212) As liberation occurs, the jivatma is freed from the bondage of birth and death and can rest peacefully. Saraswati describes this:

in *Nirvichara Samadhi* (supreme consciousness devoid of thought— waves) ... a steady state of supreme peace arises which is called Adhyatma Prasad or the placidity of the internal organ (of Chitta, ego principle, intellect and mind) giving eternal peace. (1979, p. 216)

There are various levels of bliss and higher emotions, which culminate in identity with the infinite bliss of Brahman. Saraswati simply explains: *"It is well known that one acquires bliss by Samadhi. ... the experience of the continuous flow of essential existence is the nature of bliss."* (p. 229)

Saraswati compares these inner mystical experiences to a familiar counterpart:

> just as a well favored man (or woman) is pleased to see the beauty of his (or her) face reflected in a mirror and exclaims 'Oh, how handsome I am!,' so the constant realization of one's essential consciousness gives rise to bliss. When one experiences *Aham Asmi* ('I am'), or only 'Asmi,' all other Vritti of the Chitta are restrained. Then ... the ceaseless stream of the perception of 'I am' flows on. The particular effect that arises out of the ripples of this stream is the cause of bliss. That is to say, the experience of the continuous flow of essential existence is the nature of bliss. (p. 230)

Even the pleasures of the gross body ultimately derive from the nature of Self. However, a human asleep searches for pleasures and bliss in outward forms and does not realize the hidden inner dimensions of the heart. The science of yoga, as elaborated by Saraswati, explains various states of bliss associated with the different sheaths and bodies, but the ultimate bliss of Brahmananda involves the resolution of consciousness back into its source and the shining forth of the Atman in its essential nature. Everything else is due to innumerable modifications of mind stuffs and the ego and vital principles, brought about through generations of causes and effects, which proceed from the three gunas or modes of nature. There is the sattvic bliss of purity and inner being self—awareness, the rajas desires for happiness through activity and sense enjoyments, and the tamas pleasure arising through the contact of physical bodies and sexual activity, gluttony and materialism.

As explained in the *Bhagavad Gita*, the jivatma's attention is usually engaged by the outwards fruits of enjoyment and pleasure, seeking to be lord over nature like an ego in a castle, while the ultimate state of bliss lies hidden within the depths of one's heart. Saraswati states, *"... one acquires bliss by samadhi."*

# 8. Native Spirituality

Native spiritual elders Sequoyah Trueblood and Willaru Huayta provide remarkable teachings about the sacredness of life, the origin of humankind, the extra-dimensional nature of human consciousness, spirit and soul—and the Way of the Heart.

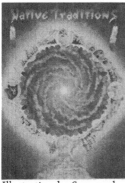

## 8a. Sequoyah Trueblood & the Sacred Law of Origin

"I define spirit as the mind of God
in motion here on Mother Earth."
Sequoyah Trueblood (in Mack, 1999)

Sequoyah Trueblood was born in the USA on December 15, 1940 to a German-English mother and Native American father. He is a blood member of the Choctaw nation with Cherokee and Chickasaw roots.

Illustration by Sequoyah

Sequoyah has lived a remarkable life, overcoming a background of abuse and cultural deprivation on a reserve and within residential schools, combat in Vietnam as a Green Beret and a Special Forces operative, and subsequently a period of drug addiction and incarceration. After undergoing healing and transformation, Sequoyah rediscovered his spiritual roots and identity and emerged as a deep and loving individual, who embodies the heart doctrine through his teaching and healing work. Sequoyah continues to live with and learn from aboriginal peoples, while conducting sacred ceremonies and facilitating healing circles and vision quests with diverse groups in Canada, the Americas and around the world.

As a pipe carrier, Sequoyah conducts healing circles and traditional ceremonies to remind us of *"the one Ceremony"* which is life itself and of the sacredness of all things. The pipe composed of a stem representing the masculine and a bowl representing the feminine embodies the ancient teaching about the male and female principles within creation. The pipe reminds us that, as men and women, we need to balance and harmonize these energies and principles within ourselves, moderating aggression and negativity, and learning respect for nature and life. Sequoyah talks of healing the pain and suffering that exist within human consciousness and the heart, so that humankind can remember themselves, their origins and the Creator. It is because humans live out of harmony with nature, that they experience such great suffering and conflict. This diminishes the quality of human life and threatens the future of society and the ecology of the living earth.

In the Native tradition, the land of the Americas (and material reality) is referred to as *Turtle Island*. Sequoyah maintains that the aboriginal teachings are required in order that humankind learns to live in harmony with each other and in balance with Mother Nature, so as to honour the sacredness of Turtle Island. He explains that humans have turned one hundred and eighty degrees away from the light of the Creator and the original teachings, and consequently do not know who they are. People live in fear, conditioned by suffering, anger and negative emotions—all of which arise from not knowing self and the Creator. Humans' minds are always set in judgment of one another, rather than in being in heart to heart relationship, with tolerance and thankfulness. Sequoyah has been instructed in spirit to help humans experience a necessary *"polar shift in consciousness and mind"*–to turn around within themselves so as to once again experience the Creator. From a psyche polarized around false ego, the individual can awaken to deeper spiritual realizations of Self. Humans can remember who they are as *"loving children of the Divine loving Creator,"* who originate from within a realm of spirit and higher dimensions.

Since 1999, Sequoyah has spent periods of time with the aboriginal tribes of northern Columbia where he was introduced to the teachings of the *Mamos*, the spiritual elders of these original peoples. The Mamos claim to be the "Elders Brothers" of both "Younger Brother"—*"hermanos menores"*—the tribes of the area, and of the "very little brothers"—the diminutive *"hermanitos menores"*—the mass of humanity on planet earth. The elders maintain that the mountains of Sierra Nevada de Santa Marta are a sacred planetary site and in fact, the *"Heart of the World."* The four tribes located there embody the four chambers of the heart, which are related also to the four directions and elements of nature. The spiritual elders to the tribes are said to serve to sustain the heartbeat and life activities of the larger planet Earth through continual cycles of prayer, meditation and activities within the realm of spirit.[12]

---

12 The tribes of these areas maintained their isolation during Spanish colonialism and afterwards because of their seclusion and a culture of invisibility and silence. In 1991, filmmaker, Alan Ereira, recounted the messages of the Kogi—one of the four tribes—in a documentary for the BBC, entitled *The Heart of the World*. Ereira explained that the

Sequoyah's accounts of meetings with the Mamos and native peoples attest to the mysterious powers, claims and practices of these adepts or elder brothers.

Sequoyah explains that as guardians of humanity: *"the mamos... are not born of this Earth. They were transferred here from other Planets to care for the internal engine, the motor that drives the space-ship Earth."* (1999) Through visions, teachings on the inner planes and direct experience, Sequoyah learned of the para-normal faculties of the Mamos, who work directly within the world of spirit, communicate telepathically and travel out of their bodies within the world of spirit and higher dimensions. The *mamas* are the spiritual leaders of this sacred Earth site, the heart of the world. The origins of this region are related to the dissolution of Atlantis and the earlier unknown history of humanity—including our extra-terrestrial origins.

The term *mamos* also refers to the sun, which is the realm of spiritual illumination. The Mamos work within the realm of *"aluna,"* the world of light, *"interacting with the ocean of spirit that is all life."* (Ereira, 1991) The Mamos' messages to Sequoyah concern the healing of the planet and human hearts and the extra-dimensional origins of life and creation.

The Mamos introduced Sequoyah to the *"Natural Law of Origin"* and asked him to communicate this to the outside world at this critical time in human history. This is the Mamos' ancient teaching about the origin of life and creation. According to the sacred *Law of Origin: In the beginning,* a light emerged from the Womb of Creation, the mystical mother. This light carried a heartbeat and was connected to the breath of life. From the Womb of Creation, the light passed into the Sun and then into the Earth, and then into humankind. Thus, humans, in the innermost dimensions of their being, embody the same light and heartbeat, which emerges from within the Womb of Creation.

Sequoyah explains that by experiencing the necessary polar shift in consciousness and mind, humans can pass beyond the realm of judgment and negativity and experience directly the worlds of spirit and the nature of the Creator. Sequoyah depicts the triune nature of the Creator as being of the spirit of *niawenhko'wa* (great blessings or thankfulness), *konnoronhkhwako'wa* (the great love) and *skennen'ko'wa* (the great peace). The great blessings, love and peace are connected to the light, breath and heartbeat emerging from within the Womb of Creation. By ceremony, prayer and thankfulness, humans can turn around

---

Mamas regard their spiritual practices and ceremonies as actually "maintaining the heartbeat" of the planet.

within themselves, face the Creator and experience the extra-dimensional nature of their origins.

Sequoyah embodies the heart doctrine and elaborates the ancient teachings of the Mamos and native peoples. Humankind has a far more mysterious nature and history than little brother imagines in his waking sleep–with his mind dominated by judgments, divided by conflict and absorbed in egoistic sufferings. In this view, we are ourselves extra—terrestrials–as the light of consciousness and the heartbeat come from the Creator and the mystical Womb of Creation. These life forces well up within us in the same way that they emerge from the Heart of the World.[13]

# 8b. Willaru Huayta: The Divine Temple & Higher Dimensions

Each person is a Sacred Temple. The alter of that temple is the heart.
The fire of love, a reflection of the greater life, burns upon this alter.
This light within must be acknowledged, cared for, and venerated.
This is the religion of the Sons of the Sun. It is that same religion of
the extraterrestrials; the universal, cosmic, solar religion.
(Huayta, 2002, p. 38)

Born a Quechua Indian, Willaru Huayta undertook spiritual quests in the jungles of the Amazon and through the Andes Mountains of Peru. He is a Chasqui or messenger for the Great White Brotherhood and embodies the ancient Incan teachings. Like Sequoyah, he brings messages pertaining to the transitional times in which we live, the extra-terrestrial and extra-dimensional nature of reality and spirit, and *"the message of the heart."*

According to Incan prophesy, five hundred years of spiritual darkness was to follow the arrival of the Spanish invaders and the Europeans. During this age of iron and wars, or of metal and coldness—Ayar Auca—humankind has been lost in darkness, destroying each other and living out of balance with nature. The western world has fallen into egoism, using the forces of nature in a negative way and dominated by the dogma of scientific materialism and greed. Willaru describes the *"alliance of black forces which subjugated and persecuted the Children of the Sun."*

However, like a long winter, the Iron Age is waning and a new Golden Age, like spring, is arising. Willaru describes the Earth as the sacred living mother,

---

13　The author is privileged to have had association with Sequoyah and to have been exposed to his profound teachings, remarkable stories and life experiences. This has been through public circles in the Kemptville-Ottawa area, native brotherhood meetings within a Correctional setting and individual contact.

the embodiment of Mother Nature, and capable of healing us with the natural medicines of clean air, water and fertility. He describes the fading of the *"plastic culture"* and the renewal of *"the spiritual consciousness of the natural solar culture."*

The ancient Inca people of the Andes followed the laws of Mother Nature, *Pachamama,* and of the Great Spirit Creator, *Pachacamag.* The Sun, *Tegsi Wiricocha,* illuminates our lives and through this light we can reach the Father Creator. Willaru explains:

> Many Incas incarnated spiritually from the heart of the Sun and worked within the laws of… the sacred fire. With love we have come and with love we have reached God. We must return to the Ways of Nature and recognize that we are a part of the sun, moon, earth, water, and air. That Mother Nature is within us and we within her. Each of our lives are divine temples of Mother Nature and Father Creator. (1997)

The Sun's rays, *"the gift of the Great Spirit,"* sustain living things through their electromagnetic energies and give life and radiance to Nature. Whereas human beings receive material bodies from the Mother Earth, their spiritual bodies are from the Sun and the Father Creator. Willaru explains that these spiritual bodies derive, not simply from the Sun we observe, but from *"another Sun that lies in another dimension,"* an invisible Sun behind the Sun.

The religion of the Sons of the Sun is based upon the Sacred Temple of the heart. According to Willaru, it is the same religion as that of the extraterrestrials. Willaru describes our early ancestors as developing extraordinary psychic and spiritual faculties which allowed them to be in tune with the great mysteries of nature. They did their scientific investigations in *"a conscious manner"* and *"moved in superior dimensions in their explorations."* Willaru describes various extra di-mensions to human life and the cosmos–including angels and archangels associ-ated with other planets and the existence of varied extra-terrestrials. He claims himself to have entered into the Mystery Schools of Peru and golden lost cities within higher dimensions, and to have travelled to the planet Venus in his subtle body to witness an advanced culture and civilization there! Willaru describes the *"priests of science"* who do not *"experience the multidimensional world of spirit"* and claims that the noble Indians of the Andes can indeed travel to other planets and move about within infinite space. The religions of the Sons of the Sun involve the acquisition of various supernatural powers and faculties—all dependent upon the mystery teachings of the Sacred Heart Temple.

Willaru explains that the *"resurrection of the dead"* of Christian teachings refers to the awakening of humanity, as we are already *"the dead."* Humankind must overcome the seven levels of false ego, associated with the seven deadly sins of pride, anger, envy, gluttony, laziness, lust and greed. We must transform hatred into love, learning forgiveness and not sitting in judgment of others. Thoughts can be brought from the mind into the temple of the heart and be dissolved through prayer and meditation.

Willaru explains three practices as the methods of the masters: the elimination of false ego, represented by the symbol of the crystal skull; the transformation of sexual energies, through esoteric sexual practice and the accumulation of the sexual energies, depicted by the symbol of the eagle eating the serpent; and thirdly, the symbol of the king and queen, representing white magic, unconditional love and service, and the culmination of spiritual consciousness through the divine marriage. The illnesses of the mind and false ego keep humans bound by the mechanics of life and according to Willaru, to patterns of recurrence (the repetition of lives) and reincarnation.

Willaru shares secrets of the esoteric sciences and explains the nature of the hidden dimensions—the fourth, fifth, sixth and seventh dimensions—related to the development of the higher being bodies, which are the basis for experience within super-sensory realms of existence. Humans are indeed already of an extra-terrestrial nature and there exists an ancient science of the Sons of the Sun, which is tied into the unknown history of humanity on this planet and within other worlds. In this view, religion is a return home to the Temple of the Heart through the reintegration with the self and experiences within the higher dimensions of existence.

These ancient teachings raise innumerable issues concerning the evolution and history of humankind and the mysteries of the world. As a contemporary teacher and spiritual messenger, Willaru makes the same claim as that of Swami Prabhupada; that an individual can transfer themselves to planets of the material and spiritual sky through the sciences of consciousness and the heart. The Heart Doctrine suggests that there is indeed an advanced science of the heart which opens doors to higher and more subtle dimensions and worlds, as well as to the deepest levels of Being and Non-Being, the Void and Plenum—the Womb of Creation.

# 9. Heart Master Adi Da: The Surrender to Love-Bliss

"This is the Highest and most Radical Teaching. Only Love, the Heart, or the Unqualified Radiance of Unqualified Consciousness, fulfills and transcends all inward paths, all experiences, and all relations of the self. Therefore, grow in the Way of the Heart until the Perfect Identity Shines as the Consciousness that transcends all bodily and mental states."
(1978, p. 512)

Adi Da is a contemporary spiritual teacher, an Avatar, a living master of the Great Tradition of esoteric teachings. Born as Franklin Jones on Long Island, New York in 1939, Adi Da has experienced profound spiritual realizations, states of samadhi and enlightenment throughout his life. He elaborates these claims in his autobiography and has certainly produced many illuminated writings and lectures. In 1970, Adi Da is said to have permanently entered the condition of Sahaj Samadhi, recovering that Identity with the Transcendental Being-Consciousness.

Throughout his life, Adi Da has experienced an inner condition which he calls *"the Bright."* He elaborates upon this state:

Even as a little child I recognized It and Knew It, and my life was not a matter of anything else. That Awareness, that Conscious Enjoyment, that Self-Existing and Self-Radiant Space of Infinitely and inherently Free Being, that Shine of inherent Joy Standing in the heart and Expanding from the heart, is the "Bright." (1995, p. 34)

Adi Da's heart was established within the Love and Bliss of the Heart, the inner Life and Identity, from the earliest years. Over time, he explored all possible realms of experience to arrive at a more complex understanding of what this condition is and the dynamics of its deep nature. Although Adi Da states, *"I have always been Seated in the 'Bright,'"* many years of mystical experiences, further enlightenment and attainment, were necessary for the nature of the Bright to become apparent to Him and for its potentials to be fully realized. He recounts:

The "Bright" had seemed to fade, progressively, in childhood and adolescence, but It had only become latent in the heart, while I followed my adventures from the viewpoint of the mind. The Heart Itself had been my only teacher, and It continually broke through in various revelations, until I finally returned to It, became It, and rose again as the "Bright." (1995, p. 382)

As a God-realized individual, Adi Da teaches and transmits to others the "way of the heart," helping them to realize the divine identity established as the All-Pervading Reality at the core of their Being. The Way of the Heart is the path towards recovering the *"Perfect Identity,"* which is *"shining as a Consciousness that transcends the body/mind complex."* The heart embodies the *"Unqualified Consciousness"* and the individual can recover awareness of this lost identity.

Adi Da describes spiritual transformation as depending upon the emotional conversion of the human heart from a condition of narcissism and self-possession to one of Divine Communion and the realization of the Light, Love and Bliss inherent to the Heart. The body-mind complex—the psychophysical being—differentiates itself from experiences, separating self from the emotional demands of life and relationships. Thus, individuals avoid deep relationships which require free emotional association and the opening of the heart in love.

In the normally subjective state of waking sleep, the individual is contracted at the heart and tied up by the *"knots"* of the heart. This heart contraction, as explained by Adi Da, entails a contraction from the All-Pervading Life Principle which is established as the root condition within the Heart. The resulting emotional dissociation cuts off the individual body-mind complex from awareness of the Universal Life Energy, one's primordial condition. The knots (or *granthi*) are the means by which ego differentiation occurs and one becomes steeped in ignorance. The individual is thus self-divided and dissociated from his/her inherent feeling-intelligence.

Adi Da depicts the process of self-examination and the change of heart required for spiritual awakening:

The heart of the usual Man, or the emotional-psychic root-being of the unawakened individual, is chronically disturbed, contracted upon itself, dissociated from the Universal Life-Principal that is its own Condition, Help, and Origin. ... The Salvation or Happiness of Man is in emotional conversion, or the conversion of the heart from the automaticities of self-possession to the conscious Realization of Ecstasy, or self-transcending Love-Communion with the Universal Principle of Being that is Life. ... We must surrender to Life

in order to be full of Life. The Life-Current is the "Holy Spirit," the Divine Effulgence or Grace whereby we may be Transformed and made One with the Living and Eternal Divine Reality. (1978, pp. 13-5)

In Adi Da's teaching, the individual Self is the Conscious Life and Light principle existing prior to the nervous system and the extended material body, and it radiates and expands from a fixed point in the region of the heart. Adi Da identifies the spiritual heart as to the right of the centre of the chest. The Free Soul intuits its Identity with the Transcendental Self and can abide in its own prior state of Bliss and Unqualified Consciousness. At different periods within his teaching work, Adi Da describes his teaching as the Way of Divine Ignorance, of Radical Intuition, of Whole-Body Enlightenment and as the Way of the Heart.

The True Self is the Transcendental Heart within the Divine Domain. When the I of the Heart opens, all phenomena appear as illusory modifications of that Radiant Self. A devotee, Bonder, elaborates upon Adi Da's revelations:

"The Heart" is God, the Divine Self or Reality. The Realization of the Heart is fully Conscious Awakening as the Self-Existing and Self-Radiant Transcendental Divine Being and Person. The psycho-physical association of Transcendental Self-Realization with the bodily heart gives rise to the capitalized term "the Heart." The Awakening to Transcendental Self-Consciousness is associated with the opening of the primal psycho-physical seat of Consciousness and attention, in the right side of the heart. One who thus Awakens generally becomes sensitive to the Current of Spiritual Energy at that location in the chest and feels the mind, or attention, falling into its *point of origin* there. Heart Master Da distinguishes the Heart as the ultimate Reality from all of the psycho—physiological functions of the organic, bodily heart. The Heart is not "in" the right side of the human heart, nor is it in or limited to the human heart as a whole, or to the body-mind, or to the world. Rather, *the human heart and body-mind and the world exist in the Heart, the Divine Being.* ... Heart Master Da proclaims and always lives ... the God-Intoxicated Realization of the Heart. (1989)

The point of origin of consciousness does not exist within the physical heart, but the heart, the mind, and the world, exist within the Heart. This mystery teaching is based upon an alternative holographic understanding of Space—wherein all things in the outer world are projections out of a Divine Realm which underlies and sustains them. The world is within the Heart instead of the Heart being contained within the physical body.

Adi Da refers to the teachings of Ramana Maharshi and the Vedic teachings in explaining the nature of the heart, the heart contraction and the "knots" of the heart. Ramana also elaborates upon the mystery of how consciousness emerges from a point source within the heart and circulates through various *nadis* or channels within the subtle dimensions:

> The effulgent light of active-consciousness starts at a point and gives light to the entire body even as the sun does to the world. When that light spreads out in the body one gets the experiences in the body. The sages call the original point 'Hridayam' (the Heart). ... The Individual permeates the entire body, with that light, becomes ego—centric and thinks that he is the body and that the world is different from himself. ... The association of the Self with the body is called the *Granthi* (knot). ... the light of active-consciousness passes through a nadi (a channel) in the body. ... When the very bright light of that active-consciousness shines in the *Amriti Nadi* alone, nothing else shines forth except the Self. ... When Atma alone shines, within and without, and everywhere ... one is said to have severed the knot ... . There are two knots. One, the bond of the Nadis and two, egoism. The Self even though subtle being tied up in the Nadis sees the entire gross world. When the light withdraws from all other Nadis and remains in the one Nadi alone, the knot is cut asunder and then the light becomes the Self. (1995, pp. 292-4)

Adi Da compares the teaching of the Radical Intuition of the Transcendental Heart to other mystical teachings—which involve raising the Kundalini energy through the spinal cord to the higher chakras. According to yogic teaching, there are seven chakras or subtle energy centres within the human's subtle anatomy. These include the crown and brow chakras associated with the crown of the head and the third eye, the throat chakra, the central heart chakra, and three lower chakras associated with the solar plexus, the navel and the base of the body, the root chakra. There are three chakras above the Heart Centre and three below it. Raising the Kundalini and other practices may allow the individual to awaken the higher chakras and thereby *"attain the subtle body in the sky of mind,"* experiencing diverse subtle realms of nature and acquiring various psychic powers. Adi Da describes this process as ultimately leading to the same Enlightenment as the Radical Intuition of the Heart, but only after long cycles of birth and death within the material and subtle realms of existence.

The Way of the Heart is the most direct route to Self–penetrating immediately to ultimate realizations:

> One Path proceeds by mystical ascent of the illusory inner self, or mind, via the Chain of Creation. The other proceeds by direct intuitive submission of the entire body-mind into the Radiant Source and Transcendental Matrix of all phenomena. (1978, p. 107)

The former path is a more gradual process of enlightenment, moving through the levels of phenomena composing the chain of creation and the different worlds of the higher psyche. Adi Da states that this route will ultimately bring one to realize the Divine Condition of the Heart. However, in Adi Da's view, the yogic and mystic teachings which focus upon the opening of the third eye (or ajna/brow chakra) involve a lower order teaching than does the ancient Heart Doctrine: *"A yogi who has fixed his Life-Force and attention into the brain-mind has not realized God or the Self."* His/her attention has simply moved into the subtle dimensions of the Realms of Nature.

States of samadhi or enlightened consciousness are rooted into the Heart. Ramana Maharshi explains:

> When the yogin rises to the highest centre of trance, *Samadhi*, it is the Self in the Heart that supports him in that state whether he is aware of it or not. But if he is aware in the Heart, he knows that whatever states or whatever centres he is in, it is always the same truth, the same Heart, the same Self, the Spirit that is present throughout, eternal and immutable. (In Adi Da, 1995, p. 390)

Since his Divine R-emergence, Adi Da exists in the state of Sahaj Samadhi and manifests various extraordinary Divine Siddhis (supernatural powers) enabling him to perceive various realms of nature and to *"meditate"* other beings. He writes:

> I spontaneously began to "meditate" countless other people, and also countless non-human beings, and countless places and worlds and realms, both high and low in the scale of Reality. (1995, pp. 371-372)

Adi Da has realized the *"Divine Guru-Siddhi,"* being able to meditate others and to transmit directly the awakened condition of the Heart. Thus he carries on his Divine Mission of Teaching, Blessing and Awakening other beings. The *leelas*—the accounts and stories—of his devotees attest to Adi Da's states of enlightenment and his capacity to envelop others within the *"Bright,"* throwing them into states of ecstasy. Wes Vaught, a devotee, recalls:

> Adi Da lifted his Feet and placed them on my head. All stress left my being. A golden balm of sweet light poured through every cell in my body. A knot opened. I let go and His brilliant Radiance washed through me. I was home. (In Lee, 1998, p. 79)

The devotee *"lives as the sacrifice of the whole body-mind"* in love and service, and this creates a *"superphysical and higher psycho-physical link"* between the devotee and the Heart Master. *"By means of the heartfelt regard or loving glance of the Spiritual Master, the devotee is Awakened, by stages, to the process of Initiation and*

*Sacrifice into the Divine Radiance."* (1978, p. 253) All of these processes involve some form of a higher dimensional physics and science.

Adi Da explains:

> there is something in the physics of the universe that makes it possible for a single or random individual to pass through the entire affair of Transformation in God, and then to bring others into the sphere of his existence, so that they may duplicate his Condition and be drawn into that entire and ultimate evolutionary cycle. (1978, p. 247)

Enlightenment is a literal change of the whole body/mind and involves some form of higher dimensional physics–exactly the physics of light, zero points, higher dimensions, holography and the like. All of this is part of what Adi Da labels *"the superphysics of literal God-realization."*

# V

# MYSTICAL DIMENSIONS
## of Consciousness, the Heart
## & the Cosmos

*"The soul of man is the spark of God.*
*... in the depths of every being there is a divine spark."*
—Hazrat I. Khan

*"I cognized the centre of the empyrean as a point of intuitive perception*
*in my heart. Irradiating splendor issued from my nucleus*
*to every part of the universal structure."*
—Yogananda

*"... the divine spark (is) buried deep in every soul. ... we must leave the*
*physical world of matter far behind and rise to the luminous world*
*above to attain the divine principle of our superior soul. ...*
*This centre which is in us, we must find."*
—Aivanhov. 1976

# 1. Spiritual or Divine Sparks: Zero Point Quantum of Consciousness and Space

Many questions arise if we attempt to scientifically or rationally explore the mysterious heart doctrine. The wisdom teachings suggest that the heart must be studied from both a physical and metaphysical perspective.

According to mystical teachings, the divine element–the hidden Self–originates from a Supreme Self. The Self *emanates* out of God or the Absolute. In contrast to the physical forces recognized within modern science, an *emanation* is a higher dimensional and metaphysical force. It is qualitatively different from the *radiation* of light or electromagnetic force. The Self emanates from within/ without through the subtle dimensions of the heart. The heart is thus a sacred place wherein the influences of higher dimensions and forces act within the human mind/body.

The most mystical dimension ascribed to Self is that as an infinitely small source at zero point levels. An invisible and indivisible, sub-atomic element–a divine element or God spark–exists within the sacred heart centre. In the terminology of modern physics, the Self is a quantum, a particle/wave or element, which exists beyond the atomic level of material organization. The divine spark can be regarded as a "quantum of consciousness" or a "quantum Self." Alternatively, it can be conceived of as a singularity condition, a point incredibly minute with no extension in external space/time. Modern scientists hypothesize that the vast universe emerged from such an infinitely small singularity at the beginning of time, out of the apparent nothingness of the quantum vacuum. The singularities of modern physics bear a profound relationship to the divine sparks described by mystics as emanating out of the mystical void and plenum. Both are infinitely small when judged from a material perspective and are rooted into higher dimensional space. At the singularity point, the finite merges into the infinite, as the individual Self merges with That Self.

The *Upanishads* compare the individual spiritual souls to sparks which are thrown off from the fire of the supreme source and which will eventually return to this underlying realm:

> As sparks innumerable fly upward from a blazing fire, so from the depths of the Imperishable arise all things. To the depths of the Imperishable they in turn descend. (*Mundaka*, ibid, p. 45)

Swami Prabhupada explains that according to Vedic teachings both the Supersoul (the Paramatma) and the atomic individual soul (the jivatma) abide within the inner dimensions of the heart. A verse of the Gita reads: *"... the Supersoul accompany(s) the individual soul in all bodies ... ."* Prabhupada elaborates upon this distinction between the Supersoul and the individual soul:

> The Vedas declare, aham brahmasmi: "I am pure spirit soul." And as spirit souls we all have a relationship with the supreme spirit soul, Krishna, or God. The individual soul may be compared with a spark emanating from the fire of the Supreme Soul. Just as the spark and the fire are of the same quality, the individual spirit soul is of the same spiritual quality as the Supreme Lord. Both share a spiritual nature of eternity, knowledge, and bliss. (1972b)

The atomic individual soul is a divine spark emanating from the fire of the Supreme Soul. The individual life is an *apparently* discrete quantum emerging from a transcendental realm of infinite Being. Prabhupada writes:

> the soul is inconceivable by human experimental knowledge. The soul is consciousness and conscious ... The Supreme Soul is infinite, and the atomic soul is infinitesimal. (1972b, p. 106)

> Every living entity is only a spiritual spark. (1972, p. 209)

> There are two kinds of souls—namely the minute particle soul (anu-atma) and the Supersoul (the vibhu-atma). ... Both the Supersoul (Paramatma) and the atomic soul (jivatma) are situated ... within the same heart of the living being ... the atomic soul, forgetful of his real nature ... requires to be enlightened ... .(1972b, p. 100)

According to yoga philosophy, a human being has seven vital energy centres within the subtle (non-physical) anatomy. These centres are referred to as the *chakras*, a term implying a wheel or vortex of energy. Of the seven chakras, the heart center is the fourth and middle chakra with three above and three below. In an authoritative text on *Layayoga*, Shyam Sundar Goswami describes these chakras:

> Each center consists of two parts—the center itself and a peripheral aspect. The center is an infinitesimal point which, from a material point of view, is zero. This point in the substratum is a power concentrated to its highest degree ... the peripheral aspect ... appears as circular radiant energy ... The *chakras* are subtler than atoms and particles. If an atom can contain a tremendous amount of energy, why should not a *chakra*, which is infinitely subtle, contain energy which is practically unlimited in quantity and capacity? (1980, pp. 144-5)

The divine or spiritual spark is the point source at the centre of the heart chakra. A similar dynamic underlies the other chakras, as all have zero point centres derived from the original heart centre.

226

In *Science of Soul: A Treatise on Higher Yoga* (1987), Swami Saraswati, describes the nature of the spiritual soul within the orbits of the heart:

> The seat of the individual soul (is) in the heart…, which may be likened to an infinitesimal poppy seed. There is no form or colour to the soul. (p. 36)

> In the innermost center of the orb of Chitta exists *Atman*, the self, like a living spark, radiant and beautiful. (p. 221)

> This luminous, gentle, diamond-like spark of the soul is enveloped by the apparel of Chitta which is snowy-white and radiantly luminous. (p. 223)

The spiritual spark is the zero point center of the bliss sheath within the heart chakra.

In explaining *Gnosticism*, D. Edwards (1996) outlines similar views:

> The true nature of the Soul is as a divine spark, which originally issued forth from the fountainhead of God. … The world is often seen as a training ground or prison for Soul as it seeks spiritual liberation, a return to its true home in the Pleroma or realms of pure spirit beyond the physical and psychic regions of matter, emotion and the mind. … Soul refers to the spark of individualized spiritual essence that dwells within the consciousness or mind.

The term gnosis derived from the Greek language means "to know." The Gnostics believe that the knowledge of God and of spiritual realities can be directly experienced. Thus "I" can be recalled, remembered or realized in its cosmic and divine origin.

Adi Da depicts the individual self as: *"… a 'seed', or 'spark' of Radiance, an atom of Original Light, located in the region of the nervous system associated with the heart core."* (1978, p. 476) This point source or atom of the Original Light is prior to time and space, matter and energy, and to all conditions or exterior relationships. Self-Realization is described then by Adi Da as an *"atomic event,"* involving the fusion of the atom with the Whole in an Infinite Brightness of Exploded Bliss. Adi Da also describes the Heart as the "Infinite Space."

Paradoxically, the Self is not *in* a human, so much as the man (woman) is in the Self. At the heart of being, the atomic point of original light is established within the underlying Infinite Heart Space. External space, in its three dimensional nature, is an outward *projection* from the underlying Infinite Heart Space—a sevenfold hyperspace. The Self is thus a conjunction of the atom of original light within the underlying higher dimensional Space of the Heart.

Some mystical teachings emphasize the quantized nature of Space as the basis for individual consciousness. The Gnostic *Gospel of Truth* of the Nag

Hammadi library depicts the "spaces" as "emanations," which exist within the underlying invisible source:

> the Father of the all was invisible, the one who is from himself, from whom all spaces come forth. ... All the spaces are his emanations. They have known that they came forth from him like children ... though truly within him, they do not know him. But the Father is perfect, knowing every space within him. ... all the emanations of the Father are pleromas, and the root of all his emanations is in the one who made them all grow up in himself. ... In time Unity will perfect the spaces. It is within Unity that each one will attain himself; from multiplicity into Unity. (Robinson, 1981 pp. 39-41, p. 47)

All individual spaces are thus rooted within the invisible pleroma and Unity, which sustains them as individual I's (eyes) of the One.

These spaces are "pleromas" as they emerge from the fullness of things (all possible potencies, in the En Soph). The zero point center is an emanation, a "quantum of original light" arising in association with a "quantum of space." The mystical conjunction of a zero-point source of original light within higher Space dimensions gives birth to individualized consciousness.

The Dalai Lama distinguishes between matter and consciousness, and explains that *"space particles"* (space quanta) are the basis for matter, while the *"mind of clear light"* is the basis for consciousness. Individualized consciousness, or the I-experience, depends upon the conjunction of the clear light with the space particles:

> the ultimate creative principle is consciousness. There are different levels of consciousness. What we call innermost subtle consciousness is always there. ... In the field of matter, that is the space-particles; in the field of consciousness, it is the clear light. These two are something like permanent, as far as continuity is concerned. ... The clear light ... is like the basic substance that can turn into a consciousness that knows everything. All of our other (kinds of) consciousnesses —sense consciousness and so on—arise in dependence on this mind of clear light. (Weber, 1986, p. 237)

Space particles are the foundation for the material realms and the *contents* of consciousness, while consciousness is of the mind of clear light, which illuminates the material or subtle world orders. Conscious experience consists of this conjunction of the mind of clear light with a quantized space particle.

According to Blavatsky, the laws of nature manifest in the material worlds are due to divine and spiritual intelligence and activity within super-sensuous states of being. These divine and spiritual forces direct or inform material process from within/without through the zero point laya centres. The laws of nature within the four dimensions of space and time are the results of activity within higher inward dimensions of being. The influx of formative forces manifesting from within the higher spiritual realm into the lower material realm is through "*holes dug in Space,*" "*invisible points,*" or "*zero-points.*"

In *The Secret Doctrine*, Blavatsky states that the relative creation of any space/time complex emerges from within the hyperspace of the Seven-Skinned Eternal Parent Space through a zero point source—beyond material differentiation. Recall Blavatsky's description: "*... "material points without extension" ... Leibnitz's monads, are the materials out of which "Gods" and other invisible powers clothe themselves in bodies ... .*" Eventually, the informing principles of the created universe will resolve back into such a zero point laya centre and the metaphysical Parent Space at the end of time. Blavatsky's concepts are compatible with modern accounts of vacuum genesis, in which singularities exist at the beginning and end of time, and a hyperspace serves as the foundation for physical manifestation.

Zero points, although infinitely small from the perspective of the manifest material world, are rooted within into higher dimensional Space and the mystical void and plenum. Zero points mark the transition between varied world orders within the hierarchies of creation. They are points at which something passes over from this world, to THAT; where the physical dissolves back into the metaphysical. They are points at which somehow the universe concentrates itself.

The basic concept of zero points can be applied to the study of the origins of the universe, to the laws of nature, which govern any quantum or superstring, to evolution, and to the study of human consciousness. All living beings, all Cosmoses, on all orders of scale—from the Universe to a quantum—are ruled through the inner dynamics of zero points: "*As above, so below.*" Thus, as we trace the laws of material nature back to their origin, we pass from physical to metaphysical dimensions. If God exists, then some such dynamics must necessarily follow, as all finite things are ultimately rooted into the infinite. Zero points mark the transition between these interpenetrating world orders. *Within,* the zero point is rooted into divine and metaphysical dimensions of existence; while *without,* the zero points give rise to a myriad of living worlds and beings clothed in different bodies.

In Blavatsky's mystical perspective, the metaphysical realm is the source of the many I's, the Monads or divine sparks, emanated from within/without. She provides varied descriptions of these:

> The Monad is a drop out of the shoreless Ocean beyond, or, to be correct, with the plane of primeval differentiation. (1888, Vol. II, p. 185)

> It (the Monad) is not of this world or plane, and may be compared only to an indestructible star of divine light and fire, thrown down on to our Earth... . (1888, Vol. 1, pp. 174-5)

If Carl Sagan wants to hone his mind for useful things, perhaps he might consider the hypothesis of divine sparks at the heart of being—as an alternative to the head doctrine or to Frances Crick's house of cards. Of course, Shirley MacLaine maintains that we all have a God spark within us, but could she really know something that the great scientists have overlooked, but which was under their noses the whole time? And how about those Kabbalists who claim that there are all these 'sparks of holiness,' differentiated out of the realm of Adam Kadmon and brought down through four interior world orders, clothed in different bodies with five different levels to the soul and human consciousness? It is useful to hone our minds for useful things.

In Kabbalah, the *Tree of Life* and the *Ladder of Jacob* provide a model of the higher dimensional zero point sources, one within the other, within the schemes of Creation. Kether, Da'at and Tipheret on the Central Pillar of Divine Will and Consciousness, can all be represented as zero point sources, as viewed from a material perspective. Each zero point portal opens up into a higher dimensional world as judged from the perspective of the plane below, or it passes into an apparent nothing.

A divine spark is stepped down into a spiritual spark, and then an electromagnetic pulse within the world of formation, and all of this brings life into the material heart and underlies the ego consciousness of everyday life. The divine spark is a zero point source emanation established in higher dimensional Space, and an underlying Unity, within which we live, breathe and have our being. The concept of a zero point element is a most mystical of dimensions ascribed to the Self.

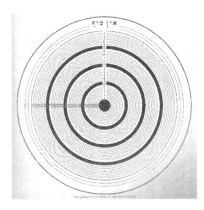

# 2. The Process of Death

Mystical views on the process of death illustrate the nature of zero point laya centres and their relationship to the material body and the psyche. A *Stanza of Dzyan* states: *"The Sons expand and contract through their own selves and hearts."* In life and death, an expansion from within/without is ultimately followed by a contraction from without/within. During life, the Self radiates within/without from the heart centre and its influences pervade the mind and body as consciousness and vitality. When approaching death, the vital energies and the consciousness principle withdraw from without/within back into the subtle dimensions of the heart.

H. P. Blavatsky describes the Monads as initially descending from the realm of spirit into matter and how this leads ultimately to *"a re-ascent from the depths of materiality"* with a corresponding *"dissipation of concrete form and substance up to the LAYA state, or what Science calls "the zero point," and beyond."* (1888, p. 620)

Various saints and seers within eastern and western spiritual traditions describe what occurs at the moments of death in terms of these principles of esoteric anatomy. The *Brihadaranyaka Upanishad* depicts the death process:

> When his body grows weak and he becomes apparently unconscious, the dying man gathers his senses about him and completely withdrawing their powers descends into his heart. No more does he see form or colour without. He neither sees, nor smells, nor tastes. He does not speak, he does not hear. He does not think, he does not know. For all the organs, detaching themselves from his physical body, unite with his subtle body. Then the point of his heart, where the nerves join, is lighted by the light of the Self, and by that light he departs either through the eye, or through the gate of the skull, or through some other aperture of the body. When he thus departs, life departs; and when life departs, all the functions of the vital principle depart. The

Self remains conscious, and, conscious, the dying man goes to his abode. The deeds of this life, and the impressions they leave behind, follow him. (Prabhavananda & Manchester, 1957, p. 108)

At death, the vital energies gather again at the heart and the spirit soul leaves the body through one of the centres, or apertures of the body, as determined by the desires, impressions and attachments accumulated through earthly existence. Some souls pass into the underworld or hell-worlds, while others, such as yogis and masters, might exit through the seventh crown chakra into the highest spiritual heavens or others might penetrate to the heart of the mysteries. Various esoteric texts and rituals are designed to guide the soul at the time of passage from this world into the afterlife.

According to Tibetan Buddhism, the energies of consciousness are distributed from the heart lotus through various "winds" to the 72,000 subtle channels (or nadis) of the body. Three major nadis (the ida, pingala, and sushumna) link the seven chakras to distribute the vital energies throughout the body, mind and psyche. At death, these winds, which serve as the foundations for conscious experience within the body, resolve back into the two major side channels (the ida and pingala), then into the central channel (the sushumna), and finally back into the *"indestructible drop"* within the heart. The Dalai Lama describes this drop as being the *"size of a mustard seed or small pea,"* white on top and red on the bottom, and as being 'indestructible' since it *"lasts until death."* (2002, p. 143)

The Dalai Lama describes the most subtle 'life bearing wind' as residing within the indestructible drop within the heart. The heart centre is called the *"wheel of phenomena"* because *"it is the residence of the very subtle wind and mind that are themselves the root of all phenomena."* (p. 139) As death approaches, all the winds from all of the nadis ultimately dissolve into the indestructible drop and then *"the clear light of death dawns."*

(At death) ... the warmth finally gathers at the heart, from which the consciousness exists. Those particles of matter, of combined semen and blood, into which the consciousness initially entered in the mother's womb at the beginning of the life, become the centre of the heart; and from that very same point the consciousness ultimately departs at death. (Rinbochay & Hopkins, 1980, pp. 9-10)

Consciousness and soul enter and exit the body/mind complex from a source within the heart.

At death, the dissolution of ego is experienced as the subtle energies of the psyche and body withdraw into the heart center. Hopkins (1980) explains that this dissolution:

induces manifestation of subtle minds, which ordinary beings fear since they feel they are being annihilated. Yogis of Highest Yoga Tantra, however, put these same states to use in the spiritual path. ... at death, all winds [subtle energies] ultimately dissolve into (the indestructible drop at the heart), whereupon the clear light of death dawns. (p. 15)

The yogi has experienced the divine or spiritual nature of Self and has no fear of death and the dissolution of ego. S/he realizes the transcendental nature of Self. In contrast, those who identify with the mind/body complex (in the mode of ignorance) are most fearful of death and the dissolution of the ego or personality. The yogis, saints and seers, through spiritual practices, essentially duplicate some of the anatomical processes which occur spontaneously in death. In dying, the life energies gather at the heart and similarly, in the mystics' struggle for self-realization and unitive states, consciousness resolves back into the divine grounds of existence, the Self within the heart.

The *Tibetan Book of the Dead* is an ancient document read to a dying person in order to enable him/her to migrate to higher rather than lower realms of after-life existence. Sir John Woodroffe explains this classic *"science of death:"*

This Text ... tells the nobly-born that Death comes to all, that human kind are not to cling to life on earth with its ceaseless wandering in the Worlds of birth and death (Sangsara). Rather, should they implore the aid of the Divine Mother for a safe passing through the fearful state following the body's dissolution, and that they may at length attain all-perfect Buddhahood. ... the nature of the Death-consciousness determines the future state of the 'soul-complex' ... .(Evans-Wentz, 1968, pp. lxv-lxix)

According to the Tibetan teachings, there are various planes of afterlife existence (or Bardos) to which the soul might gravitate or be drawn upon death. These range from the Greater and Lesser Bodies of Radiance and Ineffable Light to the hell worlds.

At death, when the final exhalation has ceased and the vital force has *"sunk into the nerve center of Wisdom"* in the heart, then the Knower will experience the Clear Light of the natural condition. This verse is intended to orient the subject to this initial afterlife condition:

O nobly-born, listen. Now thou art experiencing the Radiance of the Clear Light of Pure Reality. Recognize it. O nobly-born, thy present intellect, in real nature void, not formed into anything as regards characteristics or colour, naturally void, is the very Reality, the All-Good.

Thine own intellect, which is now voidness, yet not to be regarded as the voidness of nothingness, but as being the intellect itself, unobstructed, shining, thrilling, and blissful, is the very consciousness, the All-good Buddha." (Ibid, pp. xxxviii-xxxix)

Typically, the soul can abide only momentarily in the formless subtle realm of the void before descending into lower and lower states of Bardo experience. In the days following death, the *Book of the Dead* continues to be read aloud in order to orient the soul to the lower realms of afterlife.

In the *Bhagavad-Gita,* Krishna explains a yogic practice for spiritual attainment at death:

> The yogic situation is that of detachment from all sensual engagements. Closing all the doors of the senses and fixing the mind on the heart and the air of life on the top of the head, one establishes this situation. After being situated in this yoga practice and vibrating the sacred symbol Om ... if one thinks of the Lord and thus quits his body, he will certainly reach the spiritual planets. (Prabhupada, 1972, pp. 8, 12)

The *Bhagavad Gita,* the *Tibetan Book of the Dead* and the *Upanishads* regard death as a most important transition, the opportunity for spiritual realization and liberation. Alternatively, souls can pass into states of unconsciousness, confusion and illusion within many possible realms of afterlife existence. These possibilities make clear the importance of spiritual practices as preparation for death and eventually, for *mukti* or liberation. Ideally, consciousness would abide within the seeming Void and Mind of Clear Light, or pass into higher spiritual planes, rather than inhabiting the ghost worlds.

In Lee's (1998) account of Adi Da's life and teachings, one student recounts a story, or *leela,* in which Adi Da reportedly *"guided her through the patterns of conditional existence that are experienced in the death transition."* Connie writes:

> First there was an explosion of inner sounds. Then I felt the layers of the body-mind release and fall away. "I" was separating out from the physical body and seemed to fly upwards, whirling through dark space at incredible speed. I was moving toward an overwhelming, brilliant light. At one point, I recall slipping through a kind of "grid" as a speck of consciousness. ... I felt alive as Consciousness, at ease as the witness of mind and attention. (pp. 217-8)

After she returned to her body, Adi Da began a discourse on death and the "grid" through which we pass at death. He explained that: *"No 'one' survives in the Great Plastic of forms. Only Consciousness Itself persists, the Eternal "I," the Self-Existing and Self-Radiant Condition of all, beyond the grid of appearances."* (Lee, p. 218)

This 'grid of appearances' is similar to the 'matrix of creation' surrounding Da'at, described by the Kabbalist. Further, it is similar to the 'web' spun of Spirit and Matter discussed by Blavatsky, as *"each in turn a part of the web."* The *dream catcher* in the Native tradition has a web pattern representing the circle of life with a central hole in the web. The soul aims to escape through the central hole while the web will stay the disturbing dreams. In any case, as consciousness is freed from levels of the grid or matrix which bind it, the experience is one of resolving back into more illuminated and spacious realms and sometimes to or through a zero point portal. Imagine, every little 'I' as a speck of consciousness and Will within Space—within realms Unspeakable. Each life is just such a *"wink in the eye of Self-Existence,"* as described by H. P. B.

Lama Govinda (1988), in his presentation of Tibetan Buddhism, explicates the nature of an ultimate realization which might be achieved at death or enlightenment:

> death is ultimately illusion and ... those who identify themselves with the ultimate reality, the plenum-void (sunyata) of their inner centre, overcome death and are liberated from the chains of samsara, the rounds of rebirth in the six realms of delusion. (p. 244)

The seventh realm is within the inner centre, as the Self and Sun within Tipheret. Death can enable the transition into such higher dimensional realms, or one might continue life within the subtle worlds which constitute the six levels of the matrix or *'realms of delusion.'*

# 3. The Heart & the Spiritual Sun

The yogis and seers of ancient India held highly unusual and profound ideas about the relationship of individual consciousness to the sun. Spiritual knowledge is a result of illumination and this is related to the spiritual nature of the sun. The sun is not simply a material body related to a human's physical body, but it also has a spiritual nature related to human psychology and the inner processes of enlightenment. The sun assumes a profound importance when considered psychologically.

Miller (1974) explains the Vedic teachings:

Surya's (the Sun's) essential function ... (is) spiritual insight, as proper to gods and as hidden but to be developed in men–and as having been so developed in those ancestors who gained immortality. ... Surya is the organ of the gods' spiritual insight and therefore of enlightenment ... naturally born from the eye of the divine man, *purusa*, ... the 'overlord of sights' ... .

From the "Father of the eye" man has inherited *manas*, his mental insight, his superior understanding which marks him out among all creatures, *manas* that 'eye' by means of which the seer perceives internally ... .(pp. 87-9)

The gods are thus able to see by the light of heaven, to be sun-eyed, indeed enlightened. ... The sun ... is not only the luminous orb out in the sky, but it is the living embodiment of the light of illumination, the goal of human life. ... The rsi (seer), in his spiritual awakening, was a son of the sun and through illumination ... strove to return to his solar origin. ... The return to the solar source, the divine illumined life ... or all-round consciousness, 'all-seeing' and shining because illuminated from within. ... The sun is not merely the eye of the gods as their omniscient gaze but ... the hall-mark of immortality. Enlightenment, the vision of the golden one, or heaven, all point to a superterrestrial state wherein freedom from limitation and therefore from time is known. ... so the rsis claimed his heritage, to be united to the sun. ... that 'immortal light' ... 'abides in all living beings.' (Miller, 1974, pp. 90-4)

The Sun is a higher world of spiritual awareness, the sphere from which the inner individual originates. A human being is potentially a "Son of the Sun" and enlightenment and spiritual knowledge culminate in the realization of this solar identity. "Manas," mental insight, is that *"eye by which the seer perceives internally."* The light of consciousness and mental insight are associated with the sun, as well as with the light of heaven and the immortal light, which abides in all things. The attainment of the solar level of being brings about the *"divine illumined life"* and a form of *"all round consciousness—all seeing and shining."*

Mikhael Aivanhov, an enlightened twentieth century mystic, teaches *surya yoga,*—the yoga of the Sun. He explains that the inner dimension of Self already exists within the subtle spiritual sphere of the Sun:

> a tiny part of you, an extremely delicate substance that is part of you, lives in the Sun. No one knows what man is yet, scientists haven't begun to study the real man, we have no idea how deep he is, how rich and varied. The physical body that we can see is only part of the real man... he has other more subtle bodies, just as the Earth does. ... And, since man is made in the image of the universe, he too has an extension of himself which goes beyond his physical body, the emanations and rays which extend all the way to the Sun. In this way, man's higher self, his divine self, already lives in the Sun without his knowing it, because he can see only with his brain, his consciousness is limited to the material world. (1977, pp. 40-1)

Aivanhov recognizes that such claims sound unbelievable to most people, because they live in a world where "reality" is derived from sense-based consciousness and a materialistic philosophy—one that looks for the soul in a test tube or consciousness in the cortex of the brain.

The Sun is a higher spiritual world intricately interrelated to the material life of the individual through the inner dimensions of the heart. The heart, the Sun of the body, interconnects with the subtle higher dimensions of the Sun. Aivanhov maintains that there are vast regions of super-consciousness to be explored before one comes to the point of knowing that *"you live in the Sun."* In fact, he states: *"your whole existence is there. This part of yourself that lives in the sun is our Higher Self."* (p. 41) Mystical claims that the Higher Self exists within the Sun are not meant metaphorically but literally!

Aivanhov's descriptions of the Sun are most remarkable. It is an awesome, super-sensuous world:

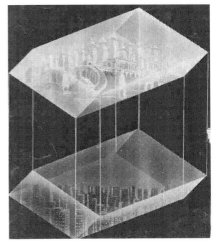

> The Sun is a whole world containing people and houses and trees and cities and oceans, with a culture surpassing anything you can possibly imagine! It is the most beautiful world imaginable; the Book of Psalms calls it the "Land of the living:" "I will walk with

237

God in the land of the living." The living are the immortal beings who live in the light, in the Sun, they are the ones who send us light. The Sun is an extraordinary world, with angels and archangels and other divinities ... It is a whole organization. ... You think the universe is merely a machine, with no soul, no mind, but everything in the universe is alive ... . (1977, pp. 36)

the Sun (is) a marvellous world full of perfect creatures, shining with light, who live there in absolute love, in absolute purity and intelligence, and whose civilization is beyond our imagination. (p. 39)

These descriptions of the inner spiritual worlds of the sun bring to mind the accounts of people who, during near death experiences, travel down a dark tunnel and emerge into the light and a spiritual realm of existence populated by spiritual beings. A mystical perspective suggests that these individuals could indeed be passing into the realm of the spiritual Sun.

Whereas the scientist looks out at the sun and stars, wondering if there is any intelligent life in the universe, the mystics explains that everything is alive, animated and informed by spiritual and divine intelligences and subtle life forces. Aivanhov explains:

a materialist is not very intelligent ... the true reality remains hidden from him. Man's mind keeps him from seeing the essential, the living side, the Source of all things, the Primal Cause. Intellectuals are concerned with the objective side, and with matter, and they have no idea of the subjective side, which is life, or the living currents, forces, fluids, emanations, quintessences, heavenly entities, planetary geniuses, and all the hierarchy of angels throughout the universe ... they sense none of that: the mind is the destroyer of reality. (1977, pp. 190-1)

Mystical, spiritual and occult perspectives regard life in all its forms as a product of divine and spiritual intelligences, Gods and Demi-gods, and a whole hierarchy of cosmic beings—all somehow divine fractions of the Unity from which they originate.

The Sun is the local source of light, heat and life within the physical solar system. The mystics related it also to the source of spiritual light, heat and life within the subtle dimensions. The sun is the central programmer and intelligence within the gross material dimensions of the solar system and of the subtle psychical and spiritual dimensions. Aivanhov depicts the Sun as radiating heat because "He" is "a sacred fire" and "loving," distributing warmth, vitality and love to all living creatures. The Sun is a living being, conscious and loving!

The Sun is the abode of the Inner Self and therefore connected to the heart. Aivanhov explains: "The Sun is a candle for us to light our hearts from." Outer and inner forms and life originate in the Sun—a spiritual world which embodies the intelligence and mind of God. Earthly objects exist there within mental and spiritual matter—rather than in physical matter—and are composed of a more subtle level of materiality of a higher more intense level of vibration. The material world is the condensation of the intelligence and images existing within the mental matter of the Sun, a stepping down of Divine Mind into lower level of creation. In Kabbalah, the Sun is associated with Tipheret, the Self and the Heart.

Aivanhov (1977) provides vivid descriptions of the Sun and its role in creating and maintaining life on planet Earth. The Sun does not act in a blind, mechanical and unconscious way, but instead is a Spiritual Being and Intelligence—an agent of the Deity:

> the Sun … is the door that leads to Heaven, he is God's representative … .No one realizes how important the Sun is. … The Sun is the origin, the father of all things, he is the Primal Cause, he fathered the Earth and the other planets; … all subtle bodies and dense bodies that earth, water, air and ether contain, all emanate from the Sun. … each element is a condensation of another, more subtle element … the Sun is the origin of all things and contains all things that exist on earth in their subtle, etheric state. (1977, pp. 18-20)

> It doesn't take much thinking to realize that the Sun is the reason for everything that exists on Earth. Ask him to tell you how he meditated and worked to bring humans to life, how he prepared the right conditions in the atmosphere, how he mixed light and heat to make life appear. (p. 205)

> The Sun sets the world in motion, the Sun regulates the lives of creatures, the Sun enables them to see, to work, to live: the Sun is the initiator of culture, civilization and progress … (p. 204)

> The Sun directs everything in the universe, like an orchestra conductor, a king on his throne. He makes a decision, gives a signal, and all the spirits he has placed here or on other planets, hasten to do his bidding. (p. 207)

Carl Sagan is so sure that with the advent of modern rational science, there is less and less for God to do. God does not have to say *"Hey flower, open"* now that we know about the sun, phototropism and plant hormones, and can explain the opening of the morning glory in terms of natural laws rather than supernatural agencies. From a mystical perspective, modern scientists are blind in their attribution of all natural phenomena to the mechanical action of cosmic laws, which happened by chance and random processes to have evolved sentient living organisms on planet earth. Scientists need to realize that there are subtle realms of mind, intelligence, information and light beyond the level of the material processes, and that these realms indeed embody spiritual and divine intelligence and forces.

To the modern mind, it might seem absurd to regard the Sun as an unsung hero. But is this dismissal of the Sun as an intelligent being and living world warranted? Aivanhov points out that while we take it for granted that human beings invented agriculture, developed science, acquired knowledge, initiated art, culture and civilization, and so on—none of this would have been possible without the Sun's existence. The Sun is the reason for everything that exists on earth and material forms and activities simply reflect processes originating within the sun in ethereal, mental and spiritual forms. Of course, such views are nothing more than delusions or pipe dreams to the materialists and reductionist who deny the existence of spirit, soul and meaningful intelligence outside of their infamous cerebral cortices. Recall Dr. Sagan's comment: *"Civilization is the product of the cerebral cortex."* For the occultist, the causes of the laws of nature are the Divine Builders, Spiritual Beings and Intelligences, and a hierarchy of beings that inform life processes from within/without. The Sun focuses divine and spiritual influences and intelligence within the solar system and is interrelated to the inner microcosm of the human being.

On the one hand, we have the physical light, heat and substance of the Sun which create and maintain organic life on earth. But beyond or within is the *invisible light* of the Sun. Aivanhov describes both phenomenal and nominal dimensions to the Solar Light:

> The world is illuminated by the light of the Sun, but there is another invisible light, which is the real light of the Sun. In Bulgaria we call it *Videlinata*, from the verb to see. *Videlinata* is the inner, invisible light of the Sun, as opposed to *Svetlina*, from the verb to shine, the external light of the Sun, or a fire, or lamp. *Svetlina* allows us to see material things, but nothing psychic, nothing in the invisible world. To capture the other light, *Videlinata*, which has endless nuances, and which is more subtle and intense than visible light, you have to be linked to the Sun, because that is where it comes from. It takes years of work, meditation, prayer and contemplation of the Sun before you are able to seize the infinitesimal amount of Videlinata which will permit you to behold the invisible world and its inhabitants. (1977, p. 208)

From a mystical perspective, materialistic scientists, like the mass of sleeping humanity, have not begun to penetrate the hidden mysteries of Cosmic Space, or, as Plato said, to *"see the Sun in his own proper place."* Although scientists have discovered and developed complex models of the sun's material processes, they have never considered the Sun to be an intelligent, living and loving Being, which is intentionally creating life on earth and involved in the scheme of human evolution. Carl Sagan and exact scientists think that all of these things happened as a result of accidents and random mutations and fortunate coincidences. Such views are regarded as being established scientifically, rather than merely philosophical speculations and metaphysical assumptions. Nevertheless, it is entirely reasonable to consider that the mechanisms of the Sun embody the intelligence and energies of more subtle dimensions and supernatural intelligence. Aivanhov suggests: *"... study the Sun's rays. ... There is no one as intelligent as a ray of Sun, no scientist or learned scholar, no genius."* (p. 217)

The Sun is a demi-God, rather than the Deity. As a representative or agent of the Absolute, it focuses divine and spiritual light, intelligence, energies and life within the solar system. On the one hand, the Sun emanates and radiates outwards throughout the solar system, but within the Sun itself is rooted into a Central Spiritual Sun—the sun and light behind the sun. The Sun also has a zero point nature rooted into a metaphysical world beyond and is constantly renewed with influences from the Absolute. The realm of the Sun is that of the spiritual spark, while the divine spark is related to the Invisible Sun–the Sun behind the Sun.

In elaborating upon the nature of the Deity, Aivanhov notes:

When God created the world, He had to limit Himself. From being Infinity ... He decided to limit Himself, to become concentrated, and He gathered Himself into a single Point from which He now projects Himself into the whole universe. (1977, p. 249)

According to Aivanhov, the universe is projected from a single point.

In *The Secret Doctrine*, Blavatsky (1888) describes the Sun and the realm behind:

This "mystery," or the origin of the LIFE ESSENCE, Occultism locates in the same centre as the nucleus of *prima material* (for they are one) of our Solar system. *"The Sun is the heart of the Solar World (System) and its brain is hidden behind the (visible) Sun. From hence, sensation is radiated into every nerve centre of the great body* ... Occult philosophy denies that the Sun is a globe in combustion, but defines it simply as a world, a glowing sphere, the *real* Sun being hidden behind, and the visible being only its reflection, its *shell*. ... the *visible* Sun only *a window cut into the real* Solar palace and presence, which reflects, however, faithfully the interior work. (*S.D. I*, pp. 40-1)

the spiritual, central sun (is) ... the *Point*; the centre (which is everywhere) of the circle (which is nowhere), the ethereal, spiritual fire, the soul and spirit of the all-pervading, mysterious ether; the despair and puzzle of the materialist, who will some day find that that which causes the numberless cosmic forces to manifest themselves in eternal correlation is but a divine electricity, or rather *galvanism*, and that the sun is but one of the myriad magnets disseminated through space—a reflection ... . (p. 270)

The "Central Spiritual Sun" or 'invisible sun' is depicted as a *"Point"* source of an *"ethereal spiritual fire,"* which is the *"soul and spirit of the all-pervading, mysterious ether."*

It is the 'Spirit of Light,' the first born of the Eternal pure Element, whose energy (or emanation) is stored in the Sun, the great Life-Giver of the physical world, as the hidden Concealed Spiritual Sun is the Light-and Life-Giver of the Spiritual and Psychic Realms. ... the "Sons of Light" ... emanate from, and are self-generated in, that infinite Ocean of Light, whose one pole is pure *Spirit* lost in the absoluteness of Non-Being, and the other, the *matter* in which it condenses, crystallizing into a more and more gross type as it descends into manifestation. (p. 481)

According to *The Secret Doctrine*, the laws of nature depend upon intelligent forces within unseen space, in various ethers and the ultimate Aether of Space itself—the "Eternal Parent Space." Blavatsky describes the Sun's subtle radiations as constituting the lower ether (or astral light), while beyond that its rays originate from within the supra-solar Aether (or Akasha).

Blavatsky and Aivanhov condemn the small mindedness and bigotry of scientists who so readily dismiss such ancient mystical teachings. Blavatsky notes: *"modern Cosmology and Astronomy now repudiate anything like research into the mysteries of being."* (p. 589) Similarly, Aivanhov notes:

What I am revealing to you about the Sun will be revealed by science, sooner or later. I didn't invent it, I rediscovered something that was known before, in the distant past. (p. 208) ... Unfortunately, man's materialistic philosophy has so reduced and weakened him that he no longer has any spiritual power, he can no longer move about in spiritual realms. Outwardly he has become more powerful with all kinds of machinery and powerful instruments, weapons of war, but inside he is growing heavier and duller and more insensitive all the time, because he doesn't understand the power of the mind and spirit. (p. 215)

The Sun is related to the origin of all things on earth: science, civilization, religion, evolution, and most importantly, the Self within the Heart. The Spiritual Spark abides within the Sun and the Divine Sparks abide within the Invisible Sun behind the Sun. Thus, near death experiences can involve a journey down a spiralling tunnel into a heavenly world populated with spiritual beings, illuminated everywhere and filled with love. All earthly things originate in the Sun, while the Sun itself originates from a Central Spiritual Sun rooted into an infinite ocean of Light.

# 4. The Universe & The Gods: Yogananda's Experience of Cosmic Consciousness

"I cognized the center of my empyrean as a point of intuitive perception in my heart. Irradiating splendour issued from my nucleus to every part of the universal structure."
(Yogananda, 1998, pp. 167-8)

A first mystical dimension ascribed to the Self involves the description of the spiritual or divine spark as the smallest of points, more subtle than any physical particle or quantum, an infinitesimal zero point condition. Another mystical dimension ascribed to the Self is that of the universe. An ancient Vedic saying declares: *"Thou art that,"* meaning you are the world. As a microcosm of the macrocosm, the individual Self, in blending with the larger SELF, reflects or contains all things within self. Thus, the Self is intimately related to the whole of the larger universe. The individual spirit soul is a seed or atom of the Supreme Supersoul, and can experience the deeper realities and the larger structures of the universe. In this way, one might know thy Self, the universe and the Gods.

Various Upanishads suggest this possibility:

Self-luminous is Brahman (God), ever present in the hearts of all. ... In him exists all that moves and breathes. In him exists all that is. ... This Self, who understands all, who knows all, and whose glory is manifest in the universe, lives within the lotus of the heart, the bright throne of Brahman. Mundaka Upanishad

As large as the universe outside, even so large is the universe within the lotus of the heart. Within it are heaven and earth, the sun, the moon, the lightening, and all the stars. What is in the macrocosm is in this microcosm ... All things that exist ... are in the city of Brahman. Chandogya Upanishad

These are the most paradoxical and unusual claims. How could the 'heart' contain the universe within itself and how might consciousness embrace such subtle realms of the inner cosmos? This ancient mystical claim illustrates the idea of a part embodying the whole as in modern holographic models within physics. Similarly, a source within the Heart Space might unfold into the larger universe.

There are a few reports within the mystical literature of individual experiences which illustrate these paradoxical ideas—about the dimensions of the spirit soul as a microcosm of the macrocosm. Paramahansa Yogananda, a twentieth century Indian saint and master of kriya yoga, was one of the first eastern sages to become prominent in the west through his work as founder of the Self-Realization Fellowship in America. In his classic book, *Autobiography of a Yogi*, Yogananda provides an extraordinary account of his realization of the fantastic possibilities inherent in the true nature of Self. The following is Yogananda's description of his experience in "cosmic consciousness," initiated by his Master striking him gently over the heart to awaken it:

> "Poor boy, mountains cannot give you what you want." Master spoke caressingly, comfortingly. His calm gaze was unfathomable. "Your heart's desire shall be fulfilled." Sri Yukteswar seldom indulged in riddles; I was bewildered. He struck gently on my chest above the heart.

At this point, Yogananda receives grace from his Master in order to *"fulfill his heart's desire."* He then experiences these extraordinary states of enlightenment and cosmic consciousness:

> My body became immovably rooted; breath was drawn out of my lungs as if by some huge magnet. Soul and mind instantly lost their physical bondage and streamed out like a fluid piercing light from my every pore. The flesh was as though dead; yet in my intense awareness I knew that never before had I been fully alive. My sense of identity was no longer narrowly confined to a body but embraced the circumambient atoms. People on distant streets seemed to be moving gently over my own remote periphery. The roots of plants and trees appeared through a dim transparency of the soil; I discerned the inward flow of their sap.

> The whole vicinity lay bare before me. My ordinary frontal vision was now changed to a vast spherical sight, simultaneously all-perceptive. Through the back of my head I saw men strolling far down Rai Ghat Lane, and noticed also a white cow that was leisurely approaching. ... After she had passed behind the brick wall of the courtyard, I saw her clearly still.

> All objects within my panoramic gaze trembled and vibrated like quick motion pictures. My body, Master's, the pillared courtyard, the furniture and floor, the trees and sunshine, occasionally became violently agitated, until all melted into a luminescent sea; even as sugar crystals, thrown into a glass of water, dissolve after being shaken.

The unifying light alternated with materializations of form, the metamorphoses revealing the law of cause and effect in creation.

An oceanic joy broke upon calm endless shores of my soul. The Spirit of God, I realized, is exhaustless Bliss; His body is countless tissues of light. A swelling glory within me began to envelop towns, continents, the earth, solar and stellar systems, tenuous nebulae, and floating universes. The entire cosmos, gently luminous, like a city seen afar at night, glimmered within the infinitude of my being. ... The divine dispersion of rays poured from an Eternal Source, blazing into galaxies, transfigured with ineffable auras. Again and again I saw the creative beams condense into constellations, then resolve into sheets of transparent flame. By rhythmic reversion, sextillion worlds passed into diaphanous lustre, then fire became firmament.

I cognized the center of the empyrean as a point of intuitive perception in my heart. Irradiating splendour issued from my nucleus to every part of the universal structure. ...

Suddenly the breath returned to my lungs. With a disappointment almost unbearable, I realized that my infinite immensity was lost. Once more I was limited to the humiliating cage of a body, not easily accommodative to the Spirit. Like a prodigal child, I had run away from my macrocosm home and had imprisoned myself in a narrow microcosm. ...

"It is the Spirit of God that actively sustains every form and force in the universe; yet He is transcendental and aloof in the blissful uncreated void beyond the worlds of vibratory phenomenon," Master explained. (1998, pp 166-8)

Yogananda offers an awe-inspiring glimpse into the hidden dimensions of consciousness, life and the universe. Is Yogananda simply exaggerating or imagining this account, or did he really objectively experience these things? If this is an objectively valid account of an awakening of consciousness within the heart and its expansion into the dimensions of the universe, then somehow there is something fundamentally fraudulent with the entire approach to consciousness found within the mainstream of western psychology, science, cosmology and education.

It is instructive to review Yogananda's experiences in order to have a clearer idea of what his account entails. The process is initiated when his master Sri Yukteswar states, *"your heart's desire shall be fulfilled,"* and then reaches over and strikes him on the chest above the heart. At this point, Yogananda feels his soul and mind stream out of his body like light, so that his awareness is interpenetrating the entire volume of space around his body and the ashram. He senses the inner activity of the plants, the soil and the ashram, while experiencing a *"vast spherical sight, simultaneously all-perceptive."* This description is of a level of samadhi, wherein consciousness interpenetrates material nature and a larger volume of space/time.

Yogananda then experiences the objects and scene surrounding him melting into a luminescent sea, with materializations of forms alternating with experiences of the unifying light. He experiences the inner dimensions of things as they crystallize out of the underlying realm of light into material forms and then dissolve back into the underlying light realm. Yogananda has united the light within himself with the unifying light of Brahman, which he describes as *"the structural essence of creation."* In doing so, he witnesses the cosmic dance of the involution and evolution of elements within an infinite Sea of Light!

Yogananda's awareness then began to envelop larger and larger realms passing from towns, to continents, the earth, the solar system, the galaxy and floating universes! Creation is revealed to involve the *"dispersion of rays poured from an Eternal source,"* which condenses or crystallizes into galaxies and constellations, which again resolve back into sheets of transparent flame. As before, Yogananda experiences the process of inward creation and dissolution, although this time at the level of the universe.

Finally, Yogananda cognizes the *"center of the empyrean."* The term empyrean from ancient and medieval cosmology refers to the highest seventh heavenly sphere consisting of fire and light. The centre of the empyrean and of the universe was *"a point of intuitive perception in his heart"*! From this point or nucleus, Yogananda experienced an *"irradiating splendour"* issuing to every part of the universal structure. Somehow, the universe as it were, concentrates itself into a point.

Yogananda's adventures in cosmic consciousness, divine and spiritual realization, illustrate the most unusual dimensions ascribed to the spiritual soul or divine spark–that it is a point source of *"omnipresent Spirit"* emerging from the unifying Light and which is interconnected to the Whole. The mystics and saints are most serious in claiming that the Self, the microcosm, is connected to the whole—of life, the universe and to God (Brahman). An atomic point or quantum of pure consciousness unfolds to embrace the universe! Yogananda's experience illustrates the statements of the Chandogya Upanishad: *"As large as the universe outside is the universe within the lotus of the heart. ... All things that exist ... are in the city of Brahman."*

In the following passage, Yogananda attempts to explain the principles behind this cosmic experience and what he calls the *law of miracles*:

> The consciousness of a perfected yogi is effortlessly identified not with a narrow body but with the universal structure. ... He who knows himself as the omnipresent Spirit is subject no longer to the rigidities of a body in time and space. The imprisoning "rings-pass-not" have yielded to the solvent: *I am He.*

> "Let there be light! And there was light." (Genesis 1:3). In the creation of the universe, God's first command brought into being the structural essential: light. On the beams of this immaterial medium occur all divine manifestations. ...

> A yogi who through perfect meditation has merged his consciousness with the Creator perceives the cosmic essence as light (vibrations of life energy); to him there is no difference between the light rays composing water and the light rays composing land. Free from matter-consciousness, free from the three dimensions of space and the fourth dimension of time, a master transfers his body of light with equal ease over or through the light rays of earth, water, fire, and air.

> "If therefore thine eye be single, thy whole body shall be *full of light.*" (Matthew 6:22) ... the liberating spiritual eye has enabled the yogi to destroy all delusions concerning matter and its gravitational weight; he sees the universe as the Lord created it: an essentially undifferentiated mass of light. ...

> *The law of miracles is operable by any man who has realized that the essence of creation is light.* A master is able to employ his divine knowledge of light phenomena ... a yogi rearranges the light atoms of the universe ... I came to understand the relativity of human consciousness, and clearly perceive the unity of the Eternal Light behind the painful dualities of *maya.* ...

> The colourful universal drama is ... issuing from the single white light of a Cosmic Source. ... "My sons are children of light; they will not

sleep forever in delusion." ... The so-called miraculous powers of a
great master are a natural accompaniment to his exact understanding
of subtle laws that operate in the inner cosmos of consciousness.
(1998, pp. 315 - 321)

This is clearly a fantastic, awesome first hand account of cosmic consciousness.
Is this the stuff of science fiction or of an ancient and ultimate science–light years
ahead of common scientific understanding?

The mystical heart doctrine provides an intriguing holographic model of
the Self (and Super Self). The Self is a point source of coherent light consciousness emanating from a realm of Eternal Light, higher dimensional Space and the
uncreated Void. Light is the structural essence of creation. A point of intuitive
perception within the heart can thus be related to the larger dimensions of the
macrocosmic universe!

Mystical teachings suggest that light has a deep, hidden, supernal nature,
unrecognized within science. When Yogananda's consciousness expands to embrace the universe, it does so at speeds greater than the speed of light! It must
as the universe is billions of light years across and his experiences lasts only
minutes. However, Yogananda is not really travelling anywhere, as the whole
universe is embodied within the point of intuitive perception within his heart.
The usual notions of time and space simply do not apply within the subtle implicate and super-implicate orders, wherein information about the whole is present
everywhere instantaneously, in omnipresent Spirit. The movement of consciousness may be experienced as expanding outwardly but involves the penetration of
the interior dimensions of being. The universe within is as vast as the universe
without.

**THE LAW IS FOR ALL**

**ALEISTER CROWLEY**

# 5. Hadit within Nuit: Every Man & Every Woman is a Star

"Each man's 'child'– consciousness is a star in the cosmos of the sun, as the sun is a star in the cosmos of Nuit."

"I lost consciousness of everything but a universal space in which were innumerable bright points, and I realized this as a physical representation of the universe, in what I may call its essential structure. I exclaimed: "Nothingness, with twinkles!" "But what Twinkles!" (Crowley, 1993, p.144)

Aleister Crowley is another major figure in modern western occultism. Crowley was infamous for his life style and his views on such controversial subjects as sexuality, drugs and religion. He called his system of ideas and practices *magick* to differentiate it from other traditions of western magic and occultism. The most basic of Crowley's writings is *The Book of the Law* (1993)—a short, poetic and symbolic manuscript, which Crowley maintains was dictated to him during a period of enlightenment and revelation while in Eygpt. Initially, Crowley claimed that the author of the work was a *"discarnate intelligence"* named Aiwass; although he later maintained that Aiwass was his own Holy Guardian Angel or Higher Self. In 1920, Crowley wrote *The Law is for All* (1993), an extended commentary on *The Book of the Law* which analyzed and interpreted its poetic verses.

The *Book of the Law* elaborates upon the mysteries of Hadit and Nuit. Hadit is an infinitely small and atomic point, which is omnipresent; while Nuit is infinite space, the root principle of creation, which allows for the manifestation of Hadit. The conjunction of Hadit and Nuit produces the tri-unity of *Ra-Hoor-Khuit*, itself a Unity, which is the foundation for all things. The conjunction of Hadit within Nuit, the supernal point within cosmic space, is the root for all manifestation. As Crowley explains: *"It is cosmographically, the conception of the two ultimate ideas: space and that which occupies space."* (1993, p. 72)

249

Hadit and Nuit are identified with various dualities; the masculine and feminine principles, yang and yin, motion and matter, the star or point of light within the darkness and emptiness of space. The term Nuit is French for night and suggests the darkness of a night sky, populated by stars—all manifestations of Hadit.

*"Every man and every woman is a star."* (1990, p. xiv) The third stanza of the *Book of the Law* suggests that each individual is so comprised in his or her magical nature as a point of divine light—a star within cosmic space. Hadit is the *"nucleolus of any star-organism."* (p. 221) Hadit, the star, exists within the infinite space of Nuit. As in Blavatsky's archaic teachings, the basic concepts are of an infinitesimal zero point source of light arising within an Eternal Parent Space—some form of infinite space or hyperspace. In *magick*, the mystical conjunction of Hadit within Nuit is the basis for all conscious experience and universal manifestation.

Crowley describes Nuit: It is *"that from which we have come, that to which we must return."* (p. 122) It is the *"hollow space"* and *"the Queen of Space."* Nuit declares herself: *"I am Infinite Space."* (p. 46) The Body of Nuit is that of the macrocosm and is symbolized by 0, zero. Nuit is the *"Great Mother"* and *"the Queen of the Stars."* Crowley refers to the *"womb of Nuit"* and the *"Scarlet Woman."* Nuit is continuous, has infinite extension or depth and possesses the power of being known.

In contrast, Hadit is: *"the sun, one point concentrating space;"* the *"infinite Stars;"* the *"winged secret flame."* Hadit is the central atom, the *"core of every star"* and *"the unit of the macrocosm."* Whereas Nuit is continuous and possesses infinite extension, Hadit is *"infinite contraction"* and *"not extended."* Hadit is an infinitely small zero point source, the core nucleus of a star or human being. Hadit is represented by the number 1 and stands for the individual conscious nature. Hadit has the power to know in contrast to the power of being known possessed by Nuit.

A human being's magical nature involves the conjunction of Hadit within Nuit:

> in the Temple called Man is the God, his Soul, or Star, individual and eternal… inherent in the Body of Our Lady Nuit. I am the flame that burns in every heart of man, and in the core of every star. (p. 162)

Every man, woman and child is thus a Star: the point-interval Star is the inner most light, the original emanation of the eternal divine essence.

The Star has a magical garment of subtle bodies, the Khabs and Khu, and it takes on a mind and body complex within the material world. In this way, the Perfect comes to experience apparent imperfection embodied within the elements of nature. Crowley elaborates upon the levels of human existence:

> Each of us is Hadit, the core of our Khabs, our star, one of the company of heaven; but this Khabs needs a Khu or magical image, in order

to play its part in the great drama, his Khu, again, needs the proper costume, a suitable "body of flesh ..." (1993, p. 245.)

Crowley describes various veils which obscure the *"secret light"* within.

The secret light of Hadit is identified with consciousness. Crowley comments: *"our light is the inmost point of illuminated consciousness."* (p. 273) Just as the sun illuminates the outer cosmos, so Hadit is an innermost point of consciousness illuminating the experiences and dimensions of the inner cosmos. Crowley notes: *"Each man's 'child'–consciousness is a star in the cosmos of the sun, as the sun is a star in the cosmos of Nuit."* (1993, pp. 300-1)

Hadit is worshiped in the center, yet its light fills the sphere to the circumference, so that all is light. (p. 83) There can be *"no regular temples"* of Nuit or of Hadit as these are incommensurable and absolutes. Crowley describes the religion of this era as the "cult of the Sun"—as this is our particular star in the outer world.

The aim within *magick* is for the individual to *"consummate the marriage of Nuit and Hadit in themselves."* (p. 84) All of life, especially love and love making, should be devoted to Nuit and her infinite possibilities for being known. Hadit knows Nuit most deeply through love. The individual is to be Hadit and to worship Her, and *"offer ourselves unto Nuit, pilgrims to all her temples."* (p. 166) The key to the worship of Nuit is: *"The uniting of consciousness with infinite space by the exercise of love ... Let love be "under" or "unto" the Body of Nuit."* (pp. 84-5) These concepts depict the mystical dimensions of love and the deepest origins of Self, the point interval Star within.

One portion of *The Book of the Law* is spoken by Nuit. The Divine Goddess states:

> I am above you and in you. My ecstasy is in yours. My joy is to see your joy. ... ye shall know that the chosen priest & apostle of infinite space is the prince-priest, the Beast; and in his woman called the Scarlet Woman is all power given. ... they shall bring the glory of the stars into the hearts of men. And the sign shall be my ecstasy, the consciousness of the continuity of existence, the omnipresence of my body. Then the priest answered & said unto the Queen of Space ... O Nuit, continuous one of Heaven, let it be ever thus: that men speak not of Thee as One but as None; and let them speak not of thee at all, since thou are continuous! ... For I am divided for love's sake, for the chance of union. This is the creation of the world, that the pain of division is as nothing, and the joy of dissolution all. (1993, pp. 45-7)

The uniting of Hadit and Nuit shall *"bring the glory of the stars into the hearts of men."* The aim of *magick* is to consummate this mystical marriage. The *Book of the Law* depicts ecstasy as a key to reality: *"Religious ecstasy is necessary to man's soul.*" (p. 151) Thus, all acts should be devoted unto Nuit, the Goddess of Infinite Space, the source of all possibilities for cosmic manifestation.

Crowley depicts the drama of creation as the unfolding of the union of Hadit with Nuit. Every man and woman is a star but this truth is forgotten in everyday life. The individual does not recognize Self during a cycle of incarnation and fails to attain true Will. As a star, each individual must come to know Divine Will and to manifest Love under Will in order to re-unite with Nuit. Hadit is perfect but this perfection is apparently lost during the soul's incarnation among the elements. Crowley explains this cosmic epic:

> each "star" is the centre of the universe to itself, and a "star" simple, original, absolute, can add to its omnipotence, omniscience and omnipresence without ceasing to be itself... its one way to do this is to gain experience, and therefore it enters into combinations in which its true nature is awhile disguised, even from itself. ... This theory is the only one which explains why the Absolute limited itself and why It does not recognize Itself during its cycle of incarnation. ... he suffers the lapse of memory of his own reality of perfection, which he has during these incarnations, because he knows he will come through unchanged. (1993, pp. 73-4)

Crowley depicts each star returning again to its original state after death and being further involved in cycles of incarnation and reincarnation:

> All elements must at one time have been separate—that would be the case with great heat. Now when atoms get to the sun, we get that immense, extreme heat, and all the elements are themselves again. Imagine that each atom of each element possesses the memory of all his adventures in combination. By the way, that atom, fortified with that memory, would not be the same atom; yet it is, because it has gained nothing from anywhere except this memory. (1993, p. 74)

The passage into the spiritual sun strips the atom of all attachments and identifications with not-I, until one is only that which remains. The soul passes through various after-life planes, shedding different bodies (the physical, astral and mental) and returning to its original divine state. As the soul withdraws into the realm of the sun, it is stripped of conditioning, of combinations and attachments, which have bound it to other elements. The Self is still itself although it retains memory of all its combinations and experiences.[1]

---

1 In modern physics, according to quantum theory, any quantum retains a "phase entanglement" or "memory" of its engagement with any other quantum with which it has participated in a singlet state. Since every quantum ultimately can be traced back to the original singularity of cosmic creation, this suggests that all quanta are ultimately inter-related in higher dimensional phase space. This is the type of memory Crowley describes as potential for Hadit.

A number of deaths unfold in the subtle dimensions of being and non-being as the garments of Hadit are dissolved; including the gross and fine bodies, and the mind. The soul passes through material and subtle deaths, until all the energies and dynamics of different matters/planes are resolved. When the dissolution is incomplete, the soul remains bound to the corresponding planes. Crowley describes the states of ecstasy following upon a complete death:

> When death is complete as it should be, the individual expands and fulfils himself in all directions; it is an omniform Samadhi. This is of course "eternal ecstasy"... .But in the time-world Karma reconcentrates the elements, and a new incarnation occurs. (1993, p. 210)

The wheel of life, death and rebirth continues until the ultimate mystical marriage is completed. Cycles of incarnation and death follow one another as the elements are re-concentrated and then dissipated once again.

This brings us to Crowley's most simple magical formula of the Universe: $0 = (1) + (-1)$. Crowley notes: *"Ultimate Reality is best described by Numbers and their interplay."* (1991, p. 31) Crowley's magick formula is a profound illustration of this:

> The Chinese ... based their whole philosophy on this primary division of the original Nothing. One must begin with Nothing; otherwise the question would arise, Whence come this postulated Something? So they wrote the equation—Zero equals plus one plus minus one $0 = (+1) + (-1)$. (1991, p. 29)

Crowley relates the plus one, $+1$, to the male yang principle; and the minus one, $-1$, to the female yin principle. In different contexts, these quantities represent heaven and earth, the sun and moon, or Hadit and Nuit. When these forces are in perfect balance, the equation is solved, the complex of differentiation resolves back into the primary nothingness. It all adds up to Zero, O.[2]

Crowley writes:

> The universe must be expressible either as $+/- n$, or as zero. That is, it is either unbalanced or balanced. ... zero, when examined, proves to contain the possibility of being expressed as $n - n$ ... . (1993, p. 195)

One might have any number of positive entities and have them balanced by an equal number of negative entities, such that it all reduces to zero. Crowley comments on this paradox: *"This thesis appears to me a reductio ad absurdum of the very basis of our mathematical thinking."* (1993, p. 95)

---

2    In physics, the comparable equation would be of the effects of gravity considered as a negative sum representing the material nature of Nuit or cosmic space and exactly balancing the positive energies/matters of the universe bound up in individual quanta. The sum adds up to zero. Scientific descriptions of vacuum genesis indeed suggest such a possibility—that the Universe adds up to nothing

On a psychological and metaphysical level, Crowley relates this magical formula or equation to the *"uniting of consciousness with infinite space by the exercise of love … ."* (p. 84) Further,

> every star is to come forth from its veils that it might revel with the whole world of stars. This is again a call to unite, or "love," thus formulating the equation $1 + (-1) = 0$, which is the general magical formula in our cosmos. (1993, p. 85)

If the opposition of the fundamental dualities is resolved, Hadit unites with Nuit in love and the riddles of the cosmos are revealed within mystical states. The spiritual atom returns to the sun stripped of binding combinations and further into the cosmic space of Nuit. The essence of love and of life is that it must be a sacrament unto Nuit. This will bring the glory of the stars into the heart of a human being.

Every man and every woman is a star but amid the dualities, contradictions, opposing forces and the madness of life, this supreme consciousness is seemingly lost. Crowley explains how the *"device of duality"* allows the soul to gain appreciation of its own perfection through experiences of imperfection:

> This soul is a particular star, with its own peculiar qualities, of course; but these qualities are all "eternal," and part of the nature of the soul. This soul being a monastic consciousness, it is unable to appreciate itself and its qualities … so it realizes itself by the device of duality, with the limitations of time, space and causality. (1993, p. 178)

The aim in magick is to gain the conversation of the Holy Guardian Angel, the higher or true Self, and resolve the magical formula $1 + (-1) = 0$. In this case, consciousness is experienced in its root nature beyond time and space, beyond causality.

> O my Son, how wonderful is the Wisdom of this Law of Love! How vast are the Oceans of uncharted Joy that lie before the Keel of thy Ship! Yet know this, that every Opposition is in its Nature named Sorrow, and the Joy lieth in the Destruction of the Dyad. … rest not in the joy of the destruction of every Complex in thy Nature, but press on to that ultimate Marriage with the Universe whose Consummation shall destroy thee utterly, leaving only that Nothingness which was before the beginning. (1993, pp. 232-3)

Consciousness issues from a point source Hadit within an infinite parent Goddess Space Nuit. As consciousness resolves back into its zero point source within infinite space, one merges into the Nothingness, the plenum and the root principles of creation. The binding of consciousness to planes of manifestation is due to broken symmetries existing between poles of existence. As forces and elements within self are resolved and balanced, the soul is freed. Ultimately, perfect symmetry is the mystical marriage of Hadit and Nuit in which only Nothingness remains: $+1 + (-1) = 0$. This simple equation expresses the most profound ideas about the inner cosmos of consciousness and the mysteries of Space. Crowley describes his own experiences of enlightenment:

> I lost consciousness of everything but a universal space in which were innumerable bright points, and I realized this as a physical representation of the universe, in what I may call its essential structure. I exclaimed: "Nothingness, with twinkles!" ... "But what Twinkles!" (1993, p. 144)

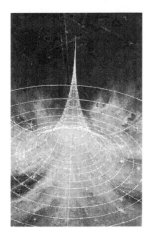

# 6. Within-Without from Zero Points

## 6a. Singularities, Vacuum Genesis & Hyperspace

The most recent ideas in modern physics and cosmology illustrate the basic concepts of zero points and their origins in metaphysical dimensions. Oddly enough, this bizarre concept—of zero point origins—is quite in keeping within emerging ideas in science, which trace the creation of the universe back to a singularity point at the beginning of time. During the last century, astronomers traced the origin of the universe back to a "big bang" creation event, currently estimated to have been about fifteen billion years ago. During the last decade, astrophysicists penetrated even further back into the origins of the universe to trace the big bang back to the first instant of time and the emergence of an infinitesimally small point source—a singularity.

Physicists describe the singularity as existing at the first $10^{-43}$ second of time and having the physical dimension of $10^{-35}$ centimetres. The infinitesimal time and size estimates of the singularity are arrived at through the physicists' understanding of the *uncertainty principle*, which limits the exactness of measurement of any quantum element or property. The singularity is the point at which the universe emerged out of a realm beyond the level of physical measurement. According to modern astrophysicists and cosmologists, the singularity emerged out of the quantum vacuum. Scientists call this creation scenario *"vacuum genesis"* and remark on its similarity to the Genesis myth. Verse two of the book of Genesis reads: *"the earth was without form and void; and darkness was upon the face of the deep."* Similarly, the idea of vacuum genesis is in accord with the ancient phrase *"creation ex nihilo,"* referring to creation out of nothingness.

Modern physicists have a very complex understanding of that so-called nothingness of the quantum vacuum. One modern physicist notes that: *"All of physics is in the vacuum"*! There are complex theories about the hidden dimensions of the quantum vacuum—a form of "hyperspace" and "big foam"—which is the basis for material creation and the laws of nature. Instead of simply being empty or void, the quantum vacuum contains all possible quanta and the laws of nature in a latent undifferentiated state. In this way, the apparent nothingness can also be described as "the plenum," that is, containing all possibilities. And so, the zero point of creation did not simply emerge out of nothing but out of a something which only appears to be nothing when judged from a material point of view. The singularity appears to pass beyond our perception into nothingness, but in reality it is emerging from a higher dimensional realm within the plenum.

Whereas the world is usually regarded as having four dimensions with three dimensions of space and a fourth dimension of time, physicists now suggest that the hyperspace within the quantum vacuum has "hidden compacted dimensions." The most advanced Kaluza-Klein theory and M-theory describes an eleven dimensional universe with four *"large dimensions"* and *"seven hidden compacted dimensions."* The laws of nature manifest within the four-dimensional space-time are described as being the manifestation of processes occurring within the higher seven dimensional space.

The vacuum genesis account of creation involves a zero point singularity emerging out of a seven dimensional quantum vacuum. This hyperspace is an eternal principle relative to the four-dimensional created universe. The quantum vacuum is also described as a *"big space/time foam,"* a root principle, which could be the basis for an infinite number of universes–all emerging out of nothingness from point sources, as sparks of eternity. Undoubtedly, the findings of modern science offer a profoundly mysterious view of the zero points of creation and the nothingness which sustains them!

The image of a point within a black circle or sphere depicts most simply the scientific or mystical idea of the emergence of a singularity out of an apparent nothingness and higher space dimensions. Mystical and occult teachings from a wide range of ancient and modern, eastern and western sources depict similar views of creation. The basic teaching of zero point sources is suggested within the Upanishads and Vedas of India, the Kabbalah and Jewish esoteric traditions, the Gnostic Christian gospels, Madame Blavatsky and *The Secret Doctrine*, M. Aivanhov of the Great White Brotherhood, Aleister Crowley, Sufi Hazrat Inayat Khan, Baha'u'llah of the Baha'i religion, Adi Da, the divine heart master, and elsewhere. Mystics and occultists have long depicted *"supernal points"* of creation as the origins of both the cosmos and human self existence.

*The Secret Doctrine* begins with Blavatsky's description of this most simple, yet profound, ancient mystical symbol:

> An archaic Manuscript...lies before the writer's eye. On the first page is an immaculate white disk within a dull black ground. On the following page, this same disk, but with a central point. The first...Kosmos in Eternity, before the reawakening of still slumbering Energy, the Emanation of the World...The point in the hitherto immaculate disk...denotes the dawn of differentiation. It is the Point in the Mundane Egg, the Germ that will become the Universe, the

All. ... The one circle is divine Unity, from which all proceeds, wither all returns ... .(1888, p. 31)

The creation of the cosmos emerges from the central point within the disk, the Point in the Mundane Egg. This is the laya centre from which cosmic differentiation begins. The circle represents the divine Unity out of which the point emerges and into which it will eventually return. Blavatsky claims that the cosmos began from such a central point and will eventually resolve back into this zero point source at the end of time when it returns to its Laya state.

Blavatsky and the Kabbalist provide profound descriptions of the root principles out of which zero points emerge, which are quite consistent with modern ideas. Blavatsky describes the Absolute (or God) as THAT which is paradoxically the void and plenum, an apparent nothingness, which is simultaneously *"the divine plenum"*—containing all potencies and possibilities. Similarly, the Kabbalist talks of the Ayin or nothingness, the En Soph—the limitless plenum and the En Soph Aur, the limitless light. This is essentially similar to the modern physicists' view of the quantum vacuum as paradoxically both empty and full, and full of electromagnetic light or zero point fields.

When describing the Eternal Parent Space, Blavatsky refers to it as *"Seven Skinned,"* that is, as having an inherent sevenfold nature which is manifest in the physical realms of creation below, as it is above. Kabbalists make similar claims in viewing the Divine Mother, Binah, as the source of the seven Sephirot created below. Although the complexity of these ideas cannot simply be explained at this time, these are absolutely astonishing correspondences between the ancient wisdom teachings of *The Secret Doctrine,* Kabbalah etc. and the newest ideas in physics and cosmology.

In modern physics, singularities exist at the level of the Planckian units where measurement becomes indefinable because of the uncertainty principle of quantum theory. When the physicist attempts to penetrate any quantum, it seemingly passes into an infinitely small mathematical point rooted into seven hidden compacted dimensions of the quantum vacuum. In fact, many of the enigmas in modern science tie into the enigmas of zero point centres, their roots in hyperspace and the nature of the void/plenum of the quantum vacuum. The wisdom of the mystics speaks directly then to critical unsolved anomalies within modern science concerning these issues. Although scientists do not generally regard singularities, quanta or the nothingness/plenum of the quantum vacuum, as having anything to do with the mystical or metaphysical, these are indeed the most mystical of concepts to the occultist.

There are complex ideas emerging in science which bear upon ancient mystical claims about the subtle nature of reality. These parallels and similarities are generally neither recognized nor suspected by contemporary theorists, but do demonstrate a fascinating convergence of scientific and mystical conceptualizations of physics, cosmology and space.

Most scientists never acknowledge or even suspect that there might be essential links between physics and the study of consciousness. According to mystical teachings, this is an error of unfathomable proportions, as all cosmoses from the microcosm (human being) to the macrocosm (the universe), embody the same principles of creation and design: *"As above, so below."* All living beings, including human consciousness, emerge from zero point sources rooted into the same underlying creative realms. Hence, from a mystical and esoteric perspective, psychologists will never understand consciousness or the heart without considering both their physics and metaphysics.

Contemporary scientific concepts provide elegant illustrations of archaic mystical doctrines. Of course, scientists have come to their understanding of the big bang singularity as a result of a century of collaborative efforts in astrophysics, astronomy and physics. The accumulation of scientific evidence and the refinement of theories have produced an astonishing account of the universe and its origins. In contrast, mystical insights arise from states of elevated and expanded consciousness, through illumination, revelation and grace. The mystic directly experiences the realities which scientists apprehend through indirect observations and arrive at as theoretical abstractions.

One contemporary author suggests that we need *"a science of the soul,"* which I would also translate into a physics and metaphysics of consciousness and the heart. In fact, the basic concepts of physics and cosmology can be applied to the study of consciousness, if we have the missing links provided by esoteric and mystical teachings. The *Within-Without from Zero-Point* series is a step in this direction—towards the synthesis of ancient wisdom and modern science. The framework developed allows us to understand how human consciousness might be related to God, to omnipresent Spirit, to the metaphysical root principles of creation, to a spiritual and soul life, and to the larger universe. These things can all be described in terms of a complex physics and metaphysics of consciousness and the heart.

To illustrate this argument, consider the statement of the mystic Sufi sage, Ibn al'Arabi: *"Know that since God created human beings and brought them out of nothingness into existence, they have not stopped being travellers."* (1981, p. 27) Is Arabi only waxing poetic or does he have some cosmic and spiritual insight into the nature of deep realities—into the nothingness out of which all things emerge? Perhaps Ibn'al is not simply a fool who knows nothing, but in fact, he knows something really profound, something about the inner depths of his being in non-being? Blavatsky and Kabbalists, and other mystics, claim that the occultist can know directly the subtle realms which underlie and sustain life. The remarkable teachings of the ancient wisdom traditions speak directly to many enigmas and mysteries of science and creation studies.

259

# 6b. Divine Sparks: The Point within a Circle

the divine spark [is] buried deep in every soul. ... we must leave
the physical world of matter far behind and rise to the luminous
world above to attain the divine principle of our superior
soul. ... I ... engraved the symbol of the knowledge of the Initiates: a
circle with a point in the center. ... Understand me once and for all:
I am speaking from experience, for me it is not mere theory, all my
life has been based on this symbol of the circle with its central point.
This center which is in us, we must find ... .

(Aivanhov, 1976, pp. 25-6)

The best symbol for a zero point is a point within a circle or sphere. If we imagine penetrating from the outside into the innermost nature of this point, it would get smaller and smaller, until it disappeared from view. The zero point would vanish into nothingness when viewed from a material perspective, as it is infinitely small and un-extended within surrounding space. A zero point cannot be measured because measurement becomes undefined beyond a certain level of physical differentiation. If we were to more accurately draw a Zero Point within the Circle, then we would draw nothing, as the point would not be perceptible to the finite senses.

Each divine spark reflects the life of the *"Self-Existing Lord,"* a point source of supernal (or supernatural) light arising out of a sea of Infinite Light. As zero point centres, these sparks are the sources of consciousness or divine light emanating out of hidden dimensions of Being/Non-Being. From within God or the Absolute, they manifest without as individual consciousness and existence.

The zero point exists within a circle which represents Space. Space is a term with complex meanings in mysticism and modern science. Most obvious are the three large spatial dimensions which extend around us into our rooms and out into the larger universe. A zero point within a circle can represent an individual existing in the world, surrounded by three dimensional space with a fourth dimension of time—which is the outward life. However, this is only the most obvious meaning of the space represented by the circle.

From a mystical perspective, this outer space which we think we know, does not exist in itself, at least not as we think it does. It is illusory, a shadow or reflection of what underlies it, which is another type of "Space." Within higher dimensional Space, all things are informed and governed by metaphysical laws, intelligence and beings. The causative realm underlies the realm of effects, as the un-manifest underlies the manifest, the metaphysical underlies the physical, and the spiritual and divine underlie the material.

The circle surrounding the zero point represents an individual in ordinary space, but more importantly, as emerging from within a higher dimensional Space. There is the *Space within* and the *space without*. Forces emerging from Space within permeate and sustain phenomena that occur in the world without. The Space within is the basis for created universes, cosmoses and the Sons. Relative space-time worlds emerge out of the Space within, empty space particles from the "Eternal Parent Space." Thus, the point within the circle can be regarded as representing the individual in relationship to the higher dimensions of this deep Space.

Aivanhov states that the point within a circle is a symbol of the initiate and that his whole life was based on the attempt to find this centre within himself, which enabled him to know the Lord and the divine life. From that viewpoint, the point within the circle represents the origin and nature of human self existence and consciousness.

Consciousness arises from the conjunction of Divine Sparks within the Divine Mother. The Zero Point reflects the qualities of the Divine Father, the Self Existing Lord; while the sacred heart Space embodies the mysteries of the Divine Mother, the seven-fold Eternal Parent Space. It is the mystical conjunction of zero point divine sparks within the nothingness/plenum and hyperspace dimensions, which ultimately give rise to human consciousness. In the depths of the Sacred Heart and the inner cosmos of consciousness are the mysterious zero point origins and dynamics.

The Zero Point Divine Spark is the Quantum Self: the point source of divine light and life, and of divine and spiritual consciousness within a human being. It is the source of the "I" in the declaration "I AM"—the Hidden Self pointed to by mystics and sages throughout the ages. Understanding the conjunction of the Zero Points within the Heart Space is a key to unlocking the mystical origins of consciousness, as well as of the universe.

From a mystical perspective, modern science is full of head knowledge but lacks the wisdom of the heart and soul, and fails to acknowledge the inner light and divine life. We fail to realize the Creator manifesting in all things and un-thinkingly believe that the world is simply what it appears to be to us in our usual conditioned and profoundly limited states of awareness dominated by ten thousand and one worries, anxieties, life interests and habits. The nature and origin of human consciousness are very deep mysteries, which can only be understood through the awakening of deep consciousness within oneself—through the processes of self-realisation and psycho-spiritual transformation.

In higher dimensional Space, all things are ultimately integrated into One unifying Source. In this vein, all the separate individuals around us in life and we ourselves are expressions of the same Unifying Life which lives through us all. We are all individual "eyes" or "I"s of "THAT," within which we live, move and have our being. Mystical experiences involve penetrating various veils of nature and awakening consciousness which allow for the realization of higher Space dimensions and experiences of the unity of things within the Inner Life. Human beings have long known in their hearts that such realities exist.

Every man, woman and child is thus a Star, a zero point source, rooted into higher dimensional Space. Such 'sparks of holiness' originate from a supernal realm within. These are the deepest and most basic concepts of the *Within-Without from Zero Points* series and the most mystical of dimensions ascribed to the Self.

# 6c. Adi Da's Zero of the Heart

In his autobiographic writings, Adi Da describes varied experiences of enlightenment and self-realization which occurred at different periods of his life. He experienced the condition of *the Bright* from the earliest childhood but surrendered this condition as he adjusted to the demands of life and explored the realms of the mind. He then experienced a "re-emergence" of the bright and the reclaiming of his Divine Identity. Adi Da describes an ultimate process of "Translation" or "Transition," whereby consciousness normally polarized around the ego identity or personality surrenders the position of Narcissus and experiences the prior condition of Self—related to the deepest Spaces of the Heart. Adi Da writes:

> In this Process of Translation, we pass as if through a point in space, at the root center of the heart. All awareness converges on that point in a kind of spiral or vortex. And that point is so small it is without dimensions, or any conceptions, or any objects. The independent self seems to dissolve in this narrow Passage. ... The Divine Translation is a matter of Transcendence of separate bodily, emotional, mental, astral, supermental, and egoic states of experience. It is a Transition through the infinitesimal space of the Heart. (1978, p. 83)

Adi Da describes Translation as involving the transcendence of the bodily, emotional and mental realms, and a movement of consciousness through the "infinitesimal space of the Heart."

Adi Da states that: *"When the soul truly awakens, it breaks out of its atomic state in the heart and Radiates through and beyond the body-mind."* (1975, pp. 103-4) The individual becomes diffused with the Radiance of Consciousness.

Adi Da describes how an individual awakened in the Heart can still move about and function in the world, although there is no sense of being identical with, or limited to, the mind and body:

"Relative to the body, I appear to reside in the heart, but to the right side of the chest. ... And I Abide there as no-seeking. There is no motivation, no dilemma, no separation, no strategic action, no suffering. I am no-seeking in the Heart. ...

The zero of the heart is expanded as the world. Consciousness is not differentiated and identified. There is a constant observation of subject <u>and</u> object in any body, any functional sheath, any realm, or any experience that arises. Thus, I remain in the unqualified State. There is a constant Sensation of "Bright" Fullness permeating and surrounding all experiences, all realms, all bodies, all functional sheaths. It is my own "Bright" Fullness, which is radically non-separate. My own "Bright" Fullness includes all beings and all things. I am the Form of Space Itself, in which all bodies, all functional sheaths, all realms, and all experiences occur. It is inherently "Bright" Consciousness Itself, which Reality is even every being's Very Nature (or Ultimate, inherent, and inherently perfect, Condition) now and now and now. ... I awakened as perfect, absolute, awesome Love-Bliss, in which the body and the mind, and every functional sheath, boiled into a solder of undifferentiated Reality. It was the madness of Dissolution into most perfect Self Awareness. (1995, pp. 364)

Adi Da describes the Divine Domain as Shining through *"an atomic window"* and hence becoming the illusory and narcissistic ego—a knot or contraction out of the Infinite. Experiences of enlightenment can involve glimpses of such inward zero point dynamics:

"... the soul ... is a "seed" or "spark" of Radiance,
and atom of Original Light ... ." (1978, p. 476)

"... body-mind arises within the soul, the atom, which
is prior to space, time, size, shape, and all relations." (1978, p. 489)

"... all souls, or all living beings (human or otherwise), are points
or atoms of the Original Light or Radiant Bright
Consciousness of God." (1978, p. 492)

"In that Process (of Re-cognition), the infinitely small space
or door of the heart, the intuition of the atomic condition
of the soul, is penetrated." (1978, p. 541)

Adi Da explains that the zero point is not in the body as such–because in reality, the mind/body and even the subtle mind/bodies are within or surrounding the zero point. All things exist within space secondary to the prior zero point condition.[3] Further, Adi Da describes *"all living things,"* human or otherwise as having such zero point origins.

For Adi Da, there is a living awareness of these profound depths of Self. He states, *"I remain Aware of the Free point in the heart ... Everything only appears to me, and I remain as I <u>am</u>. There is no end to This."* (1995, p. 408) In light of the zero point concept of Self, we can understand why Adi Da emphasizes the idea of *no seeking*—as the act of seeking itself presumes separation and the knots up the Heart. The prior condition *is*, now and now, and now. He explains: *"Conscious living is never separated from the Disposition of no-seeking, which is the Reality-Disposition of the Heart Itself."* (1995, p. 407)

The Heart Master offers profound insights concerning *"the regeneration of the Amriti Nadi."* As previously mentioned, the *nadis* are channels of conscious-ness and life energies (winds) within the subtle anatomy. Ramana describes the Heart, the Self and the channels within the inner life:

> The effulgent light of active-consciousness starts at a point and gives light to the entire body, even as the sun does to the world. ... The sages call the original point 'Hridayam' (the Heart). ... Each of the forces of the body courses along a special nadi. Active consciousness lies in a distinct and separate Nadi, which is called Sushumna. Some call it 'Atma Nadi' and others 'Amrita Nadi'.

> When the discerning one renounces egotism and the 'I am the body' idea and carries on one-pointed enquiry (into the Self), movement of life-force starts in the nadis. This movement of the force separates the Self from the other nadis and the Self then gets confined to the Amrita Nadi alone and shines with clear light. When the very bright light of that consciousness shines in the Amrita Nadi alone, nothing else shines forth except the Self. ... When Atma alone shines, within and without, and everywhere (In Adi Da, 1995, p. 393)

Severing the knot brings about the attaining of inherent Bliss of the jivatmic state and liberation from the material realms of creation, or *Moksha*.

Adi Da explains that the Self-Existing and Self-Radiant Condition of the "Bright," is what Ramana describes as the Amrita Nadi. However, Ramana refers to *"the Non-regenerated Form of the Amrita Nadi,"* which leads *"away from the world"* and the exclusive Realization of the Heart. In contrast, Adi Da describes the most perfect Realization according to His Way of Radical Understanding:

---

3    Adi Da explains that even mystical experiences of the Crown Chakra, the Sahasrar, resolve back into the point within the Heart. The Sahasrar is the lunar orbit, reflecting the light originating within the solar realm, the Bright within the Heart.

the Amrita Nadi is spontaneously regenerated, from the Heart Itself (and via the physical heart-region, but on the right side) to the crown of the head (and above), thereby permitting the Infusion of "Brightness" in the total body-mind (in a pattern that descends and then re-ascends, from the crown of the head, and above, to the base of the body, and then back again, in a continuous Circle of Life). Therefore, only the regenerated Form of the Amrita Nadi may *truly* be called the "Amrita Nadi," meaning the "Nerve of Immortality," the "Circuit of the Current of Immortal Joy," or the "Atma Nadi" ... .Only the regenerated Form of the Amrita Nadi is the Source, the Container, and the First (or Original) Form of all Energy, all centres, and all life-currents. Only the regenerated Form of the Amrita Nadi ... is the ultimate and perfect form of Reality, founded in the heart and terminated in (and even infinitely above) the aperture of the crown of the head. It is the Cycle or perfect Form of unqualified Enjoyment. It Contains and is the Source of all things, all bodies, all conditioned realms, all conditional experiences, all conditional states, and all levels (or functional sheaths) of conditionally manifested being. Its Nature is unqualified Enjoyment, or Love-Bliss. It is Self-Existing and Self-Radiant Being, or unqualified Presence. It is even every one's Real Condition at this moment, and by grace, It is experienced as such when true understanding arises and becomes the radical (and, ultimately, the most perfect) basis of one's conscious life. (1995, pp. 395-7)

These are obviously the most profound descriptions of enlightened states and the mystical dimensions of the Heart. Adi Da shares the deepest insights into the ultimate states of realization: consciousness arises within the Heart as Love-Bliss and Spiritual Force and can illuminate the crown chakra, or sahasrar, (and the whole system of chakras) while retaining its "foothold" in the heart. In this case, the source of conscious life within the heart *"moves into life"* and reverses the current that usually moves from life towards the heart. This is the *"regeneration of the Amrita Nadi."*

# 7. Remembering & Forgetting: Exile from the Kingdom

"I am seated in everyone's heart, and from Me come remembrance, knowledge and forgetfulness." Bhagavad-Gita, XV, 15

"The secret of secrets is the divine spark within each of us. Remembrance is remembering that which we already know. It is to get in touch with that divine spark that God has placed within each human being … ."

R. Frager (In Cott, 2005)

Modern psychology, philosophy, science, religion and education are simply based on contemporary ignorance, prejudices and forgetfulness. Knowing self is the missing idea in scientific theories and modern thought, and it provides a key to the enigmas of creation. One must die to levels of ego within oneself and be reborn in Self in order to realize the Kingdom and Pleroma within.

As one awakens, one realizes more and more deeply the sleepwalking state of one's former self and of the masses of humanity. Ouspensky (1949) wrote of his early experiences with self-remembering and his glimpses of man asleep:

> I was walking along the street and suddenly I saw that the man who was walking towards me was asleep. There could be no doubt whatever about this. Although his eyes were open, he was walking along obviously immersed in dreams, which ran like clouds across his face. … After him came another also sleeping. A sleeping coachman went by with two sleeping passengers. Suddenly I found myself in the position of the prince in the "Sleeping Princess." Everyone around me was asleep. … I realized what it meant that many things could be seen with our eyes which we do not usually see. … I at once made the

discovery that by trying to remember myself I was able to intensify and prolong these sensations for so long as I had energy enough not to be diverted. ... When attention was diverted I ceased to see "sleeping people" because I had obviously gone to sleep myself. (1949, p. 265)

Consciousness must be understood within oneself through the processes of self-study, self-remembering and awakening. Nothing else is serious but to awaken and to remember. Can we say, as in the Gnostic *Gospel of Truth*: *"... from the heart that you are the perfect day and in you dwells the light that does not fail. ... and speak of the light which is perfect and filled with the seed of the Father, and which is in his heart, and in the pleroma."*? Or, are our hearts and selves far from the Lord—seemingly at least?

The mystical and spiritual teachings of humanity offer inspired views on the origin and nature of consciousness, life and the universe! Human consciousness is ultimately rooted in God consciousness, in a Sea of Infinite Light, into realms of Divine and Spiritual Intelligence, and even into the Void and Plenum. These principles are elaborated in a remarkably consistent way throughout the mystical literature and are suggested by the esoteric maxim: *"Know thyself, and thou wilt know the Universe and the Gods."*

According to the mystics, saints and seers of the ages, we as individuals—as divine or spiritual sparks, Sons of the Lord and Sons of the Sun—have miraculous and awesome possibilities open to us within a vast universe of unspeakable complexity and subtlety. The individual consciousness, which emanates as the divine spark, is brought down into the spiritual realm, and then ensouled and embodied. It is qualitatively One with the Supersoul and the Lord of the Universe! I AM is a Son, a star, a divine source emanation, of the Living Father emerging from within the Divine Plenum of the vacated Heart Space. Most importantly, we can know these things directly to varying levels through the awakening of consciousness and the transformation of the Heart.

The heart doctrine is an ancient, timeless teaching of eastern and western mystical and religious traditions. The individual spirit soul emerges within/ without from a Sea of Infinite Consciousness into a contracted state of egoistic consciousness, as an 'eye' or 'I' of the Absolute. This 'I' loses its high state of transcendental realization as it descends through subtle dimensions of being, finally to be born into the material world of sense-based awareness. This is a world of distractions and attachments, of suffering, pleasures and pain, a world controlled by madmen and others in a state of forgetfulness.

The spirit soul is seemingly cast out from the realm of transcendental being, as Adam and Eve are expelled from the Garden of Eden, and sewn into the instrument of time. The spiritual soul forgets its true nature and inward relationship to the Infinite Sea of Light Consciousness and the depths of the Divine Mother, and hence lives in ignorance—exiled from the Kingdom within.

Mystical and spiritual teachings offer inspired views of the nature of consciousness and the possibilities for self-realization and attaining real I. In addition to the everyday state of sleep walking consciousness, the possibilities exist for humans to experience objective knowledge and varied subtle planes and dimensions. Moreover, we might experience states of samadhi, cosmic consciousness, and even divine consciousness within the world of emanations! The mystical and religious teachings of humanity all point to such possibilities for profound states of self-realization, cosmic insights and illumination, and God consciousness.

Are these mystics, saints and seers correct in what they proclaim? Perhaps, as materialist science maintains, humans are nothing but higher primates that have evolved through random chance and nature's mechanical processes. Perhaps consciousness originates in the mid-brain or cortical structures, and human beings have no soul or spiritual nature–or any substantive consciousness. Perhaps we should tell our sweethearts that we love them with all of our limbic systems or hormones, as scientists imagine. Maybe the 'I' does simply disappear with the breakdown of the material brain as Isaac Asimov suggests, as it was only a composite of neurons.

The prophet stated that *"the mind longs to know the secrets of the heart"* but the unenlightened mind is deluded and ignorant of Self. Unfortunately, the lives of most people are lived out in a state of waking sleep and the vast majority have no remembrance of their true nature. They do not realize the love and bliss inherent within their inner being. They do not realize consciousness as light or experience their inward depths as spiritual beings, which are reflections and emanations of the divine world. Life in the quantum vacuum is very deep indeed.

Swami Prabhupada explains the fallen position of the spirit soul:

While exploiting the gross and subtle inferior energy (matter), the superior energy (the living entity) forgets his real, spiritual mind and intelligence. This forgetfulness is due to the influence of matter upon the living entity. But when the living entity becomes free from the influence of the illusory material energy, he attains the stage called mukti, or liberation. (1972b, p. 370)

The basis of self-realization is the understanding that one is not simply the material body, nor the personal mind and emotions, and that to the contrary, the true nature of the spirit soul is of light consciousness and bliss related to the metaphysical dimensions of the heart. The opening of the heart chakra and the dissolution of the knots of the Heart, bring about Self-realization. Mystical psychologies and philosophies elaborate complex theories and methods to enable the individual to be liberated from material contamination through spiritual practices. Disciplines for the purification and refinement of the body, emotions, mind, and the attainment of consciousness all help to bring one deeper into the remembrance of Self.

Humans live in a state of forgetfulness, like the Dwarf of Ignorance depicted 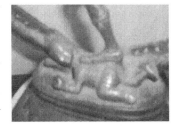 here, but the possibility exists to remember one's true nature. In fact, all of life is miraculous and it is only we, in our state of sleep, who are ignorant about the essential nature of reality and self. All of material nature exists in relationship to the deep metaphysical dimensions of existence and being, and all physics must ultimately lead to metaphysics.

The secret teachings of the Egyptian Gnostics provide this account of how the Soul forgets her true nature:

> The soul turned at one time towards Matter: she fell in love with it, and burning with desire to experience bodily pleasures, wished no more to be separated from it. Thus the world was born. From that moment the soul forgot herself; she forgot her original dwelling, her true center, her everlasting life. ... But God, unwilling to abandon the soul to its degradation with Matter, endowed her with understanding and the faculty of perception—precious gifts which would remind her of Her high origin, the spiritual world ... which would restore her consciousness of herself, teach her that she was a stranger here below. ... As soon as the soul ... has regained self-consciousness, she longs for the spiritual world as a man exiled in a strange land sighs for his distant homeland. (Doresse, 1986, p. 316)

The lost souls—who search in the unknown for meaning, pleasure and happiness to fill the void–simply do not understand Self. The soul, conditioned by the three modes of nature, tries to be lord within the realms of material existence and becomes more and more divided and fragmented through the emotional processes of identification, attachment and desires, isolation and heartbreak.

Only through mystical death and rebirth, the healing and awakening of the human heart, can the false ego or persona be dissolved and consciousness resolves back into Self and the Supreme. The ego must yield to the Bright within the lotus of the heart in order to remember our deep inward origins. Only escape from the general laws, from illusions, conditioning and forgetfulness can afford a true happiness and fulfilment in life and the afterlife. Such liberations establish us in the blissful and illumined nature of the soul, experiencing life within the nothingness with such potencies and possibilities. Paradoxically, these conditions already exist and all separation is illusory.

In the *Phaedrus*, Plato explained:

> Every soul of man has the way of nature beheld true Being; this was the condition of her passing into the form of man. But all souls do not easily recall the things of the other world.

For Plato, the soul is sewn into the *"instrument of time,"* or perhaps in modern terms into the 'matrix of creation.' Further, the goal of life is to recall or remember that knowledge which lies within our selves—within the vacated Space of the Heart. The ancient meaning of education similarly referred to bringing out that knowledge already inherent within the individual–that is cosmic and spiritual knowledge and realization. The aim of religion is to thus 're-unite' the individual soul with the Supersoul.

The realizations of the mystics are also reflected in the works of various poets who taste of the transcendent dimensions of existence, as well as in the music and literature of the world. Wordsworth, in *Intimation of Immortality*, wrote:

> Our birth is but a sleep and a forgetting:
> The soul that rises with us, our life's star,
> Hath had elsewhere its setting,
> And cometh from afar.
> Not in entire forgetfulness,
> And not in utter nakedness,
> But trailing clouds of glory,
> do we come from God, who is our home.
> Heaven lies about us in our infancy ...
> At length the man perceives it die away
> And fade into the light of common day.

And similarly, the modern rock band *Tea Party*, sings:

> ... here, here we are
> Shelter less souls
> lit by the stars
> ... because the world keeps turning

… seven circles twisting
around these moments of our lives …
… see what we are is limitless light
reflecting the stars.

*seven circles*, Tea Party

The mystical and spiritual traditions offer a view of human nature which radically opposes modern views of humans as being nothing more than higher primates, who die with physical death and the dissolution of the body—and having no deeper spiritual or soul nature. Instead, the mystics teach that all knowledge, eternal life and a state of blissful being self-existence are facets of the hidden, secret self—the human birthright, under our noses the whole time (as is suggested in the Hebrew tradition).

As it happens, however, in this accidental and strange universe, our hearts are far from the Lord, imperfect mirrors, veiled and knotted, and full of so much non-sense of the Dwarfs of Ignorance. People unfortunately do not remember Self, are not fully present, but are instead always absorbed, attached and identified with the legions of little i's which constitute the lives of sleeping humanity.

"The secret of secrets is the divine spark within each of us.
Remembrance is remembering that which we already know
It is to get in touch with that divine spark that God has placed
within each human being. In the Koran it says that God breathed from
the divine soul into Adam; another way of translating that would be
that God placed a divine spark into every human being.
And that divine spark is the secret of secrets. My master put it this way:
That spark in us could set the whole universe on fire.
Its greater than the universe itself because it's a spark
of what is infinite. And it's within every one of us.
Who we are is far more than who we think we are. (Frager, 2005)

As *Genesis* describes, there is a *Tree of Life* within the Garden of Eden, so we might long to gain the deepest knowledge, understanding and wisdom as all contained within the metaphysical dimensions of the human heart. Man, woman and children live in exile while the Kingdom exists within.

# V I

# A Fool at the Zero Point Within-Without & the Mysteries of Creation

*"... it is a kindness neither to science nor religion to leave unchallenged inadequate arguments for the existence of God. Moreover, debates on such questions are good fun, and at the very least, hone the mind for useful work. Not much of this sort of disputation is in evidence today, perhaps because new arguments for the existence of God which can be understood at all are exceedingly rare."*
—Carl Sagan, Broca's Brain, 1979

*"... the Secret teachings ... must be contrasted with the speculations of modern science. Archaic axioms must be placed side by side with modern hypotheses and comparison left to the sagacious reader. ... To make of Science an integral whole necessitates, indeed, the study of spiritual and psychic, as well as physical Nature. ... Without metaphysics ... real science is inadmissible."*
—H. P. Blavatsky, The Secret Doctrine, 1888

*"... people who define themselves as scientific, secular-liberal and open-minded are actually very narrow-minded in their scope. Instead of seeing an Infinite Intelligence manifest in the chemistry of life and in the miracle of human consciousness that that chemistry supports, they choose to perceive chance and random processes. Having closed their minds to Godliness, they simply cannot fathom what spiritual and religious people are all about. Furthermore, because they think only in materialistic terms, they close themselves off from seeing that which lies beyond matter—or within it."*
—C. Kramer, Anatomy of the Soul, 1998

# 1. ZERO POINTS:
# Winks of Self-Existence—Sparks of Holiness

THE SONS EXPAND AND CONTRACT THROUGH
THEIR OWN SELVES AND HEARTS; THEY EMBRACE
INFINITUDE. ... EACH IS A PART OF THE WEB.
REFLECTING THE "SELF-EXISTENT LORD" LIKE A
MIRROR, EACH BECOMES IN TURN A WORLD.
(Blavatsky, *Stanzas of Dzyan*, 1888, V. III, 11-12)

All Sons—a universe or an individual life—expand and contract through the Heart. This is where the zero point laya center exists—the life and consciousness principle within the material body. The Zero Point Self within the spiritual heart is rooted into the divine realms of the Eternal Parent Space and the Absolute Being/Non-Being. All cosmoses expand and contract from a point dimension, out of the infinite into the finite, to return at the end of time back to the zero point source within the Eternal. The zero point center within the Heart is rooted into the spiritual and divine realms within, while informing the psyche and material body without. Everything living in creation is informed in this way, within/without from zero points. This is truly an awesome ancient mystical teaching, which bears profound relationships to emerging scientific viewpoints.

A divine or spark exists within the vacated space at the Heart of being. This spark—the "I"—is a quantum of consciousness within the individual and it is the life principle within the material body. The Self is emanated as a zero point source of supernal light and life, rooted into the Superself, the transcendental realm of Being and Unity, or God. Within the material body, the Self is the light of consciousness, which allows for individual awareness—illuminating our thoughts, feelings, sensations and the like.

Esoteric sources elaborate sophisticated teachings about the nature and action of Self. The heart is not simply a mechanical pump but a space within which the consciousness and life principles emerge from higher dimensions. In this way, these higher subtler energies and intelligence are stepped down into the space/time complex of the material world. Thus, physical consciousness and the actions of the physical heart are manifestations of the more fundamental spiritual consciousness and spiritual heart, and derive ultimately from a zero point divine spark within the vacated Space of the Heart.

Contrary to modern thought, consciousness is substantive. The Self is a point source of consciousness, which can be equated with light. The Self is the most real, substantial entity, which persists despite the turning of the mind and the rich life interplay of sensations, desires and emotions that constitute life. Consciousness and Self are not the sum of material or psychological processes but something "other," rooted into the metaphysical domain. Similarly, the "I" is not simply a combination of material molecules, as Dr. Asimov argues, but has a deep spiritual and metaphysical nature. Human beings are thus 'winks of eternity,' divine sparks or 'sparks of holiness' embodied within levels and dimensions of existence.

It is easy to misunderstand the nature of a zero point, as we will tend to think that it exists within the four dimensional space-time continuum, like a spiritual spark within the heart. However, this is mistaken and reflects the conditioning of the materialist perspective. In fact, the zero point is not in the heart but instead, the heart and external reality exist within the Space of the Heart and its multi-dimensional zero point dynamics. Dr. Dea, a modern physicist who has studied Blavatsky, explains the unusual concept of space inherent to *The Secret Doctrine*:

> space-time came into existence by being squeezed out of a point. ... a space-time structure (is created) out of a single point! With this interpretation of space-time, certain paradoxes of nonlocality which require super-luminal speeds are no longer paradoxes. The reason is that everything is always connected because everything is really part of the same point. (1984, p. 91)

It is very difficult to grasp these ideas, because our ordinary understanding is so convoluted. The zero point centres do not exist within the heart, but rather the heart, the body, life and the afterlife, exist surrounding the zero point dynamics. All external realities are illusory projections of deep metaphysical and spiritual realities. All of creation—the universe itself—emerged from a supernal zero point. Material points without extension, or zero points, are the materials by which *"the Gods and other invisible powers clothe themselves in bodies... ."* (Blavatsky, 1888) Human consciousness is squeezed out of a point at the heart of Being!

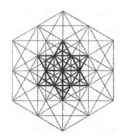

Not only is this an essential teaching of H. P. Blavatsky and the *Secret Doctrine*, but also, it is inherent within Kabbalist teachings. The manner in which the Son of the supernal triad of the Tree of Life crosses the abyss as Da'at, and descends into the Heart within Tipheret, depicts the stepping down process—from a divine source emanation into a spiritual spark, within a psychical and physical heart. The heart space within Tipheret embodies the Heart of Binah, the Divine Mother, with its inherent sevenfold nature. This means that there is an actual metaphysics to the human heart, as it is rooted into higher dimensional Space, the Eternal Parent Space of Blavatsky, the zero point fields of the quantum vacuum for the modern physicist. Kabbalah provides a profound model of higher dimensional consciousness, and the physics and metaphysics of it all. Further, at the Heart of being, we have the Zimzum contraction, the vacated Space within the Heart which allows for it all to happen.

In this view, to understand origin and nature of human consciousness, we would have to consider it through the four worlds of emanation, creation, formation and the world made. And all of these worlds surround the zero point centres, as they are is clothed in different bodies. Leat's depiction of Da'at in the world of Creation provides a profound metaphysical model of the higher dimensional nature of human consciousness and the heart. This is actually a depiction of what might be considered from an occult perspective, a God particle.

*Within-Without from Zero Points* has only begun to explore the physics and metaphysics of this all. From a mystical perspective, the origin and nature of human consciousness must be understood in terms of cosmic and metaphysical principles, which underlie and sustain all things. The microcosm of human consciousness embodies the same patterns of Creation as manifest within the dimensions of the macrocosm of the universe, and within any quantum (or element). All things embody the same inner patterns of existence, as they are parts of a living Unity.

Madame Blavatsky claims that, *"... one indivisible and absolute Omniscience and Intelligence ... thrills throughout every atom and infinitesimal point of the whole finite Kosmos."* (p. 277) The ultimate life source, God or the Absolute, or THAT, is not to be found outside of oneself in external space, but within our self in the depths of the Heart. A human I is in a sense a Zero Point rooted into metaphysical realms which inform and sustain the physical world. Consciousness derives from a "God spark" and we are all I's, eyes or individual expressions of THAT—the living Unity within.

Certainly, mystical and modern psychology are worlds apart. Mysticism suggests truly awesome possibilities for the evolution and awakening of consciousness within a profoundly mysterious and enigmatic universe. All of life issues from an Absolute intelligence and life principle, which thrills throughout every point within the finite Cosmos, and which is the source of Self. God *is micro-intervening* in the affairs of humankind, even though Dr. Sagan cannot see Him in the outer world talking to a morning glory, saying: *"Hey, flower, open."*

\*\*\*

Being brave souls in search of the unknown, we have explored the enigmatic teachings of the esoteric mystical and spiritual traditions, while attempting to relate this framework to facts, ideas, theories and enigmas within science and psychology. Could the inconceivable be conceivable? Could we really know the Self, the Universe and the Gods? Can yogis really travel to planets, along with the Mamos and other adepts? *Within-Without from Zero-Points* has only begun to suggest the mechanisms—the physics and the metaphysics of consciousness—which would allow for such an interconnectedness of the microcosms and macrocosms, and for such otherworldly possibilities. Imagine being Spiritual Children of a Lord, having the God spark within, being a Son of the Sun, and being rooted into spiritual and divine dimensions! Explorations into the ancient wisdom reveal level upon level of mystery, enigma and ignorance, and profound possibilities for human consciousness and experience. The heart doctrine is an ancient wisdom teaching evident within eastern and western traditions, and scientists are fools to ignore such profound possibilities, despite their totally otherworldly nature.

# 2. The Challenge to Science

"The universe within, then, is more vast than the universe without!"
S. MacLaine (1989, p. 101)

Mystical, spiritual and occult teachings provide the most bizarre, unimaginably complex and subtle ideas about the inner cosmos of consciousness. These ideas raise fundamental questions in every department of human inquiry about the hidden nature of life and creation, and the mechanisms of these grand cosmic schemes. If divine sparks exist at the heart of being rooted into higher dimensions and into the larger SELF, then we could begin to understand all the evidences of the psychic sciences and reports of mystical and spiritual experiences. We might even understand how a human can pass down a tunnel into a light realm like the Sun and encounter spiritual beings; or, how we might know many lives; or, how Yogananda might experience cosmic consciousness through a point of intuitive perception within his heart. We might even understand why Isaac Asimov prefers his nothingness, while Adi Da prefers the Bright.

Of course, it is easy for sceptics to dismiss all mystical teachings as simply irrational, superstitious or fanciful, even without bothering to learn what is actually taught. Unfortunately, given the fragmented state of contemporary science and psychology, and the materialist assumptive framework and the intentionally 'dummied down' educational system in western society, we do not consider the possible metaphysical causes and origin of things. Scientists and philosophers look for the causes of physical manifestations in other physical manifestations, but not in the realm of an underlying metaphysics. They think that the "I" is built up somehow by the molecules of the body; that consciousness is produced by the cerebral cortex and midbrain within the head; that metabolic energies provide the life spark within the heart; and that the dying brain produces only illusions of an afterlife. However, these are only assumptions and prejudices, which have not been established on a factual scientific basis. No one really understands these great mysteries. The mysteries of consciousness are the intergalactic questions yet to be resolved, but I have tried to at least sound the postal code and beat around the bushes.

Hence, we are all fools who know nothing. Understanding any part—without understanding its relationship to the whole—is not understanding but ignorance. From a mystical perspective, humans live in ignorance and modern scientists are little-bit scientists, fixated on the parts at the expense of the whole. They fail to penetrate to the depths of matter or Self—into the causative realms wherein any part is related to a greater Unity. They study everything in isolation. Psychology is considered quite separate from the studies of physics, astronomy, cosmology, biology and medicine. Mind scientists do not ask; what is the physics of consciousness? How is human consciousness related to the larger solar system or universe? How might the biology of the body/brain be sustained by subtle intelligence and vital principles? Or, what is the basis for the subtle dimensions of existence and the physics of afterlife? Yet such issues should and must be seriously addressed. If we take all the evidences for psychic and mystical experiences seriously, they point to all kinds of new questions within every domain of science.

Gurdjieff states that in order to understand a human you have to understand the universe, but to understand the universe, you have to understand a human or oneself. The laws are everywhere the same. As a microcosm of the macrocosm, the hidden and subtle dimensions of human beings are interrelated to the hidden and subtle dimensions of the world. 'I' is an eye of the Absolute, rooted into higher dimensional spaces—the plenum and the Unity, which sustains all things. Quantum interconnectedness implies that in higher dimensional spaces, we are all ultimately holograms of the whole event. If we want to understand the origin of the universe, we can attempt to understand the origin of our own consciousness and Self. Both emerge as singularities and are rooted into higher dimensional spaces—spiritual and divine realities.

We can ask how God might micro-intervene to open the morning glory flower. All things are created and sustained by metaphysical causes—the sun, the flower and Dr. Sagan. However, we cannot expect to see the metaphysical causes acting externally within four-dimensional space-time; like angels pushing and pulling the planets, or a God-like little man inside the flower opening it with some mechanical apparatus and saying *"Hey, flower, open."* Things are much more subtle than that and yet the existence of angels and other supernatural entities need to be investigated.

Mystical psychologies and cosmologies provide awe-inspiring views of the nature of human consciousness, the heart and the universe. Our personalities and separate identities are indeed masks or veils which obscure some unknown Self in a grand scheme of cosmic involution and evolution. The situation is one of an immortal Actor restricted and confined by the many little i's of life, yet lived out in a state of conditioning and forgetfulness. Mysticism is an ancient science that is light years ahead of modern science in understanding the ultimate origin of things. If Swami Prabhupada is correct and yogis can travel to the planets of the material and spiritual sky using psychic/spiritual powers and if consciousness is squeezed out of a zero point within the vacated space of the heart, then scientists should be studying the cosmos of consciousness. The route to human self-knowledge may well be the route to space exploration and to unveiling the mysteries of creation.

Although mystical possibilities sound wonderful and inspiring, this does not make them true. Dr. Sagan makes this point in his essay on *Night Walkers and Mystery Mongers*, in which he criticises what he calls the *"borderline belief systems."* Dr. Sagan notes that if such things as astral projection, spiritualism, extrasensory perception, astrology, elves and goblins were possible, then indeed the world would be a more interesting place. However, he notes that because such possibilities might *"charm or stir us,"* this does not guarantee their truth and there is no such compelling evidence. Dr. Sagan goes on to tell us that the claims of the borderline sciences do not compare to the elegance of the data and discoveries made in modern times with *real science*:

> In my opinion the claims of borderline science pall in comparison with hundreds of recent activities and discoveries in real science, including the existence of two semi-independent brains within every human skull; the reality of black holes; continental drift and collisions; chimpanzee language; massive climatic changes on Mars and Venus; the antiquity of the human species; the search for extraterrestrial life; the elegant self-copying molecular architecture that controls our heredity and evolution; and observational evidence on the origin, nature and fate of the universe as a whole. (1979, p. 62)

Actually, Dr. Sagan's main point is certainly not true. Mystical views of the nature of creation are definitely more profound and awesome than are those of Sagan's version of modern science. Of course, this does not make them true, but it also does not make them false.

From a mystical perspective, it looks absurd to regard Dr. Sagan gazing out into the universe, thinking with Broca's brain and wondering if there is any intelligent life out there in the accidental universe. Should humans be content to restrict their quest for knowledge and search for meaning to the study of such matters as the dualities of the brain, chimpanzees learning language, black holes and continental drift, and the like, when there are such lucid models and massive evidences suggestive of mystical, spiritual and divine possibilities? The issues of spirit and soul, of consciousness and afterlife, are profoundly important and essential to understanding the meaning of human life and existence; and unfortunately, these areas are almost totally ignored within science, psychology and modern philosophy. We need to get to the heart of the matter and determine what is science and what is pseudo-science. Dr. Sagan describes the *"mystery mongers"* as *"pretenders to arcane and occult knowledge,"* but we must wonder seriously who is pretending and who really knows. Our explorations of mysticism pose profound enigmas, which scientists are fools to ignore.

Perhaps we should experience more humility and awe in the face of unknown possibilities, and consider why modern scientists and psychologists think that they know so much more about the nature of life and the universe than do the many mystics, saints and seers, and the Heart Masters. Who really knows more: Dr. Hawking who thinks that we do not need God now that his quantum gravity theory can smear out the big bang singularity, but who fails to notice when he irritates his wife; or the former Mrs. Jane Hawking, who tells us that she believes that the answers lie in the lap of God and within the heart?

Mysticism does not contradict the *facts* of science. Rather, it is scientists' rigid adherence to a simplistic, mechanistic and materialist position, which leads them to prejudge and mindlessly dismiss mystical claims. Blavatsky noted in this regard:

> Occultism does not deny the certainty of the mechanical origin of the Universe; it only claims the absolute necessity of mechanicians of some sort behind those Elements (or *within*)—a dogma with us. ... It is easy for an astronomer ... to build a theory of the emergence of the universe out of chaos, by simply applying to it the principles of mechanics. But such a universe will always prove, with respect to its scientific human creator, a Frankenstein's monster; it will lead him into endless perplexities. The application of the mechanical laws only can never carry the speculator beyond the objective world: nor will it unveil to men the origin and final destiny of Kosmos. (1888, p. 594)

Normally, scientists simply close their eyes to the endless perplexities instead of venturing into the unknown. However, the mystical and spiritual teachings provide alternative ways of interpreting the facts and theories of science itself, and of understanding contemporary enigmas. Everything takes on new significance if the parts are considered in relationship to the whole and in relationship to underlying metaphysical causes. Mystical teachings do provide all kinds of testable hypotheses, if we are ingenious enough to begin from first principles and draw out the implications and applications of such theories—within different domains of inquiry.

Most importantly, mystical studies entail self-study, the awakening of consciousness and the transformation of the heart. In this way, the most advanced scientific methods require the individual process of psycho-spiritual transformation and include the scientist in the equation. Ordinary science is limited by the ordinary state of egoic consciousness and the commonly conditioned psycho-pathology of humankind. In contrast, mystical science includes the scientist him/herself in the equation and demands more, not less, from the seeker after truth. The key to the mysteries lies in understanding the nature of consciousness within oneself—by inner experience, sensation and taste.

The ideas and hypotheses presented in *Within/Without from Zero Points* may seem totally preposterous to many, even to those who believe in God and spiritual realities. This is odd really, since if God exists and is omnipresent, omnipotent and omniscient, then indeed it does imply that everything in the manifest universe is ultimately part of one Undivided Whole, and that all knowledge and potency is present throughout the higher dimensions of Space. Normally, people live with this split between what they feel in their hearts and what they know in their minds. In a mystical paradigm, the God hypothesis and its corollary, the soul hypothesis, should be taken seriously. Humans need to work from this point of view in a creative manner in order to understand how all these mystical possibilities may indeed be true and how certain patterns of intelligent design are inherent to nature.

What then is at the Heart of Being? What might be the soul physics for a new age? This is a task for the new millennium—to develop a comprehensive and scientific approach to spiritual technologies, the study of consciousness, and the physics and metaphysics of the heart and soul. This is also the task taken up in the *Within-Without from Zero Point* series, to develop this approach and to illustrate its relationships to modern scientific concepts and insights. The fool at the Zero Point Institute has begun these explorations of mysticism and science, but we have to delve more widely in order to elaborate the ancient wisdom teachings.

It is more than a hundred years since Blavatsky completed *The Secret Doctrine* and unfortunately, scientists are still far from having taken up her challenge of exploring the occult side of Nature. Her comments from 1888 still hold true today:

> Now that (scientists) have studied nature in the length, breadth, and thickness of her physical frame, it is time to remove the skeleton to the second plane and search within the unknown depths for the living and real entity .... (p. 610) ... this failure of the scientists to discover the truth is entirely due to their materialism and contempt for transcendental sciences. (p. 600)

Indeed, humans might have both the heart and physics, and even a higher dimensional physics to their own hearts and Selves!

# 3. A Fool at the Zero Point: Towards a Mystical Science of the Heart

I have attempted to seek out the truth of mystical and spiritual teachings by assuming the role of the fool who knows nothing but who seeks to understand the ultimate mysteries. In doing so, I have delved into the rich esoteric literature without dismissing any possibilities—no matter how bizarre they might initially seem. Of course, it is hard to imagine any more seemingly bizarre notion than that offered by the scientists themselves, who propose the zero point origin of the vast universe.

A significant body of mystical, spiritual and religious writings identifies the Self most intimately with the heart. Christ, Krishna, the Lord, the individual Self and the Super-Self, the Perfect Identity, are all claimed to exist within the abode of the sacred Heart Space. Although, not all mystical teachings articulate the heart doctrine, this theme is widely evident throughout the esoteric literature and is surely worthy of scientific investigation and individual consideration. Similarly, doctrines about zero points, higher dimensions of Space and metaphysical causes, are widespread within mystical teachings and are clearly related to emerging scientific concepts.

I have taken mystical claims about the nature and origin of human consciousness and compared these with modern psychological ideas, as well as with ideas in modern science and creation physics. The most bizarre point of all—the zero point—is proposed as a starting point for understanding the origin of consciousness within a human being *and* the origin of the universe or cosmos. Supernal points are described within the mystical, occult and spiritual literatures as in the scientific literature. However, whereas scientists apply zero point concepts to understanding the origin of the universe or the nature of quanta, the mystics apply it also to understanding Self and the origin of consciousness.

Certainly, mainstream psychology/science and mystical teachings offer strikingly different views of the origin and nature of human consciousness. If we are to speak off the top of our heads, we will simply take consciousness to be produced by material processes within the brain, a fortunate by-product of a long chain of random and accidental cosmic, sub-atomic and biological causes. When physical death occurs, the "I" simply dissipates and is no more, as a human being has no soul or spiritual nature. A century of mainstream science and psychology has embraced and reinforced this viewpoint or dogma.

In contrast, *The Secret Doctrine* of Madame Blavatsky and the heart doctrine of the mystical and spiritual traditions suggest that the deep origins of consciousness involve subtle and complex metaphysical, cosmic, spiritual and divine causes. The individual spirit soul, like a universe, emerges from within/

without through zero point dynamics from the perfect symmetry and Unity of Infinite Being/Non-Being into a contracted state of egoistic consciousness. The divine spark of a Cosmos or of an individual is an 'eye' or 'I' of the Absolute—a singularity rooted into the underlying Unity. Thus, every man, woman and child is a Star in their magical nature—a wink in the eye of Self-Existence, another Space Particle.

Shirley MacLaine states that each human being has a *"God spark"* within and that we need a *"physics of consciousness"* in order to understand such possibilities. What would such a God spark be and how might there be a physics of consciousness? Blavatsky and the mystics of the ages have provided lucid doctrines depicting metaphysical views pertaining to these issues, which link the study of consciousness intimately to the study of physics, metaphysics and cosmology. In light of *The Secret Doctrine*, modern psychology appears to be a science of sleepwalkers, full of head learning but devoid of soul wisdom. Modern conceptualizations of consciousness ignore the fundamental issues of the nature of space, matter and force. It is as if scientists assume that consciousness has no deep connection to the world which sustains it, or the higher space dimensions and quantum vacuum states, within which we live, move and have our being.

Mystical teachings align the study of consciousness with the study of physics, metaphysics and cosmology. How else are humans to ever understand the possibilities for out of body experiences, ghosts, life after death, states of illumination and cosmic insight, reincarnation and self liberation? If we search out all the unexplained, yet scientifically documented paranormal experiences and phenomena, then we realize that there is something far stranger happening with respect to human consciousness and the cosmos than the *head scientists* have ever imagined. Occult teachings provide this kind of perspective and suggest that a physics and metaphysics are necessary to provide a comprehensive explanation of consciousness and the heart, and the multi-dimensional holographic nature of existence. In order to comprehend the origin of human consciousness and life within the material body, we must penetrate the veils of the heart which conceal the ancient wisdom of Self. Certainly, we have very interesting alternative hypotheses about the nature of consciousness—the zero point teaching and the heart doctrine—to compare with the head doctrine of modern science.

Recall Swami Prabhupada's comment that, *"you come to God by studying these physical laws"* —because God is the ultimate source of everything. If God and supernatural agencies exist, then the study of the laws of nature must bring us back to this source. If God exists, then there has to be some form of *"microintervention"* even in the opening of the morning glory flower. If God exists, then the mechanisms of phototropism, life energies and the opening of the flower to the Sun are all based on spiritual intelligence and forces operating within the domain of the natural world. According to mystical teachings, consciousness and the life principle—even within Dr. Sagan himself—emerge through such a microintervention point within his heart, as it does in the Sun!

Dr. Sagan suggests that the cerebral cortex and the hierarchy of neural networks within the brain produce consciousness. The head doctrine has its hypothesis: that consciousness has no supernatural origin but rather is produced by material processes. Yet, when we examine this dogma, we find that there are many unanswered issues and enigmas within this alleged scientific explanation. In fact, there is no substantive evidence to support scientists' claims to understand consciousness or its origins. Even Dr. Crick, whose work is at the forefront of scientific theory, describes his theory as possibly being a *"house of cards,"* which collapses if you touch it.

Of course, the same criticism could be applied to the Heart Doctrine. I have not substantiated its validity. The material presented raises as many questions and issues as it attempts to explain. However, we have only begun to examine aspects of extremely complicated issues. Recall Dr. Sagan's comment that, *"new arguments for the existence of God which can be understood at all are exceedingly rare."* The *Within-Without from Zero Points* series is attempting to provide such new arguments for the existence of spiritual realities and for God. Unfortunately, scientists generally have no idea of the profound depth and rationality of mystical, occult and spiritual teachings, and therefore do not carefully weigh these doctrines before dismissing such multidimensional views of reality and Self. *Within-Without from Zero Points* represents a serious scholarly effort to address this glaring failure by articulating a mystical perspective within a rational psychological and scientific framework.

There are certainly many radical implications to mystical doctrines. What could be the physics and metaphysics of the divine or spiritual sparks and the subtle planes of existence? What is time and space, which seem so real and yet are described as illusory? To understand mystical doctrines requires a radical transformation in our understanding of all things: time, space, matter, energy, dimensions, mind, consciousness, fullness and emptiness, life and death—but most importantly, of Self. Instead of disproving the ancient wisdom teachings, the newest theories emerging in science make these teachings increasingly more intelligible—rather than less. The synthesis of mysticism and science indeed points toward the possibility of a science of the soul and *a soul physics* and as well as a science of mystical creation. There is every reason to consider seriously the soul hypothesis and the many implications of such viewpoints. At least, it all makes sense to the fool at the zero point. Perhaps, as Schwartz and Russek suggest:

> "If the 20th century has been, so to speak, the Century of the Brain,
> then the 21st century should be the Century of the Heart."
> (Pearsall, 1998, p. xiii)

An understanding of the heart doctrine and of zero point dynamics would certainly introduce a new paradigm for the 21st century. Unfortunately, the madness and collective psychoses and psychopathology of modern times suggests sadly that most of the sheep people, or sheeple, have already lost their souls and the population of the earth has been deliberately *"dummied down"* by the pseudo-elite illuminate, psychopaths and perverts who rose to the top of the waters of life—like scum. The mysteries of the heart doctrine are the teachings which could awaken human beings to their hidden nature and possibilities, as we are ourselves 'extra-terrestrial beings.' Humankind is faced with the alternatives of sinking into a new world psychiatric disorder or else, truly bringing about a new age of awakening, enlightenment and participation in the larger cosmos.

In *The Book of Tokens*, P. Case (1968) presents a meditation on the nature of the Fool. The Fool is numbered as zero in the Tarot deck and represents Self:

I am,
Without beginning, without end,
Older than night or day,
Younger than the babe new-born,
Brighter than light,
Darker than darkness,
Beyond all things and creatures,
Yet fixed in the heart of every one.

A Zero Point fixed in the Hearts of every one. This is the Quantum Self, one with THAT SELF. At the Heart of Being, the Fool is one "I" of the Absolute. Science must come to mysticism in order to penetrate the mysteries of consciousness and the heart.

# About the Author

Christopher Patrick Holmes was born in Sussex, England on October 7, 1949 and raised in Ontario, Canada. He graduated with a B.A. from Carleton University, Ottawa in 1971 and a Ph.D. in clinical psychology from the University of Waterloo in 1978. Christopher taught at York University, Downsview (Toronto) Ontario over an eleven-year period amidst controversy over his investigations of mystical and spiritual psychology, science and psychical phenomena. He co-founded three centers with Anita J. Mitra–the Institute for Mystical and Spiritual Science, Maple, Ontario, the Rainbow Centre in Toronto and Zero Point in the Ottawa valley. Christopher worked for twelve years as a forensic psychologist with young offenders and adults within the Ontario Ministry of Corrections. Since 2003, Christopher has dedicated himself to writing and furthering the aims of the Zero Point Institute for Mystical and Spiritual Science, while learning and working with Miss K. In 2010, the Zero Point Institute opened in Kemptville, Ontario. Christopher maintains a website at www.zeropoint.ca and hosts a bi-monthly radio show with co-host James A. Moffatt on www.bbsradio.com.

Christopher has studied the issues of consciousness, mystical and spiritual psychologies, modern physics and ancient metaphysics, for over thirty five years. In addition, he has experienced various paranormal phenomena, states of illumination and awakening. The *Within-Without from Zero Points series* presents a provocative alternative view of the nature of consciousness and human existence consistent with the esoteric religious teachings of humankind and with modern physics and science. The WWZP series also provides a model of intelligent design based upon the archaic concepts of zero point centres and the higher dimensions of Space. Christopher has additional books on G. I. Gurdjieff, *The Secret Doctrine* of H. P. Blavatsky, and a collection of assorted writings.

# BIBLIOGRAPHY

Abhayananda, S. *History of Mysticism: The unchanging Testament.* Atma Books, Olympia, Washington, 1996.

Adi Da. (Da Love Ananda, Buddha Free John). *The Knee of Listening: The early-life ordeal and the radical spiritual realization of the divine world teacher.* Dawn Horse Press, California, 1995.

———. *The Enlightenment of the Whole Body.* Dawn Horse Press, California, 1978.

———. *Compulsive Dancing.* Dawn Horse Press, Clearlake Highlands, California, 1978b.

Adolph, E. The Heart's Pacemaker, *Scientific American*, March 1967.

Aivanhov, O. *The Spendour of Tipheret.* Complete Works, Vol. 10, Editions Prosveta, France, 1977.

———. *Love and Sexuality*, Complete Works, Vol. 14, Editions Prosveta, France, 1976.

Arabi, I. *Journey to the Land of Power: A Sufi Manual on Retreat.* Inner Traditions, New York, 1981.

Asimov, I. The Subtlest Difference. In Abell, G. & Singer, B. eds. *Science and the Paranormal.* Scribner's Sons, New York, 1981.

Baha'u'llah. *The Seven Valleys and the Four Valleys.* Baha'i Publishing Trust, Wilmette, Illinois, 1978 (1945).

Bakan, P. Two streams of consciousness. In Pope, K. & Singer, J. (Eds.), *The Stream of Consciousness.* Plenum Press, New York, 1978.

Bawa. G. The Mind is in the Heart. *Psychology Today.* Interview, April 1977.

Benner, J. *The Impersonal Life.* DeVorss & Co. Publishers, Marina del Rey, California, 1988 (1941).

Bhikshu, K. *Sri Ramana Gita (Dialogues of Maharshi).* Tiruvannamalai, India, 1966.

Blavatsky, H. *The Secret Doctrine: The syntheses of science, religion and philosophy.* Theosophical University Press, Pasadena California, (1970) 1888.

———. *The Voice of the Silence.* Theosophical University Press, Pasadena, California, (1976)1889.

———. *Isis Unveiled: A master key to the mysteries of ancient and modern science and theology.* Theosophical University Press, Pasadena, California, 1976 (1877).

————.*Transactions of the Blavatsky Lodge of the Theosophical Society*. The Theosophy Company, Los Angeles, 1987.

Boehme, J. In *Personal Christianity: The Doctrines of Jacob Boehme*. Ed. by F. Hartmann. Frederick Ungar Publishing Co., New York, 1954.

Bonder, S. Beyond Peripheral Existence. *The Laughing Man*. Dawn Horse Press, Clearlake, CA, Vol 2,1981.

Brown, B. *New Mind, New Body: Bio-Feedback: New Directions for the Mind*. Bantam Books, Toronto, 1974.

Capra, F. *The Tao of Physics: An exploration of the parallels between modern physics and eastern mysticism*. Fontana/Collins, Great Britain, 1976.

Case, P. *The Book of Tokens*. Builders of the Adytum, Los Angeles, 1968.

Chalmers, D. The Puzzle of Conscious Experience. *Scientific American*. Dec.1995.

————. What is a Neural Correlate of Consciousness? www.u.arizona.edu. 2000.

Chinmoy. G. *Yoga and the Spiritual Life*. Tower Publications, New York, 1970.

Cohen, J., Phipps, J. *The Common Experience*. Tarcher, Inc., Los Angeles, 1979.

Collin, R. *The Theory of Celestial Influence: Man, the Universe and Cosmic Mystery*. Robinson & Watkins, London, 1980.

Cott, J. *On the Sea of Memory: A journey form Forgetting to Remembering*. Random House, New York, 2005.

————. *Visions & Voices*. Doubleday, New York, 1987.

Crick, F. *The Astonishing Hypothesis: The Scientific Search for the Soul*. Touchstone Books, London, Great Britain, 1995.

Crookall, R. *The Interpretation of Cosmic & Mystical Experiences*. James Clarke & Co., London, 1969.

Crowley, A. *The Law is for All*. New Falcon Publications. Phoenix, Arizona, 1993.

————. *The Book of Thoth*. Samuel Weiser, Inc. York Beach, Maine, 1991.

————. *Magick: In theory and practice*. Magickal Childe Publishing, Inc. New York, (1929) 1990.

Dalai Lama. *The Universe in a Single Atom: The convergence of science and spirituality*. Morgan Road Books, New York, 2005.

————. *Advice on Dying: And living a better life*. Atria Books, New York, 2002.

Davies, P. *The Mind of God: The Scientific Basis for a Rational World*. Touchstone Book, Simon & Schuster, New York, 1992.

———. *The Mind of God: The Scientific Basis for a Rational World.* Touchstone Book, Simon & Schuster, New York, 1996.

———. *Superforce: The Search for a Grand Unified Theory of Nature.* Touchstone Book, New York, 1984.

———. *God and the New Physics.* Touchstone Book, Simon & Schuster, New York, 1983.

Dea, J. Space, Time & Matter: Modern View vs the Secret Doctrine. *Symposium on H. P. Blavatsky's Secret Doctrine.* Wizards Bookshelf, San Diego, 1984.

Doresse, J. *The Secret Books of the Egyptian Gnostics.* Inner Traditions International, Rochester, Vermont, 1986.

Edwards, D. *Gnosis-Overview.* Deane@netcom.com. Dec. 1996.

Eudes, J. *The Admirable Heart of Mary.* P.J. Kenedy & Sons. New York, (1680) 1948.

Evans-Wentz, W. *The Tibetan Book of the Dead.* Oxford University Press, London, 1968.

Ey. H. *Consciousness: a phenomenological study of being conscious and becoming conscious.* Indiana University Press, Blomington, Indiana, 1978.

Fadiman, J., Frager, R. *Essential Sufism.* Castle Books, New Jersey, 1997.

Fortune, D. *The Mystical Qabalah.* Ernest Benn Ltd., London, 1935.

Francis, J. *The Mystic Way of Radiant Love: Alchemy for a new creation.* Heart Blossom Books, Los Altos, California, 1998.

Freud, S. *The Future of an Illusion.* Alfred Knopf, New York, 1914.

Gibran, K. *The Prophet.* Alfred Knopf, New York, 1968.

Gordon, H. *Channeling into the New Age: The "Teachings" of Shirley MacLaine and other such gurus.* Prometheus Books. Buffalo, New York, 1988.

Goswami, S. *Layayoga: An Advanced Method of Concentration.* Routledge & Kegan Paul, London, 1980.

Govinda, A. *The Way of the White Clouds; A Buddhist pilgrim in Tibet.* Shambala, Boston, 1988.

———. *Foundations of Tibetan Mysticism.* Rider & Company, London, 1962.

Greeley, A. Mysticism goes mainstream. *American Health: Fitness of Body and Mind.* Jan./February 1987.

Greene, B. *The Elegant Universe: Superstrings, hidden dimensions, and the quest for the ultimate theory.* Norton & Co., New York, 1999.

Grof, S. *The Holotropic Mind; The three levels of human consciousness and how they shape our lives.* Harper, San Francisco, 1993.

Gurdjieff, G. *All and Everything: Beelzebub's Tales to His Grandson.* Routledge & Kegan, London, 1950.

Haisch, B. *The God Theory: Universes, zero-point fields, and what's behind it all.* Red Wheel/Weiser, San Francisco, 2006.

Halevi, Z.S. *A Kabbalistic Universe.* Weiser, New York, 1977.

Hall, M. *The Secret Teachings of All Ages: An encyclopedic outline of Masonic, Hermetic, Quabbalistic and Rosicrucian Symbolical Philosophy.* Philosophical Research Society, Los Angeles, 1978.

———. *Man: Grand Symbol of the Mysteries.* Philosophical Research Society, Los Angeles, 1972.

Hawking, S. *A Brief History of Time: From the big bang to black holes.* Bantam Press, New York, 1988.

Heline, C. *Occult Anatomy and the Bible.* New Age Press, Los Angeles, California, 1937.

Horgan, J. *The Undiscovered Mind: How the human brain defies replication, medication, and explanation.* Touchstone Books, New York, 1999.

———. Can Science explain Consciousness? *Scientific American.* July 1994.

Huayta, W. The Awakening. Lecture in Peru, September, 1997.

———. Planetary Mission of the Extraterrestrials. Lecture in Cuzco, Peru, 1998.

———. The Inca Prophecy. 03/28/00. *Tone* magazine, Ottawa, March 2002.

James W. *The Principles of Psychology.* Holt, New York, 1890.

———. *Psychology: Briefer Course.* Collier Books, New York, 1972, (1892).

———. *Varieties of Religious Experience.* A Mentor Book, New American Library, New York, 1958.

Jastrow, R. *Genesis Revealed.* Science Digest, Winter 1979/ Summer 1980.

———. *God and the Astronomers.* Warner Books, New York, 1978.

———. *Until the Sun Dies.* Warner Books, New York, 1977.

Jones, B. *The opposite of gravity is hate.* bjon@ix.netcom.com. 1996.

Khan, H. *Spiritual Dimensions of Psychology.* Sufi Order Publications. Sante Fe, New Mexico, 1982.

———. *The Sufi Message of Hazrat Inayat Khan.* Volume 1. Barrie and Rockliff, London, England, 1960.

Kramer, C. *Anatomy of the Soul*. Breslov Research Institute, Jerusalem, 1998.

Kuhn, T. *The Structure of Scientific Revolutions*. University of Chicago Press, Chicago, 1962.

Lassen, N., et. al. Brain function and blood flow. *Scientific American*. 239, 62, 1978.

Leat, *The Secret Doctrine of the Kabbalah: Recovering the key to Hebraic Sacred Science*, Inner Traditions, Rochester, Vermont.

Lee, C. *The Promised God-Man is Here*. Dawn Horse Press, California, 1998.

Leith, Holography, *Scientific American*, 1976.

Levi, H. *The Aquarian Gospel of Jesus the Christ*. De Vorss & Co., Santa Monica, California, 1975.

Luria, I. *The Kabbalah: A Study of the Ten Luminous Emanations*. Research Centre of Kabbalah, Israel, 1984.

Lewin, R. Is the brain really necessary? *Science*. December 1980.

Mack, J. *Passport to the Cosmos: Human transformation and alien encounters*. Three Rivers Press, New York, 1999.

MacLaine, S. *Going Within: A Guide for inner transformation*. Bantam Books, New York, 1989.

Mead, G. *Pistis Sophia*. University Books, Inc.. Secaucus, New Jersey, 1974.

Miller, J. *The Vedas: Harmony, meditation and fulfilment*. Rider & Co., London, 1974.

Mills, W. *Tone* Magazine. Ottawa, Ontario, April, 1999.

Mishra, R. *Yoga Sutras*. Doubleday Anchor Books, New York, 1973.

———. *The Textbook of Yoga Psychology*. Julian Press, Inc., New York, 1971.

———. *Fundamentals of Yoga*. Lancer Books, New York, 1969.

Moffatt, J. *But I'll Know My Song Well*. Zero Point Publications, Kars, Ontario, 2002.

Moses of Leon. *The Book of Concealed Mystery*. Continuum Publishing, London, 2000.

Natsoulas. T. Consciousness, *American Psychologist*. pp. 906-914, October 1978.

Neisser, U. *Cognitive Psychology*. Englewood Cliffs: Prentice-Hall, 1966.

Nicoll, M. *Psychological Commentaries on the Teachings of G. I. Gurdjieff and P.D. Ouspensky*. Robinson & Watkins, London 1975.

Ornstein, R. *The Psychology of Consciousness*. Penguin Books, Markham, Canada, 1972.

Ouspensky, P. *The Fourth Way*. Vintage Books, Random House, New York, 1957.

———. *In Search of the Miraculous: Fragments of an unknown teaching*. Harcourt, Brace & Jovanovich. New York, 1949.

———. *Tertium Organum: A Key to the Enigmas of the World*. Vintage Books, New York, 1970 (1922).

Overbye, D. The Universe according to Guth. *Discover,* June, 1983.

Padmanabhan, K. *Teachings of Sri Bhagavan*. Prabha Printing House, Bangalore. 1980.

Pagels, H. *Perfect Symmetry: The Search for the Beginning of Time*. Simon and Schuster, New York, 1985.

Pearsall, P. *The Heart's Code: Tapping the Wisdom and Power of Our Heart Energy*. Broadway Books, New York, 1998.

Pelletier, R. *Towards a Science of Consciousness*. Delacorte Press, New York, 1978.

Penfield, W. *The Mystery of the Mind*. Princeton, Princeton University Press, 1977.

Prabhavananda, S. & Manchester, F. (Eds.) *The Upanishads: Breath of the Eternal*. New American Library, New York, 1957.

Prabhupada, A. *Bhagavad-gita: As it is*. Bhaktivedanta Book Trust, Los Angeles, Ca., 1972.

———. *Bhagavad-gita: As it is: Complete Edition*. Collier Macmillan Publishers, New York, 1972b.

———. *Easy Journey to Other Planets*. Bhaktivedanta Book Trust, Los Angeles, Ca.,1977.

———. *Consciousness: The Missing Link*. Bhaktivedanta Book Trust, Los Angeles, Ca., 1980.

Radin, D. *The Conscious Universe: The Scientific Truth of Psychic Phenomena*. Harper Collins Publ., New York, 1997.

Ramana Maharshi. *The Sage of Arunacala*. By Mahadevan. Allen & Unwin, London, 1977.

Rinbochay, L., Hopkins, J. *Death, Intermediate State and Rebirth in Tibetan Buddhism*. Gabriel, Snow Lion, Valois, New York, 1980.

Robinson, J. (Ed.). *Nag Hammadi Library*. Harper & Row, San Francisco, 1981.

Roth, G. The Quest to find Consciousness. *Scientific American*, Special Edition, *MIND*. 2004.

Ryle, G. *The Concept of Mind*. Hutchinson, London, 1949.

Sagan, C. *Billions and Billions: Thoughts on life and death at the brink of the millennium*. Random House, New York, 1997.

————. *The Demon-Haunted World. Science as a candle in the Dark*. Random House, New York, 1995.

————. Interview, *Psychology Today*. Jan/Feb. 1996.

————. *Contact*. Pocket Books, New York, 1985.

————. *Cosmos*. Random House, New York, 1980.

————. *Broca's Brain: Reflections on the Romance of Science*. Random House, New York, 1979.

————. *The Dragons of Eden: Speculations on the Evolution of Human Intelligence*. Random House, New York, 1977.

Sagan, C., Druyan, A. *Shadows of Forgotten Ancestors: A Search for who we are*. Random House, New York, 1992.

Saraswati, Y. *Science of soul: A Treatise on Higher Yoga*. Yoga Niketan Trust, New Delhi, India, 1987.

Sarma. K. (Translator) of Bhagavan Sri Ramana. *Revelation*. Centenary Publication, Tiruvannamalai, India, 1980.

Science Digest, Editors. *How Does the Heart Keep Time?* p. 90, August 1983.

Searle, J. *The Problem of Consciousness*. Www.eco.soton.ac.uk.

Shah, I. *The Way of the Sufi*. Jonathan Cape, London, 1968.

Shapley, H. *Beyond the Observatory*. Scribner's Sons, New York, 1967.

Sherwood, L. *Human Physiology: from cells to systems*. West Publishing Co., New York, 1989.

Sperry, R. Structure and Significance of the Consciousness Revolution, in *Revision*, Vol. 11, Summer 1988.

————. Emergence. In *The Omni Interviews*. Omni Press Books, New York, 1984.

Strange, J. A Search for the Sources of the Stream of Consciousness, in Pope, K. & Singer, J. (eds). *The Stream of Consciousness*. Plenum Press, New York,1978.

Subbaramayya, G. *Sri Ramana Reminiscences*. Jupiter Press, Madras, India, 1967.

Sylvia, C. *A Change of Heart*. Warner Books, New York, 1997.

Talbot, M. *Beyond the Quantum*. Bantam Books, New York, 1987.

Tart, C. *Transpersonal Psychologies*. Harper & Row, New York, 1975.

Trueblood, S. Healing Circle, Kemptville, Ontario, 1999.

———. Letter to John Mack and the Center Family, Feb. 1999.

Underhill, E. *Mysticism: A study in the nature and development of Man's spiritual consciousness.* New   American Library, New York, 1974.

Vaysse, J. *Towards Awakening: An approach to the teaching left by Gurdjieff.* Harper & Row, San Francisco, 1979.

Waley, M. *Sufism: The Alchemy of the Heart.* Aquarian/Thorsons, London, 1993.

Walker, K. *Venture with Ideas.* Samuel Weiser, New York, 1965.

Watson, J. *Behaviorism.* Norton, New York, 1924.

———. Psychology as the behaviorist views it. *Psychological Review,* 1913, pp. 158-177.

Weber, R. *Dialogues with Scientists and Sages: The Search for Unity.* Routledge & Kegan Paul, New York, 1986.

Weinberg, S. *The First Three Minutes: A Modern View of the Origin of the Universe.* Bantam Books, New York, 1979.

Whinfield, E. *Teachings of Rumi.* Octagon Press, London, 1979.

Yogananda, P. *Autobiography of A Yogi.* Self Realization Fellowship. Los Angeles, California, 1998.

# Zero Point Publications

Kemptville, Ontario, Canada K0G-1J0

# WITHIN-WITHOUT from ZERO POINTS

## Book I I

# MICROCOSM-
# MACROCOSM

Scientific and Mystical Views on the Origin of the Universe,
the Nature of Matter & Human Consciousness

"... "material points without extension" are Leibnitz's monads, and at the same time the materials out of which the 'Gods' and other invisible powers clothe themselves in bodies. ... the entire universe concentrating itself, as it were, in a single point."

*H. P. Blavatsky, The Secret Doctrine, Cosmogenesis, 1888*

"... all the so-called Forces of Nature, Electricity, Magnetism, light, heat, etc., are in esse, i.e., in their ultimate constitution, the differentiated aspects of that Universal Motion. ... for formative or creative purposes, the Great Law modifies its perpetual motion on seven invisible points within the area of the manifest Universe."

H. P. Blavatsky, *The Secret Doctrine, 1888*

"It is necessary to notice that in the Great Universe all phenomena in general, without exception wherever they arise and manifest, are simply successively law-conformable 'Fractions' of some whole phenomenon which has its prime arising on the Most Holy Sun Absolute."

G. I. Gurdjieff, 1950

*Microcosm-Macrocosm* explores the newest theories in physics and creation science–including materials on superstrings, higher dimensions, singularities, the quantum vacuum and the holographic principle in science and in the psychology of consciousness. It draws from ancient metaphysics—particularly *The Secret Doctrine* of H. P. Blavatsky (1888), esoteric Judaism and Kabbalah, and the cosmology and metaphysics of G. I. Gurdjieff. This is a challenging and provocative work with deep insights into the Divine Mystery teachings and a unique critique of modern science philosophy. It provides a shocking alternative view of the zero point origins of human consciousness and cosmos.

Zero Point Publications, ISBN 978-0-9689435-1-9     $30

# UPCOMING...

## WITHIN-WITHOUT from ZERO POINTS

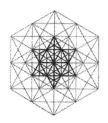

### Book I I I

### TRIUNE MONADS IN SEVEN DIMENSIONAL HYPERSPACE

Scientific and Mystical Studies of the
Multi-Dimensional Nature of Human Existence

*Monads* draws from the teachings of Madame Blavatsky, Kabbalah and Judaism, Gurdjieff and a wide range of mystical doctrine about the multidimensional nature of human existence. Esoteric teachings identify the abode of the 'I' as within the human heart, where a triune Monad element is established within a Seven Dimensional Eternal Parent Space which underlies and sustains our normal physical four-dimensional space-time complex. Such ideas from mystical sources bear profound relationships to theories in advanced physics as to the nature of Space itself, quantum interconnectedness and higher dimensional superstring elements at zero point levels. A triune and sevenfold Monadic Essence spins a Web of Spirit, Soul and Matter within a Seven Dimensional Virtual Reality out of the Aethers of the void and plenum, the quantum vacuum. In order to illustrate the necessity for such an alternative understanding of reality, this work examines evidences for out-of-body experiences, Sheldrake's fields of extended mind, enigmas posed by heart transplant patients and twin studies and an interpretation of other paranormal investigations.

### Book I V

### A FOOL AT THE ZERO POINT

An *Autobiographic* Tale about the Strange Case of Professor Z, the
Mysteries of Love and Ecstasies of the Heart & the Horror of It All

Christopher, by the grace of God, will provide an autobiographical account of his life experiences, his psychical and mystical experiences, his life struggles and relationships, and an account of awakening to the horror of it all. This work includes materials on Christopher's struggles for academic freedom at York University, his twelve years of work in correctional centres as a forensic psychologist, his life and loves, and his awakening to psychopathology of the world elites with their plans for committing genocide against the human race.

# GOD, SCIENCE
# &*THE SECRET DOCTRINE*

The Zero Point Metaphysics and
Holographic Space of H. P. Blavatsky

## Christopher P. Holmes, Ph.D.

*"Deity ... is in every point of the universe."*
*(S.D.I, p. 114)*

"... the Secret teachings ... must be contrasted
with the speculations of modern science. ... To
make of Science an integral whole necessitates,
indeed, the study of spiritual and psychic, as well as physical
Nature. ... Without metaphysics ... real science is inadmissible."
H. P. Blavatsky *(S.D., 1888)*

H. P. Blavatsky's *The Secret Doctrine* was published in 1888 and is relatively unknown in modern times. As it happens in this strange universe, Madame Blavatsky over a century ago anticipated numerous modern concepts concerning the creation of the Universe and the mechanisms of the laws of nature—including the holographic paradigm in psychology and physics. Blavatsky articulated the concept of the zero point or singularity origin of the Cosmos and of the Sons, and a profound alternative view of the nature of the Aether and higher Space dimensions.

Blavatsky states: *"... 'material points without extension' (zero-points) are ... the materials out of which the 'Gods' and other invisible powers clothe themselves in bodies ... the entire universe concentrating itself, as it were, in a single point."* Dr. Holmes has grasped the profound meanings of this claim and related these ancient mystical teachings to the newest ideas in physics and science; as well as to explorations of human consciousness, spirit and soul, and the mysteries of the Heart. *God, Science & The Secret Doctrine* raises the ultimate question of the existence or non-existence of God—and what we mean by this term.

Holmes plunges the reader into the deep places of the occult and the new frontiers of science to come up with a lucid and provocative book. It unseals many of the Secret Doctrines mysteries as it weaves the seeming opposites of spirit and science into a new synthesis. It is a must read for those wishing to understand the complex and seemingly impenetrable world of Helena Blavatsky alongside the newest ideas of quantum theory. Holmes has created something of his own tour de force in *God, Science and the Secret Doctrine*. His book is destined to serve as a guidebook for all those that follow. (Donna Brown, *The Esoteric Quarterly*, 2009)

Zero Point Publications, ISBN 978-0-9689435-6-4    $24.95

# ZERO POINT TEACHINGS

Selected Articles and Writings
of Mystical Psychologist & Scientist

## Christopher P. Holmes, Ph.D.

The zero point teachings are a portal of some sort to awaken you to a higher dimensional model of yourself and the structure of reality—to view the world in a magical and mystical way. The basic idea is that all living beings, including yourself, have a zero point centre within and this is the means by which *"the Gods and other invisible powers clothe themselves in bodies"*—as explained by mystic scholar Madame Blavatsky in *The Secret Doctrine* (1888). Just as the scientists conceive that the huge universe grew from an infinitesimal singularity out of the quantum vacuum, so also, I suggest that you also have such a hidden zero point or singularity source condition--a singular I within the Heart. Further, we ourselves emerge *"out of nothingness"* in some mysterious way unknown to modern science and contemporary understanding.

This selection of articles and writings is drawn from the _www.zeropoint.ca_ web site and from Christopher's varied books, and includes original socio-political writings posted to the zero point website, but then withdrawn. This book includes materials on the origin and nature of human consciousness, the mystery teachings of the heart doctrine, Kabbalah and *The Secret Doctrine*, modern physics and quantum theory, a commentary on the psychopathology of humanity based on the teachings of G. I. Gurdjieff, book, movie and music critiques, and much more. It provides an overview of the mysteries of consciousness and the heart, and a view of the psycho-pathology of humankind upon planet earth.

Zero Point Publications, ISBN 978-0-9689435-7-1        $30

# PSYCHOLOGICAL ILLUSIONS

Explorations of the Gurdjieff
Fourth Way Teaching

## Christopher P. Holmes, Ph.D.

The central illusion of humankind is that we *"know self."* The components of this illusion concern the different powers or capabilities which men and women think that they possess but which in reality they do not. Four primary illusions or misunderstandings concern the human faculties of consciousness, the unity of I, the possession of will (or the capacity to do) and the existence of the soul. The fourth way psychology begins with a study of humans as they are under the conditions of mechanical life and then describes the psychology of man's *possible evolution*. Humans can awaken and experience new states of consciousness, attain a unity of "I" and real will, and thus attain the soul. Unfortunately, wrong ideas and convictions about the nature of consciousness, unity, will and the soul are major obstacles to self knowledge. If we can begin to understand these illusions, then there is a chance of escape, of awakening and evolution.

According to Beelzebub, the central character in Gurdjieff's *Tales*, the three-brained beings on planet Earth are microcosmoses or *"similitudes of the Whole."* As such, they have the possibility of not only serving local cosmic purposes, feeding the earth and moon as part of organic life on earth, but also of experiencing sacred being-impulses—attaining varied levels of objective reason and individuality and even of *"blending again with the infinite."* (1950) As a microcosm of the macrocosm, a human being can potentially coat higher being-bodies for the life of the soul, instinctually sense cosmic truths and phenomena, and maintain existence within the subtle realms of being after death–achieving different levels of immortality. Unfortunately, humankind came to exist only in waking sleep states of automated consciousness, perceiving reality topsy-turvy, conditioned by pleasure and self love, and wasteful of their sacred sexual substances. Human beings no longer realize their deeper cosmic purposes and possibilities, or attain real "I."

*Psychological Illusions* explores the psychology, metaphysics and cosmology of the fourth way teaching. This includes material on the *Ray of Creation*, the fundamental cosmic laws, the alchemical crystallization of *higher being-bodies* for the life of the soul, and the miraculous possibilities existing for the evolution of the individual human being. The Gurdjieff fourth way teaching is a profound and coherent system of esoteric teaching about the horror of the situation for humanity asleep living under their psychological illusions.

Zero Point Publications, ISBN 978-0-9689435-2-6    $24.95

# "The Slugs"

## On G. I. Gurdjieff's
### *Beelzebub's Tales to his Grandson*

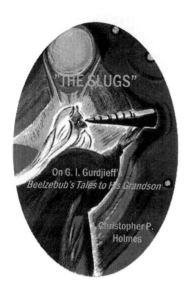

## Christopher P. Holmes, Ph.D.

"This Most Great Foundation of the All-embracing of everything that exists constantly emanates throughout the whole of the Universe and coats itself from its particles upon planets–in certain three-brained beings who attain in their common presences the capacity to have their own functioning of both fundamental cosmic laws of the sacred Heptaparaparshinokh and the sacred Triamazikamno—into a definite unit in which alone 'Objective Divine Reason' acquires the possibility of becoming concentrated and fixed."—Beelzebub recounting the teachings of Lord Buddha (Gurdjieff, 1950, pp. 244-5)

*Beelzebub's Tales to His Grandson* is undoubtedly one of the most profound and mysterious books among the sacred literature of the world. The framework of ideas, claims and objective science offers a fundamentally alternative view of the miraculous nature of life–a perfectly coherent, intelligible and astounding account of "All and Everything." In the light of *The Tales*, all of modern thought and understanding is so much 'pouring-from-the-empty-into-the-void.' The 'sorry scientists' of 'new format' have no conception of the great inscrutable mysteries of Nature and the subtle inner dimensions of human beings. *Beelzebub's Tales* is a work not only of myth, allegory and fantasy, but also about the secrets of 'objective science' and the psychology of the soul.

Human beings are potentially similitudes of the whole–particles of the Great Universe. In this way, everything is some Divine Fraction-a law conformable portion of the whole. Behind essence is real I, behind real I is God, or at least the Most Most Holy Sun Absolute. Beelzebub provides strange and provocative tales for his grandson Hassein, about the hidden dimensions of those strange three-brained beings on planet Earth, the principles of esoteric science and the meaning and purpose of it all—for living, breathing creatures who might attain a "real I."

The Author: Christopher Holmes is a mystic scientist and consciousness researcher, a clinical and forensic psychologist. He has studied the Gurdjieff work for over thirty years, as well as pursued broader investigations of human consciousness and the physics and metaphysics of creation.

Zero Point Publications, ISBN 978-0-9689435-4-0          $25

# Zero Point Radio

# Live two-hour Internet Radio Broadcasts

### every second Saturday

In North America: 4 to 6 p.m. Eastern Time, Every Second Saturday
1 to 3 p.m. Pacific, 10-12 pm GMT

Dr. Christopher P. Holmes hosts an online internet Radio Broadcast through www.bbsradio.com. Previous broadcasts are available for online listening at the Zero Point archive service. These include shows on the zero point hypotheses, the magical formula of 137, on consciousness and the heart doctrine, the metaphysics of *H. P. Blavatsky's The Secret Doctrine,* the insanity of humankind and the criminality of the elites. James A Moffatt serves as commentator and interviewer, with invited guests. Shows archived at www.bbsradio.com.